Fodor's EXPLORING

THE GREEK ISLANDS

FODOR'S TRAVEL PUBLICATIONS

NEW YORK • TORONTO • LONDON • SYDNEY • AUCKLAND

WWW.FODORS.COM

© Automobile Association Developments Limited 2004,
2007 Maps © Automobile Association Developments
Limited 2000, 2004 (registered office : Fanum House,
Basing View, Basingstoke, RG21 4EA, UK. Registered
number 1878835).

Published in the United States by Fodor's Travel, a
division of Random House, Inc., and simultaneously in
Canada by Random House of Canada Limited, Toronto.
Published in the United Kingdom by AA Publishing.

Fodor's and Fodor's Exploring are registered trademarks
of Random House, Inc.

ISBN: 978-1-4000-1769-0

Fourth Edition

Fodor's Exploring the Greek Islands

Authors: **Anthony Sattin and Sylvie Franquet**
Revision Verifier: **Sylvie Franquet**
Revision Editor: **Stephanie Smith**
Original Photography: **Steve Day, Terry Harris,
Bob Moore, Anthony Sattin, James Tims**
Cartography: **The Automobile Association**
Cover Design: **Fabrizio La Rocca, Tigist Getachew**
Front Cover Silhouette: **R. Matina/age fotostock**
Front Cover Top Photograph: **AA Photo Library**

Printed and bound in Italy by Printer Trento srl
10 9 8 7 6 5 4 3 2 1

A02985

How to use this book

ORGANIZATION

The Greek Islands Are, The Greek Islands Were
Discusses aspects of life and culture in the contemporary Greek Islands and explores significant periods in their history.

A–Z
Breaks down the islands into regional chapters, and covers places to visit, including walks and drives. Within this section fall the Focus On articles, which consider a variety of subjects in greater detail.

Travel Facts
Contains the strictly practical information vital for a successful trip.

Hotels and Restaurants
Lists recommended establishments throughout the Greek Islands, giving a brief summary of their attractions.

ABOUT THE RATINGS
Most places described in this book have been given a separate rating. These are as follows:

▶▶▶   **Do not miss**

▶▶   **Highly recommended**

▶   **Worth seeing**

MAPS
To make each particular location easier to find, every main entry in this book has a map reference to the right of its name. This comprises a number, followed by a letter, followed by another number, such as 176B3. The first number (176) refers to the page on which the map can be found, the letter (B) and the second number (3) pinpoint the square in which the main entry is located. The maps on the inside front cover and inside back cover are referred to as IFC and IBC respectively.

Spelling of place-names
Visitors to Greece will find variations in the spelling of place-names on road signs and maps. In this book the transliteration of the Greek names into Roman letters follows a recognized convention, but where another version may be more familiar (eg, Athens, Crete, Corfu, Rhodes) this is also used. The names of the islands are given in the Greek alphabet (in capital letters) on the pages that introduce the groups of islands.

Contents

5

Sylvie Franquet has been touring the Greek Islands for more than 20 years and writes full time for the AA and other publishers.

Anthony Sattin is the author of several highly acclaimed books, most recently *The Gates of Africa*. He is also a travel writer and a regular contributor to *The Sunday Times*.

Our Greek Islands

Young Greeks have a word—*halara*—which they use for 'take it easy', 'let it go', 'stay cool', 'chill out', and nothing better expresses the spirit of the islands. *Halara* encapsulates the dream of island life, of bare rocks jutting out of the azure sea, a shady corner in a whitewashed village, a cooling swim in crystal water, the prospect of crunchy bread, crisp calamari and crisper salads, a lazy sleep during the heat of the day and then the many pleasures of lingering taverna nights.

But this is a dream of the islands in summer, when it is easy to move around, but less easy to find a seat in a good restaurant, a quiet beach, a clear view of the star exhibits in the museums or a quiet night in many hotels. Summer is also when prices rise with the temperature and when the sense of community fades a little as islanders find themselves outnumbered by visitors.

We are more than fair-weather friends—we love the islands out of season, in spring and early summer, when the sun is warming but the water still icy, the air full of hope, and in early autumn when the wind blows the visitors away but when all the seductive charms of the place are still very present. Tourism to the islands is mostly concentrated on the four months over summer, but that is beginning to change as culture, sports and spas lure visitors to the islands out of season and as some - though not all - places stay open to welcome them.

Young Athenians have their own version of *halara*. *Parne plateia?* they ask, *shall we go to the square?* It's another way of saying *let's go and hang around*. And that, after all, is what attracts us to Greece—the prospect of hanging around, of chilling out and taking it easy in sight of great beauty, in the company of warm, welcoming and often fascinating people and in the presence of significant history. Greece, for all its rush to modernize, remains a place of its own and nowhere more so that the places far from the city. No wonder we fall for the lure of the Greek Islands.

Anthony Sattin and Sylvie Franquet

The Greek Islands Are

There are more than 1,400 Greek islands, many of them merely tiny uninhabitable rocks breaking through the surface of the smooth sea. The islands account for only one fifth of Greece's total land mass, yet their magical combination of brilliant light, hard land and diamond-clear air dominates many people's image of Greece.

IONIAN AND AEGEAN Greece's islands are mostly scattered to either side of the Greek mainland. To the west is the Ionian Sea, bounded by Greece and Albania to the east, Italy and the Adriatic to the north and west and the Mediterranean to the south. Within the Ionian Sea lie the Ionian Islands. To the east of the Greek mainland is the Aegean Sea, with Macedonia and Thrace to the north, the rest of mainland Greece to the west, Turkey to the east and Crete to the south. Cradled in the waters of the Aegean are the Cyclades ('the

> ❏ Lawrence Durrell's words still ring true: 'You should see the landscape of Greece. It would break your heart.' (*Spirit of Place*, London, 1969) ❏

Circle', from the ring they form around Dílos), the Dodecanese ('the Twelve'), in the southeast, the islands of the Northern and Eastern Aegean, the Saronic Islands, the Sporades ('the Scattered'), Évvoia, cheek by jowl with the mainland and, in the far south, Crete.

ISLAND LANDSCAPES Geology, topography and climate have combined in Greece to create some of the most stunning scenery in the Mediterranean, helped by a legendary blue sea. The Greek Islands are mostly the peaks of an otherwise submerged landmass. Their appearance is so varied that it is impossible to make generalizations: many of the larger islands have extremely fertile districts, as in the interior of Náxos, for example, while some smaller islands appear to have been worn down to the bare rock.

Other small islands, such as Paxoí and its tiny neighbour Antipaxoí, in the Ionian Sea, are very fertile; Paxoí is almost entirely given over to olive cultivation while Antipaxoí is dedicated to grapes. Even between neighbours, the difference can be striking: while Thásos is green and gentle, nearby Samothráki is little more than a forbidding peak jutting out of the sea.

Older Greeks swear that Poseidon sliced Évvoia off the mainland with his trident

10

CLIMATE Crete, Europe's most southerly land mass, enjoys mild winters and early springs on its southern coast and yet has snow on its peaks for much of the year (snow has fallen as late as April).

The winter islands would be unrecognizable to most summer visitors; clouds and rain strip colour from the often windswept land, the light can be dull and the sea stormy, although there are still fine days, especially on Crete and in the Dodecanese islands.

Spring comes later the farther north you go and can be a joy to follow, from Crete and the Dodecanese in the south to Corfu farther north. For many people, late spring and early summer are the best times to visit, when the sun is not too strong and the islands are as green and flower-filled as they will ever be, although

Agriculture still plays an important part in the islands' economy

the seas are still cold. Summers are usually hot and dry; rainfall is rare, which is one of the reasons why so many people are attracted to the islands. In September, however, although the winds pick up and the ferry service becomes less dependable, the sun is still very evident and the blue sea is at its warmest.

❏ In ancient times, the Aegean was divided into different areas: the Thracian Sea in the north, the Ikarian Sea in the east, the Mirtoan Sea in the southwest and the Sea of Crete in the south. You may still hear these names used in some places. ❏

❏ As Greek sailors know, Aegean winds are unpredictable and none more so than the *meltémi*. It can blow out of nowhere, get up to Force 7 or 8 on the Beaufort scale and last for an hour or a week. Perhaps more than any other single factor, the *meltémi* is responsible for the streak of resignation in the islanders' character: when control over something as basic as leaving an island is regularly taken out of your hands, what can you do but shrug your shoulders and head for the nearest *kafeneío*? ❏

Times have changed for the Greek islanders. On some islands, the quiet life dependent on the olive or grape harvest has become a distant memory and new opportunities have arisen. At the same time, people from the mainland have found new value in the old island life.

THE ISLAND DREAM 'Of all peoples,' wrote the German poet Goethe, 'the Greeks have dreamed the dream of life best.' Many visitors, seeing islanders going about their life—eating food grown and gathered locally, living with uplifting natural beauty, their families around them and with time to spend with each other—envy the life they have dreamed. There is another side to it, of course. Island life can be a nightmare: earthquakes have devastated islands such as Zákynthos and Kefalloniá; men plying the seas, or diving beneath them, fail to return; hardships increase as work and seafood become scarce, while every winter storms cut off the more remote islands for weeks at a time, making food, fuel and water run short. These things do not intrude in the foreigner's rosy vision of the islands but, just as much as the summer sun, they have shaped the character of every islander you meet.

OLD HABITS Traditional island life was arranged around the seasons and orchestrated by three characters: the policeman, the priest and the teacher. In many places it still is. All three are still to be found sitting in the taverna or *kafeneío*, or strolling along the waterfront at sunset. Many of the values they stand for are still upheld—Greeks are still extremely religious and family ties are still central (how many Three Brothers' Restaurants are there?)—but life around them has changed. On many islands, students no longer need to go to Athens to be educated: television and new technology have brought the islands closer to the city, while tourism has given contact with people from all over the world. This has changed island habits. Many men no longer rely on the land or their boats for their livelihood and a woman at work is no longer a sign of a man's failure to provide for his family. But at the same time as the old ways are being questioned on the islands, another group of people are finding them of great value.

RENEWED INTEREST Last century, particularly in the 1950s and 1960s when Greece was heavily influenced by the United States and the city was *the* place to live, islanders were seen as backwards. A quarter of all Greeks now live in Athens, but many of them trace their origins to the islands. As the

12

The kafeneío *is usually a men-only affair*

Young girls' expectations differ from those of their mothers and grandmothers

city becomes more crowded, they dream of returning: many go back for Easter and other holidays, but some find work that allows them to spend the summer near the blue Greek waters. They and some of the many Greek islanders who emigrated to South Africa, Australia and elsewhere, have become part of the summer crowd, renovating the old stone houses that year-round islanders have left for the comforts of modern homes, upholding the more traditional attitudes, and only running for the boats when the autumn (fall) wind bites.

MEETING THE PEOPLE In spite of the vast numbers of tourists visiting the islands, locals can still be extraordinarily hospitable to strangers: the Greek word *xénos* means both foreigner and guest. You might not be invited into people's homes, but even on a first meeting—out strolling along the waterfront or lingering over a coffee or *ouzo*—islanders are usually welcoming and open.

Their hospitality, like so much else on the islands, is shaped by the sea. History has taught islanders to be wary of invaders; you might be met with suspicion if you hint of any plans to settle, but otherwise you are welcome because you have stopped on their island, of which they are justifiably proud. On many occasions you will find yourself being shown around or told anecdotes about the place with a mixture of candour, wit and humour.

How do people survive on the Greek islands? How do they earn their money? The answer might seem simple for people who are surrounded by the sea. But as fish and sponge stocks have been depleted, islanders have had to look elsewhere for their livelihood.

SHIPPING For people who live surrounded by the sea, earning a living on it would seem to be an obvious option, and so it still is. The proximity of islands to each other made it possible for Greeks to sail early on in history and since then they have been renowned as a nation of sailors. With a population of just 11 million, Greece still dominates the global shipping industry, with 25 per cent of global maritime trade. However, the nature

❏ The tiny island of Oinoússes, off Chíos, is famous for its shipping families, who own as much as a third of all Greek ships. Fleeing from the Turks after the 1820s massacre on Chíos, they arrived in Sýros, were impressed by the shipyards and went home determined to set up a shipping business. 'When you're an Oinoussian', said one islander, 'from the time you're born, all you hear is ships.' ❏

of the industry is changing fast, to a more corporate way of doing business, and many Greek ship owners are floating their companies on the international stock exchanges.

TRADITIONAL TRADE Until the 1940s and 1950s, most islands were dependent on the business (usually agricultural) from which they had always earned their living: olives, grapes or wine and wheat for trading off the island and dried and fresh fruit and vegetables, chickens, goats and dairy products for sale or barter among themselves. In some places this sort of existence is still possible, but the effect of the exodus of young men to the mainland is still easily seen on many islands: fields are left to turn into scrub because the islanders are either too old or too young to do the hard work.

FAMOUS EXPORTS In 1900, currants accounted for half of Greece's total exports, while other products included lead and other ores, olive oil,

Not so many islanders as in the past work on small farms, like this one on Náxos

wine, honey and sponges. Some of these, most noticeably sponges, have now become too scarce to be a going concern. But olives and their oil, honey, wine and marble from Páros are still valuable export commodities.

TOURISM The second of Greece's three big money-spinners is the country itself. Since the 2004 Olympic games in Athens, the Greek government is working hard to enhance the country's international image as a tourist destination. The islands are still mostly perceived as a summer destination, at the most for four months of the year, but the aim of the Ministry of Tourism Development is to create a year-round industry, and create 150,000 new jobs in the next ten years. There will be a new emphasis on sports such as yachting, golf and diving, on developments in spa and health tourism, and on eco-tourism.

Tourism touches every part of the islands' economy: local farms produce food for hotels and restaurants, wineries produce wine, new hotels and housing keep the construction industry running. A lot of money is being made, and the people from the mainland, particularly from Athens, are increasingly interested in going to the islands for the summer season to take their share in the profit.

Shepherds are a rare sight as more islanders head for Athens

With tourists providing a ready market, fishing is still a viable trade

BRINGING IT BACK HOME The third mainstay of the Greek economy is money sent home by Greek émigrés. Nearly six million Greeks live abroad, among them people as diverse as Kalymniot sponge divers working in Florida, wealthy ship owners of Oinoússes operating out of New York and other world financial centres and the 300,000-strong Greek community in Melbourne.

While travelling around the islands, it is as common to see churches being repaired and libraries equipped through the generosity of expatriate Greeks as it is to find their large houses shut up when the summer has ended.

15

When tourism on the Greek islands started becoming big business in the 1960s, it seemed like a beneficial exchange: foreign visitors could enjoy the islands' beauty and culture while islanders could earn some much-needed income. Now in a growing number of places both islanders and tourists are having doubts.

In summer a space on the beach is as scarce as shade

THE LOOK OF THE LAND Every visitor has an image of the Greek islands. It probably includes a small landing-place, a waterfront with a *kafeneío* and whitewashed houses on a hillside. Once commonplace, such a view is becoming increasingly hard to find in the wake of a building boom that has transformed the islands. New hotels, apartment buildings and villas appear each season, many without zoning permission. But, as one owner in the Cyclades explained, pointing to a hotel that had appeared, illegally, in front of his building, 'The planning office is far away in Sýros. It will take them forever to come to check and then they'll do nothing'.

WILDLIFE IN DANGER It is not only the views that are disappearing. The Greek islands are home to rare plants and animals which are now endangered too. Loggerhead turtles, for instance, are being forced off the beaches where they breed, in places like Zákynthos, frightened away by the noise and lights of hotels and disco-bars, though thankfully they are being increasingly protected. Plant life is exposed to risk too: in his introduction to *Wild Flowers of Crete* (Athens, 1987), George Sfikas writes, 'if human interference continues at the same rate without immediate steps being taken to protect nature in Crete, it will soon be ecologically destroyed.'

THE HUMAN COST Flora, fauna, the landscape—and people. Many tourists seem to believe that by paying money to visit Greece, they have bought the right to behave as they like and to find the sort of facilities with which they are familiar. In doing so they have changed life on the islands, often destroying the very things, such as the quiet, the undeveloped shoreline and the wildlife, that they had hoped to find here.

Greek politics are a stormy affair, providing fodder for animated discussion in many an island kafeneío. *In the 1980s and early 1990s the political scene in Greece was dominated by the elderly but charismatic and controversial leader Andréas Papandréou. Since his death in June 1996, things have been a little calmer.*

GREECE'S CONSTITUTION Under the 1975 constitution, Greece is a democracy headed by a president and ruled by an elected government with a majority in the 300-member single-chamber parliament, the *Voulí*. Members are elected for a four-year term, while the president is in office for five years. Greece joined the European Community (EC) in 1981, which became the European Union (EU) in 1992, and it joined the euro zone in 2001.

RELATIVE STABILITY The past few years have been a time of relative political stability for Greece. The Greek government has worked hard to become a more mature and stable member of the EU. The success of the 2004 Olympic Games and in the European football cup gave Greece an amazing boost of confidence. That year, too, the Greek people, tired of many years of socialist PASOK rule, elected the leader of the New

Democracy Party, Konstantinos Karamanlís as their prime minister. His priority was to clean up public life from corruption.

TWO PARTIES Greek politics today is dominated by two parties, the Panhellenic Socialist Movement (PASOK) and the conservative New Democracy (ND). Konstantine Karamanlís, the current prime minister, is leader of the ND. Minority parties have had a growing appeal, and there is a strong feeling that Greeks politics are likely to become less polarized in the near future.

17

❑ The Greeks, who pride themselves on having invented politics, enjoy voting and love nothing more than to settle down for a good argument about politicians and how to solve the ills of their country and the world. You have been warned! ❑

Politics are often on the kafeneío *menu*

The Greek Orthodox Church touches every part of life. Priests play an important part in everyday living and are as often seen in kafeneía as conducting formal church services. Alongside the Orthodox Church, some minority religions have survived the passing of history.

18

EAST AND WEST The division of the Christian Church into Roman Catholic and Eastern Orthodox reflected a gap in the culture, politics and economies of the eastern and western provinces of the Roman Empire as much as a theological split. The final break occurred for two reasons: Rome's desire for supremacy in theological matters and a doctrinal difference over the divine nature of Jesus. The differences reached a head in 1054, when the pope and the patriarch excommunicated each other.

THE ORTHODOX CHURCH The Orthodox Church has some 150 million followers, but Greece is the only country where Eastern Orthodoxy is

❏ Small wayside shrines are a familiar sight on island roads. Often designed in the shape of a house or basilica surmounted by a cross, they are built in thanks to particular saints for their blessings. Inside the shrine will be an icon, an oil lamp and a bottle of oil, just as there were at the roadside shrines of pagan gods in ancient Greece. Then, as now, travellers paused to pray and to refill the lamp with oil. ❏

the state religion. During the Turkish occupation, the Orthodox Church played a crucial role, giving Greeks a sense of common identity and later providing a focus for nationalist sentiments. It was a churchman who first raised the Greek flag in defiance of Turkey in 1821 (see page 45). The Church kept Greeks in touch with their literature, art and music.

Almost all Greeks belong to the Orthodox Church. When they have something to celebrate, they go to church. When in trouble, they light candles in supplication. When afflicted, they make offerings to icons, praying that the saint will intercede for them. In a changing world it is the Church that is holding families and communities together.

ROMAN CATHOLICISM IN GREECE
Although the majority of Greek Christians are Orthodox, there are small Catholic communities, a reminder of centuries of Italian influence. Catholic communities can most often be found on islands that

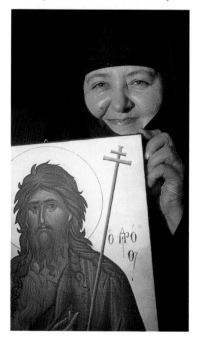

Saints are believed to intercede through their icons

were formerly Venetian or Genoese possessions. Tínos and Sýros, with their important Catholic shrines, are notable examples.

MUSLIM AND JEWISH COMMUNITIES

Most of Greece's Muslims are descended from Ottoman traders or from officials who settled throughout the empire as administrators. After World War I Greece and Turkey

The priest is still very much part of the village life

The church plays a social role and keeps the traditions alive

'exchanged' nationals in a swap of land and people.

Many Muslims were shipped to the nearest point out of Greece. For some that meant the Dodecanese, which were in the hands of the Italians at that time. Kós and Rhodes saw the greatest influx and today have two of the largest Muslim communities in the islands.

At one time Greece boasted one of the oldest Jewish communities in Europe, but more than 65,000 of Greece's 80,000 Jews were taken prisoner by the Nazis during World War II. Few survived the concentration camps—less than 100 in Rhodes and none at all on Kós. The number of Jews in Greece was further reduced after the war, when many emigrated to Israel. Around 6,000 Jews live in Greece today, of whom half are in Athens, and a small number on Corfu.

❏ Icons have a special function in the Orthodox Church, being seen as a medium through which the divine makes itself accessible. Before making icons, both painter and material must be spiritually cleansed. During the Eucharist, the saints represented are believed to be present through their icons in the same way that the wine and wafer are Jesus's blood and body. ❏

The Greek year is punctuated by festivals. There are saints' days every day of the year and many traditional festivals are maintained locally, celebrating everything from harvest to the arts. The Lent Carnival is a time of freedom and excess. If you are lucky enough to be on an island during a festival, join in for a glimpse of real island life.

PARAMONI Below are listed the days of festivals, but remember that most religious celebrations in Greece occur on the eve of the holiday. At Easter, for instance, Sunday is mainly a day for family get-togethers. On the previous evening, however, there are candle-lit processions and prayers and, around midnight, the wonderful *Anástasi* service, ending with the greeting *Christós Anésti!* (Christ has risen).

TAKING PART Greeks are extremely welcoming to outsiders: if you happen to be on an island at a time of public celebration, feel free to join in. For religious celebrations, Orthodox church services are generally more informal than those of Roman Catholic or Protestant churches. People come and go, children run around and, provided you are suitably respectful, you will be welcome. A list of the more popular holidays

❏ For most Greeks, their name day—the day of the saint after whom they are named—is more significant than their birthday. They will celebrate and be given presents on their saint's day rather than their own birthday. This has a dual function: it ensures that everyone remembers the day and it ties the person, through their name and their saint, to the Greek Orthodox Church. ❏

and festivals is given below. The dates of some religious holidays are set according to the Eastern calendar and will change each year. To find out more about these and civic holidays and festivals, contact the National Tourist Organization of Greece (see page 268).

January 1: New Year's Day, Feast of St. Basil (national holiday); 6: Epiphany (national holiday), Blessing of the Waters, Piréas.
February Carnivals throughout Greece, celebrations in the Ionian Islands (particularly Kefalloniá), in Athens and on Skýros, with its outrageous goat dance; 25: Ágios Riginos (patron saint of Skópelos).
March Start of Lent (national holiday), Feast of the Purification; 25: Independence Day; Evangelismós (Feast of the Annunciation: national holiday), celebrations held on Tínos and Ýdra.
April *Son et lumière* shows start in Athens, Corfu and Rhodes Town

With so many saints' days you are almost certain to encounter a festival

Easter is the most important festival in the Greek calendar

(until October); Palm Sunday and Easter Saturday: celebrations for Ágios Spyridon (patron saint of Corfu; also 11 August and first Monday in November); Easter (national holiday); 23: Ágios Georgios (patron saint of Skýros).

May 1: May Day (national holiday); 8: Ágios Thomás; 21: Anniversary of the union of the Ionian Islands and Greece (celebrated particularly in Corfu Town), Ágios Konstantínos and Agía Eléni; end of May: Navy Day—celebration on Ýdra of the great Independence hero Admiral Andréas Miaoúlis (1769–1835).

June Pentecost (national holiday); Athens festival of arts at Herod Atticus theatre (which runs until September); Classical drama festival (Itháki); 20: Ágios Pnévmatos (Holy Spirit Day); 29: Ágioi Apóstoloi Pétros, Pávlos.

July Rhodes wine festival, Thásos ancient drama festival (see pages 218–219), wine festival at Réthymno (Crete); 17: Agía Marína; 20: Ágios Ilías (celebrated on hilltops dedicated to the Prophet Elijah); 27: Ágios Pantelís.

August Dionysia wine festival (Náxos), Hippocrateia festival of arts (Kós), Irákleio festival (Crete), Lefkáda festival, Santoríni (Thíra) music festival; 6: Feast of the Metamórfosi (Transfiguration) of

Most celebrations occur on the eve of the festival

Jesus; 15: Panagía (Assumption of the Virgin: national holiday), Agía María, Ágios Panagiótis (notable celebrations on Tínos, Páros, Lésvos and Kárpathos); 30: Ágios Aléxandros/Agía Aléxandra.

September 8–9: Eorti Tis Armatas (Battle of the Straits) regatta on Spétses, celebrating defeat of the Ottoman navy in 1822.

October 26: Ágios Dimítrios/Agía Dimítria; 28: Óchi day (the major patriotic festival with parades, etc; national holiday).

November 8: Feast of the Archangels Ágioi Michaíl and Gavriél; 14: Ágios Fílippos; 25: Agía Katerína; 30: Ágios Andréas.

December 5: Ágios Savvás; 6: Ágios Nikoláos; 9: Agía Ánna; 12: Ágios Spýros; 15: Ágios Eleuthérios/Agía Eleftería; 25: Christmas (national holiday), Ágios Chrístos/Agía Christína; 26: Sinaksis Theotokou (national holiday); 27: Ágios Stéfanos.

Greeks love to spend evenings talking, laughing, drinking and eating. A meal is always shared, wine flows freely and bread is abundant as both body and spirit are satisfied. Mealtimes tend to be late, leisurely and, above all, are there to be enjoyed by everyone.

Typical lunchtime scene at this pleasant Corfu taverna

LOST TRADITIONS? Greek cuisine has changed dramatically in the last 50 years as television, tourism and the modern world have put rural traditions in touch with a more global urban lifestyle. Food was simple and the ingredients dictated by the seasons. Meat and cheese were luxuries for most people. One result of the emigration of islanders and the arrival of foreigners is that in many places Greek cuisine has been reduced to the standard tourist dishes of Greek salad, *moussaká* and *souvláki*. However, the Cretan Diet has been shown in several studies to be one of the healthiest in the world, with a good balance of fresh fish, pulses, fruit and vegetables.

EATING HABITS Greeks eat little in the morning, so hotel breakfasts are often poor. It may be better to shop for a picnic breakfast of bread, fruit and rich, thick Greek yogurt with honey. In comparison with most visitors, Greeks eat the main meals of the day late: in Greek homes lunch is usually served after 2pm and dinner at 10 or 11, although restaurants do serve meals earlier than that. Children are welcome and Greek cuisine offers several dishes suited to their taste.

Many dishes are cooked in the morning, so food is often lukewarm, sometimes cold, but Greeks do not complain as they believe that hot food is bad for the stomach.

ORDERING FOOD Before ordering, Greeks ask the waiter what's cooking, as specialities are often not on the menu. You may want to look at the menu to familiarize yourself with the Greek names of food or to get an idea of the price range, but ask the waiter if there is anything else. Either go and look in the kitchen, or see what others are eating.

MEZÉDES Starters or *mezédes* are served with *ouzo* or beer as a

> ❑ *'The food...*food was something he [the Greek Katsimbalis] was passionate about...Between great carnivorous gulps of food he would pound his chest like a gorilla before washing it down with a hogshead of *rezina*. He had drunk a lot of *rezina* in his time: he said it was good for one, good for the kidneys, good for the liver, good for the lungs, good for the bowels and for the mind, good for everything.'
> Henry Miller, *The Colossus of Maroussi* (London, 1942) ❑

Little snacks are one of the instant pleasures of Greek cuisine

complete light meal or at the beginning of a larger meal. As soon as Greeks arrive in a restaurant drinks are ordered, a variety of dishes is put in the middle of the table to be shared by everyone and the evening is under way. Anything served in portions smaller than a main course will do, but there are a few classics: *choriatikí* or Greek salad, *tzatzíki* (yogurt with cucumber and garlic), grilled *féta* cheese, *ochtapódi* (grilled or boiled octopus), *melitzanosaláta* (aubergine salad), *taramá* (fish-roe salad), *kalamarákia* (fried or stuffed squid), *dolmádes* (stuffed vine leaves), *gígantes* (baked butter beans), *keftédes* (meatballs), *skordaliá* (garlic sauce with mashed potatoes), *saganáki* (fried cheese), *spanakópitakia* and *tiropitákia* (spinach and cheese pastries).

MAIN COURSES Greeks are the biggest meat-eaters in Europe. The most common meat dishes are *souvláki* (lamb, veal, or pork kebabs), *brizóles* (chops), *keftédes* (meatballs), *biftékia* (Greek hamburger), and *kotópoulo* (chicken). On special occasions a spit-roast lamb (*arní psitó*), goat (*katsíki*) or suckling pig may be

available. Other traditional dishes are *pastítsio* (baked macaroni), *imám baïlnti* (stuffed aubergines with tomato sauce), *moussaká* (an oven dish with layers of chopped meat, aubergine and béchamel) and *gemistá* (stuffed tomatoes or peppers). Fish tends to be more expensive and is normally priced by the kilo. It usually comes grilled or baked.

FOR A SWEET TOOTH Traditionally tavernas do not serve desserts; at most there may be watermelon or another fresh fruit. This does not mean no desserts are available. The *zacharoplasteío* (pastry shop) usually offers ice-cream, French pastries and syrupy Greco-Turkish sweets such as *baklavás* (sweet filo pastry stuffed with nuts and honey), *kataïfi* ('angel hair' soaked in honey), *galaktoboúreko* (custard tarts) and *loukoumádes* (honey puffs).

In the heat, traditional Greek coffee is often replaced by a **frappé** *or iced Nescafé*

One of the pleasures of the Greek islands is to stroll around on a warm evening, your mouth watering, choosing where to eat dinner. But how to get past that pushy waiter and find the perfect taverna, or an authentic Greek meal?

LOCAL KNOWLEDGE

Greeks love going to restaurants with company or *paréa*, a group of friends or the extended family. Like Greek cuisine itself, Greek restaurants are easy-going, apart from a few more formal places in Athens and Mýkonos. The best advice is to choose a restaurant where you can see the local Greeks eating, remembering that they dine later in the evening (see pages 22–23). This may well mean giving the sea and the often tourist-orientated waterfront a miss and venturing inland. Simple tavernas, filled with Greek families, frequently produce the most delicious food and their waiters do not need to tout for business (see pages 279–283).

WHERE TO EAT An *estiatório* is the closest thing to a restaurant, sometimes with French or Italian cuisine. A *tavérna* is a straightforward place with plastic-covered tables and a menu of *mezédes*, grills and stews. A *psarotavérna* specializes in fresh fish. These can be tiny beach cabins, where fishermen cook the day's catch, or expensive waterfront tavernas with superb displays of fish, lobster and other types of seafood. A *psistariá* is a grill house specializing in char-grilled meats which often serves *kokorétsi*, a sausage made of offal, or lamb chops.

The *kafeneío* is the coffee shop where from morning till evening men sip coffee or play cards and backgammon. In small villages without tavernas the woman of the house may serve home-cooked food or offer local cheese. *Ouzéri* serve *ouzo* or wine accompanied by *mezédes*, which can be anything from char-broiled octopus to cucumber sticks. Greeks love the *zacharoplasteío* for its neon-lit counters laden with syrupy *báklavas*.

Waiters often tout for customers, but Greek families dining out are a better advertisement

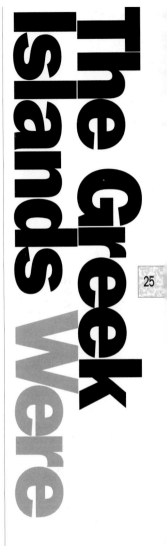

The Greek Islands Were

The world of Greek mythology—of gods, demi-gods, nymphs, furies and heroes—is a complex one. Most ancient Greek art and literature drew heavily on mythology for its subjects and although many early works have been lost, enough survive to provide a precious record of these monumental stories.

IN THE BEGINNING... There were different versions of the creation myth, but one of the most widely accepted began with Chaos, the unshaped mass from which an ordered universe was formed. Chaos gave birth to Ge (or Gaia), the earth-goddess. Then Ge, without a partner, gave birth to Uranus (sky), whom she later married. Their many children included Ourea (mountains), Pontus (sea), the Cyclops, the Hundred-Handed and the Titans including Phoebe (the moon), Hyperion (a sun god) and Kronos. Ge also gave birth to Oceanus, the stream that encircled the earth, dividing the land of the humans from the underworld.

THE EARLY GODS Into this ordered world came gods who helped maintain the order. They were described as being related—a family—no doubt reflecting the growing importance of the family unit in Greek society. The founders of this heavenly family were Ge (earth) and Uranus (sky). Uranus feared his children and threw them into Tartarus, deep in the earth. Ge, wracked with pain, made a sickle and urged the Titans to strike out at their father. When Uranus next came to Ge's bed, Kronos cas-

The Cyclops Polyphemos is blinded by Odysseus and his crew

trated him, threw his genitals into the sea and became ruler of the world. But Kronos then feared that he would suffer the same fate as his father, so he ate his children Demeter, Pluto, Poseidon, Hera and Hestia. When his youngest was due, his wife Rhea tricked Kronos into swallowing a stone instead, hurried off to Crete and gave birth to Zeus. When Zeus was grown, he forced Kronos to vomit up the children in his belly and himself became ruler of the gods.

THE OLYMPIAN GODS With Kronos out of the way, the world was divided between his three sons: Poseidon was given the water, Pluto the underworld and Zeus the earth. Zeus's wife Hera, champion of heroes, is most frequently depicted as being jealous of Zeus's recurrent extramarital relations. They are seen as the mother and father of the gods, although only two of their legitimate children—Ares and Hephaistos—were admitted to the Olympian Twelve. The others were Athena, Apollo, Artemis, Poseidon, Aphrodite, Hermes, Demeter, and Hestia.

CULT FIGURES As well as the gods, a range of cult figures appeared in Greek mythology. Among those whose tales have survived into our own time are Midas, the king who was given the double-edged ability to make everything he touched turn to gold and Orpheus, whose love for the wood-nymph Eurydice led him to brave the horrors of the underworld.

THE DESCENT OF MAN Earlier Greeks accepted that man grew out of the earth, like animals, plants and all other living things, but the poet Hesiod (*c*8th century BC) claimed the

Poseidon and Anymone in Chaniá Archaeological Museum

gods made the first race of humans from gold, the second race of silver, the third of bronze. They were followed by the Homeric heroes and last of all by his own age, of which he wrote, 'never by day they cease from toil and woe, nor by night from being worn' (*Theogony*). It is at this point in the story of Greece that history begins to overtake mythology.

Hermes is often represented in the full flower of youth

❏ Among the best early sources for mythology are:
Homer: The *Iliad* and the *Odyssey* are the oldest surviving works of Greek literature.
Hesiod: The *Theogony* presents the creation myth and the genealogy of the gods.
Pindar: The *Victory Odes* from the Olympic Games are peopled by athletes and gods.
Aeschylus, Sophocles and Euripides: The 5th-century dramas of these Tragic Poets are based on the same sources as Pindar.
Pausanius: His *Guide to Greece* was written around AD170.
Apollodorus: His *Library* of mythology draws heavily on Pausanius and the Tragic Poets. ❏

The religion of the Ancient Greeks was peopled with a great number of deities, connected to each other through a series of legends about the creation and early times of the universe. Many gods were personifications of aspects of the world around them (earth, night, spring) or of human life (love, discord, wisdom).

The great god was Zeus, son of Kronos, who lived on Mount Olympus with his wife Hera. His brothers Poseidon and Pluto ruled the sea and the underworld respectively. Also on Olympus were the other major gods: Athena, Apollo, Artemis, Aphrodite, Ares, Hephaistos, Demeter, Hestia and Hermes. As well as the Olympian gods, there was a host of lesser deities: the Furies, Harpies, Nymphs and Sirens. In addition, there were demi-gods: deified heroes like Heracles and Perseus, who lived on earth but became gods on their death. Ancient Greeks tried to understand the will of the gods by consulting oracles (most famously at Delphi and Dodona), interpreting dreams and looking for a variety of signs, from flights of birds to a clap of thunder.

The better-known gods of Ancient Greece include:

Aeolus God of the winds, which he kept in a cave in the Aeolian Islands.
Aphrodite The beautiful goddess of love and marriage, said to

According to Homer, Aphrodite was the daughter of Zeus and Dione

have sprung from the sea near Kýthira.
Apollo Twin of Artemis, born on Dílos. Skilled with the lyre and bow, he was regarded as the sun god (Homer called him radiant) and later also the god of all progress.
Ares Son of Zeus and Hera, the terrible god of war and lover of Aphrodite.
Artemis The huntress was a virgin goddess, often connected with the moon.
Asklepios God of medicine, worshiped at Epidáuros in the Peloponnese and on Kós.
Athena Together with Zeus and Apollo, one of the sacred trinity, often shown as the prudent warrior. As the goddess of wisdom, both practical and intellectual, she was the patron of the city of Athens.
Demeter Great mother-goddess, responsible for the fruitfulness of the Earth and mother of Persephone.
Dionysos Also known as Bacchus, he taught men how to grow grapes and was the god of wine. Dionysia or bacchanalia, riotous celebrations or orgies, were famous throughout antiquity.
Eris Goddess of arguments and sister of Ares.
Eros God of love.
Gaia Earth-goddess. Born from Chaos, she gave birth to Kronos, ruler of the earth before Zeus.
Hebe Goddess of youth.

Dionysos with panther, from the House of Masks at Dílos

Nyx Goddess of the night and mother of doom, death and sleep.
Oceanus God of the ocean.
Pan God of shepherds and nature.
Persephone Daughter of Demeter. She was abducted by Pluto and became goddess of the underworld. When found by her mother, she agreed to spend part of the year underground (winter), the rest above.
Pluto God of the underworld, brother of Zeus and Poseidon.
Poseidon God of the sea, brother of Zeus and Pluto.
Priapus A fertility god, usually shown as an ugly satyr with huge genitals.
Rhea Wife of Kronos and mother of Demeter, Hera, Hestia, Poseidon, Pluto and Zeus.
Uranus God of the sky and father of the Titans, the Cyclops and, according to one legend, Aphrodite.
Zeus Son of Kronos and both brother and husband to Hera. Born on Crete, the leader of the gods presided over them on Mount Olympus.

Zeus, the supreme divinity

Hecate Goddess of darkness and witchcraft, who roamed the earth on moonless nights with a pack of ghostly, howling dogs.
Helios A sun god, but not to be confused with Apollo. Helios rose on his chariot from the ocean in the morning and returned there at night.
Hephaistos The friendly god of fire, a blacksmith who lived on Límnos.
Hera Sister and wife of Zeus; the goddess of marriage and motherhood. The mother of Hebe, Ares and Hephaistos, she was often seen as a jealous wife—understandable, given Zeus's serial infidelities.
Heracles Later known as Hercules, he was worshiped as a demi-god for completing the famous 12 labours.
Hermes The messenger of the gods. A complicated deity, the epitome of many fine qualities but also associated with theft and cunning.
Hygieia Goddess of health; Asklepios's daughter.
Kronos Son of Heaven and Earth, he ruled the world until deposed by his son Zeus.
Luna A moon goddess.
Metis Aunt of Zeus, by whom he fathered Athena. Metis was eaten by the god when she was pregnant which is why Athena was born from his head.
Muses The nine daughters of Zeus and Mnemosyne, they were attributed to different kinds of poetry.
Nike Goddess of victory, most famously portrayed in the statue found on Samothráki, now in the Louvre, in Paris.

It is hard to travel anywhere in Greece without hearing of some of the key events in the country's long and illustrious history. The chronology below will help to put those events in context. (Note that many of the earlier dates given are approximations only.)

3200–2000BC	Cycladic civilization
2800–1000BC	Bronze Age
2600BC	Rise of Minoan civilization
1600BC	Height of Mycenaean civilization
1500BC	Thíra's volcano explodes
1450BC	Knosós palace destroyed
1184BC	Fall of Troy
1100–100BC	Iron Age and Dorian invasions
900–750BC	Creation of city-states
776BC	Probable date of first Olympic Games
750–700BC	Homer
650BC	Birth of Sappho (Lésvos) Aígina mints first Greek coins
570–480BC	Pythagoras (Sámos)
500–323BC	Classical period
490BC	Battle of Marathon
480BC	Battle of Salamis
478BC	Dílos, centre of Maritime League
460–45BC	First Peloponnesian War
460–377BC	Hippocrates (Kós)
458BC	Aeschylus' *Oresteia*
456BC	Euripides' first tragedy
442BC	Sophocles' *Antigone*
431–04BC	Second Peloponnesian War
425BC	Aristophanes' *Acharnians*
399BC	Trial and death of Socrates
380s/370sBC	Plato's *Republic*
359–36BC	Philip II of Macedonia
336–23BC	Alexander the Great
323–146BC	Hellenistic period
146BC	Romans sack Corinth, annex Macedonia and Greece
146BC–AD410	Roman rule
AD58	St. Paul on Rhodes
AD95	St. John's revelation on Pátmos
AD395–1453	Byzantine rule
AD476	End of the Roman empire (western)
AD727–843	Iconoclasm: banning of icons in Eastern Church
AD824–961	Saracen rule in places
AD961	Byzantines retake Crete
1054	The Great Schism
1088	Monastery of St. John founded on Pátmos
1096	First Crusade
1204	Fourth Crusade: Constantinople taken. Venetians claim right to Ionian and other islands

1210	Venetians take Crete
1309	Knights Hospitallers of St. John arrive on Rhodes
1453	Constantinople falls to Ottoman Turks
1522	Rhodes falls to the Turks
1541	El Greco born in Crete
1649–69	Venetian-Turkish war, ends with Irákleio falling to Turks
1797	Napoleon takes the Ionian Islands
1799	Ionian Republic declared
1815–64	British rule in the Ionian Islands
1821–27	War of Independence
1822	Chíos massacre
1823	Solomós writes the *Hymn to Liberty*
1827–29	Aígina capital of Greece
1827	Defeat of Turkish fleet at Battle of Navaríno
1828–31	Ioánnis Kapodístrias rules
1833	Accession of King Otto
1834	Athens becomes Greek capital
1854–57	Piréas blockaded by British and French fleets
1863–1913	King George I
1864	Ionian Islands annexed
1882–93	Corinth Canal cut
1883–1957	Níkos Kazantzákis
1901	New Testament (and *Iliad*) published in demotic Greek
1910	Venizélos becomes prime minister
1912–13	Balkans War. Greece takes Crete, Macedonia and Northern and Eastern Aegean Islands
1941	Greece invaded by Nazi Germany
1947–67	Constitutional monarchy
1967–74	Dictatorship of the Colonels
1974	Restoration of the Republic
1974	Turks invade Cyprus
1981	Greece joins European Union (EU)
1996	Andréas Papandréou dies
2003	Greece is head of the European presidency for a year
2004	Athens Olympic Games. Konstantine Karamalís from the New Democracy party becomes prime minister

Around 3200BC, a civilization emerged in the Cyclades that endured for more than 1,000 years. From this period come the first recognizably Greek art and some of the country's most wonderful ancient treasures.

A SEA CHANGE Perhaps the single most important change that occurred during the Bronze Age was the development of techniques for working metals, most commonly copper. As ore was transported through the Aegean, the Cyclades found themselves at the hub of new trade routes. From these elements a distinctive culture developed.

CYCLADIC ARTS AND CRAFTS Islanders began to live in larger communities, preferring hilly and, if possible, rocky sites for their settlements, close to the sea but easily defended. As well as metal, marble—found in excellent quality on Náxos and Páros—began to be worked into images that are among the finest creations of the human imagination. Pottery developed into an art.

Most of the objects that survive from this period were found in graves. Cycladic graves were rectangular, built of stone slabs and filled with objects that might be of use to the deceased in the afterlife: marble vessels, zoomorphic clay pots, bronze weapons and tools, amulets of clay or semi-precious stones and the marble figurines that have come to characterize Early Cycladic art.

AN UNSOLVED MYSTERY No one knows what purpose these figurines of startlingly modern appearance might have served. Were they cult figures? Divinities of life and death? Fertility figures?

The famous Faistós Disk has never been deciphered despite the endeavours of numerous experts

31

❏ The Cycladic era is often divided into three periods: Early Cycladic I, 3200–*c*2800BC; Early Cycladic II, *c*2800–*c*2300BC; Early Cycladic III, *c*2300–*c*2000BC. ❏

The function of clay discs known as 'frying pans', usually covered with geometric designs, is also puzzling. The accepted theory is that they were used for cult purposes, but you wonder what cult could the 'frying pans' decorated with ships, in the National Archaeological Museum in Athens, have served?

Few periods of Greek history offer as many attractions and mysteries as that of the Minoans (c2600–c1450BC). Their origins are obscured by myth, their dramatic ending has long been a matter of speculation, but what is certain is that the wonderful objects that have survived, particularly from their palaces on Crete, are proof beyond doubt of the grandeur of Europe's first civilization.

MINOS AND THE MINOTAUR

According to legend, Crete was ruled by King Minos whose wife, Pasiphae, fell in love with a bull. From their union came a frightening creature, half-man, half-bull, called the Minotaur, for whom Daidalos, the great architect, built a labyrinth under Minos's palace at Knosós. Every nine years a group of young Athenians were sent into the labyrinth, never to be seen again.

32

THE AGES OF THE MINOANS It is difficult to separate fact from fiction with the Minoans. The Greek historian Thucydides (c460– c400BC) wrote that King Minos was 'the first ruler we know of who possessed a fleet and controlled most of what are now Greek waters': this is supported by the growth of coastal settlements on pre-Minoan Crete. Other commonly accepted facts about the Minoan period include (using Professor

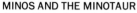

Bull's head from Knosós

N. Platon's period division, *Crete*, London, 1966):
Pre-Palace (2600–1900BC): communities were established and growing, stone and metals were worked and burial rituals became increasingly elaborate.
Old Palace (1900–1700BC): insecurity elsewhere in the region led the Cretans to unite under a few leaders, a concentration of power and wealth which led to the building of palaces at Archánes, Faistós, Knosós, Mália and Zákros. This period ended with a huge earthquake around 170BC.
New Palace (1700–1450BC): the old settlements and palaces were reconstructed after the earthquake in a grander style.
Post-Palace (1450–1100BC): Greek-speaking Achaians took over power from the Minoans.

THE OLD PALACE PERIOD After 2000BC, several extraordinary palaces were built on Crete. Very little is known about who built them, or why, so we can only marvel at the objects found in them, such as the hieroglyphic writing (still not deciphered), the brightly coloured pottery known as Kamáres ware and the finely worked jewellery, including the famous 'Hornet Pendant' from Mália, made around 1700BC, just before a massive earthquake destroyed all of the Minoan palaces.

THE BULL AND THE LABYRINTH The Minoans held complex rituals involving the bull, the animal sacred to the sea-god Poseidon. Decorations have shown the importance of a bull-leaping ceremony and there is a convincing theory that it was for this,

A fine gold amulet with two bees holding a drop of honey, found in the Palace of Mália on Crete

today. Knosós was once again the scene of the Minoans' most sacred rituals and seat of their power. It is from the new palaces that the great Minoan frescoes have been salvaged, startling for their realism and exuberance. Similar realism appears on the surviving pottery, particularly on the jars showing octopuses, dolphins and other sea life.

Around 1450BC, this great period of the Minoans came to an end when buildings across the island were destroyed. Was it by fire, perhaps, or a tidal wave caused by the eruption of Thíra's volcano?

once every nine years, that unwitting or unwilling Athenian youths were brought to Knosós. Another theory suggests that the labyrinth was not a place but a series of rituals or dances, a mystic approach to Poseidon, who was, appropriately, enough called the 'Earth Shaker'.

THE NEW PALACES After the earthquake, the Minoan civilization was still vigorous enough for new palaces to be built, the ruins of which we see

Huge píthoi *like these, for storing wine and olive oil, were found in most Minoan palaces in Crete*

❏ When Theseus, son of King Aegeus of Athens, went to kill the Minotaur, Ariadne, the daughter of King Minos, gave him a ball of thread which allowed him to retrace his steps through the Labyrinth. After killing the Minotaur, Theseus fled Knosós with Ariadne, but then abandoned her, asleep, on Náxos. His punishment was immediate: sailing home to Athens, he forgot the arrangement he had made with his father: to change his black sails for white ones if he had survived. His father, seeing the black sails and believing that his son was dead, killed himself. ❏

In the 15th century BC, power and influence shifted from the islands of Greece to the mainland, in particular to Mycenae, the Peloponnesian kingdom where, according to Homer, Agamemnon, leader of the Greeks' army to Troy, ruled. By the time Homer was telling his tales, the Mycenaeans were history and the Archaic period (c700–c500BC) was witnessing the birth of the city-state.

The alleged golden funerary mask of King Agamemnon

a rectangular hall entered through a porch and vestibule. At the centre of the *mégaron* was a hearth, surrounded by four columns.

Mycenaean tombs were just as accomplished, their central chambers covered with a dome of cut stone, sometimes well over 9m (29ft) high. Huge blocks of stone, carefully cut and fitted together to make high walls, gave rise to the term 'Cyclopean', used to describe Mycenaean fortifications which can still be seen today at sites such as Tiryns and Mycenae itself.

THE DORIC INVASION Disaster overtook the Mycenaeans, as it had the Minoans and in their place came the Dorians, Greek-speaking people from the north. The Dorians are often described as having ushered in a 'dark age', but evidence suggests otherwise. Being warriors in troubled times, by necessity their settlements evolved into fortified towns and this was the germ from which the Classical city-states and ancient Greece as we think of it, grew. Alphabetic writing also appeared in their time, as did Greek colonies in Asia Minor, the idea of the gods on Mount Olympus and Homer, who came at the height of a great tradition of storytelling.

MYCENAEAN POWER (c1500– 1125BC) The people who took control of Crete from the Minoans and who attempted to control trade in the Aegean, as legend tells us King Minos did, came from Mycenae, a town in the northern Peloponnese, north of the Saronic island of Spétses. It was during this era that many of the events that inspired Greece's epic poets took place.

THE BASIS OF GREEK ARCHITECTURE The roots of Greek architecture can be traced to the Mycenaeans. A great Minoan palace, such as Knosós, rambled over the hillside with its hundreds of chambers, but the Mycenaeans favoured a controlled symmetry. The main component of their palaces was a *mégaron*,

THE ARCHAIC ERA The period loosely called Archaic saw important changes to the society of the islands. There were significant shifts of population as colonies were founded

Archaic sculptures were often a strange interpretation of foreign, mainly Egyptian, statues

❏ The term 'Spartan', still in use today, refers to characteristics exemplified by one of the two great city-states of the Archaic period. Lycurgus, the Spartan lawmaker, believed that people were distracted by the decorations on buildings, so he banned them. A similar theory was expressed about the home, which led to the creation of a uniquely unembellished city. The Spartans were just as single-minded in their behaviour and, to keep the citizens fighting-fit, both boys and girls were forced to exercise. ❏

across the Mediterranean. As Greek culture spread, so did the influence of Greek ideas, of poetry, philosophy and architecture. The most important change was undoubtedly the rise of the city-state (*polis*). Greece was divided into about 1,500 of these. Notable city-states on Crete included Górtys (the most powerful), Polyrriniá, Lató and Praísos.

There had never been anything like the *pólis* before. For the first time, ordinary people had a part to play in the running of their community. Regarding themselves as independent political and military units, city-states fostered their individual identities in times of peace but formed leagues or alliances with others when it was expedient. The most powerful cities to emerge were Sparta and Athens, usually bitter rivals.

❏ According to Homer, among the men who followed Agamemnon and Achilles to Troy, 'Euboea [Évvoia] sent the fiery Abantes, the men of Chalcis, Eiretria and Histiasa, rich in vines...Those from Dulichium and the sacred Echinean Islands... Odysseus next, leading the proud Cephallenians, masters of Ithaka' (*Iliad* Book II).

From Homer's list it is clear that during the Mycenaean period the islands all had separate and recognizable identities, each with a number of ships, a leader, a band of warriors and a community at home to which they hoped to return one day. ❏

A row of magnificent Mycenaean lions guards the waters of the Sacred Lake in Dílos

At the height of the Classical period, around the 5th century BC, Athens achieved the glory for which she is still renowned. In poetry and sculpture, in warfare and politics, the Greeks and particularly the Athenians shone. By the time of Alexander the Great (336–323BC), the vitality of Athens was exhausted, but her achievements have not been lost.

CLASSICAL GREEKS United at the beginning of the 5th century BC by a common enemy in the form of the Persians, who threatened the Delian league (effectively Athens' empire), the people of Athens and her colonies emerged with a common identity and with artists and poets to question and refine it.

THE GLORY OF ATHENS Much that we admire about ancient Greece—the Parthenon, lifelike statues, moving drama, the political force of democracy or the wisdom embodied in treatises such as Plato's *Republic*—was conceived or already flourishing during the Classical period. The power

Top: Pericles, Athens's great statesman. Below: Alexander the Great in battle at Issus in 333BC

and wealth that ensued after Athens had fought off the Persians and taken control of most of the Cyclades and Dodecanese was shared among the Greek people.

Although not all classes were entitled to vote—women and slaves were prohibited—those who could had a more active hand in the administration of power than the average voter of today: for example Pericles, the most famous Athenian general, was voted out of office by an electorate he had temporarily angered, shortly before his death in 429BC.

THE PELOPONNESIAN WARS Athens was not the only great city-state. Corinth and Sparta were her rivals for trade in the eastern Mediterranean. Although they had all banded together to face the Persian threat, they

Lidded Greek amphora

were also suspicious of each other. From 460 to 445BC Athens fought against the Peloponnesian League but it was Corinth, not Sparta, who was at the forefront of the conflict. Athens was victorious in that she had her maritime empire acknowledged in the peace treaty, though only at the cost of handing back territory gained on the mainland. After a mere 14 years they were fighting again: Athens lost the Second Peloponnesian War (431–404BC), but all parties were so weakened by the conflict that they were unable to prevent the rise of the Macedonians (Philip II and Alexander the Great) in the 4th century BC.

ALEXANDER THE GREAT In 338BC, Philip II of Macedonia defeated the Athenians and Thebans in his single-minded attempt to unite the diverse and widely scattered city-states under his control. Two years later Philip was succeeded by his son, Alexander III, the Great. The 5th-century BC Greek historian Herodotus identified *hellenikón*, Greekness, as 'shared blood, shared language, shared religion and shared customs'. The remarkable Alexander lost no time and showed little mercy, in extending the concept: having conquered the Persians (334–327BC) and taken control of the land between Greece and Afghanistan, he hoped his culture would provide a common bond between the diverse people of his empire that would allow them to trade and thrive.

THE HELLENISTIC IDEAL Alexander was said to have founded over 70 new cities (though it was really many

fewer). The generals who divided up the empire on his death, at the age of only 33, carried on where he had left off. These cities were the perfect vehicle for spreading Greek culture.and, in the process, for Hellenizing conquered people by introducing Greek institutions, constitutions and language. This was an attempt not so much to convert new subjects to Greek ways as to establish Greek colonies to rule over new territories: 300 years after the founding of Seleucia in Persia, for example, the only people with Greek names were those who actually had Greek fathers.

With new cities came new rulers and new courts, all wishing to emulate the cultural achievements of Athens. Alexandria, with her library and her great thinkers and writers, did this so successfully that Athens was eclipsed as the cultural centre of the Hellenistic world. This set a precedent that the emerging Romans were only too happy to follow: Rome annexed Greece more than a century before Cleopatra committed suicide and Alexandria was taken. Even under Roman rule, however, Greek remained the common language of the lands conquered by Alexander.

❑ The Greek alphabet, from which ours has evolved, was adopted from the Phoenicians in the 8th century BC. By the Classical period, it was taken for granted that a man of wealth could read. In Athens during this period, at least half of the male population was literate. ❑

The Romans regarded themselves as the inheritors of the achievements of ancient Greece and were more tolerant of the Greeks than of many other subjects. With the decline of the Western Empire and the move of the Emperor Constantine to Constantinople, the Greeks found themselves part of a glorious civilization—that of Byzantium.

ROME'S EMPIRE The Roman conquest of Greece started in 215BC. The Macedonians, under Perseus, were defeated in 168BC when Athens was taken. Corinth fell in 146BC. Under Roman rule, the city-states survived, with Corinth, as the principal city and Athens, as the artistic and spiritual centre, attracting special favour. In Greece, the Romans stressed continuity, while the hallmarks of Roman presence—the security of the *Pax Romana* and the building of roads and of aqueducts and other irrigation works—brought wealth and an increase in population.

The Byzantine icon of the Virgin and Child from Skiádi on Rhodes

❑ Religious subjects dominated Byzantine art, but in the 8th century, differences of belief led to what is known as the Iconoclastic Controversy. While Iconoduli worshiped icons (religious images), Iconoclasts wanted them banned and they were until the Empress Theodora had them legalized in AD843. ❑

IMPERIAL GREECE The Romans loved Greece and many emperors made the journey from Rome. Nero is said to have competed in the Olympic Games and danced and sung at the Temple of Zeus at Kassiópi, on Corfu. In AD122, the Emperor Hadrian visited Athens, having been deified by the Greeks and calling himself Olympian Zeus. He rebuilt the city, added the suburb of Adrianopolis (approached through Hadrian's Arch), built his library and completed the Temple of Olympian Zeus.

CHRISTIANITY St. Paul is credited with bringing Christianity to Greece and in the mid-1st century he visited the great mainland cities, as well as several islands. The Greeks took to Christianity with a passion, converting pagan temples into churches and some local deities into saints. In those early years, they also provided martyrs, including the Ágioi Déka (Holy Ten) of Crete, who were killed by the Romans for their faith.

BYZANTIUM In the 4th century AD, Emperor Constantine had a vision of a cross on which was written *Hoc vinces* ('By this you shall win'). It was a defining moment in history: in

Byzantine church near El Greco's birthplace in Fódele

AD330, having made Christianity the state religion, he moved his capital to Byzantium, which he renamed Constantinople (now Istanbul). After 65 years the empire split into two. The Eastern (Byzantine) Empire—the more vital—was based on Greek culture, Roman regulations, Christian morality and the wealth of the eastern Mediterranean.

In AD476 the Western Empire was overrun by 'barbarians,' but under the Emperor Justinian (AD527–565), Byzantine fortunes revived, lost provinces were restored, the entire imperial law was codified and the empire's defences were strengthened; it was at this time that many of the islands' *kástri* were built.

BYZANTINE ARTS AND ARCHITECTURE As well as the *kástri*, the Byzantines built glorious churches and cathedrals throughout the empire. Many have survived on the Greek Islands. Byzantine art and architecture blended Greek and oriental elements into a new form. Literature was written in a form of Greek that was increasingly removed from the spoken language. Drama and poetry were ignored, while writers concentrated on theology, history and philosophy. Byzantine painting,

The Temple of Olympian Zeus in Athens, built by the Emperor Hadrian on earlier foundations, is the largest temple in Greece

also blending eastern and western elements, made rich use of colours, particularly gold.

THE END OF BYZANTIUM The Byzantine Empire had to fight for its existence from the very beginning. Persians, Arabs, Egyptians, Seljuks, Turks and Venetians all sought to undermine it, but in the end the very brilliance of Constantinople and the jealousy of the provinces in its power, were its downfall. The fatal blow was struck not by unbelievers, but by Christians—Crusaders—who sacked the city in 1204.

In the 11th century Byzantium gave Venice trading rights in Greece in return for protection against the Normans. Before long Byzantium needed to counter Venetian power by encouraging the Genoese. But in 1204 the Venetians deported the Crusader army that sacked Constantinople and ushered in a period of diverse foreign rule.

THE CRUSADERS When the Seljuk Turks captured Asia Minor and Jerusalem, some Christian kings, seeing commercial and political advantage behind religious justification, sailed east to recover the Christian holy places from Muslim control. Christian power bases were established in the region, some of them taken from the Byzantines; Cyprus, for instance, was taken by England's Richard I during the Third Crusade. The Fourth Crusade (1202–04), undertaken with the blessing of the Latin Pope, saw the sack of

The Knights of Rhodes defeated the Turks in the naval battle of Embro

Constantinople and the creation of a Latin Empire of Romania. In the dismemberment of the Byzantine Empire, the Greek mainland was divided among Flemish, French and German barons, owing only nominal allegiance to the new Latin emperor.

VENETIAN MIGHT The power of Venice was based on its navy. The dominant sea power of the eastern Mediterranean, rich from carrying trade between eastern ports and Europe's capitals, Venice had been the obvious choice to provide a shipping service for the Crusading armies, both for the strength of its navy and for the rapacious ambition it shared

40

with the Christian knights. Part of the payoff was Venetian control of most of the Aegean, which helped Venice to secure the shipping routes to Alexandretta and the Black Sea as well as to Alexandria. The Venetian aristocracy controlled the republic's new possessions, most noticeably the Orsini family in Kefalloniá and the Sanudi, who became the dukes of Náxos and thus effectively controlled the Cyclades.

CHANGING TIMES The Venetians continued to add to their possessions in the Aegean: in 1204 they acquired Crete, valued for its grain and sugar; they held the island until it was captured by the Turks in 1669. Évvoia was bought in 1209 and, until its capture in 1470, served as an excellent maritime base. The Venetians faced increasing competition from their commercial rivals the Genoese, who had been enlisted by the Byzantines in 1261 to help bring down the Latin emperor in Constantinople. When that succeeded they were given control of the islands of Chíos, with its lucrative mastic trade and Lésvos, while in 1267 the Genoese occupied the Golden Horn at Constantinople and controlled trade to and from the Black Sea.

WANING POWER Some time around 1354 a new and irresistible force appeared in Europe for the first time: within 200 years the Ottoman Turks

❏ Crusaders on their way to the Holy Land showed little interest in Greece and her islands. The most influential Crusader presence appeared only after the collapse of the Eighth and final Crusade (1270–72) when the Christians were forced to flee the Holy Land: the Knights Hospitallers of St. John, an order founded to care for sick pilgrims in Jerusalem, arrived on Rhodes in 1309 and, until their defeat by the Turks in 1522, were a significant force in the islands and in eastern Mediterranean trade (see pages 168–169). ❏

The Siege of Constaninople in 1453, taken from the Turkish Story of the Nations

had seized control of much of the eastern Mediterranean. At the time, the Venetian Republic was still adding to its strategic possessions: Tínos and Mýkonos were taken in 1390 and four years later Venice even had control of Athens, which it held until 1402. But in 1453, only two years after the Venetians took Aígina, both Venetians and Genoese failed to respond in time to prevent the Turks capturing Constantinople. In September 1453, rather belatedly, the Pope issued a Bull calling for another Crusade, but there was no response. The Genoese ceded control of the Black Sea trade, the Knights of St. John were forced out of Rhodes in 1522 and one by one the heavily fortified Venetian posts fell to the Turks, although Tínos held out until 1715.

Greece was too close a neighbour for the Ottoman Turks to leave in foreign hands. But the sultan in Constantinople (Istanbul) had little interest in this newly acquired territory. Having been treated as the private property of European rulers, the Greeks found themselves neglected by the Ottomans (1453–1827).

42

SECURING NEW TERRITORIES

After setting up their capital in Constantinople, the Turks took more than two centuries to capture all the Greek islands. One legacy of this period is the islands' ruined fortresses, many of them sacked by Kheir-ed-Din Barbarossa. Born and brought up on Lésvos, Barbarossa made his reputation raiding European ships and establishing, under Turkish sovereignty, the kingdom of Algiers. In 1535, Sultan Suleiman (the Magnificent) appointed Barbarossa High Admiral of the Ottoman fleet. Within three years, Barbarossa's notoriously ruthless tactics had ensured Turkish domination of islands and sea in the golden age of the Ottoman empire. He died in triumph in Constantinople in 1546.

OLD WAYS PRESERVED

The Ottomans were generally negligent in their occupation of Greece. They regarded the Greeks and other Christians as lesser beings, from whom they required obedience, particularly concerning taxes. At the time of the Ottoman conquest, Patriarch Gennadius guaranteed obedience and

The Turks lift the siege of Rhodes

regular taxes in return for self-government. Although in this way the Church became an instrument of foreign rule, it also had an important role to play in creating the national identity by preserving Greek and Byzantine traditions.

THE BITTER YEARS The British ambassador to Constantinople in 1622 complained that Turkish rule was so hard that he had to ride for three or four days in Greece to find food for himself or his horse. Taxation had its effect, as had the taking of children to be trained as Janissaries (imperial soldiers), a practice that was stopped later in the 17th century because it affected people's ability to pay taxes.

> ❏ The Orthodox Church still commemorates 28 May each year, remembering that Tuesday in 1453 when Constantinople, centre of the Eastern Empire and of the Orthodox Church, fell to the Ottoman Turks. ❏

THE PHANARIOTES Not all Greeks suffered. In the 17th century, some official posts became available to them. In 1669, Panagiotaki, a Greek Christian from Chíos, was appointed Dragoman to the Porte, in effect a secretary of state to the sultan. Other Greeks were appointed to govern territories, or as assistants to senior officials. Most lived near the Patriarchate, beside Constantinople's lighthouse, the *Phanar*, and were known as Phanariotes.

THE TURKISH LEGACY Considering how long the Turks occupied Greece, very little has survived from then, mostly as a result of a backlash against Turkish institutions and property after independence. Notable

❏ As Orthodox Christians, the Greeks found support in the 18th century from Russia, particularly under Catherine the Great. In 1783 she took the Crimea and forced the Sultan to allow Greek ships to trade under the Russian flag. This new status boosted the fortunes of Greek traders while depriving the Turks of mercantile support. ❏

exceptions include the mosques and houses in old towns such as Rhodes, Chaniá on Crete and Myrína on Límnos.

Monuments of the Turkish legacy, like the Defterdar Mosque on Kós, are often neglected in Greece

43

The French Revolution; the weakening of the Ottoman Empire; the conviction of Western aristocrats that Greece must rediscover her glory; rebellions and atrocities within the Greek territories; and growing opposition to the Turkish occupation by sympathizers elsewhere in Europe—all these factors helped create the circumstances that brought about Greek independence.

THE ORIGINS OF THE STRUGGLE

Although in some places (particularly on the islands previously held by the Venetians) there was initial relief when the Ottoman Turks arrived as the new masters, from the beginning of the Turkish occupation Greeks had fought for their independence. Not for a Greek nation—there had not been one for so long that most would not have understood the concept—but at least for freedom from what was, for many people, in effect slavery. In the last decades of the 18th century, Catherine the Great of Russia promoted the cause of Greek Christians, but events took a more significant turn when Napoleon

44

Bonaparte took the Ionian Islands from Venice in 1797. Two years later a combined Russo-Turkish force captured them and created the autonomous Septinsular Republic and for the first time in 350 years the islanders had at least the pretence of governing themselves.

CULTURAL SIGNALS The movement toward independence had interesting cultural indicators. While Smyrna-born scholar Adamántios Koräis was working in Paris on reviving classical Greek, groups in Europe were raising awareness of Greek aspirations. They included the *Filikí Etaireía*, founded in 1814 in Odessa by three Greek merchants and the Philomuse Society in Vienna which numbered the Bavarian king and the Russian czar among its supporters. The British poet Lord

A wreath on Byron's statue in London commemorates the cause that was dear to him as well as to many other foreigners

Byron, who first visited Greece in 1807, was one of many classically educated foreigners who sympathized with the Greek cause, while the arrival in European capitals of Greek antiquities did much to win over the western public.

ACTION The Metropolitan of Pátra raised the Greek flag on 25 March, 1821, a date still celebrated as Greece's national day. Nothing that occurred in the ensuing struggle for independence was as simple. European governments condemned the move, but public opinion was for Greek independence. Early Greek successes led to a power struggle between rival groups. In April 1824 the death of Lord Byron at Messolóngi increased international support for the cause and when Messolóngi fell to the Turks in 1826, British, French and Russian fleets were sent to pressure the Turkish sultan. It ended in conflict, with the Turkish and Egyptian navies being destroyed at Navarino in October 1827, ending the long period of Turkish control of the Greek seas and paving the way for independence.

THE CONTINUING STRUGGLE It took the Greeks until the middle of the 20th century to take possession of the land they regard as their own. During the reign of King George I of Greece (1863–1913) the British relinquished the Ionians (1864) and Crete was finally won in 1913, following the Balkan Wars. In 1897 Greece went to war against the Turks and was defeated. The resultant upheavals saw the advent of one of the country's most able and best-loved rulers, Elefthérios Venizélos, who took Greece into another conflict with Turkey (1912–13), this time to emerge with considerable territorial gains, including the eastern Aegean islands.

In 1921, having supported the Allies during World War I to their advantage, the Greeks again went to war with Turkey. Turkey had undergone considerable changes of its own under the leadership of

Ioánnis Kapodístrias, Greece's first president after independence

❏ Count Ioannis Capo d'Istria (later spelt Kapodístrias) from Corfu was one of the most powerful Greek politicians during the independence struggle. With the Treaty of Adrianople (1829), Greece won its autonomy. Kapodístrias had already been elected governor and when the new state was created he became its first president. He provoked strong opposition by ignoring the constitution and in October 1831 he was assassinated. As a result, the European powers imposed a monarchy on the country. ❏

Kemal Ataturk and the Greeks were crushingly defeated. The consequences were catastrophic: around a million and a half Greek refugees were forced out of Turkey, back to their homeland. It took Greece until the 1950s to recover from their arrival.

45

Greece emerged from World War II in a state of crisis and immediately slid into civil war. Since then it has been ruled by monarchs, military dictatorships and mainly socialist governments. Only now is it enjoying an extended period of stability for the first time.

ÓCHI! In August 1940 the Italians tried to provoke the Greeks into joining World War II by sinking one of their battleships in Tínos harbour. They failed. Two months later they demanded the right to march Italian troops across Greek soil, to which the head of Greece's government, General Metaxas, gave his famous response—'Ochi!' (No!)—still commemorated with a public holiday. Early victories against the Italians in Albania led to a German occupation of Greece in 1941. With the help of British commandos a bitter resistance

46

❏ The Dictatorship of the Colonels from 1967 to 1974, led by Colonel George Papadópoulos, marked the low point in modern Greek history. Executions, mass imprisonment, the hounding of public figures (even the beloved Melína Merkoúri) and inept administration were typical of the junta. In 1974 the Colonels were forced from power and a referendum also ended the monarchy. ❏

The actress Melína Merkoúri was a strong opponent of the junta

campaign was waged and in 1944 most of Greece was liberated from the rule of the Germans.

CIVIL WAR Even during the German occupation, rival resistance groups had begun fighting each other. From December 1944, after the government returned from exile, Greece became an ideological battleground. It was by now surrounded by Communist regimes in Albania, Bulgaria and Yugoslavia. After right-wing parties won the 1946 elections, the United States offered massive financial and military aid. Although internal Greek politics were polarized, the country came under increasing American influence, joining NATO in 1951. Continued American backing created the climate (and some say gave instructions) for the 1967 military coup that stopped George Papandréou's Centre Union Party from taking power.

THE EUROPEAN IDEAL Since the downfall of the Colonels and the monarch, Greece has been a republic keen to measure itself by European standards. Democracy was encouraged and living standards improved under Konstantine Karamanlís, a hard-line conservative who also lobbied for entry into the European Union. Greece joined the EU in 1981, the year of her first socialist government, led by Andréas Papandréou. In 2004, Karamanlís was elected prime minister, leaving behind PASOK rule for the time being.

PASOK The major force in recent Greek politics has been Papandréou's PASOK (Panhellenic Socialist Movement). With a decisive majority, it ruled from 1981 until its scandal-ridden government was brought down in 1989 by a bizarre coalition of left- and right-wing parties. In 1990 the right-wing New Democracy Party was voted in with a small majority, but although its austerity plans seemed to be approved, humiliation over the creation of an independent Macedonian state brought back Papandréou's PASOK with a large majority in 1993. Ill health forced Papandréou to step down in 1995 and he died the following year.

THE PRICE TO PAY Despite the image of wealthy shipping families, Greece is not a rich country. There has been extraordinary economic and social change since World War II, with growth in housing, education and health care (although the last still

cannot be taken for granted). At the same time there has been hardship, a move away from the countryside and islands to towns where living conditions for many remain poor.

Andréas Papandréou at the height of his powers

The multi-millionaire shipping magnate Aristotle Onassis

❏ 'Macedonia...is Greek—always has been, always will be.' So says one particularly plain-speaking sticker that has appeared all over Greece. In 1991, one of the provinces of the former Yugoslavia proclaimed independence under the name of Macedonia. As part of northeastern Greece is also called Macedonia (and only passed from Turkey to Greece in 1913), Greece vigorously opposed the new state using the name, fearing that in time it will call for the unification of Macedonian lands. As a strange compromise, both the UN and the European Union recognized the new state under the name of The Former Yugoslav Republic of Macedonia (FYROM). ❏

'Don't mention the Turks'… Greeks are still bitter about the Turkish occupation of their country. The proximity of the two countries, and recent events, have ensured that Greeks remain suspicious of Turkish intentions.

WHEN TURKS WERE MASTERS There are obvious historical reasons for Greek mistrust of Turkey. From a religious point of view, it was the Turks who brought an end to the Greeks' spiritual centre, the Orthodox capital of Constantinople. Politically, the centuries of Turkish rule have also left bitter memories. The Greek state was built upon the rejection of Turkey, independence coming only after Greeks had taken up arms. While Greeks wrapped their actions in the cloak of romance, the Turks were always seen as barbarians: no one mentions Greek atrocities in the War of Independence but the Turkish massacre of the islanders of Chíos caused international outrage.

A NEW ERA The last islands were handed back to Greece in the 1940s, but that has not eased fears about Turkish expansionist policies. Independent Greece is as uneasy as ever about its neighbour. There are few Ottoman buildings left intact in Greek towns, few mosques left unconverted and Turkish artefacts are conspicuous by their absence in Greek museums, but despite all the Greek efforts to

On a clear day the coast of Turkey is easily visible from the beach in Kós

erase traces of the occupation, the Turks still loom large. Nor will the rest of the European Union adopt Greece's attitude of condemning Turkey since they fear alienating a strategically valuable ally (Turkey's stand during the 1991 Gulf War was evidence of this strategic value).

CYPRUS In 1974, the Greek military junta, headed by former secret police chief General Ioannídes, attempted to stage a coup in Cyprus to overthrow the independent Cypriot leader Archbishop Makários. The coup failed to dislodge the archbishop but still provoked an aggressive Turkish response: some 30,000 Turkish troops helped Turkish Cypriots divide the island into two separate entities, taking at least a third of the land even though Turks accounted only for some 18 per cent of Cyprus's population. The Greeks attempted to fight back and for a few days a full-scale war between the two enemies looked likely, until international diplomacy defused the situation. Although only

Turkey has recognized Turkish Cyprus as an independent state and has, apparently, settled mainland Turks on the northern part of the island, enforcing their position with a considerable garrison, the international community has held back from implementing the anti-Turkish measures that Greece has demanded for the simple reason that Turkey is too valuable an ally to alienate. A status quo now appears to be observed, giving Greece justification for blocking Turkey's application for membership of the European Union.

TROUBLE IN THE 'GREEK LAKE'

Greek islands fringe the western coast of Turkey and sit on the vital shipping lane from the Bosphorus to the Mediterranean. The Turks complain of having to sail through what has become a 'Greek lake', while the Greeks watch Turkish movements with alarm. The isolated positions of some Greek islands make the situation even more difficult: there is a story circulating in the Dodecanese, for instance, that if the population of Kastellórizo drops below 200 the island will revert to Turkey. Greek officials deny this as vigorously as they protest invasion of Greek air space by the Turkish air force: Greek jets are scrambled periodically in response to these aerial 'invasions'. From its side, Turkey protests at the heavy Greek military presence on the island of Límnos, so close to the Turkish mainland.

The Archbishop Makários waving at a crowd of Greek Cypriot supporters

THE FUTURE As the futility and trauma of the exchange of Greek and Turkish populations showed in the 1920s, there are no quick solutions to this crisis between neighbours. Differences in religion, history and self-image, in economies and military standing, will always remain.

A negotiated settlement, an easing of tension and, especially, a solution to the Cyprus problem will have to come about before relations will begin to improve—more easily said than done. Mutual suspicion is inevitable, in view of the long history of conflict.

Turkish tombstones dumped outside the Archaeological Museum in Irákleio, Crete

The famous porch of the Eréchtheion, supported by Caryatids, thought to be aristocratic maidens in the service of Athena

ATHÍNA (ATHENS) Greece's capital city has such a reputation for traffic and pollution problems that many visitors head straight out for the islands. However, the capital has changed dramatically in the last five years, particularly since the 2004 Olympics. It is unlike anywhere else in Greece, it's a wonderful place to spend a few days strolling around, especially in spring and autumn. The Acropolis, of course, is essential viewing, despite the crowds and several of the city's museums complement visits to the islands by their displays of island artefacts and antiquities, which bring the islands' history vividly to life.

There is no escape from the ancient Greeks, even in modern-day Athens

ANCIENT BEGINNINGS Athens has grown enormously in the past few decades, but its centre remains clustered around the Acropolis and Areopagus hills, where the first settlement grew, around 3000BC. Athens played her part in the Mycenaean and Dorian periods but did not really shine until the 8th century BC, when, under the protection of the goddess Athena, the city dominated the Greek world, its wealth and power attracting intellectuals and artists still influential today.

ATHENIAN GLORY The Persian King Darius attacked the rising city-states of Athens, Sparta and Corinth in 490BC, but his formidable army was defeated by a smaller Athenian force at Marathon. Ten years later the Persians returned under King Xerxes with the largest army ever seen. The Athenians were strongest at sea: after Athens was destroyed, the Greek navy outmanouvred the Persians at Salamis and forced them to withdraw. The glorious city that attracts us today—the city of the Parthenón, the Eréchtheion and the Temple of Athína Nike, of Phidiass famous statue of Athína, Herodotus' histories, Socrates' philosophy and Sophocles' and Aristophanes' dramas—rose out of the 5th-century BC reconstruction of the city.

▶▶▶ CITY HIGHLIGHTS

Acropolis
see pages 54–55

Museum of Cycladic and Ancient Greek Art
see pages 58–59

National Archaeological Museum
see pages 56–58

USEFUL NUMBER
Airport (tel: 210 353 0000)

FOREIGN RULE Athens's power was already waning when the Macedonians—Philip and his son Alexander the Great—sought her help with their eastern ambitions. Alexandria and Pergamon began to challenge her cultural supremacy, though even after the Roman conquest (146BC) Athens was revered for her achievements. Roman emperors, especially Hadrian, added to her beauty, while shipping treasures off to Rome and then later to Constantinople. By the 3rd century AD they were unable to defend her and the city was sacked by barbarians.

THE MODERN CITY Fifteen hundred years of foreign rule—Byzantine, Catalan, Neapolitan, Venetian, and Turkish—eventually left Athens a heap of derelict housing crouching around the Acropolis. For the capital of the newly independent Greek state, King Otto I (1833–62) planned new districts along neoclassical lines, their broad avenues now forming the centre of the modern city. Athens has changed greatly since the Olympic Games in 2004, with new metro lines and a tram way, a new ring road around the city and a new airport. A pedestrian area in the centre now allows visitors to walk from one archaeological site to the other.

ISLAND DREAMING More and more people dream of leaving Athens and returning to the islands of their birth or parentage. Those who stay in the city flee to the islands in the summer, so if you want to see Athens in full swing, visit in spring or autumn (fall): winter is cold and can be wet; summer is hot and many shops and restaurants close.

TOURIST INFORMATION

The Greek National Tourist Organization (GNTO) has moved its administrative headquarters out of the centre to Odós Tsokha 7 (tel: 210 870 7000; www.gnto.gr; *open* Mon–Fri 9–4.30), but still has a great deal of information. More practical is the tourist office at the airport (tel: 210 353 0445) or at the more central and very helpful information office at 26a léoforos Amalias, Syntagma (tel: 210 331 0392; *open* Mon–Fri 9–7, Sat–Sun 10–4), opposite the National Garden. These offices have useful information on ferries, accommodation, sights and more. In the summer there are City of Athens Information Booths all over the capital (tel: 195; www.cityofathens.gr).

53

The picturesque streets of old Athens are a reminder of the simple village life on the islands

Athína (Athens)

A STROLL THROUGH THE AGORÁ

After visiting the Acropolis it is a pleasant stroll down to the Agorá and the area of Monastiráki via the hill of Áreios Págos (Areopagus). Just below the entrance to the Acropolis, stairs ascend to the site of Areopagus, with various ancient and Roman foundations and good views over the entire area. From here it is possible to continue to the southern entrance of the Agorá.

OPENING TIMES IN GREECE

Opening times of monuments and sights vary greatly in Greece from year to year and from day to day. There is often a difference between winter and summer as well. To make sure of the opening times call in advance, or check with the Ministry of Culture (tel: 210 820 1100; www.culture.gr).

The Acropolis is still the heart of Athens, often visible from wherever you are when the smog clears

▶▶▶ Akrópoli (Acropolis)   52B2

(Tel: 210 321 0219)
Open: 8–7.30 in summer; 8.30–3 in winter (hours change frequently). Admission charge (free Sun Nov–Mar).
Metro: Akrópóli. Bus: No. 230

The Ancient Greeks always built their acropoli on high places, a safer bet and also a step closer to the gods. The Athens Acropolis was already a cult place when the Athenians erected their magnificent temples and buildings here in the 7th century BC. After the Persians set fire to Athens and sacked the Acropolis in 480BC, the ruins were at first kept as a reminder, but 50 years later Pericles rebuilt the city in all its splendour. The remaining buildings are still a testimony to the magnificent achievements of Greece's Golden Age. The weathered stone glows in the sun, seductive to our modern eye but looking rather different from the original buildings, painted in bright colours and with dressed-up statues covered in golden trinkets.

Even before it was finished, the massive gateway or **Propýlaia**, constructed between 437 and 432BC by the architect Mnesikles, was considered as great an achievement as the Parthenon. The graceful **Naós Apteroú Níkis (Temple of Athena Nike)**, built between 427 and 424BC by Kallikrates, was surrounded by a marble wall sculpted with war scenes and figures of the winged Victory. According to legend, this is where Aegeus waited for the return of his son Theseus from Crete, and where he jumped to his death after Theseus forgot his promise to signal victory over the Minotaur by hoisting a white sail.

Today the site, as the city itself, is dominated by the **Parthenón**, but in Classical times the temple, less important than the Eréchtheion, was mostly hidden by other buildings. Hundreds of books have been written about the perfection and optical illusions of the vast Doric temple, but a simple wink of the eye reveals its magnificence and harmonious proportions. It was built in Pentelic marble between 447 and 438BC by the architects Iktinos and Kallikrates. Phidias completed the sculptures in 432BC, including the 10m (33ft) high bronze statue of Athena which stood in front of the temple and was visible from Cape Sounion. The statue was taken to Constantinople and later lost. Most of the Parthenón sculpture is in the British Museum in London, some in the Louvre in Paris and the rest in the Acropolis Museum. Over the years the Parthenón has been put to many uses, from Greek and Roman temple to Byzantine church, Frankish cathedral and Ottoman mosque.

The last great monument on the Acropolis is the complex **Eréchtheion**, built on an older sanctuary and dedicated to Poseidon, whose spring provided the temple's inhabitants with water, and to Athena, whose sacred olive tree grew on this site. The famous southern Porch of the Caryatids or Maidens was used for rituals. Four of the original caryatids are displayed in the **Mouseío Akropóleos (Acropolis Museum)** (*Open* Tue–Sun 8–6.30, Mon 11–6.30 in summer; Tue–Sun 8–2, Mon 11–2 in winter), which houses some magnificent sculpture from the Acropolis including fragments of the Parthenón frieze and the unique 6th-century BC *korai*—statues of young maidens attending Athena.

The **ancient Agorá** (*Open* daily 8–7.30, in summer; 8–3, in winter. *Admission charge*), northwest of the Acropolis, was the market place and the centre of Athens's political and social life. Its buildings cover a large area and date from the 5th century BC to late Byzantium, making the site difficult to understand. Among the ruins is the 5th-century BC **Thiseío (Theseum)**, the best-preserved ancient building in Greece. It was a temple to Athena and Hephaistos, though the adventures of Theseus are depicted on its frieze. The museum, in the **Stoá Attálou (Stoa of Attalos)** (2nd-century BC, reconstructed between 1953 and 1956), has 6th- to 4th-century BC pottery and fine red-figure dishes.

BEST VIEWS OF THE ACROPOLIS

There is a good view of the Acropolis from Odós Aiólou, where the rock rises up at the end of the street, and from the area around the Naós Aiólou (Tower of the Winds) at night when the site is illuminated. The views from the nearby pine-wooded hills of Arditóu, Filopáppou and Lykavittós are excellent, and make for the ultimate picnic with a view.

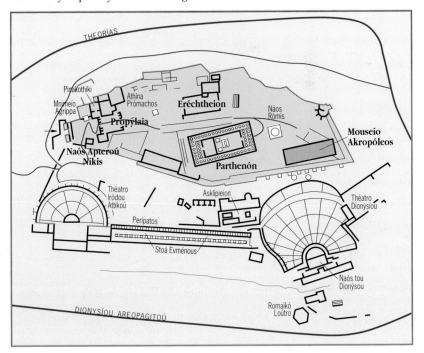

Athína (Athens)

MOUSEIO BENAKI (BENAKI MUSEUM)

The Benáki Museum (corner of Odós Koumbári and Vasílissis Sofías; tel: 210 367 1000; www.benaki.gr. *Open* Wed–Sat 9–5, Sun 9–3, Thu 9–midnight. *Admission charge*) houses the wonderful collection of the Egyptian Greek, Antoine Benáki. The museum contains Egyptian antiquities and Ottoman manuscripts, a superb collection of folk costumes and crafts from the Ionian islands, as well as several paintings by the Cretan-born El Greco.

Many of the best archaeological pieces from the islands are in the National Archaeological Museum, including these vases from Thíra (Santoríni)

►►► Ethnikó Archaiologikó Mouseío (National Archaeological Museum)   52C4

Odós Patissíon 44 (tel: 210 821 7717) Open: Tue–Sun 8–7.30, Mon 1–7.30 in summer; Tue–Fri 8–3, Mon 10.30–3, Sat–Sun 8.30–3 in winter. Admission charge. Trolley buses: Nos. 1, 2, 3, 5, 6, 7, 8, 9, 11, 13, 15. Metro: Victoria

The National Archaeological Museum is one of the top museums in the world, with an astounding collection of the world's finest Cycladic, Minoan, Mycenaean and Classical Greek art. The best finds from the islands have made their way here, some of them as the prize exhibits, so a visit is essential to get a complete picture of the archaeological sites on the islands.

The visit starts with three prehistoric rooms, the first of which (room 4) often renders visitors speechless as it is packed with the rich treasures discovered by the archaeologist Heinrich Schliemann in the chamber tombs at Mycenae (see pages 86–87). Most famous of all is the **Funerary Mask of Agamemnon** (No. 624), named by Schliemann for its supposed connection with the words from the *Iliad*: 'He was the King of Men... distinguished among many and outstanding among heres.' There is the silver **bull's head with golden horns** (No. 384) and the earliest known depiction in Europe of a historical event, on the silver **Siege Rhyton** (No. 481). Almost every case contains objects of extraordinary refinement, including gold seals with hunting scenes (Nos. 33–35) and a delicate duck-shaped vase in rock crystal (No. 8638). To the left of the central gallery, in the pre-Mycenaean room (room 5) are neolithic figurines, pottery and jewellery from the Thessalian plain. In the **Cycladic room** (room 6), on the central gallery, the finds are arranged island by island. The largest female figurine (No. 3978) and a beautiful large head (No. 3909) were discovered on Amorgós, while the amazing harpist and flute-player (Nos. 3908 and 3910) come from Kéros, near Amorgós. The excellent marble figurines (6195, 6140.21 and 6140.22) come from Náxos, as do the finely decorated vases, some in the shape of animals.

Most of the remainder of the ground floor is devoted to sculpture, arranged chronologically and showing clearly the developments from immobile stylized statues of the early Archaic period to the free and more naturalistic masterpieces of the Classical period. Rooms 7–13 are devoted to Archaic sculpture from the 7th to the 5th centuries BC. Room 7 has the first statue listed in the museum's catalogue, the **Artemis of Nikandra** (No. 1), discovered on

FOLK ART FROM THE ISLANDS

The Mouseío Elliníkis Laografias (Museum of Greek Folklore), (Odós Kydathinaíon 17, Pláka; tel: 210 322 9031. *Open* Tue–Sun 10–2. *Admission charge*) is a must for anyone interested in the fast-vanishing traditions of most of the islands. It houses an important collection of folk art from the mainland and the islands, including ceramics, shadow puppets, embroideries, jewels and costumes, as well as a series of murals by the primitive artist Theophilos (1873–1934) who came from Lésvos.

Dílos. Rooms 8–13 contain many *kouroi* and steles, of which the best examples are the **kouros from Mílos** (room 9, No. 1558), the exquisite **Stele of Marathonomachos** (No. 29) and the strong, graceful **Kroisos** (No. 3851) from around 530BC. The extraordinary bronze **Poseidon of Artemision** (room 15), found in the sea near Évvoia, has the perfectly balanced body of an athlete, muscles tensed as he prepares to throw his trident. The impressive **Eleusinian relief** (No. 126) in the same room shows Demeter and Persephone with the young Triptolemos, from about 430BC.

Among the Classical steles from 5th-century BC graves in rooms 16–17, note the delightful **relief of the actors** (room 17, No. 1500), where Dionysos, lying on the bed, is worshiped by an actor holding a mask and by two drummers. The exquisitely carved funerary **Stele of Hegeso** (room 18, No. 3624) expresses sorrow and a kind of despair in a very subtle and dignified way. Quite poignant for anyone from the islands today is the **Stele of Demokleides** (room 18, No. 752), showing a man sitting on a rock, his head resting in sorrow, with his prow and high waves in front of him, suggesting that he died far from home.

Room 20 has a small Roman copy of Phidias's Athena (No. 129), the cult statue from the Parthenón. Does the 'jockey' belong with the jumping horse (room 21, No. 15,177)? The question continues to divide experts, but most people who see the 2nd-century BC bronze statue tend to marvel at the passion and the tension of the boy and the racing horse. It is hard to imagine what else the boy might have been designed for.

In the middle of room 28 stands the **Youth from Antikýthira** (No. 13,396), a large bronze statue from about 340BC, discovered in many pieces near Antikýthira. The statue is a masterful portrait of a relaxed, confident and

BOOKSHOPS

The international bookshops in Athens are the best place to stock up on books about Greece and the islands.

● Eleftheroudákis (Odós Panepistimíou 17; tel: 210 322 9388) has good guidebooks and books about both ancient and modern Greece.

● Compendium (Odós Níkis 28; tel: 210 322 1248) is smaller but well stocked with English-language books on Greece, and plenty of fiction.

● Lycabettus Press (tel: 210 363 5567) has published several interesting guidebooks to individual islands such as Pátmos, Spétses, Náxos, Kós etc.

● The museum shop sells quality plaster casts of the masterpieces of sculpture from museums all over Greece, as well as good copies of famous Greek frescoes and icons.

The magnificent statue of Poseidon was found on the same shipwreck as the Little Jockey in room 21

The vivid Hellenistic portrait of the unnamed philosopher was found off the coast of Antikýthira

WHAT'S ON?
English-language listings of films, theatres, concerts, lectures and other entertainment can be found in the monthly *Athenian* magazine, the daily *Athens News* newspaper and the excellent weekly *Athenscope* magazine. Another good source for listings is *Kathimerini*, the supplement with the *Herald Tribune* news-paper. For those who read Greek, the *Athinórama* weekly or its website www.athinorama.gr are both excellent.

totally harmonious youth. Room 30 has another treasure from Antikýthira, the Hellenistic **Head of the Philosopher** (No. 13,400), which shows the man, wrinkles and all. This is in direct contrast to the earlier Classical **Head of the Boxer** (room 28, No. 6439). The 2nd-century BC **Poseidon** (No. 235) supported by a dolphin, dominating the room, once adorned the Poseidon Temple in Mílos. The 1st-century BC **Man from Dílos** (No. 14,612) looks anxiously towards the future (as well he might—Greece was a Roman province by then), while in the **Group with Aphrodite and Pan** (No. 3335), made around 100BC and also from Dílos, Pan is held back by Eros while seducing the naked, shy Aphrodite. Rooms 41–43 contain Roman sculpture, including some pieces from the islands.

On the upper floor, rooms 49–56 house the **Vase Collection** with amazing pottery from the Geometric period, black-figure and red-figure vases and white *lekythoi* (containers for oil or perfume), many of which came from Eretria on Évvoia. In room 48, the **Thíra Exhibition** contains various finds from excavations on Thíra (Santoríni), including pottery, bronze objects and the famous frescoes from Akrotíri, remarkably well preserved having been covered by volcanic pumice for so long. These wall paintings have provided much essential information about life on Thíra at the end of the 16th century BC. The best-preserved frescoes are the **wall-painting of the fisherman**, where a naked young man holds two bunches of fishes and the strange **wall-painting of Spring**, which shows a Thiran landscape before the volcanic eruption, with swallows and flowers.

▶▶ **Monastiráki** 52B2

Monastiráki, the area between the Agorá and Syntágma, is famous for its Sunday morning flea market and also for its restaurants and budget hotels. Monastiráki metro stop is useful for the area around Syntágma and Pláka.

▶▶▶ **Mouseío Kykladikís kai Archaías Elliníkis Téchnis (Museum of Cycladic and Ancient Greek Art)** 53D2

Odós Neofítou Douká 4, Kolonáki (tel: 210 722 8321; www.cycladic-m.gr)
Open: Mon and Wed–Fri 10–4, Sat 10–3. Admission charge
All buses for Plateía Syntágmatos (Syntagma Square)
Sometimes also referred to as the Goulandrís Museum, this fine collection was amassed by a wealthy shipping magnate who was a keen patron of the arts. The Nikolas P. Goulandrís Foundation opened the museum in 1986, with astonishing displays of Cycladic art, as well as Minoan and Mycenaean sculpture and pottery.

Unlike many other museums in Greece, it exhibits and labels every object perfectly, allowing even the most casual

*Helmet worn by the
Athenian army general
Miltiades*

JUST A BIT OF TORSO

'There remains only a fragment of the torso, just the two breasts, from the base of the neck to above the navel. One of the breasts is draped, the other uncovered. What breasts! Good God! What a breast! It is apple-round, full, abundant, widely spaced from the other; you can feel the weight in your hand. Its fecund maternity and its love-sweetness make you swoon. The rain and sun have turned the white marble yellow, a tawny colour, almost like flesh...How one would have rolled on it, weeping! How one would have fallen on one's knees before it, hands joined!... A little more and I'd have prayed'. The French writer Flaubert describing a statue in the Archaeological Museum, from *The Letters of Gustave Flaubert, 1830–57*, edited and translated by Francis Steegmuller (London, 1954)

GREEK MUSEUMS

'The least expert haunter of such places must surely feel the difference between other museums and those of Athens, which contain hardly anything but masterpieces exhumed on or near the spot where they took life. You may not be a connoisseur, but in presence of original marbles undishonoured by the proximity of even excellent copies, your eyes become cleansed and sharpened and you see as you never saw before.' Ethel Smyth, *A Three-Legged Tour in Greece* (London, 1925)

These exquisite marble figurines inspired many 20th-century artists

visitor to understand the intricacies of Cycladic art (see page 31). In the basement are a café and a shop with expensive copies of the figurines on display. The first floor is mainly devoted to Cycladic marble figurines (3200–2000BC). The stylized 'violin' figurines (case 3) are among the most common types of early Cycladic sculpture, with a long stem for the neck and two symmetrical shapes for the chest and the voluptuous hips. In case 5, the more intricate Plastira type of early Cycladic figurines have facial details and well-formed buttocks. The majority of these statues are female, but there are a few rare examples of male torsos, such as the one with a folded arm in case 9. Cases 22 and (especially) 26 hold some of the best and most impressive figurines, where it seems the artists were more confident and more masterful in handling of the marble.

Some of the works have an astonishingly modern feel to them—perhaps because the smooth, simple lines of Cycladic sculpture have inspired some famous 20th-century artists, including Modigliani and Henry Moore. The entire second floor of the museum has been dedicated to Ancient Greek art including Minoan and Mycenaean ceramics, Geometric pottery, Archaic art, bronze vessels and some lovely Tanagra—female terracotta figurines (4th century BC, displayed in case 40).

Go through a lovely cool courtyard (with cafeteria) to reach the adjacent neoclassical Stathatos mansion. This was the former home of the 19th-century German architect Ernst Ziller, designer of the Olympic Stadium and the Presidential Palace. This is the sumptuous annexe of the museum, used for those exhibitions and other displays of a temporary nature.

Athína (Athens)

Monastiráki has few of its original market stalls left, but a flea-market fan can still discover a bargain or two

ETHNIKOS KIPOS (NATIONAL GARDEN)
The National Garden offers welcome shade to both Athenians and visitors. It was formerly the private palace garden, stocked with plants shipped from all over the world in the 1840s by Queen Amalia. There is still an amazing variety of trees and shrubs. On the southern side is the Záppeio, a grand exhibition hall and some elegant café terraces.

NAÓS AIÓLOU (TOWER OF THE WINDS)
The Syrian astronomer Andronikos of Kyrrhos designed this octagonal tower in the 1st century BC as a water clock, compass, weather vane and sundial. Each side represents one of the eight winds, each personified by a different figure flying through the air. Underneath each figure was a sundial.

GAZI AND PSÍRRI
The old working area of Psírri, north of Ermou, is now a happening place with bars, clubs, trendy shops and restaurants, and so is the quarter of Gazi, west of Ermou, where artists and intellectuals hang out. In this area is also the small Maria Callas Museum (Technopolis, Odós Pirás, Gazi; tel: 210 346 0981) for devotees of the singer.

▶▶ Pláka   52C2

The Pláka is definitely the most atmospheric part of Athens. Its pedestrian streets wind steeply up the hill towards the Acropolis, lined with lovely neoclassical houses, flower-filled balconies, café terraces, Greek ruins and stunning views of the Parthenón. Part of it is now very touristy, with mediocre but expensive tavernas, tacky souvenir shops and endless crowds in the evening.

Stroll off the main streets of the city in search of the quieter squares, the little museums and the archaeological sites to enjoy its beauty. The **Monument of Lysikrátous▶▶** (Odós Lysikrátous) is an elegant marble structure from 335BC and nearby are the **Sanctuary of Olympian Zeus▶▶** (*Open* Tue–Sun 8.30–3. *Admission charge*), the largest temple in Greece and **Pýli Adrianoú (Hadrian's Arch)▶▶**. The **Naós Aiólou (Tower of the Winds)▶▶▶** is easily the loveliest and best-preserved building in the **Romaïkí Agorá (Roman Forum**, Odós Aiólou. (*Open* Tue–Sun 8.30–2. *Admission charge*).

▶ Plateía Omonoías (Omonia Square)   52B3

All roads in Athens seem to lead here. The whole district surrounding the square has a somewhat run-down air but the lively **meat and vegetable markets▶▶**, the 'bazaar' area, and the nearby National Archaeological Museum (see pages 56–58) make it a useful stop. Despite a recent face-lift, the once beautiful square still looks drab.

▶▶ Plateía Syntágmatos (Syntagma Square)   52C2

This is the centre of government, business and tourism in the capital: the best area to look for banks, as well as tourist and travel offices. Up the hill are the **Greek National Parliament (Voulí)** and the **Tomb of the Unknown Soldier**, guarded by the Evzónes, soldiers in traditional mountain costume. Across the street stands another Athens institution, the Hotel Grande Bretagne, one of the capital's grandest hotels. Political demonstrations frequently take place in the square, also adding to the traffic chaos.

Getting around Athens and Piréas

Airport Athens's international airport, Elefthérios Venizélos, is 26km (16 miles) east of the city at Spáta.

Buses and Metro Athens' extensive network of buses and trolley buses runs from 5am to midnight. Tickets are inexpensive, but must be bought in advance from kiosks, individually or by the 10 and cancelled on the bus. Tourist office offers a city map with metro lines and bus routes, and the website www.oasa.gr offers info on how to get to all of Athens' sights. Tickets are inexpensive, day and week tickets are available from kiosks and all public transport stations, but exclude the airport. Tickets must be bought in advance and cancelled on board. A new 24-hour tramway runs from Léforos Amalias, south of the National Garden to Glyfada and Néo Faliro (south Piréas), offering a quicker escape to the beaches near Athens (www.tramsa.gr).

Taxis Athenian taxis are inexpensive, but make sure the meter is switched on and that the display is on zero when you get in. The legal surcharges, for luggage, Christmas and Easter bonuses and double fare after midnight, are displayed in English in every taxi. A tip of 10–15 per cent is customary. Any other charges are robbery.

Ferries and Hydrofoils www.gtp.gr and www.greek-islands-ferries.gr offer timetables, prices and availability for all the ferries from/to Greece and the Greek islands; you can make reservations online. Departure times are announced in the *Herald Tribune* supplement (*Kathimérini*), and the tourist offices in the centre and at the airport have a daily printout of departure times on their windows. All ferry schedules are subject to change. Most shipping agents in Piréas have offices around the Metro or on Plateía Karaïskáki. There are fixed quays for departures to each island group, so make sure you have enough time to look for it as the port is huge.

The hydrofoils and high-speed catamarans are twice as fast as the ferries, and often cost twice the price. They are more subject to weather conditions than the ferries, but in summer it is best to book tickets in advance. Most hydrofoils and catamarans leave from Zéa Marína in Piréas.

Piréas, a port since antiquity, has now grown into a city in its own right

LEAVING THE AIRPORT
The X95 express bus links with the city centre approximately twice an hour, 24 hours a day. The journey can easily take one hour or even two. There are taxis and a metro (line 3, from 6am–midnight) to Syntágma Square. The X96 leaves twice an hour, 24 hours a day, to Piréas.

ATHENS-PIRÉAS-ZÉA MARINA
The easiest and fastest way to get from Athens to Piréas is by metro (line 1) every 10 minutes from 5am–midnight to and from Omonoías, Monastiraki, Victoria and Thissio. Bus 40 leaves from Syntágma Square, bus 49 from Omonoías to the ferry docks, also from 5am–midnight. Bus 904 leaves from Plateía Karaïskák, 200m (220 yards) to the left coming out of the Piréas metro station) to Zéa Marína.

Most foreigners visit Piréas to catch one of the island-bound ferries

Kríti (Crete)

KRÍTI (CRETE) The most southerly of Greece's major islands has been getting a bad press for insensitive tourist development and much of it is deserved. Away from the resorts, however, it is still 'the Great Island', rich in history and tradition, important historical sites and excellent museums, beautiful landscapes, an incomparable variety of flora and still a few idyllic, out-of-the-way beaches.

IN THE BEGINNING: MYTH AND FACT Most people arriving in Crete have heard of Minos, the legendary king who already belonged to ancient history when the Athenians built the Parthenón. Minos' wife, Pasiphae, gave birth to the Minotaur, half-man, half-bull, who was contained in a great labyrinth beneath King Minos' palace. There is no proof for any of this, but great palace complexes have been found across the island, dating from 2000 to 1450BC. For want of any more accurate name, the people who built them have been called Minoans, after the legendary king. Enthusiasm for the splendours of this civilization is often tempered by a sneaking suspicion that the Minoans sacrificed humans. The sudden demise of the Minoan era,

Kríti (Crete)

Page 62, top: Lasithiou Plateau
Right: some coastal towns, like Ágios Nikólaos, have kept their charm despite rapid development

64

when the palaces are thought to have been destroyed by an earthquake or a tidal wave, remains a mystery. However, it heralded the end of Crete's golden age and by the time Athens was enjoying her glory, the island had become a backwater.

ROME AND CHRISTIANITY Crete, an important prize for anyone wanting to control the eastern Mediterranean, was always hard-won: the Romans attempted invasions in 71BC and again in 69BC, but only succeeded in controlling Crete until 67BC by getting Cretan to fight with Cretan. From the Roman era to the Byzantine, the island flourished economically, though there was little social advancement. Christianity spread through the island: St. Paul is believed to have visited Crete around AD50, the famous Ágioi Déka (10 martyrs) were put to death at Górtys and after the conversion of the empire to Christianity many splendid churches and chapels were decorated with extraordinary frescoes.

VENETIAN AND TURK Venetian nobles won control of Crete after the sack of Constantinople (1204). They encouraged farming, stripped out timber for their shipyards and used the excellent harbours as way stations for east–west trade. When the Turks took Constantinople in 1453 many Byzantine scholars fled to Crete, stimulating a period of artistic excellence, the Cretan renaissance. The Venetians built magnificent fortifications to fight off the Turks, but by 1649 the island was lost.

INDEPENDENT IDENTITY Turkish rule was negligent at best and the memory of the occupation is still bitter. The Cretans fought regularly for their independence, which was not won until 1913. In May 1941, Nazi Germany invaded the island, Allied defences crumbled and the Cretans found themselves fighting again. For four years they suffered great brutality, but by the start of 1945 Cretan partisans and Allied intelligence officers had penned the Germans into Chaniá and were in control of most of the island.

THE NATURAL WORLD While Crete's capital and main towns are all along the coast, Cretan tradition is an agricultural one. The island's history and the character of its people are shaped by the geology of the country, which is dominated by mountains. Zeus, the father of ancient gods, was born in the Cretan mountains, great Minoan cities were built in them and resistance to Nazi Germany was centred up there. It is in the mountains that Crete's age-old traditions have been best maintained and where its spectacular catalogue of rare flora and fauna finds refuge.

ARTISTIC HERITAGE Crete is known for its legacy of painters and writers, from El Greco to Níkos Kazantzákis, creator of Zorba the Greek. There is also a strong tradition of folk music, of *mantinádes* (improvized poems, accompanied by the lyre), of songs glorifying history, songs for the table and songs for the road. Equally strong is the tradition of dances: one is said to represent the legendary hero Theseus leading his companions out of the Labyrinth. It is often performed for tourists in tavernas, the leader guiding his companions with his handkerchief.

THE CRETAN CHARACTER

'The Cretan character—warlike, proud, compulsively generous to a friend or stranger in need, ferociously unforgiving to an enemy or traitor, frugal day-by-day but prodigal in celebration—was, of course, strongly influenced by the landscape of dramatic contrasts in which the islanders lived... From subtropical vegetation with banana trees, carobs and orange groves, a mountain village, only 15km away as the crow flew, but probably sixty on foot, seemed to exist in a different world and a different climate.'
Anthony Beever, *Crete: The Battle and the Resistance* (1991)

65

MODERN THREATS

In the 1960s much of Crete was underdeveloped and many Cretans were extremely poor. This has changed, in part because tourism has brought cash and work to the island, but at a price. Large tracts of the north coast have been spoiled by sudden, unplanned development. In some places the situation is so bad that hoteliers have been known to wish for an earthquake of Minoan proportions to bring it all down and give them a chance to do it differently. Tourists preferring to go elsewhere, as they are beginning to do now, may have the same effect. But the greater part of the island has been relatively untouched by this development and the farther you go from main roads, the more likely you are to see something of the individual customs and character that Cretans have fought so bitterly and so often to defend.

Kríti (Crete)

USEFUL NUMBER
Tourist information
(1 Xanthoudídou, oppo-
site the Archaeological
Museum, tel: 2810
24630; *Open*
daily 9–9, in summer;
8.30–2.30, in winter.

WHAT'S IN A NAME
The capital of Crete was
known as Irákleio in
antiquity, when it served
as a minor harbour for
Knosós. The Saracens, in
the 9th century, built a
stronghold (near the old
Venetian fort) which they
called Rabdh al-Khandah,
the Fortress with a Moat.
The Greeks then turned
the Turkish word for
moat—*khendek*—into
Khandákos, which was
further corrupted in sev-
eral European languages
into Candia, by which the
whole of Crete was then
known. During the 19th-
century Hellenist
movement, the ancient
name of Irákleio was
revived and in 1923 the
capital officially changed
its name.

►►► Irákleio (Iráklion)   64C2

Irákleio, the capital of Crete, has a reputation for being charmless and crowded—true, perhaps, but it is still a fascinating city. A visit is sure to be rewarding, even if it is only long enough to see the superb Minoan artefacts in the Archaeological Museum and Irákleio's Venetian monuments, not to mention the important Minoan site of Knosós nearby (see pages 83–85). As to the living city, the market and the pedestrian streets around it have plenty of local colour and character.

On the **Plateía Venizélou►** stands the fine **Morazíni Fountain** (see panel opposite), surrounded by restaurants, car-rental offices and shipping agencies. On 25 Avgoústou (the street leading from the square to the port), **Ágios Márkos►** was the first church built by the Venetians and is now an art gallery (*Admission free*). The elegant Venetian **Loggia** is nearby. Farther down, 10th-century **Ágios Títos►** (*Admission free*) has been reconstructed several times, lastly in the 1800s. It contains the relics of the saint who first brought Christianity to Crete. Seat of the Orthodox Archbishopric in Byzantine times, of the Roman Catholic Archbishopric under the Venetians and of the mosque during the Ottoman period, it was reconsecrated in 1925 and is an interesting architectural hybrid.

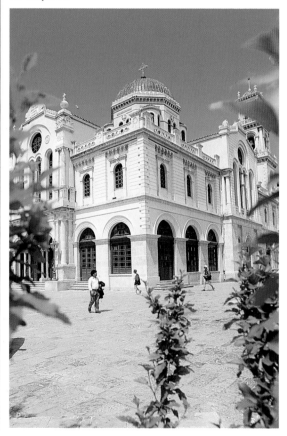

The square in front of the Ágios Minás cathedral is quieter and more typical than busy Plateía Venizeloú

The **Church of Agía Aikateríni▶▶** (Plateía Ag Aikaterínis. *Open* Mon–Sat 9–6, Sun 10–6. *Admission charge*) is a beautiful old building in the shadow of the imposing **Ágios Miná Cathedral** (*Open* daily 7am–8pm. *Admission free*). Connected to the monastery of St. Catherine in Sinai, Egypt, it contains a wonderful collection of icons, the most famous being a series by the near-contemporary (and maybe even teacher) of El Greco, Mikhális Damaskinós.

The magnificent **city walls▶** (*Admission free*) withstood the 21-year-long Ottoman siege of the city, during which 30,000 Christians and 117,000 Turks died, but which ended with the city falling in 1669. Only a small stretch is accessible: from the bastion of St. Antonio it is possible to walk on the 16th-century Venetian walls (4km/2.5 miles long and 60m/196ft wide in places) to the Martinengo Bastion and the **Táfos Kazantzáki (tomb of Kazantzákis)▶** (see page 91). The epitaph on his simple tomb reads, 'I believe in nothing, I hope for nothing, I am free.' More Venetian fortifications can be seen near the port: the **Koúles▶** (*Open* Tue–Sun 8.30–3. *Admission charge*), a well-preserved 16th-century fortress with a Lion of St. Mark guarding the doorway; and the boat sheds known as the **Arsenali▶** (*Admission free*), both restored. Up from the harbour, the **Istorikó Mouseío Krítis (Historical Museum of**

see page 91

THE MORAZÍNI FOUNTAIN
The fountain is Irákleío's most famous legacy from the Venetian period. It was ordered in 1628 by the Venetian Governor Francesco Morazíni. The basin is decorated with a relief of sea gods from Greek mythology. Water spouts from the mouths of four lions. Once upon a time a giant Poseidon rose up from the upper pool, but the colossus went missing during the Turkish occupation.

67

Kríti (Crete)

UNDERSTANDING THE MINOANS

To get a better understanding of Knosós and the various Minoan sites all over the island, as well as of the fascinating Minoan civilization in general, it makes sense to visit Irákleio's Archaeological Museum at least once before and once after visiting the rest of the island.

Crete) ►► (Sofoklí Venizélou, tel: 28102 83219. *Open* Mon–Fri 9–4, Sat 9–2, in summer; Mon–Sat 9–3, in winter. *Admission charge*) contains an excellent collection of Byzantine, Venetian and Ottoman art, Cretan folk art, the books and furniture of Níkos Kazantzákis and the only El Greco painting on Crete, the *View of Mount Sinai and the Monastery of St. Catherine* (c1570).

The **Archaiologikó Mouseío (Archaeological Museum)** ►►► (Odós Xantoudídou 2, tel: 28102 24630. *Open* Tue–Sun 8am–7pm, Mon 1–7.30; winter closing 3pm. *Admission charge*) houses the world's greatest collection of Minoan art: most local finds have been kept on the island. Ground-floor exhibits are arranged chronologically from Neolithic and Minoan through the Post-Minoan, Classical, Hellenistic and Roman periods. A magnificent collection of frescoes from the Minoan palaces is on the upper floor.

Some fascinating neolithic finds (room I) came from the Cave of Eileithyia (see opposite), such as the **fertility goddess** (No. 2716). Also of interest here is the **Vassilikí pottery** (case 6). Room II has a collection of finds from the Protopalatial period (2000–1700 BC), mainly from Knosós and various mountain sanctuaries dedicated to Zeus. Most exceptional are the early **Kamáres vases** (see cases 26–29) and the **faience** (case 25), which represent detailed façades of a Minoan town. Room III holds more superb **Kamáres ware**, mainly from

The wonderful murals confirm the sophistication of Minoan Crete

Faistós, especially the fruit bowl (No. 105,800) and the *krater* with flowers (No. 10578). The star item of this room, however, is the undeciphered **Faistós Disk**, the earliest known example of printing. The New Palace period (1700–1450BC) represented the peak of the Minoan civilization, proved by the exhibits in room IV: the **lily vases** from Knosós (case 45), the **jug of reeds** (case 49), the **bull's head rhyton** (case 51) and the astounding bare-breasted **snake goddess** (case 50). One of the most amazing objects is the **checker board** (case 57), made of ivory, gold leaf and rock crystal, from Knosós. Room V shows the decline of the New Palace period (1450–1400BC) with the Mycenaean influence discernible in most of the exhibits. The large number of **Egyptian objects** suggests a flourishing trade between Crete and Egypt, while the clay house from Archánes (case 70a) looks very much like Cretan houses today. The finest **jewellery** is on display in room VI, as well as two superb **helmets** (case 82), one of boar's tusks. Finds from smaller sites and villas (room VII) from throughout the Palace period show the richness and abundance of the Minoan life. Note especially the **pendant of two bees** (case 101). Room VIII has magnificent

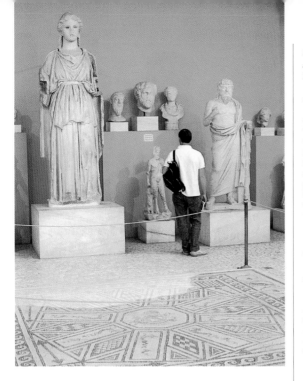

Statuary in the Archaeological Museum, Irákleio

A TROUBLED ODYSSEUS
'He [Odysseus] also was on his way to Troy, but the force of the wind drove him out of course past Malea to Crete. He escaped the storm with difficulty and managed to get into the dangerous harbour of Amnisos, where is the cave of Eileithyia.'
Homer, *Odyssey* Book XIX

FISH LIFE
The Hellenic Centre for Maritime Research has opened Cretaquarium, the largest aquarium in the Eastern Mediterranean, at the old American Base of Gournes, 15km (9 miles) east of Irákleio (tel: 28103 37801; www.hcmr.gr. *Open* daily 10–5.30. *Admission charge*). There are 32 tanks with a total capacity of 1,600,000 litres (352,000 gallons) of seawater. There are 50 viewing points to observe the 4,000 sea creatures, and special cameras allowing visitors to check out the 'hidden' spots in specific tanks.

ANCIENT VOTIVE OFFERINGS
Greeks today hang aluminium votive offerings in the shape of a baby or of some part of the body by icons in churches and chapels in the hope of being cured of an ailment. This is nothing new, as the votive offerings in the Archaeological Museum show. In room II, in the case against the back wall, are ancient representations of several parts of the body, found at mountain shrines. They look much like the *ex votos* found in Classical shrines of Asclepius, the healing god, and are definitely the predecessors of today's aluminium versions.

items from Zákros, including the **rock-crystal rhyton** and the **jug with the Argonauts** (cases 109 and 111). The naturalistic terracotta statues (room IX, case 123) give a clear idea of what Minoans looked like, while the large collection of fine seal stones portrays scenes from daily life. Room X shows merely a repetition of former glory with strong Mycenean influences and rooms XI and XII show the later Dorian and Egyptian influences. Room XIII is filled with sarcophagi and bathtubs.

The upper-floor rooms (XIV–XVI) display tiny fragments of frescoes mounted on a painted background. Most of these superb wall paintings are from the New Palace period of Knosós.

Around Irákleio Amnisos►, one of the closest beaches to Irákleio, was important in Minoan times as the main harbour for Knosós. The fresco of the lilies, now in the Irákleio Archaeological Museum, was found in a villa here. Nearby is **Neiradaspílios** or the **Cave of Eileithyia►►**, noted for its large stalagmites. The cave is closed, but it is sometimes possible to get a key from the guardian on the site of Nirou Hani in Háni Kokkíni, 7km (4.5 miles) farther east (not on Mondays).

Fódele► is a lovely village surrounded by a fertile valley. It has Byzantine chapels and a church, but its biggest claim to fame is as the supposed birthplace, in 1541, of Doménico Theotokópoulos, better known as the greatest of Cretan painters, El Greco (see page 70). There is nothing to support the claim, but the memorial with his bust on the main square (offered in 1934 by the Spanish University of Valladolid) and the so-called **El Greco House** across the river seem enough to attract visitors.

For **Knosós►►►** see pages 83–85.

Crete fell to Venice after Constantinople was sacked in 1204. Some 250 years later, when Constantinople fell to the Turks, the island offered refuge to Byzantine artists. Out of this mixing of influences came a school of painting that was essentially Cretan.

A 14th-century fresco in the church of St. Cristos Kakodiki, Crete

The Byzantine inheritance After the Turks captured Constantinople on 28 May 1453, refugee Byzantine painters moved to Irákleio, reviving what was becoming a stagnant tradition and bringing to it a new elegance, seen in the frescoes that survive in a number of churches from the second half of the 15th century.

The Cretan School Fresco painting in Crete quite suddenly stopped at the end of the 15th century as the artists moved to the mainland. In their place came icon painters, some of whom travelled to Venice and returned suitably impressed with the ideas of the Renaissance. The most famous of these was Michális Damaskinós. Having worked in Venice, Damaskinós returned to Irákleio and began working on large-scale pictures that fused elements from Byzantine tradition with new Venetian ideas and which epitomize the 'Cretan School'.

There is a statue of El Greco (above) in the park named after him in Irákleio. Below right: his View of Mount Sinai and the Monastery of St. Catherine

El Greco The village of Fódele makes the loudest claim to be the birthplace of Doménico Theotokópoulos. The painter later known as El Greco (1541–1614) spent very little time on Crete, travelling to Italy and settling in Toledo, Spain by 1577. His paintings developed out of the Cretan School, initially adhering to its traditions of religious subjects, spiritual intensity and richness of colour, adding credibility to the theory that he studied in the school of Agía Aikateríni monastery in Irákleio.

WHERE TO SEE THE PICTURES IN CRETE
For early 15th-century work, see the frescoes in churches at Varsamónero, at Apáno Sími (near Viannos) and at Agía Paraskeví in the Amári valley. As for Michális Damaskinós's work, six of his larger paintings hang in the Church of Agía Aikateríni, Irákleio and others in the Istorikó Mouseío Krítis (Historical Museum of Crete) (see pages 68–69). The only El Greco painting on display in Crete is his *View of Mount Sinai and the Monastery of St. Catherine*, also in the Historical Museum.

Drive

Réthymno to Irákleio

This drive between two of Crete's largest towns crosses the island's rural heart, passing ancient and Byzantine ruins and farming villages. (Allow six to seven hours; 125km/77 miles). Allow time to get off the winding mountain roads by nightfall.)

Leave Réthymno eastwards, following signs for Arkádi (22km/13 miles). In Plátanias, turn right at the sign for Arkádi, cross under the new road and climb up through olive groves towards Mount Psiloreítis. In Amnátos look out for the **Sacred Church of Panagíos Merkoúri** (right) and continue to the monastery of **Moní Arkadíou**, a national monument (*Open* daily 9–7. *Admission charge*). Founded in the 11th century, the monastery was a focus for the Cretan rebellion against Turkish rule. The 16th-century church, a unique example of Cretan rococo, has a simple, double-vaulted interior. The adjacent **museum** has a collection of religious artefacts (*Open* daily. *Admission charge*).

Leave Arkádi on the track past the cafeteria, to Eléftherna and continue through the village to see the post-Minoan settlement of **Archaía (Ancient) Eléftherna▶**. Return to Old Eléftherna and turn left to Margarítes (4km/2.5 miles), famous for ceramics. Some 5km (3 miles) beyond Margarítes, a right turn leads to Pérama and the **Melidóni cave▶ ▶**

(*Open* daily 10–5 in summer. *Admission charge*), where some 300 Greeks, mostly women and children,

Arkádi is a shrine for the victims of the Cretan rebellion

were killed by the Turks in 1824. Back at Melidóni village, take the left turn off the square to a junction. Turn left along the Mylopótamos Valley through Garazó to Axós, high on the mountain. The 8th-century BC acropolis of **Ancient Axós▶** (*Open* daily. *Admission free*) is signposted.

From Axós, continue past Anógia to the junction with signs to the right for **Idaío Ántro (the Idean Cave)** (see page 92) and left for Irákleio. After 14km (8.5 miles) the road winds down past the site of **ancient Tílisos** (see page 95) to Irákleio.

TOURIST INFORMATION (ÁGIOS NIKOLAOS)
The tourist office is at 21A Odós S. Koundourou beside the bridge (tel: 28410 22357; www.agiosnikolaos.gr. *Open* 8.30–9.30). The staff is very helpful, and provides a free town map, information on the whole Lasíthiou region, a money change and assistance with accommodation.

ESSENTIAL READING
Crete by John Freely, (London, 1988)
The Cretan Runner: His Story of the German Occupation by George Psychoundakis, translated and introduced by Patrick Leigh Fermor (London, 1998)
Falling for Icarus: A Journey Among the Cretans by Rory MacLean (London, 2005)
Crete by Booker Prize-winning novelist Barry Unsworth about his journeys through Crete, capturing the rich history of the island, the Cretan culture and the Cretan people (London, 2004)

Fishing nets laid out to dry in the sun at Ágios Nikólaos

►► Ágios Nikólaos   65D2
One of the prettiest port-towns on Crete, Ágios Nikólaos has over the last decades developed into a resort of international renown, often compared to St. Tropez in France. It is certainly not the place to go in search of the 'old Crete', but it has nevertheless managed to retain some of its charm. Most attractive of all is its setting on the Gulf of Mirabéllo and its harbour, connected by a small canal to the deep Voulisméni lake. Catching the early-evening breeze on one of the many lakeside terraces is one of the more pleasant occupations Ágios Nikólaos has to offer. The town's name comes from the early Byzantine church on the peninsula of Liména, the **church of Ágios Nikólaos►**, notable for fine frescoes from the 8th, 10th and 11th centuries. Crete's second finest collection of antiquities is housed in the **Archaeological Museum►►** (Odós Palaiológou. *Open* Tue–Sun 8.30–3. *Admission charge)*, which has a wealth of finds from the nearby sites of Agía Fotiá near Siteía, Mochlós, Kritsá and Mýrtos. In the same building as the Tourist Office there is a tiny **Museum of Folklore Art►** (*Open* Sun–Fri 10–4. *Admission* inexpensive). The **church of Panagía Vrefotrófou►**, near the bus station on Odós Meletíou, dates from the 12th century.

Around Ágios Nikólaos The road to **Eloúnta►►** is lined with mostly luxurious hotel complexes, so it comes as no surprise that the pretty fishing hamlet of Eloúnta gets quite crowded in the season. On days when the water is calm and clear it is possible to get a glimpse of the underwater ancient site of Oloús. Boats can be rented for the excursion to the peninsula of **Spinalógka►►** (*Open* daily 9–6. *Admission charge)*, where the Venetians built an impregnable fortress and, in 1579, made it an island by cutting a canal. Later, until as recently as the 1950s, there was a colony for people with Hansen's disease (leprosy) here. Another day trip is to the villages of **Krítsa and Lató►►►** (see page 88) and the **Lasíthiou Plateau►►►** (see pages 88–89).

Chaniá, with the snow-capped White Mountains in the background, is one of the most frequently photographed views on Crete

73

▶▶ Archánes   64C2

Surrounded by vineyards, the villages of Káto Archánes and Páno Archánes produce much of Crete's table wine. Páno Archánes, a lively town at the foot of Mount Ioúhtas, has been beautifully restored. It was built over the site of a larger Minoan town. The remains of four people, discovered in 1979 in the **Temple of Anemospília▶**, led to the controversial suggestion that when the temple was struck by an earthquake the Minoans were practicing human sacrifice. Neither this nor the other Minoan sites in the area (a villa in the centre and the burial ground in nearby Foúrni) are open to the public, but there is a small **Archaeological Museum▶** (centre of the modern town. *Open* Wed–Mon 8.30–3. *Admission free*) with finds from the area. About 8km (5 miles) higher up into the hills, **Vathípetro** has views over the green valleys. The remains of a **Minoan villa▶** (*Open* Mon–Sat 8.30–2; ask in museum in Archánes), built around 1580–1550BC, were found with rooms filled with household objects and agricultural equipment. Southeast of Archánes at **Trapsanóu▶** potters still make *pithoi*, the large urns seen on Minoan sites. South of Archánes, at Houdetsi, the musician Ross Daly runs a **Museum of Musical Instruments▶▶** (*Open* daily 10–8, Mar–Oct; www.labyrinthmusic.gr).

▶▶▶ Chaniá   64A2

The historic centre of the city of Chaniá is the most picturesque and beautiful in all Crete. Elsewhere, Chaniá, the island's capital until 1971, feels like a bustling modern town. Package tourism has spread to the new town and to nearby beaches, but the area around the Venetian harbour remains as attractive as ever. With the usually snow-capped White Mountains looming over it, Chaniá is the perfect base to use for exploring the more remote parts of western Crete. The harbour is especially lively during the evening *volta*, when young and old stroll along the waterfront. The huge 17th-century **Mosque of the Janissaries▶**, near Plateía Sindriváni, is now an art gallery. **Kastélli▶▶** is a Byzantine fortress later fortified by the Venetians.

ROOMS WITH A VIEW

Several Venetian mansions on and around Chaniá's waterfront have been converted into guest houses and hotels, all with splendid views. There is something for every budget, from the elegant Casa Delfino to the much cheaper Hotel Manos.

ST. JOHN THE HERMIT

St. John the Hermit is thought to have lived and died in a cave near the Katholikó monastery on the Akrotíri peninsula. Every 7th of October a *paiyíri* is held in his honour: the previous day busloads of pilgrims walk from Agía Triáda monastery to Gouvernéto to attend all-night services. The next morning they walk to the cave, where an emotional service is held. At the point where the saint died, the water that collects in the cistern is believed to be holy.

One of the pleasures of old Chaniá is a stroll along the paralía *in search of that perfect setting for a sunset drink*

The scant remains of the ancient **acropolis of Cydonia**, one of the three most important Minoan towns on Crete, have been excavated on Odós Kandanoléon. In the yacht harbour, at the bottom of Kastélli, look for the 16th-century Venetian **Arsenáli** (now the Centre for Mediterranean Architecture) and walk along to the lighthouse at the end of the harbour wall. A tower on the other side of the **outer harbour** houses the **Naval Museum▶** (*Open* daily 9–4. *Admission charge*), where Chaniá's long and exciting seafaring past is brought to life.

The **Archaeological Museum▶**, housed in the Venetian church of San Francesco (Odós Chálidon. *Open* Tue–Sun 8.30–3, in summer; 8.30–2, in winter. *Admission charge*), includes a considerable collection of Minoan pottery, lovely 3rd-century Roman mosaics and tablets inscribed with Linear A and Linear B, the Minoan and Mycenaean scripts. Past the museum lies the cathedral and Odós Skridlóf, a tourist bazaar where leather-workers still sell traditional footwear. Nearby is the central market, whose colourful stalls are piled with fresh local produce.

Around Chaniá Akrotíri▶, the peninsula north of Chaniá, is developing into a wealthy suburb. On top of the Profítis Ilías hill, the **tomb of Elefthérios Venizélos**, father of modern Crete and his son, stands in the middle of a pleasant garden that has wonderful views. Farther inland, **Agía Triáda▶▶** (*Open* daily 8–2 and 4–8. *Admission charge*), one of the most famous monasteries in Greece, was founded by a Venetian family in 1634. Some 4km (2.5 miles) away are the fortress-like **monastery of Gouvernéto▶** and the **Katholikó monastery▶**, where a cave contains the tomb of St. John the Hermit.

On the mountainous **Rodópou peninsula▶**, west of Chaniá, is the **monastery of Goniá▶** (*Open* daily 8–2 and 4–8. *Admission free*) with spectacular views. Its monks are proud to show their small collection of 17th- and 18th-century icons as well as the remains of a Turkish shell which is incorporated in the eastern wall of the monastery.

74

Walk

Old Chaniá

There is more to Chaniá than water-side cafés and souvenir shops. Not far away, beautiful old houses and atmospheric streets are a reminder of the port's long and illustrious past. (Allow three hours, including breaks.)

Starting at Plateía Venizelóu, walk up Odós Kaneváro, the main street of the Venetian town of La Canae. Some noble mansions can be seen on Odós Lithínon (first left), quite a few now turned into guest houses. At the top of this street is the **Venetian Archives and Financial Exchange►►**, from 1623. Going back down Lithínon, Odós Psaromiligón on the left leads past the remains of **Minoan Cydonia** (no access). Returning to Kaneváro, turn left and then take the first left (Odós Ágios Márkos) past the **ruins of a monastery►** to Plateía Ágios Títos, with won-derful views over the harbour and coast. Steps from the square lead to the imposing ruins of the **Palace of the Rector►►**, the centre of gov-ernment for western Crete during the Venetian period, and down to the waterfront. Turn right, past the **Arsenáli►** (Venetian boat sheds) and walk along the breakwater to the minaret-like **lighthouse►**, pausing to enjoy the views.

Returning to the Arsenáli, continue along the waterfront to Plateía Venizelóu. Odós Zambelióu leads off the square into the picturesque **Jewish Quarter**, which has many nar-row houses. Odós Kondiláki (first left), another fine Venetian street, leads to Odós F. Portoú. Turn right, with the city wall and bastion on your left and then right into Odós Doúka, which

leads back to Zambelioú and turn left. Just past a row of medieval houses, Odós Moshón, a passageway of steps with the only surviving **Venetian chapel** (15th-century), leads to Odós Theofanoú and the **Casa Delfino** (17th-century). Climb up the hill, turn right into Odós Zambelioú and then first right into Odós Theotokópoulos, with Turkish houses (wooden upper storeys) near the bottom. Turn right onto one of the old town's most beautiful streets, Odós Angeloú, which brings you back to the waterfront.

Chaniá's lighthouse stands on the harbour breakwater

Kríti (Crete)

GENERAL HADZIMICHALIS
On 18 May 1828, the fortress of Fragko Kástelo was besieged by the heroic General Hadzimichális and 1,000 Cretan rebels, but the general and his men were slaughtered by a Turkish army of 14,000 under the command of Mustafa Pacha. The villagers buried the remains after the Turks left and Hadzimichális was placed in the crypt of Ágios Harálambos. At dawn on the first anniversary of the battle, villagers reported seeing the *drossoulítes*, the ghosts of the general and his men, walking across the field where they died and then disappearing into the mist.

The most superbly set of all Minoan sites, Faistós overlooks the fertile Messára plain

HENRY MILLER IN FAISTÓS
'Below me, stretching away like an infinite magic carpet, lay the plain of Messara, girdled by a majestic chain of mountain ranges...At the very gates of Paradise the descendants of Zeus halted here on their way to eternity to cast a last look earthwards and saw with the eyes of innocents that the earth is indeed what they had always dreamed it to be: a place of beauty and joy and peace...Phaestos contains all the elements of the heart; it is feminine through and through.'
Henry Miller, *The Colossus of Maroussi* (London, 1942)

▶ **Chóra Sfákia**   *64B1*

The small harbour of Chóra Sfákia, on the south coast, comes alive only during late afternoon, when crowds of tired hikers return from the Samariá Gorge (see page 93) to catch a bus from here to Chaniá or Réthymno. Most of the portside *kafeneía* cater only to tourists, but the calm and beauty of the place are restored once the buses leave around 7pm. Nearby **Loutró▶**, accessible by boat or road, is a quieter option in this region; it has a small beach overlooked by a Turkish castle. East of Chóra Sfákia is **Fragkokástelo▶▶**, an isolated, crumbling Venetian fortress (see panel). The beach below is superb.

▶▶▶ **Faistós**   *64C1*

Tel: 28920 42315. Open: daily 8–7.30, in summer; 8–5, in winter. Admission charge; free Sun. Buses daily from Irákleio

The setting of Faistós is magnificent, with sweeping views over the Messára plain and both Mount Díkti and the twin peaks of Mount Psiloreítis. This was the second most important Minoan city and the capital of Messára, with two harbours, Mátala and Kómmos. The site, like most other Minoan cities, was inhabited during the neolithic era, but what remains today are the ruins of the grand New Palace built around 1700BC, incorporating some of the foundations of the Old Palace, built around 2000BC and destroyed in an earthquake 300 years later. The New Palace was destroyed by the same disaster that brought down the other Minoan palaces in 1450–1400BC. Faistós was inhabited afterwards and remained an autonomous state until the end of the 3rd century BC when it was again destroyed, during a war with Gortýna.

Unlike Knosós, the site has not been reconstructed, leaving scope for the imagination to fill in the gaps. The Palace is approached from a **Grand Stairway**, past the remains of the first palace and the **Theatral Area**. Beyond the storage rooms is the Central Court with the remains of what was a grand façade. A corridor to the north leads to the **Royal Apartments** with the large **Peristyle Hall** and the **Lustral Basin**. Across the Central Court are the **Prince's Rooms** with a small peristyle hall and beside it the workshops in which perhaps the oldest metal forges in the world were found.

It is thought that about 50,000 people lived near the palace and the ruins of their villages are scattered all over the Messára plain. A 45-minute walk or a short drive away from Faistós, **Agía Triáda**▶ ▶ (tel: 28920 91564. *Open* daily 10–4.30, in summer; 8–3, in winter. *Admission charge*) is a Minoan villa complex, perhaps the summer residence of the king of Faistós. Nearby Agía Triáda was abandoned in 1897 after the Turks killed most of the inhabitants. The villa or palace dates from around 1550BC and some of the finest Minoan artworks discovered here are now in the Irákleio Archaeological Museum.

These giant píthoi, *still in place in the magazines, were used for storing grain, olive oil and wine*

77

THE FAISTOS DISK
The famous clay disk, dating from 1700–1600BC, (see illustration on page 31) was stamped with seals on both sides, with hieroglyphics spiralling from the middle. The hieroglyphics represent persons, body parts, tools, flowers, animals and ships. So far the disk has not been deciphered but it is thought that these hieroglyphics were typical of Minoan Crete.

Greece in the summer is all sun and scorched earth, but in spring and autumn it is a different place, full of flowers and the scent of blossoms. With more than 2,000 species of plants—160 not seen anywhere else in the world—Crete, even more than most of the islands, is a botanist's dream.

PLANTS IN DANGER
Of the species endemic to Crete, six are in danger of immediate extinction as their habitat is systematically destroyed. Fifteen more are threatened and 78 others are rare. (These figures are taken from George Sfikas's excellent handbook; see the panel opposite.)

*Top: wild cistus
Below: islanders often have colourful displays of flowers in their gardens and balconies*

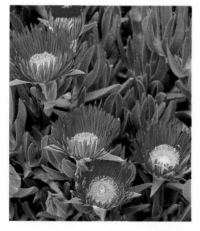

The seasons Summer visitors to the Aegean could be forgiven for thinking that the flora is nothing but olive trees and geraniums. The usual pattern of hot dry weather means that by July, most flowers are reduced to brown sticks by the roadside. In spring, however, even the most barren islands are likely to have a burst of flowers. The ruins at sacred Dílos are scattered with red poppies, the olive groves of Paxoí are luminous with white blooms, while Zákynthos lives up to the nickname the Venetians gave it—the flower of the Levant—with its fields full of wild flowers.

Spring arrives in different places at different times: mid- to late February in southern Crete and perhaps as late as May or early June in more mountainous regions. This is the season to walk in the islands, when the days are warmer, the air rich with the scent of aromatic foliage. While the Aegean summer has the same effect on plants as the northern winter, in cooler, higher places there are still flowers to be found, while certain species of cyclamen and crocus bloom between October and December.

Flowers of Crete Nowhere on the Greek islands is there such an abundance of flowers as on Crete. Its 8,311sq km (3,208sq miles) provide a variety of terrains, each of which is suited to different species and subspecies of plants. Of the 700 species of plants endemic to Greece, at least 160 are found on Crete and nowhere else.

Crete's coastal strip is only a few metres wide in some places and, because of tourist development, much at risk. Plants that thrive on the salty terrain include sea daffodils and lilies, stonecrops, various species of convolvulus as well as tamarisk and jujube trees. In autumn, crocuses and sea squills bloom on the shore.

The lowland plain covers the area from the littoral across the hills and lowest mountain slopes, up to approximately 300m (985ft). As this is intensively cultivated, in many places wild flowers have disappeared, but survivors may include poppies, Cretan ebony, lupins, chrysanthemums, gladioli, species of ranunculus and euphorbia and many other unexpected treasures.

Higher ground between 300 and 800m (980 and 2,600ft), including the Omalós, Lasíthiou and Nída plains, is the place to find brilliant brooms and wild

78

orchids, asphodels, cyclamens, anemones and convolvulus, thyme, clematis and several types of cistus and phlomis. Of the trees, the pink blossoms of the Judas trees are especially dramatic.

The mountainous regions of Crete used to be differentiated by whether or not they had trees, but deforestation has robbed even the subalpine regions of its forests. Clumps of trees have survived here and there, like the small forest near Mourniés, in eastern Crete. In areas ranging in height from 800 to 1,800m (2,600 to 5,900ft), look in the summer for several unique tulips, including the delicate pink-tinged Tulipa bakeri, endemic to western Crete. Crocuses, anemones, saxifrages, alyssums and species of centaury can also be found. Higher up, trees disappear altogether and plants are mostly herbaceous or bulbous, with some shrubs that can survive in the cold. Here may be found rock-cress (flowering in June), vetches, alkanets and violets.

Hillside bloom at Réthymno

79

Crete's other distinct botanical habitat is its gorges, most famous of which are the Samariás, Imriotico and Coutraliotico. Usually running north–south, from the uplands to the sea, they are good places to look for rock plants, including campanulas, endemic *Symphyandra cretica*, certain types of flax, also endemic to Crete and *Scabiosa minoana*, which has two subspecies endemic to specific regions of the island —*minoana* to the Mount Díkti gorges, *asterusica* to Mount Cofinas.

Every year more fields with rare and endemic flowers are cleared for the rapid development of the tourist industry

FLOWER BOOKS

If you want more information about plant life on Crete, the following books will be of interest:
Anthony Huxley and William Taylor, *Flowers of Greece* (London, 1977)
George Sfikas, *Wild Flowers of Crete* (Athens, 1993)
Marjorie Blamey and Christopher Grey-Wilson, *Wild Flowers of the Mediterranean* (UK 2004)
Oliver Rackham and Jennifer Moody *The Making of the Cretan Landscape* (UK 1997)

The ancient town of Gourniá must have looked much like the large mountain villages of Crete today, with small houses clustered around a few cobbled streets

►► Gávdos   64B1

The isolated island of Gávdos, some 40km (25 miles) off the southern coast of Crete, is Europe's southernmost point. Locals believe that theirs was the island of Calypso, visited by Odysseus and known in Roman times as Clauda. Ferries dock at Karabé, from where it is an hour's walk to the capital, Kastrí. Today it is hard to believe that Kastrí had 8,000 inhabitants in the Middle Ages. Now, only five families remain amid the crumbling houses. There are good beaches, but food and water can be in short supply. The island gets incredibly hot in summer, when small ferries make three weekly trips from Palaiochóra via Sóugia, as well as three weekly trips from Chóra Sfákia. Out of season there are only erratic connections.

►►► Gortýs   64C1

The remains of **ancient Gortýna**►►► (tel: 28920 31145. *Open* daily 8–7 (5 in winter). *Admission charge*) are scattered over the whole area of Ágioi Déka and modern Gortýs. The site was inhabited from the neolithic period, but Gortýna only became an important commercial power in the 8th century BC. In the 3rd century BC Gortýna conquered Faistós and its harbour Mátala. After it sided with Quintus Metellus against Knosós, the Romans made it the capital of the Province of Crete and Cyrenaica (North Africa and Egypt) in 67BC. The island's first centre of Christianity after St. Paul appointed Titus as bishop in AD67, Gortýna remained the capital during the Byzantine era until the Saracens sacked it in AD824.

The site is important for its excellent remains from several periods. One of the most prominent, by the entrance, is the ruins of the 6th-century three-aisled **basilica of Ágios Títos**, still revered as one of Crete's most important Christian monuments, as the shrine inside shows. Behind the basilica is the *agora* (marketplace) and the Roman **Odeion** with the famous **Law Code**, a series of huge stones engraved around 500BC with laws and rulings (see panel). They are written in a Doric Cretan dialect, in a system called *boustrophedon*, 'as the ox ploughs', meaning that one line must be read from left to right and the next from right to left. Across the river are the remains of a Hellenistic theatre, built over the acropolis of ancient Gortýna. Fragments of the walls remain, probably the ones Homer meant when he mentioned the 'walled city of Gortýna' in the *Iliad*. On the other side of the main road are the remains of the **Praetorium** (governor's house) and a Nymphaeum among many other ruins.

Nearby is the village of **Ágioi Déka►►►**, or the Holy Ten, named after 10 early Christians martyred for their faith around AD250 by the Romans. A chapel was built over a crypt which supposedly contains their remains. These 'Holy Ten' are among the most important Cretan saints: martyrs not just for their faith but also for their island against a foreign occupation.

►►► Gourniá 65D1

Tel: 28410 24943. Open: Tue–Sun 8.30–3. Admission charge
Ancient Gourniá is the best preserved of the Minoan towns, set beautifully against hills and overlooking the sea. Little visited today, it is extremely pleasant to stroll around and gives a rare insight into how ordinary Minoans liked to live. The narrow cobbled alleys between Gourniá's small houses are not so very different from the old mountain villages of Crete today.

The site was inhabited from the early second millennium BC, but what remains today is from the New Palace period (c1500BC). The town was destroyed in 1450BC by the same unknown disaster that struck Knosós and other Minoan palaces. In the centre of the site is the so-called palace (probably the governor's house) and an open courtyard believed to have been the *agora*. In the houses a large number of tools and objects from different trades were found, showing that the people of Gourniá were engaged in carpentry, fishing, pottery and weaving.

THE FIRST LEGISLATION IN EUROPE
Plato mentions Gortýna in his *Laws* as one of the best-governed states, as well as being among the wealthiest and most powerful of all the cities in Crete. Gortýna's 5th-century BC constitution was incorporated into the Law Code, the earliest legislation in Europe. It reveals a hierarchical society in which people were divided into three classes: free citizens, serfs and slaves. In the law courts of Gortýna, every conviction needed to have at least one witness.

81

THE LAW CODE ON ADULTERY
'If someone be taken in adultery with a free woman in her father's house or brother's or husband's, he shall pay one hundred staters; but if in someone else's house fifty; and if with the wife of an apeitairos ten; but if a slave with a free woman he shall pay double; and if a slave with a slave five.'
Quoted in R. F. Willets, *The Law Code of Gortyn* (1967)

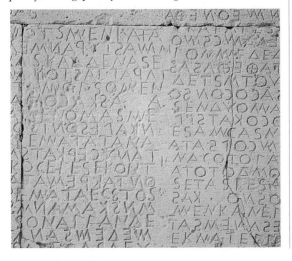

According to tradition, the Law Code was received by King Minos when he visited Zeus on Olympus

Kríti (Crete)

A GOOD DRIVE

Most people take the quick coastal road from Irákleio to Ágios Nikólaos or the Lasíthiou Plateau. The inland roads may be more winding and slower, but the drive is much more pleasurable. The hilly countryside is beautiful and the villages and tiny churches are a far cry from the coastal resorts.

VISITING CHURCHES

Many of the old churches in the interior of the island are often closed, which is disappointing for visitors who have come to see their famous frescoes. The dedicated traveller can always try to find the keeper of the key. Start by asking at the nearest *kafeneío*: news travels fast in these villages and there is a good chance that the key will appear.

Not all traditions are lost: the old men still watch the world go by from the kafeneío or barbershop

▶ Ierápetra   65D1

The centre of a thriving agricultural industry, Ierápetra is a modern, unattractive city. Most visitors come here for the sandy beaches nearby, but also worth visiting is the small **Archaeological Museum▶** (tel: 28420 28722. *Open* Tue–Sat 8.30–3. *Admission charge*) and the Venetian fort. In summer excursion boats make the trip to the nearby Hryssí islet, which has excellent beaches. The southern coast of Crete boasts the warmest climate in Europe and close to **Árvi▶**, west of Ierápetra, there is a lovely gorge surrounded by banana and pineapple groves.

▶ Kastélli Kissámou   64A2

To distinguish itself from the many Venetian castles called *Kastélli*, the town still uses its ancient name Kíssamos, a legacy from the days when it was the port of the powerful inland town of Polyrrinía. Parts of the Venetian castle walls are still visible, and a small archaeological museum is due to reopen. The town has a laid-back atmosphere, and some great beaches near by.

▶▶ Kastélli Pediádos   65D2

Kastélli is the main village in the middle of the picturesque and little-visited farming region known as the Pediáda. The Venetian castle after which the village was named has disappeared, but Kastélli is pleasant enough, with a few taverns and *kafeneía*. More rewarding would be a drive through the lovely surrounding countryside, through tiny old villages where there are some amazing medieval churches. Near Pigí is the site of **Ágios Pandeleímon▶▶**, where parts of a 10th-century basilica, built over a spring, are incorporated in the 13th-century church, which has some very early frescoes. Two Byzantine churches, **Ágios Nikólaos** and the frescoed **Ágios Giórgios▶**, stand at the foot of Mount Díkti, near Xidás. Above Kastélli to the east is the site of the once-important **ancient city of Lýttos▶**, once a rival of Knosós, but very little remains. The **Moní Agárathou▶**, near Sabás, one of Crete's oldest monasteries, was built to house the sacred icon of the Assumption of the Blessed Virgin, found nearby. The 15th-century church **Isódia Theótokon▶▶**, near Sklaverochóri, has 15th- and 16th-century frescoes.

1 West Court
2 Corridor of the
   Procession
3 Central Court
4 Grand Staircase
5 Hall of Colonnades
6 Queen's Apartments
7 King's Apartments
8 Hall of Double Axes
9 Throne Room
10 Theatral Area
11 Royal Road

▶▶▶ Knosós   64C2

Tel: 28102 31940. Open: daily 8–7 (5 in winter)
Admission charge
Bus: No. 2 from bus station 2, on the waterfront near the quay,
Irákleio. Visit at opening time, or at midday with hat and
water, to avoid the worst crowds

The palace of Knosós, with its 1,300 rooms and alabaster throne, exerts a magical attraction. This may have something to do with the fact that, until a century ago, Knosós was no more than a legend—the place where King Minos was said to have lived, where his wife gave birth to the Minotaur, for whom the Labyrinth was constructed and where human sacrifices are believed to have been made in ancient times.

Knosós was built some time after 1950BC and damaged in an earthquake around 1700BC. Much of what we see now, such as the foundations of the Royal Palace, the Little Palace, a caravansary and other buildings, covering more than 2ha (5 acres), belongs to the reconstruction in the New Palace period; at this high point in Minoan civilization, the palace and the city around it would have held as many as 100,000 people. Around 1450BC all the Minoan buildings except Knosós were destroyed. It is still unclear what happened; perhaps an earthquake or a war, or a tidal wave caused by the massive volcanic eruption that blew Thíra apart. Knosós survived, albeit under Mycenaean control; Homer mentions King Idomeneus of Knosós joining the war against Troy.

In 1380BC Knosós too was destroyed by fire. Its remains lay buried under a growing mound until they were discovered by Sir Arthur Evans at the beginning of this century (see pages 86–87). Much of Evans's reconstruction of the palace was enlightened guesswork and while it has protected many of the ruins from the elements and perhaps made the site easier for us to understand, it has certainly intruded upon the ancient ruins.

EVANS'S RECONSTRUCTION

As Sir Arthur Evans uncovered the great palace of Knosós, he was faced with an increasingly urgent problem. Because of the bad state of preservation of much of the palace, because it was a several-storey building on a hillside and because the Cretan winter is cold and wet, he had to protect the site as best he could. Evans, who had paid for the site with his own money and obviously felt he had proprietorial rights, decided on a reconstruction. While the Throne Room was roofed over to preserve the floor and the throne itself, in other places Evans took what some consider unwarranted liberties, in particular with the Grand Staircase and the upper rooms. Much of his reconstruction is based on pure guesswork. In our own time, when archaeology has become such an exact science, Evans's actions are being increasingly criticized, for while most of today's visitors to Knosós come to see the Minoan ruins, much of what they actually see is a 20th-century concrete rebuilding by Evans.

Kríti (Crete)

84

Long, narrow storage rooms still contain the huge píthoi *or storage jars*

The story of the Labyrinth may have been based on fact, for Knosós is hard to negotiate in any particular order. Try wandering around to get a sense of the ground plan, then return to look again. Knosós needs imagination as well as patience, for much of it is either very ruined, heavily reconstructed or under restoration.

The site (see page 83) is entered through the **West Court (1)**, leading into the **Corridor of the Procession (2)**, named after its frescoes (now in the Archaeological Museum in Irákleio, like all the others). Follow the inevitable crowds to the **Central Court (3)**, which divides the site in two and which would have been enclosed by the walls of the surrounding buildings. On the west side of the court are the ceremonial chambers, to the east the royal apartments.

The royal apartments are reached via the **Grand Staircase (4)►►**, one of the great architectural achievements of prehistory, which originally continued for another two storeys above the Central Court. The part that still exists leads down from the court to the **Hall of Colonnades (5)** and would have continued, around a light well, farther down the hillside. Off the Hall of Colonnades lie the **Queen's Apartments (6)►►►**, which archaeologists believe would have been brightly decorated and comfortable—qualities that were as important to the Minoans as to us. Beyond are the bathrooms, one with a clay bath and another with a toilet. The main attraction here is the drainage system, a series of terracotta pipes which appear to have carried off not just dirty water but also sewage. The queen, it seems, used a flushing toilet.

Pipework has been found all over the palace, forming a drainage system which not only brought fresh water from Mount Juktas but could also have coped with even the worst storms. It was unparalleled in the world until

The original frescoes at Knosós have been replaced by reproductions, while the originals are shown in Irákleio's Archaeological Museum

THE MINOTAUR
Among the treasures that survived at Knosós there were bull's-head libation vessels, shrines in the shape of bulls' horns and a wonderfully preserved fresco showing a group of men and women involved in bull-leaping, one man having gripped the bull by its horns and leapt over its head. This striking image calls to mind the myth of the Minotaur, the beast said to inhabit the Labyrinth at Knosós, to whom young men and women from Athens were offered as sacrifice.

ARIADNE'S DANCING FLOOR
Homer, describing the god Hephaistos decorating the shield of Achilles, gives a vivid impression of celebrations at Knosós, perhaps on the dancing floor in the theatral area: 'Youths and marriageable maidens were dancing on it with their hands on one another's wrists, the girls in fine linen with lovely garlands on their heads and the men in closely woven tunics showing the faint gleam of oil and with daggers of gold hanging from their silver belts. Here they ran tightly round, circling smoothly on their accomplished feet...and there they ran in lines to meet each other. A large crowd stood round enjoying the delightful dance, with a minstrel among them singing divinely to the lyre, while a couple of acrobats, keeping time with his music, threw cart wheels in and out among the people'.
Homer, *Iliad* Book XVIII

85

Roman times. Back up the Grand Staircase, above the Queen's Apartments, are the so-called **King's Apartments (7)**. These are a series of rooms connected by double doors, leading to the **Hall of Double Axes (8)**, named after the motif carved into its blocks.

Across the Central Court lie the palace's most intriguing and atmospheric chambers, starting with the **Throne Room (9)**. This has stone benches and an alabaster throne, one of the oldest in the world, though archaeologists are divided over its date (was it Minoan or later Mycenaean?) and its function (was it for a king or a priest?). Beside it is a chamber with a sunken floor, clearly used for ritual cleansing. Its place beside the throne room suggests the close relationship between religion and state in Minoan times and perhaps the possibility of there having been a priest-king. Stairs lead up to chambers reconstructed by Evans. Their functions, however, are not known.

Reproduction **frescoes** have replaced several of the originals, some of which are now on display in the Archaeological Museum in Irákleio (see panel opposite). A priest-king looks over the Central Court, dolphins adorn the Royal Apartments and a bull charges at the northern portico. Beyond the entrance, past the gatehouse and lustral bath, also used for ritual purification, lies the **Theatral Area (10)**, whose stone platform is surrounded by amphitheatral stone seating for about 500 people, clearly an area for ceremony or entertainment. Leading away from the Theatral Area is the **Royal Road (11)**, a paved road that runs as far as the present main road to Irákleio, towering above you.

The old road is thought to have run right across the island. It has been excavated on the other side of the modern road and runs past a couple of reconstructed town houses to the Small Palace, which, along with the caravansary, a Roman villa, the so-called Royal Villa and a royal tomb-chapel, is closed to the public.

As late as the mid-19th century, when excavations had already revealed so much about ancient Rome and Egypt, many of the antiquities of ancient Greece lay waiting to be uncovered. With the advent of an inspired amateur in the 1870s, all this began to change, but many questions still remain to be answered.

Heinrich Schliemann (1822–90) In the 1870s, Greek archaeology was transformed by the arrival of a wealthy German called Heinrich Schliemann. Having made a fortune as a trader, he retired from business to fulfil his ambition of proving the truth behind Homer's epics. He started on the coast of Asia Minor by uncovering the site of Troy. In 1876, with Homer still as his guide, he uncovered the remains of an extraordinary warrior civilization at Mycenae. And in 1878, on Itháki, he identified what he believed to be Odysseus' palace.

The critics Not everyone greeted Schliemann's discoveries with enthusiasm, least of all the professional archaeologists whom he had upstaged. His methods, certainly far from scientific, were called into question and many of his claims ridiculed. While he did make mistakes, most obviously with the so-called 'jewels of Helen', which turned out to be from another Trojan period, he was clearly vindicated for his belief in Homer's historical accuracy. In 1878, perhaps spurred on by Schliemann's Mycenaean discoveries, a Cretan antiquarian, Mínos Kalokairinós, began to dig near Irákleio and uncovered storerooms full of large pottery jars. Could these be the remains of the great city of Knosós, also mentioned by Homer? Schliemann was soon on the site, but was unable to acquire the rights to work on it.

Heinrich Schliemann, the excavator of Troy, arrived on Crete with his copy of Homer in hand, hoping to uncover a major Minoan palace, but didn't get permission to excavate

The circle of graves inside the citadel in Mycenae, excavated by German archaeologist Heinrich Schliemann

Sir Arthur Evans (1851–1941) Oxford-educated Evans, formerly keeper of Oxford's Ashmolean Museum, arrived in Athens in 1893 to study Schliemann's Mycenaean seals. He saw similar seals in an Athens antiques shop, whose owner said they came from Crete, where women used them as charms to help with breast-feeding. In 1898 the Turks lost control of Crete and two years later Evans had bought the mound called Kefala, where the large pottery jars had been found and was ready to start excavating. Within a very short time it became clear that this was to be a major discovery: the Knosós that Homer mentioned, but belonging to a civilization much older than that of the Mycenaeans and Achaians. As nothing was found to give a name to the period or the people who inhabited Knosós, Evans felt free to invent. Remembering that mythology credited King Minos, son of Zeus and Europa, with building the city of Knosós, Evans called the people and their age, Minoan.

Halbherr at Faistós While Evans was excavating Knosós, an Italian enthusiast was at work on another site on the island. Federico Halbherr had been working on Crete for some years, excavating more recent sites, but at the turn of the century he was digging at Faistós. He was just as surprised as Evans when his excavation of the palace shed more crucial light on the Minoans. Schliemann had caused a sensation by proving that the heroic age depicted by Homer had actually existed. Between them, Evans and Halbherr provided proof for the period that preceded the Homeric age.

The continuing challenge It is 100 years since Evans discovered Knosós, yet despite the wealth of architectural details, it is still not known who the Minoans were, what language they spoke, nor what they believed in. However, there are still many sites to be excavated on Crete and these may provide the answers. In the meantime we remain ambivalent, attracted by the beauty of Minoan buildings and artefacts, horrified by the idea that they might have made human sacrifices.

Schliemann was convinced of the historical truth behind Homer's epics and proved his point by discovering Agamemnon's citadel at Mycenae in 1874

FURTHER READING
Arthur Evans, *The Palace of Minos* (London, 1921). His own account.
Dilys Powell, *The Villa Ariadne* (London, 2004). On archaeology and modern Crete.
Jacquetta Hawkes, *Dawn of the Gods* (London, 1972). A vividly written study of the Minoan and Mycenaean civilizations.
Brian M. Fagan (ed.), *Eyewitness to Discovery* (Oxford, 1996). First-person archaeological accounts, includes Evans and Schliemann.
Rodney Castleden *Knossos: Temple of Goddess* (Athens, 1997)
Sylvia L. Horwitz *The Find of a Lifetime: Sir Arthur Evans and the Discovery of Knossos* (London 2001)
N. P. James *The Ring of Minos: The Palace of Knossos* (CV Visual Arts Research S.) (London 2005)

▶▶▶ Krítsa and Lató 65D1

Krítsa, one of Crete's largest villages, is set dramatically against hills and surrounded by olive and carob groves. Although it is one of the most popular day-trip destinations from Ágios Nikólaos, Krítsa has maintained much of its character as well as its weaving traditions. The **church of Ágios Geórgios Kavousiótis**▶ has early 14th-century frescoes. A signposted path to the right on the road into town leads to the finest Byzantine church on Crete, **Panagía Kerá**▶▶▶ (Our All-Holy Lady. *Open* Mon–Fri 8.30–3, Sat 8.30–2. *Admission charge*). Believed to have been founded in the 13th century, with 14th-century additions, it is worth visiting for its extraordinary and well-preserved frescoes. The church has three aisles: the central one—the oldest—is dedicated to the Assumption of the Virgin, the south to St. Anne, the Virgin's mother and the newer north to St. Anthony. Together, they show clearly the artistic flourish of the late Byzantine empire.

Past Panagía Kerá, the right turn leads to the ruins of **Lató Etera** (*Open* Tue–Sun 8.30–3. *Admission free*). The setting is dramatic, covering two neighbouring hilltops and the saddle between them, with fine views over the Krítsa plain and the Gulf of Mirabéllo. Lató Etera, the region's most important city in the Archaic period, was built around the 7th century BC, about 800 years after the great Minoan palaces were destroyed and yet it shows strong Minoan influences. The best-preserved part is the **agora**, or marketplace, surrounded by a town hall, *stoas* (roofed colonnades) and a sanctuary.

▶▶▶ Lasíthiou 65D1

The Lasíthiou Plateau, a basin set into Mount Díkti (2,147m/7,042ft), is famous for its 10,000 windmills, traditionally used to pump water to the fields or as grain mills, most of which no longer work. The soil here has always been very fertile—every bit of land is cultivated—and it was heavily populated even in antiquity. A circular road connects the villages along the plateau starting from **Tzermiádo▶**. (The drive alone is worth the trip.) Nearby is the oldest inhabited site, the **Cave of Trápeza▶▶**, where 7,000-year-old neolithic tombs were discovered, like miniature houses (*Open* at all times; torch essential). Uphill is the 11th-century BC site of **Karfí**, where statuettes of fertility goddesses were found (now in the Irákleio Archaeological Museum). Ágios Giórgios has a tiny **folk museum▶** (*Open* Jun–Aug daily 10–3. *Admission charge*) in a farmhouse, which explains the daily life of a farmer. Most people go to **Psichró▶** and the nearby **Diktaío Ántro (Diktean Cave)▶▶** (*Open* daily 10–6.30; 4 in winter). The latter is one of several places which are claimed as birthplaces of Zeus (see panel). Nearby, off the circular road before Krási, the 12th-century **convent of Panagía Kardió-tissa▶▶** has some superb well-restored frescoes from the 14th century, that were undiscovered until the 1960s.

THE DIKTEAN CAVE
Legend has it that this cave was where the goddess Rhea gave birth to Zeus. Zeus's father Kronos feared that he would lose his throne to a son, so in an attempt to prevent the prophecy from being fulfiled, he ate all his children. At the birth of Zeus, however, Rhea fooled Kronos into eating a stone instead and hid her son in this cave. Whatever the truth, the cave must have been a cult centre for the Mother Goddess and for Zeus, since offerings were discovered going back to Classical times.
   When visiting the cave, take a torch and nonslip shoes. If you want to miss the crowds, visit in the early morning.

One of the most popular excursions from Ágios Nikólaos is a drive through the beautiful Lasíthiou countryside. The Lasíthiou Plateau is often called the Valley of the Windmills, though most are no longer functioning

▶ Mália   *65D2*
Modern Mália is a rather ugly beach resort with a dwindling old town. Its main interest lies in the nearby **Palace of Mália▶▶▶** (3km/2 miles east of Mália, tel: 28970 31597. *Open* Tue–Sun 8.30–3. *Admission charge*). The site has a fine setting, near the sea and with the Lasíthiou mountains in the background, and resembles Knosós without the reconstructions and without the usual crowds. The site has the same history and ground plan as the two more important Minoan cities, Faistós and Knosós, but is much easier to grasp than either of them.

   Excavations have uncovered remains of the second palace to occupy this site, built soon after the first palace was destroyed in about 1700BC and inhabited until it too was destroyed around 1450BC. As at Knosós, there is a vast Central Court in which it is believed bull-games were held, surrounded by royal apartments, cult rooms and granaries. Recent excavations outside the palace area have revealed houses, probably part of a large Minoan town.

THE JEWELS FROM MÁLIA
A rectangular mausoleum called Chryssolákos (Golden Pit) was found near the Minoan palace at Mália. The burial chambers, which seem to date from the Old Palace period, were filled with gold objects. Some of these treasures, such as the famous gold amulet in the form of a couple of bees holding on to a drop of honey (illustrated on page 33), are in the Irákleio Archaeological Museum, but a large number are exhibited in the Aegina Collection in London's British Museum.

The extraordinary caves at Mátala are no longer inhabited, but they continue to fascinate busloads of tourists

ROADSIDE SHRINES

All over Crete and the rest of Greece, there are small roadside shrines. Many visitors believe that they were built for someone who died there in an accident, but that is not completely true. These shrines are sometimes built by the victim of an accident or his family in honour of their favourite saint, in thanksgiving for allowing their survival. At other times they are erected as a simple act of devotion or piety. Inside there is usually a picture of the saint, an oil lamp, small bottles of oil and matches. The people who put up the shrine in the first place may take responsibility for maintaining it, cleaning and lighting the lamp. Passers-by will often leave coins to help with the maintenance of the shrine.

THE OLD ROAD

A new highway connects Kolymvári on the north coast with Palaiochóra. It saves time, of course, but the old road from Kaloudianá makes for an even more spectacular drive. There are some quiet villages on the way, mostly untouched by package tourism and enjoying wonderful views across the mountains.

PALAIOCHÓRA IN LITERATURE

In *The Last Lemon Grove* (London, 1977) Jackson Webb gives a wonderful description of how an American survived his lonely stay in Palaiochóra.

▶▶ Mátala   64C1

Mátala, on the southern coast, may no longer be the 'hippie' beach it once was, but it is still one of the island's most beautiful. The man-made caves cut into the cliffs, probably ancient tombs inhabited by early Christians, were famous for their foreign hippie community in the 1960s and 1970s. The place has now been cleaned up and although the caves still attract crowds, they are locked at night. The underwater remains of **ancient Mátala**, an important harbour under the Romans, can be seen from the cliffs on the northern side of the cove. On the other side of Ákra Líthino (Cape Líthinon) is **Kaloí Liménes**, a big harbour for oil tankers. A small chapel marks the spot where, according to tradition, St. Paul first landed on Crete.

▶▶ Myrtiá   64C2

Lost among olive groves and vineyards, the picturesque village of Myrtiá has a single attraction for visitors, as a sign in a dozen languages makes clear: it was the home of the family of the writer Níkos Kazantzákis. The **Kazantzákis House▶**, the town's most imposing villa (next door to Zorba's *kafeneío*) has been turned into a museum containing memorabilia of the writer and his family (tel: 28107 42451. *Open* Tue–Sun 8.30–3. *Admission charge*). A 20-minute video in four languages tells the story of the author's life and work.

▶ Palaiochóra   64A1

Palaiochóra, once a remote fishing hamlet with a crumbling castle, is now a laid-back and popular family beach resort, with many small hotels. In summer, daily excursion boats leave the harbour for the site of **ancient Lissós▶**, but walking there is also possible. The site contains the remains of a healing temple or Asklepion, a theatre and some houses.

Farther on, Soúgia is a small hamlet near **ancient Syia▶**, a former port whose remarkable 6th-century basilica contains a fine mosaic pavement depicting deer and peacocks surrounded by vines.

Of all modern Greek writers, none is as familiar to non-Greeks as Níkos Kazantzákis. As might be expected of someone who has been several times nominated for the Nobel Prize for Literature, there is more to Kazantzákis's work than Zorba the Greek.

Before *Zorba* Born in Irákleio in February 1883 and educated at the University of Athens and at the Sorbonne, Níkos Kazantzákis began his career by writing books describing his travels in foreign countries. He went on to write 22 plays, nine film scenarios, a history of Russian literature (he lived in Russia for two years), articles for newspapers and journals and an epic poem, *The Odyssey*. He also held the post of minister without portfolio in 1945. But it is on his novels that his reputation rests, in particular *The Last Temptation of Christ* and *Zorba the Greek*.

Alexis Zorba Kazantzákis's best-known novel, set in Crete, tells the story of Alexis Zorba, a 'free spirit' who gives his all to pleasure as he does to work and shows the English narrator of the story how to stop worrying and start living. The narrator also witnesses the growing relationship between Zorba and Madame Hortense, an old woman down on her luck—'a sort of blonde walrus who had been cast up, half-rotting, on this sandy shore', as Kazantzákis describes her in his typical, overblown style. In the background, Crete before the days of tourism comes memorably to life.

The *Zorba* **effect** Not even in his wildest dreams could Kazantzákis have predicted the success of *Zorba*. In 1964, seven years after Kazantzákis's death, the film of the novel was released with Anthony Quinn as Zorba. To foreign audiences, Quinn's vital hero epitomized the spirit of modern Greece, just as Míkis Theodorákis's *bouzouki* music characterized its sound. As a result, the name 'Zorba' has been widely adopted by Greek hotels and restaurants and Theodorákis's soundtrack remains the anthem for the island way of life.

FREEDOM AND DEATH
This was perhaps Kazantzákis's most powerful work. Setting his story in the time of the 1878 Cretan revolt against Turkish rule, he brilliantly catches the spirit of the time, particularly the terror and the belief in sacrifice that drove the Cretans in their determined fight for independence.

KAZANTZÁKIS'S MEMORIAL
Celebrated now as one of the most important Greek writers of the century, Kazantzákis was less appreciated by his countrymen during his lifetime. Because of his freely expressed thoughts on politics and history and his much publicized doubts about Christianity, he spent most of the later part of his life abroad, banned from returning to Greece and excommunicated by the Orthodox Church. One explanation of why he was buried on Irákleio's city ramparts and not in a cemetery was because the Church authorities denied him burial, a decision that must, to them, have seemed fully justified after his story *The Last Temptation of Christ* was filmed in 1988.

Above left: many hotels put on Greek dancing, in an attempt to convey Zorba's joie-de-vivre
Left: Níkos Kazantzákis

91

Kríti (Crete)

THE IDEAN CAVE

According to legend, the *Kuretes* (young warriors) danced around in the cave and beat their bronze shields so that the crying of baby Zeus would not be heard. One of the first things archaeologists found upon excavating the cave were votive offerings in the shape of bronze shields, one of which is now in the Irákleio Archaeological Museum. It is thought that the ceremony was re-enacted here at celebrations of Zeus's birthday.

MOUNTAIN CLIMBING

Crete is a small paradise for walkers and mountain climbers. The Mountaineering and Skiing Club of Irákleio (EOS, Odós Dhikeosínis 53, Irákleio; tel: 28102 27609 between 8.30pm–10.30pm; www.interkriti.org/ orivatikos/orivat.html) provides information and also organizes trips inland. There are several books on walking in Crete, including *Walks and Treks in the White Mountains of Crete* by Loraine Wilson (London, 2002) and *Western Crete: Walking in the Kissamos* by Alan Hall (London 2006).

USEFUL NUMBERS (RÉTHYMNO)

Tourist information (Odós Venizélou. *Open* Mon–Fri 9–9, in summer, tel: 28310 29148). Réthymno's branch of the Greek mountaineering club has great information on the nearby mountains (tel: 28310 57766; http://eos.rethymnon. com

The monastery of Préveli is dedicated to St. John the Theologian, whose ancient Byzantine icon is preserved in the church

▶▶ Psiloreítis 64C1

Mount Ida (2,456m/8,055ft), the peak of the Psiloreítis range, is the highest in Crete. At the end of a rough road from Anógia, above the beautiful Nida Plateau, is the **Idaío Ántro (Idean Cave)▶▶** (closed at the time of writing), which claims, along with the Diktaío Ántro (Diktean Cave; see page 89), to be where Rhea gave birth to Zeus and hid him from his father Kronos. A cult place probably before the Minoan period, it remained the most sacred cave until well into Roman times, mentioned often by ancient writers. There is an altar in front of the cave and a labyrinthine corridor leads to the 60m (197ft) high main cavern.

The ascent to the summit starts either behind the cave or at the **Spílaio Kamarón (Kamáres Cave)▶**, where the first Kamáres pottery (now in the Irákleio Archaeological Museum) was discovered.

▶▶ Réthymno 64B2

Réthymno, Crete's third largest town and an important harbour, has preserved its historical centre from Turkish and Venetian times remarkably well; a new resort area sprawls along a beautiful beach to the east of the old town. Out of season it is a rewarding place to stroll and an excellent base for exploring the nearby mountain ranges. Seen from the sea, a 16th-century **Fortress▶▶** dominates the town (*Open* Tue–Sun 8–8; earlier closing in winter. *Admission charge*). It claims to be the largest Venetian castle ever built. Much of it is ruined, but at sunset, the views are great and there is a pretty, domed mosque with a fine

Behind the inner harbour and lighthouse lies the most atmospheric part of Réthymno

mihrab, indicating the direction to Mecca. Opposite the entrance is the **Archaeological Museum▶** (*Open* Tue–Sun 8.30–3. *Admission charge*), which includes a collection of Roman finds. The **Historical and Folk Museum▶** (Odós Vernárdou. *Open* Mon–Sat 9.30–2, in summer. *Admission charge*) gives a good insight into rural life and traditions. In the heart of town near the 17th-century **Venetian loggia**, now a library, is the 17th-century **Rimondi fountain**, adorned with spouting lion heads. Nearby on Odós Ethníkis is a restored grand Venetian/Turkish house, now the **Centre for Byzantine Art▶**, with a fine café on the roof terrace. Enjoy the views over the town from its minaret.

Places to visit from Réthymno include the **monastery of Arkádi** (see page 71). Also within easy reach are the pretty village of **Spíli▶▶**, with its old alleys and extraordinary lions'-head fountain and, farther south, the monastery of **Préveli▶▶**, a centre of Cretan resistance against Ottoman rule and, later, during World War II, against occupation by Germany.

▶▶▶ Farángi Samariás (Samariá Gorge)   64A1

Tel: 28250 67179. Open: May–Oct, daily 6 am–3 pm May–Oct (conditions permitting). Admission charge

The spectacular Samariá Gorge, a 16km (10-mile) long canyon running from Omalós down to the beach at Agía Rouméli, offers a popular but strenuous downhill hike, suitable for anyone who is used to long walks and is reasonably fit. The trail starts from **xilóskalo** (literally 'wooden stairs') and drops down about 1,000m (3,300ft) in the first 2km (1.2 miles). After that it becomes flatter, with a wealth of wild flowers, especially in spring. The gorge is named after the 14th-century **church of Óssia María▶** in Samariá (almost halfway) which was abandoned after the villagers were relocated in 1962. Beyond the church, the path follows the river and becomes even more spectacular as it gets closed in by steep cliff walls, reaching what are popularly known as the *sidiróportes* (iron gates), where it is almost possible to touch both sides of the gorge. The valley soon widens and, a little farther on, reaches the gate of the White Mountains National Park. From here it is about another half-hour's walk to the beach. Lucky walkers might just spot the famous *kri-kri*, the rare Cretan wild goat, which is protected here in the National Park.

PRACTICALITIES FOR THE SAMARIÁ GORGE
The easiest (and often the *only*) way to do the hike in a day is to buy a day trip from a travel agent. If you prefer to walk by yourself, or to stay on the south coast, early morning public buses from Chaniá go to the top of the gorge near Omalós (1.5 hours). The first buses from Réthymno and Irákleio to Chaniá continue straight to Omalós. The walk takes 4 to 5 hours to Agía Rouméli, from where several boats a day leave for Chóra Sfákia. From there, several buses daily, especially in the late afternoon, return to Chaniá and one to Réthymno.
Wear good walking shoes, take a picnic and enough to drink, a hat, sunscreen and, in summer, swimsuits for the beach at the end.

THE WHITE MOUNTAINS
'The high mountains had the austerity, the extravagance and sometimes the melancholy of the backgrounds of primitive religious paintings in Italy (though not the softness) or the vertigo of those insane and toppling crags—steel grey on purple, or ice blue on asbestos white—that surround the saints and martyrs on the ikons of Byzantium.'
Patrick Leigh Fermor, in his introduction to George Psychoundákis, *The Cretan Runner* (1955)

USEFUL NUMBER (SITEIA)

Tourist office (Odós Karamanlí, tel: 28430 28300. *Open* Mon–Fri 9.30–2.30, 5–8.30, Sat am only).

LINEAR A AND LINEAR B
The term 'linear' differentiates these early scripts from the even earlier hieroglyphic ideograms also used by the Minoans; instead of pictures they use abstract groups of lines. Linear A, which has never been deciphered, was a new script used from the beginning of the New Palace period (*c*1700BC). Although it is not known which language it is, there are suggestions that it is related to the pre-Hellenic languages of western Anatolia, where the Minoans originally came from. Linear B, a modification of Linear A, is known to have been used at Knosós for palace inventories from 1450BC. It has been deciphered as Mycenaean Greek and is therefore regarded as the first Hellenic language.

Tóplou monastery was built as a fortress against the Turks who destroyed the original building

▶ **Siteía**   *65E2*

A harbour town and the capital of Crete's eastern province, Siteía struggles to compete with the beauty of the surrounding hills. The modern town has preserved few reminders of its long history, but still has some of its old sleepy charm. Modern Siteía is built on the site of **ancient Iteía**, an important Minoan port and the supposed birthplace of Mysonas, one of the seven sages of ancient Greece. East of the town, at Pétra, this partly excavated Minoan settlement has yielded what was probably a palace and storage rooms. Siteía flourished under the Venetians, the much-restored **fortress** above the town being one of the few reminders of this period. First devastated by an earthquake in 1508, it was then sacked by the Turkish admiral Kheir-ed-Din Barbarossa.

The excellent **Archaeological Museum**▶▶ on Odós Pisokefaloú (tel: 28430 23917. *Open* Tue–Sun 8.30–3. *Admission charge*) has finds from the nearby excavations, mainly from Zákros (see below) and some evidence that a post-Minoan culture did exist in this area after the destruction of the Minoan palaces around 1450BC. Among the treasures is a collection of rare Linear A tablets. The charming **Museum of Folklore**▶ (Odós Kapetan Sifnos, tel: 28430 22861. *Open* Mon–Fri 10–2, also Wed 5–8pm. *Admission charge*) contains local costumes and embroideries. The waterfront, with several restaurants, bars and good *zacharoplasteía* (pastry shops) gets lively at night.

Around Siteía Many visitors to Siteía travel on eastwards to the famous palm-fringed beach of **Váï**▶▶ (see page 97). On the way, near **Agía Fotiá** (where the largest early Minoan cemetery was found), is the fortified **Moní Tóplou**▶▶ (tel: 28430 61226. *Open* 9–1, 2–6, Apr–Oct. *Admission charge*), one of the richest monasteries in Greece. After the stark exterior, the interior is remarkably beautiful and contains the amazing 18th-century **icon of the Greatness of the Lord**▶▶▶ by Ioánnis Kornáros, one of the masterpieces of Cretan art. Set into the exterior wall is the historic **Tóplou inscription**▶▶, an appeal by the people of Ítanos to the Egyptian King Ptolemy VI, made in 146BC, asking for help against their enemies from Ierápytna (Ierápetra). **Ítanos▶**, on the most northeasterly tip of the island, has the scattered remains of both a Minoan and a Roman Acropolis. At nearby **Palaíokastro▶▶** is the largest Minoan town so far found. Visitors can wander through the remains of streets and houses. On the other side of Siteía, **Móchlos▶▶** is a charming and quiet little fishing harbour, a reminder of how most of Crete used to be not so long ago. An important archaeological site has been discovered on Psíra island in front of the harbour, with a Minoan settlement from after the 1450BC disaster.

Quiet Zákros is believed to have been a major Minoan seaport, that traded with Egypt and other countries in the Middle East

▶▶ Tílisos   64C2

At the edge of the village of the same name is **ancient Tílisos▶** (*Open Tue–Sun 8.30–3. Admission charge*), whose three Minoan villas from the Neopalatial period (c1700BC) are still surrounded by rich farmland. The remains of House A suggest an elegant construction with a colonnaded court. House B is less well preserved, while the refined House C has evidence of a drainage system and a cult room. Both A and C have stairways, indicating that they had at least one more floor.

▶▶ Zákros   65E1

From Áno Zákros, a sleepy town surrounded by lush vegetation, a memorable two-hour walk (see panel) is an alternative to the bus ride to the lovely fishing harbour of Káto Zákros. The **Palace of Zákros▶▶** here is Crete's fourth largest Minoan palace (*Open Tue–Sun 8–7; 3 in winter. Admission charge*). Although it is much smaller than Knosós, Faistós and Mália, much of the town that surrounds it has been preserved. Zákros was most probably an important trading port with Egypt and the Levant. The new palace was built around 1600BC and destroyed in the 145BC disaster, perhaps by tidal waves caused by Thíra's volcano (a lot of pumice was found at the site).

GORGE OF THE DEAD
The 11km (7-mile) walk from Áno Zákros to the Minoan site near Káto Zákros passes through a magnificent ravine known as the Gorge of the Dead. Follow the road towards Káto Zákros for the first half hour, until a path to the left goes up to the ravine. Getting down into the gorge can be tricky, but once down by the riverbed the path is marked with red. Surrounded by wild vegetation and high cliff walls, you start to understand how the place got its name: the Minoans buried their dead in caves in the cliffs. From the end of the gorge, make your way back on to the road that leads to Káto Zákros and the palace.

Kríti (Crete)

One of the undeveloped and wonderful beaches in southern Crete, near Ierápetra

BEACHES ON CRETE
There is very little happy news to report on Cretan beaches. Package tourism has spoiled many of the once world-famous splendours, like Váï and Mátala and even where land access is difficult—as, for instance, to the most remote beaches on the south and west coasts—crowds of day trippers arrive by boat in summer. So even if you find that beach of your dreams, with white sand, good swimming, hills or greenery behind and no development, you won't be alone. And since these out-of-the-way beaches have no facilities or services, when visitors leave their waste behind them, it stays there...

INTERNATIONAL FERRIES
There are ferries in summer from Irákleio to Ancona (Italy), Haifa (Israel), Çesme (Turkey) and Cyprus, although not all of these operate regularly.

SUNKEN TREASURES
Many historic treasures still lie on the sea bed near the coasts of the islands. This is the main reason why scuba diving is not permitted in most Greek water; a rare exception is Mýkonos. The Greek government is still hoping to recover these treasures one day.

Beaches
Irákleio There are no great beaches around the capital. Amnísos, to the east, is the cleanest, but has continuous noise from aircraft. The coast farther east is one built-up resort after the other, each with a thin strip of pebbly beach. Beaches are better along the Gulf of Mália, but most have been developed. The beach near the Minoan palace at Mália is pleasant for a swim. Of the overdeveloped beaches west of Irákleio the best (but near a power station) is Amoudári. More trendy Agía Pelagía, with a good beach and clear water, is often less crowded.

Agía Galíni This popular package resort on the south coast has only a small beach, but boats go to beaches farther west. Ágios Geórgios is the most popular cove, but the better one is Ágios Pávlos. Mátala beach, overlooked by the cliff, remains truly spectacular, even if it is completely overrun in summer. Léndas's long beach is popular with nudists and the former crowd from Mátala.

Ágios Nikólaos The best near the town are the sandy, clean beach of Almýros and some pretty sandy coves near Istro. Eastwards towards Gourniá and Pachiá Ámmos the beaches are often dirty and polluted. Móchlos is cleaner.

Chaniá The town beach and Akrotíri beaches, Stavrós especially, are usually crowded. Westwards, the best are Chryssí Aktí or Golden Beach, increasingly built up but good, and Kalamáki, which has excellent swimming. From Chaniá to Kolymvári the coast is one long line of development and the beaches are not very clean. Falasarná, near Plátanos, is a long and isolated stretch of fine sand.

Chóra Sfákia Chóra Sfákia is a popular resort with a tiny beach. Boats run to the tranquil beaches of Gávdos island, Sweetwater Beach with cool springs and Mármara with

CONNECTIONS

Ferries run from Irákleio to Piréas, Íos, Mýkonos, Páros, Skíathos, Skýros, Tínos, Thíra, Náxos, Thessaloníki, Kárpathos, Kásos, Rhodes, Sýros, Amorgós, Kálymnos, Chálki, Milos and Pátmos. There are also excursion boats in summer to Thíra and the major Cyclades.
From Ágios Nikólaos and Siteía there are links with Thíra, Kýthnos, Mílos, Piréas, Sérifos, Sífnos, Sými, Kárpathos, Kásos, Chálki, Rhodes, Folégandros and Síkinos. Chaniá and Réthymno offer services to Piréas, while from Kastélli Kissámou there are ferries to Antikýthira, Kýthira and Piréas. Check the ferry connections on www.cretetravel.com as the timetables vary between summer and winter. There are also several high-speed catamarans to Piréas from the different harbours on Crete.

rock formations. Agía Rouméli has a pebble beach, Plákias is still good but development is coming fast. Nearby are smaller secluded coves such as Damnóni, Amoúdi and the spectacular Palm Beach, but they too are far from empty.

Ierápetra Near Ierápetra is Long Beach, a good stretch of sand. Agía Fotiá is an attractive beach set in a green valley, but Makrýgialos, once a magnificent beach, is now getting increasingly developed. Westwards the beach at Mýrtos, a small white resort, is a better option.

Palaiochóra Palaiochóra has a superb sandy beach, which so far is not too crowded, and more unspoiled beaches are within walking distance. Daily boats go to the wonderful, almost tropical beach of Elafonísi (no longer a secret), with white sands and warm turquoise waters. Elafonísi island can be reached by wading through the shallow water.

Réthymno The wide, sandy beach in town is packed, but the water is cleaner away from the harbour. The coast east-wards has fine beaches near Balí, but

most of it has given in to serious development. There are sandy beaches towards the Georgioúpoli resort, but the currents can be dangerous.

Much of Mália has been overrun by package tourism and space is short on its beach

Siteía Palm-fringed Váï is still a magnificent and exotic beach, even if the palm trees are now fenced in. If the crowds in summer get too overwhelming, there are emptier beaches 1.5km (1 mile) away near Ítanos. There are excellent sandy beaches south of Palaíkastro and a small pebble beach near Káto Zákros. Farther south, dirt paths lead to deserted sandy beaches near Xerókampos.

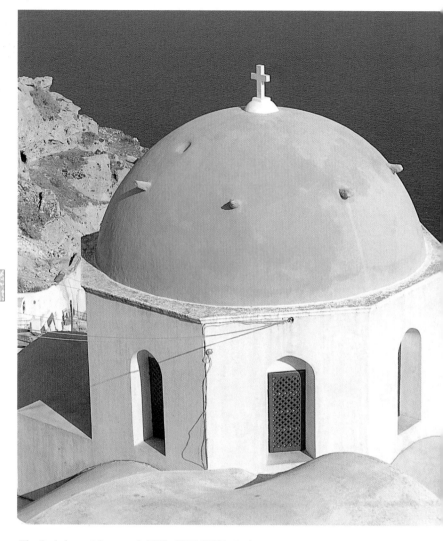

The Cyclades match everyone's dream of the perfect Greek island

THE CYCLADES Perhaps more than the other island groups, the Cyclades fulfil most visitors' expectations of how Greek islands should look. And yet, as the largest island group, they offer a great variety of landscape and character, from the dramatic cliffs of Thíra (Santoríni) to the lush valleys of Náxos. The Cyclades are the peaks of a mountain range beneath the Aegean, a fact most easily appreciated when looking at the volcanic caldera of Thíra.

FIRST CULTURE In an age when sea travel was constantly hazardous, the relative proximity of the Cyclades to each other allowed islanders to trade among themselves earlier than elsewhere; from this sprang the enigmatic Cycladic civiliazation of the period around 3000BC (see page 31). The remarkable artefacts attributed to this culture appeal to modern taste, particularly the carved figures with their clean lines and restrained movement.

The Cyclades
Amorgós (ΑΜΟΡΓΟΣ)
Anáfi (ΑΝΑΦΗ)
Ándros (ΑΝΔΡΟΣ)
Dílos (ΔΗΛΟΣ)
Folégandros
  (ΦΟΛΕΓΑΝΔΡΟΣ)
Íos (ΙΟΣ)
Kéa (ΚΕΑ)
Kímolos (ΚΙΜΩΛΟΣ)
Kýthnos (ΚΨΘΝΟΣ)
Mílos (ΜΗΛΟΣ)
Mýkonos
  (ΜΨΚΟΝΟΣ)
Náxos (ΝΑΞΟΣ)
Páros (ΠΑΡΟΣ) and
  Antíparos
  (ΑΝΤΙΠΑΡΟΣ)
Sérifos (ΣΕΡΙΦΟΣ)
Sífnos (ΣΙΦΝΟΣ)
Síkinos (ΣΙΚΙΝΟΣ)
Sýros (ΣΨΡΟΣ)
Thíra (Santoríni)
  (ΘΗΡΑ)
  (ΣΑΝΤΟΡΙΝΙΗ)
Tínos (ΤΗΝΟΣ)

EARLY POWER The name 'Cyclades' is derived from the Greek word for circle or ring: at the centre of the ring of islands lies Dílos (Delos), long respected as a place of both religious and political importance. In the 5th century BC, the creation of the Delian League brought cohesion to the islands. Subsequent Athenian Confederacies also kept the islands together, but they were no match for the powers that swept through the Aegean in the coming centuries: Egyptians and Romans, Vandals and Goths.

FOREIGN RULE AND INDEPENDENCE The Cyclades were nominally held by the Byzantines until the sack of Constantinople in 1204, after which they were ceded to Venice, which divided them among the adventuring sons of her aristocracy. The Venetian Sanudos, who claimed the title of dukes of Náxos, were the most powerful of these families, but not even they held out against the Turks, who

Cyclades

100

BEST BEACHES
● Mylopótamos and
Manganari (Íos), for the
summer 'scene'
● Paradise, Super
Paradise and Panormas
(Mýkonos)
● Kolymbithrès (Páros)
● Pláka (Náxos)
● Roúkounas and
tamarisk-lined Klisídi
(Anáfi)

then controlled the archipelago until Greek independence. The importance of the Cyclades to the independent Greek state was immediately apparent: the port of Ermoúpoli on Sýros became its principal commercial and shipping centre and one of the eastern Mediterranean's main coaling stations. It remains a busy port and is still the administrative capital of the Cyclades.

LANDSCAPES AND LIFE Surrounded by a dramatic landscape of rock and olive trees, of green terraces, golden sand and brilliant blue sea, the islanders have created an architecture of simple lines and smooth surfaces, painted white

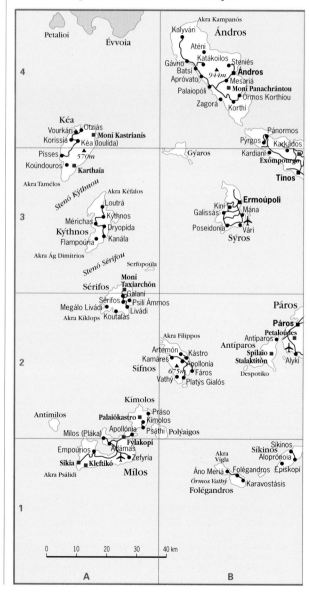

and blue—the colours of the Greek flag—which has much in common with the art of their Early Cycladic ancestors.

The islands within easy reach of Piréas were among the first to be developed. But even on Mýkonos, famous (some would say notorious) the world over for its nightlife, much of the island's original character remains intact. While, in summer, some of the islands can seem to have sold their soul to tourism, out of season, with the high sea crashing on the beaches and ferry arrivals limited, island life is the same as it ever was. Visit some of the smaller villages, stop and talk to a farmer or a fisherman and experience the Cycladic inheritance firsthand.

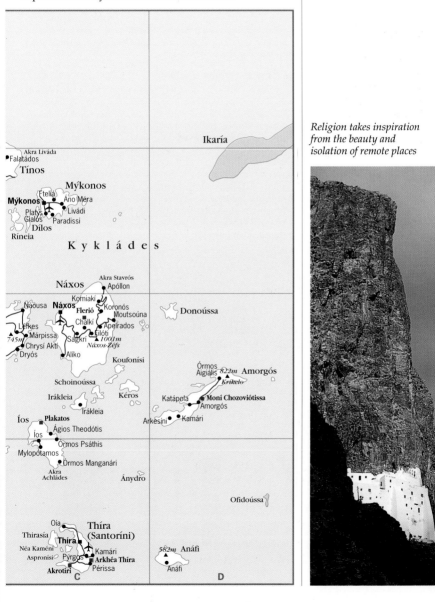

Religion takes inspiration from the beauty and isolation of remote places

101

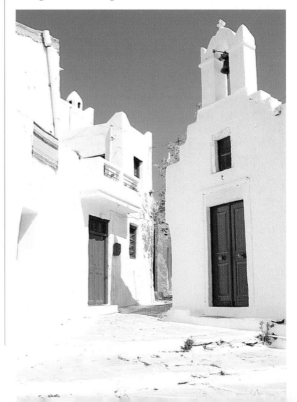

USEFUL NUMBERS
Port Authority (Amorgós)
tel: 22850 71259
Tourist information
(Ándros: Gávrio. *Open*
Jun–Sep) tel: 22820
71770; www.andros.gr
(Anafi) tel: 22860 61253

AMORGÓS

Amorgós, the dramatically rugged island that starred in Luc Besson's film *The Big Blue*, is still a low-key place, though more visitors head this way each summer.

▶ Amorgós Town (Chóra)   *101D2*

The island's capital, built around a 13th-century Venetian castle, has more than 40 chapels and churches, including the smallest one in Greece, **Ágios Fanoúrios**, which can hold a congregation of three. Outside the town a path leads towards the striking white **monastery of Chozoviótissa▶▶** (*Open* daily 8–1 and 5–7. *Admission donation*), founded around a miraculous 11th-century icon of the Virgin. Downhill is the main harbour, Katápola and a track leading past **ancient Minoa▶**, with the remains of a temple of Apollo, to the site of **ancient Arkesíni▶**, with a burial site and some houses.

▶ Órmos Aigiális (Eyiáli)   *101D2*

This harbour in the northern part of the island is a good base for the nearby beaches and walks to the villages of Tholária, Langáda and Potámos or a climb up the peak of Kríkelo (780m/2,560ft), with its splendid 5th-century **church of Theológos▶▶**.

Beaches

The only sandy beach on the island is near Órmos Aigiális, though farther north there are a few pleasant coves. From Amorgós Town a trail goes down to the pebble beaches and coves of Agía Ánna. Near Kamári there are fine secluded beaches at Moúros, Notiná and Poulopódi, all with good swimming.

CONNECTIONS
Amorgós has ferry links with Náxos, Páros, Piréas, Schoinoússa, Sýros, Donoússa, Mýkonos, Rhodes, Kós, Kálymnos, Astypálaia and Rafína. Hydrofoils run to Piréas, Mýkonos, Náxos, Páros and Sýros. Excursion boats operate to Rafína, Páros, Náxos, Sýros and Tínos.

The Chóra in Amorgós has more than 40 churches, including the smallest one in Greece

102

ANÁFI

According to legend, Anáfi, a small and idyllic island, was pulled up from the sea by Apollo to give refuge to the Argonauts. Today it offers refuge to people escaping nearby Thíra, though there is just a small stretch of paved road and few tourist facilities.

► Anáfi Town (Chóra)   *101D1*

The island's 300 inhabitants live in Anáfi Town or the port of Ágios Nikólaos. At first sight, the former looks like a windswept ghost town, but closer inspection reveals friendly *kafeneía* and sheltered terraces.

The island's main attraction is the **monastery of Panagía Kalamiótissa►►**, three hours' walk away from Anáfi Town, less from Kálamos, reached by daily boats. The path up to the little monastery offers spectacular views.

Beaches

Klisídi is a lovely tamarisk-lined beach near the harbour. An hour's walk away is the island's best beach, Roúkounas, with sandy dunes and shade under the trees. Farther down are some superb coves and the secluded Monastiri beach.

ÁNDROS

Green, pine-forested Ándros has long been a favourite holiday destination for Greek families. Other Europeans are slowly arriving, attracted by the cosmopolitan atmosphere combined with traditional village life.

►►► Ándros Town (Chóra)   *100B4*

The oldest part of the island's capital is built on a rocky tongue of land, while a later addition was built on the hillside. It is filled with marble pavements, elegant squares and 19th-century mansions. A 13th-century Venetian **kástro►** sits on a rocky islet reached by an arched bridge. The modern galleries of the excellent **Archaeological Museum►►►** (tel: 22820 23664. *Open* Tue–Sun 8.30–3. *Admission charge*) contain a fine statue of Hermes, Byzantine and Venetian marbles and finds from the

---

CONNECTIONS
Anáfi is linked by ferry with Thíra, Píreas, Íos, Náxos, Kythnos, Sérifes, Sífnos, Milos, Tinos, Folégandros, Páros and Sýros.

103

THE GOULANDRÍS FAMILY
The extremely wealthy and famous Goulandrís shipping magnates, originating from Ándros, put their island on the map of the art world when they opened two museums in Ándros Town. The Archaeological Museum contains the beautiful statue of Hermes of Ándros, on display until 1981 in the National Museum in Athens. The Museum of Modern Art has wonderful collections of contemporary Greek and European work. After all that, it comes as no surprise that both the square at the heart of the Ándros Town and its main street carry the Goulandrís name.

GREEN ÁNDROS

The countryside of Ándros is perfect for hiking. The strong prevailing winds keep it cooler than most islands, even in summer, and freshwater springs are abundant. The countryside is dotted with lovely Venetian dovecotes and there is an interesting system of dry-stone walling around many fields and orchards. The Andriots, noted for their hospitality, are always proud to show off the beauty of their island.

CONNECTIONS

Ferries from Ándros serve Rafína, Tínos, Mýkonos, Sýros, Amorgós and Thíra. A summer hydrofoil service operates to Tínos, Mýkonos, Páros, Náxos, Íos and Amorgós.

ancient fortified town of Zagorá. Close by, the excellent **Museum of Modern Art**►►► (*Open* daily Wed–Sat 10–2, 6–8, Sun 10–2, in summer; Sat–Mon 10–2, in winter. *Admission charge*) has a remarkable collection by modern artists including Picasso, Matisse, Rodin and Braque.

► Batsí 100B4

Ándros's main resort, Batsí, has a fine fishing harbour and a beautiful but crowded beach. The walk up the mountain to the picturesque villages of Káto and Áno Katákolos, Aténi and Arní is rewarding. Farther along the coast is the 7th-century BC site of **Palaiopólis**►. Most of the once-grand former capital has now disappeared.

► Gávrio 100B4

Gávrio is the island's main harbour, on the more sheltered west coast. A short walk away is **Ágios Pétros**►►, a 20m-high (65ft) Hellenic round tower, perhaps once a royal tomb, later converted into a watchtower.

►► Korthí 100B4

Korthí village is isolated from the rest of the island by a high ridge. The nearby convent of **Zoödóchou Pigís**►► (*Open* mornings) is a Byzantine school, converted into a monastery during the 14th century and into a convent in the 1920s. North of Korthí is Palaiókastro, which has a crumbling Venetian castle.

►►► Mesariá 100B4

Mesariá is a picturesque medieval village near the **monastery of Panachrántou**►►, the finest on the island. It was probably built in the 10th century and is still surrounded by impressive defensive walls.

► Zagorá 100B4

Most of the finds from this ancient fortified town are in the Ándros Archaeological Museum. This site, which was never built over, is spectacular, with steep cliffs on three sides.

Beaches

The beaches near Chorá often suffer from the *meltemi* wind, but there are some excellent ones: Achla near Ágios Nikolaos monastery, and to the south Pidima tis Grias, a superb sandy beach. Batsí gets crowded, but Aténi to the north has gorgeous coves. Ágios Pétros southeast of Gávrio is a huge sandy beach.

Panachrántou, the most ancient of Ándros's monasteries, has recently celebrated its 1,000th birthday

More important in the calendar than Christmas, Easter in Greece is a magical time of traditions, prayers and, later, of treats as well. It is also a time when many quiet island villages are suddenly filled with celebrating Athenians. If you are lucky enough to be on the islands for the festival, prepare to rejoice.

The tradition Greeks take their celebrations seriously and none more than Easter, a time of celebration rather than mourning. It is usual for people to return to their place of origin and both ferries and hotels fill up at this time of year. The islands of Ýdra, Pátmos, Sýros and Tínos are particularly noted for their Easter festivities. On Good Friday, after church bells have tolled, the *Epitáfios*, a symbolic bed for Jesus, decorated with flowers, is carried through the streets.

Easter celebrations are intense

The rising In keeping with a religion that emphasizes joy, the main event of Orthodox Easter takes place at midnight on Easter Saturday: the bells toll again, lights are dimmed in churches and a priest calling *Christós Anésti* (Christ has risen) offers a lighted candle to the community. People light their own candles from the priest's, make the sign of the cross in smoke on the threshold of their houses and then leave the candle to burn down while they eat. The traditional late-night dish is *mayarítsa*, a soup of tripe and rice.

The Easter slaughter Few restaurants serve dinner on Easter Saturday as islanders are saving their appetite for the following day's Easter feast. During the previous day

or two, a great slaughter will have taken place and on Easter Sunday every family that can afford it will roast a lamb. The summer barbecue is often brought out for the first time after winter in order to roast it.

On the Thursday before Easter, there is also a tradition of painting hard-boiled eggs red. Some are used in *tsouréki* (see panel) while others are saved for a holiday game: the eggs are knocked together two at a time and the holder of the last unbroken egg is considered lucky.

FASTING
Patience Gray wrote in her wonderful book *Honey from a Weed* (London, 1986): 'From Advent until Christmas Eve and from Ash Wednesday until midnight on Easter Saturday the diet is reduced to the consumption of dried beans, lentils, rice, spaghetti and weeds. The normal standbys—goat, lamb, pork, fresh cheese, eggs and often fish, as well as olive oil, are eliminated. As the diet of island Greeks was already restricted, one marvelled at their ability to deprive themselves still further.'

EASTER BREAD
Of all the traditional Easter fare on the Greek islands, the most common is *tsouréki*, a sweet twist-bread, usually flavoured with mastic from Chíos. A red-painted egg is usually inserted into the dough and baked into the bread as it cooks.

Lamb on a spit for the Easter feast

Three of the lions from the stunning Lion Terrace are now in the Arsenale in Venice

GETTING THERE
The entire island of Dílos is an archaeological museum and can only be visited as a day trip. Boats leave Mýkonos harbour daily from around 9am for the 40-minute ride, returning from around 1.30pm. This allows visitors three hours on the site, enough for most people. Tickets for guided or non-guided trips are best bought in advance from the booths on the quay, rather than from a travel agent. Note that most tickets sold on Mýkonos do not include the admission to the site (which, incidentally, is closed on Mondays). In summer there are hydrofoils from Páros three days a week.

THE DELIAN GAMES
In antiquity, the Delian Games were as famous as the Olympics. Both were religious festivals held in honour of the gods, who were believed to be delighted to see humans enjoying themselves on their account. Homer confirmed this in his *Hymn to Apollo*:
'But it was on Dílos, Phoibos, that your heart especially took delight, Where the long-robed Ionians gathered together With their children and wives on your sacred street;
There in boxing and dancing and singing They think of you and rejoice, when they hold your contest.'

DÍLOS (DELOS)

▶▶▶ Ancient Dílos   101C3

Open: Tue–Sun 8.30–3

Leto, the pregnant mistress of Zeus, was pursued all over the world by his jealous wife Hera, until the winds brought her to Dílos. Poseidon struck the island with his trident and anchored it with four columns of diamond, while Leto gave birth to Artemis on the nearby island of Ríneia and to Apollo under a date palm on Dílos's Mount Kinthos. The dry, barren island, which immediately started to flourish, was to become one of the most sacred places in Greece.

Cyclades

ODYSSEUS TO NAUSICAA
'Never in my life have I seen such another, man or woman: I'm amazed as I look upon you. In Dílos once I did see something like you, a young palm-spire springing up beside Apollo's altar....'
Homer, *Odyssey* Book VI

The Ionians, who considered Apollo the father of Ion, the founder of their race, made Dílos their religious capital. The rising Athenians became increasingly jealous of Dílos's power and tried everything in their might to diminish it. The Athenians tricked the oracle in Delphi into ordering a purification of Dílos: in 426BC, they went as far as forbidding all births and deaths on the island! The island flourished again in the 3rd and 2nd centuries BC as one of the great trading centres of the eastern Mediterranean, especially after the Romans declared it a free port. Mithridates and his pirates plundered the island twice, in 88 and 69BC, killing more than 20,000 people, a blow from which Dílos never recovered.

KEEPING DILOS CLEAN (ANCIENT STYLE)
'Do not wash anything in the spr[in]g, or sw[im in t]he spring, or [th]ro[w] i[n]to the spri[ng manure or anything els]e. Pe[nalty]: 2 [s]acr[e]d drachmas'.
Inscription relating to the sacred spring of the nymphs, Dílos, 5th century BC

Excavations on the island started in 1872 and continue today. The site is large, but easy to visit as everything is clearly labelled. The **Sacred Way**, once lined with grand statues, leads to the **Sanctuary of Apollo** and the **House of the Naxians**, originally fronted by a huge statue of Apollo. There are three subsequent **temples of Apollo**. Towards the museum is the **Sanctuary of Dionysos** with the often-photographed marble phalluses on pedestals. The **Agora of the Italians** leads to the 6th-century BC **Temple of Leto** and the **Dodekatheon**, dedicated to the 12 Olympian gods. Beyond lies the dried-up **Sacred Lake** and beside it the impressive 7th-century BC **Avenue of the Lions**. The **museum** has some fine Hellenistic and Archaic sculpture, mosaics, murals and daily objects from private houses. A path leads up to the **Terrace of the Foreign Gods**, with the 1st-century BC **Sanctuary of the Syrian Gods** and several temples dedicated to the Egyptian gods Serapis and Isis. Farther up is the **Sacred Cave**, site of the oracle of Apollo and **Óros Kynthos** (**Mount Kinthos**) (110m/360ft), with excellent panoramic views over the entire island. At the foot of Mount Kinthos, in the **Theatre District**, well-preserved private houses and streets give a good feel of what life on Dílos must have been like. The 2nd-century BC **Theatre** once seated 5,500 people, but is now ruined. The houses date from the Hellenistic and Roman period, some still decorated with exquisite mosaics. In the **House of Dionysos** there is a superb mosaic of Dionysos seated on a panther. The **House of the Dolphins**, the **House of the Masks** and the **House of the Trident** also have fine mosaics.

One of several giant phalluses on Dionysian pedestals near the Sanctuary of Dionysos

The Greeks had no word for religion—that came with the Romans—nor did they have sacred texts. Ancient Greeks had their own ways of establishing relationships with the gods.

READING THE SIGNS
'...if the bird flying from right to left disappears from view the omen is favourable; if it raises its left wing, flies away and disappears the omen is unfavourable; if flying from left to right it disappears on a straight course the omen is unfavourable; but if after raising its right wing, it flies away and dis-appears the omen is favourable....'
6th-century BC divination from Ephesus, quoted in F. Sokolowski, *Lois sacrés de l'Asie mineure* (1955)

GREEK GODS
The 5th-century BC histo-rian Herodotus wrote, 'Not till the day before yester-day, so to speak, did the Greeks know the origin of each of the gods, or whether they had all existed always and what they were like ...It was Homer and Hesiod who created a theogony for the Greeks, gave the gods their epithets, divided out offices and functions among them and described their appearance.' (*The Histories*)

ANCIENT AND MODERN
It was common practice in ancient Greece to make offerings at times of illness at the shrines of gods or heroes associated with healing (notably Asklepius). Offerings were often clay effigies of the afflicted body part, a habit that modern Greeks con-tinue by bedecking holy icons with metal effigies of their afflicted parts.

The ritual of pouring a libation to the gods is depicted on a black-figured vase

Of gods and men Greeks had a very clear view of who their gods were. They were mostly related to each other, but each was associated with a specific area of human experience. The primary gods lived on Olympus and also in the world of men, sometimes associated with certain cities. However, gods and men were not on equal terms: men needed to do their utmost to keep the gods happy—all of them, because to ignore one particular god was to risk being cut off from a sphere of human interest.

Understanding the will of the gods Greeks knew about the gods from mythology, from Homer and Hesiod in par-ticular. There were priests and priestesses, but no unifying religious institution. Instead, Greeks relied on what they believed was a more personal relationship with the gods. The most direct way to understand the will of the gods was via the oracles, the most famous being at Delphi, Olympia, Siwa (in Egypt) and Dílos. Seers did not speak the will of the gods, like the oracles, but they knew how to interpret signs (see panel).

108

How to make your god happy The gods were happy when humans remembered them in their prayers and paid their respects by observing daily rituals and making offerings to temples and cult shrines. This observance ran throughout Greek society: fathers made sacrifices for the household, while priests and civil leaders did so for the people. There was a calendar of dates on which sacrifice was due to certain gods. Sacrificial offerings were either animals, slaughtered on site, or dry offerings, like grain or fruit. The most common form of sacrifice was for the thigh bones of a slaughtered animal to be wrapped in fat and burned on an altar. The meat could then be eaten by the mortals. To give thanks to a god, one might make a donation to the temple or cult centre.

Fun and games The gods loved fun and games and activities held in their honour had to reflect this. Greeks sang, danced, recited poetry, enacted dramas and held carnivals to delight the gods. Competing in athletics was also acceptable. The Olympics were the most prestigious of several athletics meetings held to honour them; games held on Dílos were similarly famous. Not only did these observances encourage a common Greek identity, they also allowed Greeks to feel they had a relationship with the gods: humans sacrificed and prayed and in return the gods granted wealth, health and happiness.

Mysteries and afterlife The dead in Homer's epic stories are mere shades of themselves, left to wander aimlessly in the underworld, with the occasional taste of heaven or hell. However, there were secret rites—the mysteries—that might improve things in the afterlife. Initiation was via a long and extraordinary ritual. The most important were those connected to Demeter and Persephone at Eleusis, near Athens, but the mysteries connected to the great gods at Samothráki were still sufficiently important for Roman emperors to make the long journey to the island after the start of the Christian era.

One of the finest temples on the islands, the Temple of Aphaia on Aígina is associated with women, wisdom and light

GREEK ATHEISM
The power of the Greek religion lay not in texts but in its universality: people paid their respects to the gods and observed the necessary rituals. But in the 5th century BC there was a religious crisis in Athens as philosophers and scientists began to question the nature and the very existence of the gods. 'About the gods I cannot declare whether they exist or not', stated the intellectual Protagoras. Soon after, it seems, the common good or the common will exerted itself and there was a backlash against such thinkers: one of the charges levelled at Socrates, whom the oracle at Delphi had called the world's wisest man, was that he did not recognize 'the gods that the city recognizes' and that he searched 'into things under the earth and above the heaven'. He was sentenced to death for his thoughts in 399BC.

USEFUL NUMBER
Actéon Travel near the
port in Íos Town provides
tourist information. *Open*
daily in summer
8am–9pm; also sells
ferry tickets) tel: 22860
91088;
www.iosgreece.com

CONNECTIONS
Ferry services from
Folégandros operate to
Piréas, Thíra, Íos,
Síkinos, Sífnos, Mílos,
Kímolos, Kýthnos, Náxos,
Páros, Sérifos and Sýros.
There are additional sum-
mer services to Mýkonos,
Crete and Rhodes. Daily
boats run to Íos during
the summer.
 From Íos, ferries run to
Piréas, Náxos, Páros,
Thíra, Sýros, Síkinos,
Folégandros, Anáfi,
Sífnos, Kímolos, Kýthnos,
Mílos and Sérifos.
Hydrofoils serve
Mýkonos, Náxos, Páros,
Thíra, Sýros and Irákleia.

HOMER ON ÍOS
One story has it that
Homer's ship, on a trip
from Sámos to Athens,
was forced to call at Íos
and that while in port the
poet died. Another tradi-
tion claims that Homer's
mother was from the
island and that the poet
chose to return to this
place to die.

*Opposite: the blue-domed
Byzantine churches of the
Chóra are a little oasis
away from the nightlife
crowds*

FOLÉGANDROS

The high barren cliffs of Folégandros always deterred
eager invaders, until recent years. Now tourists have discovered this peaceful and quiet island.

▶▶ Folégandros Town (Chóra)   *100B1*

The island's capital, perched on a cliff high above
the harbour of Karavostásis, is a delightful village with
pretty squares, tree-shaded *kafeneía* and a 13th-century
Venetian **kástro** surrounded by solid two-storey houses.
A steep path leads to the **church of Koímisis Theotókou**
with spectacular views and, beneath it, the stalactite cave
of **Chrissospiliá**, accessible only to experienced climbers.

Beaches

The beaches near Karavostásis are average, but there is a
superb small-gravel beach at Katergó, reached by boat or
after a hard walk. Buses from Folégandros Town pass
close to the various beaches on the southwest coast of the
island: Angáli is the busiest, while nudism is tolerated on
Firá and sandy Ágios Nikólaos. From Áno Meriá a path
leads to the more secluded beach of Vígla.

ÍOS

Íos, one of the prettiest Cycladic islands, has a reputation
for good beaches and an even better nightlife. For these
reasons it attracts a particularly large number of tourists.
Depending on your idea of fun, you will either love it or
loathe it!

▶ Íos Town (Chóra)   *101C1*

A pretty, whitewashed village with a host of Byzantine
churches, the island's capital bursts with life at night when
music blares from countless bars and discos. The nearby
port of Gialós has excellent fish tavernas. Two to three
hours' walk away, above Ágios Theodótis, the Venetian
fortress of Palaiokástro overlooks the site of ancient
Aigina and a Byzantine church. A longer walk or a trip by
boat gets you to the ancient town of Plakatos, at the northern end of the island, where a tomb is believed to be that of
Homer, who is said to have died on Íos. Every year on 15
May, there is a Homer festival, when the villagers carry a
flame from the harbour to the grave.

Beaches

Good beaches and an easy lifestyle are what Íos is really
about. Gialós beach is nothing special; better is Koumbára,
20 minutes away, less crowded and mostly nudist.
Mylopótamos is a superb but very popular sandy beach.
For one of the most beautiful beaches on the island, walk,
or take a bus or boat, to Órmos Manganári, in the south, or
head to Ágios Theodótis or Psáthis on the east coast.
 Note that, although sleeping on the beach was always
the thing to do on Íos, these days it is better not to. With a
growing number of people looking for a good time,
reports of theft and violent crime have increased dramatically. The police, in response, is really tough. They will try
to convince people to make use of the official campsites
and can be very unfriendly towards those who do not take
their advice.

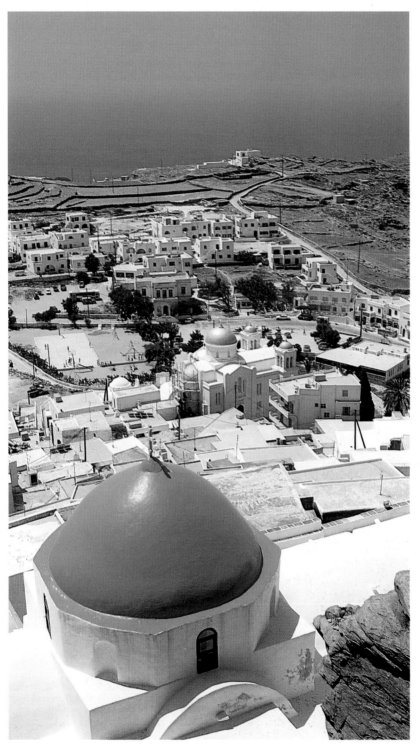

USEFUL NUMBERS
Tourist Information on the quay (Kéa) tel: 22880 21500
Tourist information (Mílos, on the quay in Adamas) tel: 22870 22445; www.milos-island.gr

KÉA

The closest Cycladic island to the capital, Kéa has long been a favourite weekend escape for Athenians.

►►► Kéa Town/Ioulída (Chóra)   100A4

Red-tiled houses are set tight against the hills. The crumbling Venetian **kástro** was built on the acropolis of ancient Ioulis; a few stones from the Apollo Temple remain. The **Archaeological Museum►** (tel: 22880 22079. *Open* Tue–Sun 8.30–3. *Admission free*) has finds from local sites, but the best are in Athens. East of the town, the striking 6th-century BC **Lion of Kéa►►►** was chiselled out of rock. A pleasant walk leads to the 18th-century **monastery of Panagía Kastrianís►**, famed for its miracle-working icon. *Kaíki* (small fishing boats) go south to **ancient Karthaía** and its remains of a Temple of Apollo.

Beaches

The best beach near the harbour, Korissía, is Yialiskári, lined with eucalyptus trees. Písses has a large beach with tavernas. Koúndouros has several sandy coves but is more developed. Otziás is a popular resort.

KÍMOLOS

Known in antiquity for sea urchins and to the Venetians for silver, the unspoiled volcanic island of Kímolos long survived on the export of chalk (*kimolía* in Greek).

►► Kímolos Town (Chóra)   100A2

The gleaming white houses of the capital, perched on the ridge above the working windmills, are overlooked by a wonderful Venetian **kástro►** and the beautiful 14th-century **church of Chrisostómos►►**. All boats arrive in the tiny harbour of Psáthi.

Beaches

Práso has a good beach and hot springs, with several shady secluded coves nearby. Elliniká's coarse sand, overlooked by capes, is the island's best.

KÝTHNOS (THERMIÁ)

Older Greeks come here to soak in the thermal spas and more recently it has become popular with big yachts.

► Kýthnos Town (Chóra)   100A3

The inland capital has little action and few attractions beyond its interesting churches, particularly 17th-century **Ágios Saba**. Boats dock at Mérichas, where most tourists stay. Some 3km (2 miles) away is the island's 19th-century spa of **Loutrá**. Farther north, on Akra (Cape) Kéfalos, is the medieval **Palaiokástro►**. From Kýthnos Town, a fine 6km walk leads south to the **Dryopída**, the former capital and the nearby **cave of Katafíki**.

Beaches

The nearest beach to Mérichas is unexceptional Episkopí. Towards the south, Flampoúria is the better beach. Loutrá has an adequate beach with tavernas and there are several secluded coves around Kanála.

CONNECTIONS
From Kéa, ferries operate to Lávrio (mainland), Kýthnos, Sýros and Ándros. There are hydrofoil links with Piréas and (summer only) Kýthnos, Mílos, Sérifos, Sífnos, Kímolos and Rafína. Ferries from Kímolos serve Piréas, Mílos, Kýthnos, Sífnos, Sérifos, Folégandros, Íos, Páros, Thíra, Síkinos and Sýros. There is a summer hydrofoil service to Mílos, Sífnos, Sérifos, Kýthnos, Kéa and Rafína. Boats operate to Mílos in summer.
Ferries operate from Kýthnos to Piréas, Sérifos, Sífnos, Kímolos, Mílos, Kéa, Thíra, Folégandros, Íos, Síkinos, Crete, Ándros, Kárpathos, Sýros and Lávrio. In the summer hydrofoils serve Kéa, Sérifos, Sífnos, Kímolos, Mílos, Rafína, Mýkonos and Tínos.

112

MILOS BOAT TOUR
Boats leave from Adámas at 9am for a tour around the island, well worth it for the excellent views on the black volcanic rock formations and the stops for swims at otherwise inaccessible beaches. Boats stop at the huge underwater cave of Sikia, and the old pirate lair of Kleftiko, with its superb volcanic eroded rocks.

MÍLOS

The island that is best known for a world-famous statue has fertile, rolling countryside, but is scarred by a long (and continuing) tradition of quarrying.

▶ Mílos Town/Pláka   100A2

This is an attractive capital but more modern than those on other islands. The **Archaeological Museum▶** (tel: 22870 21629. *Open* Tue–Sun 8.30–3. *Admission charge*) has mainly finds from ancient Fylakopí, the oldest site on the island. Inhabited from the third millennium BC, Fylakopí has revealed evidence of both Minoan and Mycenaean settlement. The museum also has a plaster cast of the Venus de Milo. The original, now in the Louvre in Paris, was found in 1820 by a local farmer, in a cave near the theatre of ancient Melos. The **Folklore museum▶▶** (tel: 22870 21292. *Open* Tue–Sat 10–2 and 6–9, Sun 10–2; shorter hours in winter. *Admission charge*), in the old quarter, has a fine collection of Milian costumes and old photographs.

Above the town there are breathtaking views over the Aegean from the Venetian **kástro▶▶** and the chapel of Panagía Thalassítra. Between the town and the harbour, Adámas, are 1st-century AD **Christian catacombs▶▶** (*Open* Tue–Sun 8–7. *Admission free*), where thousands of bodies were buried in rock-cut corridors. Below the town lie the extensive remains of **ancient Melos▶▶**, including a huge temple podium and a well-preserved theatre. Below it is the lovely fishing harbour of **Klíma**.

Beaches

Adámas is popular but mediocre. The island's second resort, Apollónia, has a sandy (though often windy) beach. Tree-lined Plathiéna is the first choice near Mílos Town, but the island's best beach is the remote sandy Palaiochóri.

Photogenic Klíma with the typical boat houses on the waterfront

THE VENUS DE MILO
After its discovery in 1820, the statue was apparently given to the French for safe-keeping from the Turks, but the two arms broke off in transit. Safe-keeping, however, has turned into ownership: it was given to Louis XVIII, who put it on display in the Louvre, where it remains one of the star attractions.

CONNECTIONS
Mílos is linked by ferry with Piréas, Kímolos, Kýthnos, Sérifos, Sífnos, Thíra, Folégandros, Crete, Íos, Páros, Síkinos, Sýros, Kárpathos, Kásos and Rhodes. Hydrofoils run in summer to Kéa, Kímolos, Kýthnos, Sífnos, Thíra, Piréas and Sérifos.

USEFUL NUMBERS
Tourist Police
(waterfront) tel: 22890
24106
Airport tel: 22890 22327
Hoteliers Association of
Mýkonos (on the quay)
tel: 22890 24540;
www.mykonos-
greece.com)

MÝKONOS

Mýkonos was originally a stopover for those en route to the nearby island of Dílos (Delos, see pages 106–107), so it has a long tradition in the service of tourism. Although dry, windy and barren, it is one of the most visited of all the Greek islands and its famous windmills are one of the most photographed sights in Greece. In spite of this, Mýkonos has managed to maintain its postcard-like beauty *and* a cosmopolitan flair, although few of its Greek traditions survive. It is no longer *the* gay resort of the Med, but it still attracts its share of 'beautiful' people.

Now the most popular of the Cycladic islands, Mýkonos was originally only visited as a stop on the way to Dílos

A NIGHT ON THE TOWN
The legendary nightlife of Mýkonos Town still throbs, but, comes at a price. At sunset head for the terraces of Le Caprice, Galleraki or the Kastro bar in Little Venice. Pierro's, on the main street, was the first gay bar on the island, and it still draws a large crowd of beau monde, straights, gays and drag queens. The Scandinavian Bar near the east end of the waterfront is popular with a young trendy crowd, as is Astra on Odós Enoplon Dinameon, with the country's best DJs. Space disco on Odós Laka goes on until the early morning. Run by the same people is the more laid-back El Pecado on Odós Polikandrioti.

▶▶▶ **Mýkonos Town (Chóra)**   *101C3*

Ferries arrive at the big newer harbour, but the heart of the town still beats around the old fishing port, its waterfront lined with elegant terraces from which to see and be seen. Its maze of streets was intended to confuse pirates; now full of designer boutiques and trendy bars, they still bemuse visitors. Cars are forbidden, so the only way to explore the town is by walking and getting lost. The cubist whitewashed houses are well looked after, decorated with the traditional bright blue woodwork, masses of flower-pots and, often, with a cat asleep on the stairway.

Just past the Dílos jetty is the bizarre asymmetrical church of **Panagía Paraportianí▶▶** and the **Folklore Museum▶** (*Open* Mon–Sat 5.30–8.30pm, Sun 6.30–8.30, Apr–Oct. *Admission free*), which has a vast collection of paraphernalia relating to the island. Farther along is **Alefkándra▶▶▶**, the most picturesque and the trendiest quarter of the capital. It is known as 'Little Venice' because of its tall Venetian houses, built right on the water's edge. Here and elsewhere in the town, visitors may be surprised to encounter one of the resident Mýkonos pelicans which roam the streets and pose vainly for photographs. On the rise beyond Alefkándra, whitewashed windmills complete the picture. Inland from here is the **Maritime Museum▶▶** (Odós Évoplon Dynaméon. *Open* daily 10.30–1, 6.30–9, Apr–Nov. *Admission charge*), which has fine model ships and other nautical items. Next door is the **Traditional House of Lena** (*Open* daily in summer 6pm–9pm. *Admission free*). Here, a typical 19th-century house, complete with its original furnishings and equipment, has been turned into a lovely museum. The **Archaeological Museum** (*Open* Tue–Sun 8.30–3. *Admission charge*) has a few artefacts from Dílos.

Elsewhere on the island, the village of Áno Méra offers the most traditional atmosphere and its 16th-century **monastery of Panagía Tourlianí▶** (*Open* daily 9–2. *Admission free*) has Cretan frescoes and lovely baroque woodcarvings. Nearby stands another monastery, **Palaiokástro**, set in an oasis on a barren hill (*Open* daily 9–2. *Admission free*).

Beaches

Mýkonos has magnificent beaches and coves, nudism is widely allowed and scuba-diving is legal, unlike in most other places in Greece. An excellent network of buses serves most of the beaches, as do daily boats from Mýkonos Town's harbour and Ornos Bay. The good beaches near the capital—Megáli Amnos in town, popular but average Ornos and more pleasant Ágios Stéfanos—all have developments. Ágios Ioánnis is more secluded and has a little chapel on its pebble beach.

The south coast has excellent beaches, but as this is what most people come to find on Mýkonos, even these can get crowded, with boats arriving all the time in summer. Platýs Gialós is a fine family beach, Psárou is a delightful sandy bay with paths to the fashionable, mainly nudist, Paradise Beach (Paradíssi) and, in the next bay, Super Paradise, once only gay but now a mixed nudist beach. The island's longest and probably finest beach is Elía. If that is still too busy, head for the superb beaches of Agrári, Livádi and Lía Ammóudia in the next bays. The north coast beaches often get strong winds; Mýkonos is notorious for the unpredictable *meltemi*. Ftelía, on Panórmos Bay, is the best for windsurfing.

Some of the picturesque windmills near Little Venice are now up for rent

The lovely narrow streets in the Chóra become more colourful every year, as tourism increases

CONNECTIONS

Mýkonos has ferry links with Ándros, Piréas, Rafína, Sýros, Tínos, Amorgós, Kálymnos, Ikaría, Schoinoússa, Kýthnos, Kéa, Pátmos, Léros, Nisyros, Sífnos, Skíathos, Thessaloníki, Kós, Rhodes, Síkinos, Sérifos, Folégandros and (summer only) Íos, Páros, Náxos and Thíra. Hydrofoils and catamarans run in summer to Tínos, Piréas, Sýros, Páros, Náxos, Ráfina, Íos, Thíra and also to Anáfi.

Greek civilization grew up alongside the water. Both the nature of the country, with its scattered islands and its position astride a major sea route have ensured that navigation remains important to Greeks, whose shipping magnates, such as Onassis and Niarchos, have become wrapped in legend.

ANCIENT JOURNEYS

It was not only trade that led people in ancient Greece to hoist their sails. The holy isle of Dílos, the sanctuary of the Great Gods at Samothráki and the health spa and hospital on Kós were but three of many centres that could be reached only by boat. Today, when it is possible to fly to so many islands, it is often those islands that can still be reached only by boat that make the greatest impression on the visitor.

THE SHIPPING NEWS

Shipping is still so important a business in Greece that a daily shipping newspaper is published in Athens, *Naftemborikí*. It is a finance and business newspaper, but it lists the following seven days' domestic sailings from Piréas and other Greek ports, as well as international arrivals and departures. If is also available at www.naftemporiki. gr, in Greek. Up-to-date information on sailings from the islands is available on www.gtp.gr and www.greek-islands-ferries.gr with timetables, prices and availability for all the ferries from/to Greece and the Greek islands. Departure times on the day and for the next day are announced in the *Herald Tribune* supplement (*Kathimérini*).

Classical Greek light sailing ship

Early shipping It was the readiness of Greek ships, so Homer tells us, that allowed Agamemnon to collect the army that sacked Troy. That should come as no surprise. The early civilizations of the Greek world—the Minoans, Mycenaeans and Phoenicians—were primarily naval powers, their success based on an ability to move people and goods across the water. The power of Antony and Cleopatra collapsed when their fleets were defeated by Octavian just off Lefkáda.

Without maps or navigational aids, without motors or rows of oarsmen, early sailors needed to stay close to land. This was easy in the Greek islands, many of which were close enough for a sailor to see his destination before setting sail.

A long tradition Romans and Byzantines, Venetians and Turks—the foreign powers that controlled the islands—often came to rely on the skill of local sailors. Most famously, Kheir-ed-Din 'Barbarossa', the 16th-century corsair, born on Lésvos, ended his life as grand admiral of the Turkish fleet. After independence, the Greeks were quick to build up their fleet and Ermoúpoli on Sýros, the new nation's main port, was the most important coaling station in the eastern Mediterranean.

Modern fleets Greek shipping magnates such as Onassis and Niarchos made their fortunes building oil tankers and after the glorious days of the 1970s there were more than 4,000 registered Greek ships. Oil crises, fear of a socialist government (elected in 1981) and stiff competition from Asian shipping corporations brought a sharp reversal of fortunes for the Greek tycoons. But for as long as her islands are surrounded by sea, Greece will remain a seafaring nation.

NÁXOS

Náxos, the largest and highest of the Cyclades, is also the most fertile, with an abundance of cultivated valleys and orchards. The island, centre of the Cycladic group, is just as rich in historical remains, having been continuously inhabited for some 5,000 years. The interior is a great place for hikers, with beautiful trails and old paths connecting the villages. Náxos is equally blessed with some amazing, and more often than not deserted beaches. Despite all the beauty, it is relatively unspoiled by tourism, perhaps because of its size and viable farm economy.

▶▶▶ Náxos Town (Chóra)   101C2

The island's harbour has plenty of charm and is surprisingly laid back for the capital of such a large island. Bourgos is the lower part of the old town, with two-storey

USEFUL NUMBERS
Tourist information (near the ferry landing) tel: 22850 24525 (emergency)/25201; www.naxos-island.com
Tourist Police tel: 22850 22100

The long causeway connecting Náxos Town with its symbol, the gateway on the islet of Palátia

houses and gardens full of bougainvillaea and almond trees. The most picturesque part of the old town is higher up around the 13th century Venetian Kástro▶▶. The maze of narrow alleys of the old town hide many grand mansions built by the Venetian aristocracy in the 13th century, and are still home to the island's Catholic community, and now many local artists.

In 1627 the Ottomans founded a Jesuit school where Nikós Kazantzákis studied for a while. It is now the **Archaeological Museum▶▶▶** (tel: 22850 22725. *Open* Tue–Sun 8.30–3. *Admission charge*), housing a large and interesting collection of Cycladic figurines, Mycenaean pottery, Roman glass and a famous mosaic of Europa. Near the entrance of the Kastró is the Della Rocca-Barozzi Museum▶▶ (tel: 22850 22387. *Open* daily 10–3, 7.30–10, in summer. *Admission charge*) with fascinating guided tours through the Venetian mansion and the family's collection of objects going back to the 15th century, illustrating the Venetian history of the town. On the square stands the 13th-century Catholic Cathedral (*Open* guided visits daily in summer 5.30–7pm. *Admission charge*).To the north of the port, an ancient causeway connects the town with the islet of Palátia, where Ariadne was abandoned. The 6th-century BC **Temple of Apollo▶** was never finished and only the monumental gateway, a symbol for Náxos, is still standing.

ARIADNE'S ISLAND
According to mythology Náxos was the island where the Minoan princess Ariadne was abandoned by her husband-to-be Theseus, on their return from Knosós, where he had killed the Minotaur. The god Dionysos found her and married her and, as he was the god of wine and the good life, they lived happily ever after. Some believe that this story illustrated the decline of Crete and the rise of the Cycladic culture, although archaeologists dispute the dates. Whatever the truth, it inspired many artists over the years, including the composer Richard Strauss, who took the story as the theme for his opera *Ariadne auf Naxos.*

Filóti and its pretty Cycladic houses with red-tiled roofs and colourful shutters

VENETIAN HOMES
Pirgi or fortified Venetian manor houses, built between the 14th and 18th centuries, are typical of Náxos. As the island was the seat of Venetian dukes, many of the Italian nobility were given land according to the feudal system. Every aristocratic family had a house in the *kástro* in Náxos Town as well as a *pýrgos* to keep their possessions safe from pirate raids. Some 30 of these buildings have survived and it may be possible to rent a few of them.

▶▶▶ **Apeírados (Apíranthos)**   *101C2*
Arguably the most beautiful village on Náxos, Apeírados, with its un-whitewashed houses and balconies, clearly shows a Cretan influence. The winding streets are paved with marble while the core of the village is built around a Venetian *pýrgos* or fortified tower. On the *plateía* at the entrance is the village church of Koímisis tis Theotókou, with an unusual three-tiered bell tower, and farther inward the small **museum**▶▶ (if closed ask for the guard).

▶▶ **Apóllon**   *101C3*
The pretty fishing village of Apóllon has become too commercialized for its own good, as it tries to make the most of the daily arrivals of tour buses. However, the scenery along the road to it is magnificent. The star attraction lies in a nearby ancient marble quarry, home to a ***kouros***▶ (statue of a naked young man) which would have stood over 10m (33ft) tall. The unfinished 7th-century BC statue was probably a representation of the god Dionysos; at over 30 tonnes, it is the largest but not the finest *kouros* on the island.
  Nearby is delightful **Komiakí**▶▶, the island's highest village, where *kitron* liqueur was first distilled. From here a mountain trail leads to the ridge and on to an amazing marble staircase which goes steeply down to the lush village of **Myrísis**▶.

▶ **Chalkí**   *101C2*
The small town of Chalkí has several fine churches, one of the oldest and the most beautiful being the church of **Panagía Protóthronis**▶▶ (*Open* mornings only. *Admission free*). On the main square is the **Vallindras Distillery**▶▶ (tel: 22850 31220. *Open* daily 10am–11pm, in summer; 10–5 in winter) where they still make the local lemon liqueur, *kitron*, in the traditional way. The church is overlooked by the imposing and remarkably well-preserved **Pýrgos Grazia (Frangopoulos)**, a fortified Venetian villa set amid olive trees and orchards. A pleasant walking path leads up to the village of **Moní**▶ with wonderful views over the

Tragéa valley. This beautiful and fertile area, rich in interesting villages, little churches and historical sites, is one of the best places to explore unspoiled Náxos (see the Drive on page 122). Just before Moní is the 6th-century **church of Panagía Drosianí**►► (*Open* daily 10–7, in summer), which has marvellous frescoes.

►► Filóti   101C2

The pleasant town of Filóti lies on the slopes of **Náxos-Zéfs (Mount Zas)** (1,001m/3,283ft), the highest peak in the Cycladic islands and one of several places contesting the honour of being the birthplace of the god Zeus. A path leads to the summit of the mountain, offering spectacular views (allow two or three hours and be sure to check directions before you go because the path is not always easy to follow). To the south of the peak, another trail leads to a fortified 15th-century monastery, **Moní Fotódotou**, built on a rise and looking more like a castle than a religious centre. The ground-floor church is well preserved.

►► Flerió (Melanés)   101C2

One of several Naxian quarries used in antiquity, the Flerió quarry, covering a considerable area, contains two 6th-century BC *kouroi*, presumably abandoned because of flaws in the stone.

► Sagkrí   101C2

Káto Sagkrí► is a small village with the remains of a Venetian villa standing on a barren hill. The area around **Áno Sagkrí**► is dotted with Byzantine chapels and churches. From the village, a path leads southwards to the **Temple of Demeter**►► (*Open* Tue–Sun 8.30–3. *Admission charge*), built on a hilltop with amazing views over the surrounding countryside. East of the village is the 17th-century **Bazeos Castle**► (tel: 22850 31402. *Open* daily 10–5, 6–9. *Admission free*), now a beautiful cultural centre.

Satellite islands near Náxos

The small islands between Náxos and Amorgós, home to peaceful, traditional communities, are becoming increasingly popular, especially with young Greeks. Facilities tend to be basic, where they exist at all, but there are some good beaches to be found. There are, especially in summer, frequent ferries to Piréas, Náxos, Páros, Sýros and Sérifos, as well as a daily boat to Náxos and a hydrofoil

The cultivated valleys of Náxos often come as a surprise to visitors used to the barren landscapes of the other Cyclades

Cyclades

WALKING COUNTRY
The Náxos countryside has countless good walking trails. For walks other than the one described opposite, look out for the excellent German-published book *Walking Tours on Náxos* by Christian Ucke, available in local bookshops.

CONNECTIONS
Náxos has ferry links with Piréas, Páros, Sýros, Thíra, Íos, Amorgós, Koufonísi, Schoinoússa, Crete, Donoússa, Kárpathos, Rhodes, Sámos, Anáfi, Astypálaia, Irákleio, Ikariá, Kásos, Síkinos, Chálki, Folégandros, Foúrnoi, Kastellórizo, Pátmos, Leípsoi, Léros, Kálymnos, Kós, Nísyros, Tílos, Sými and (in summer) Mýkonos. There is a summer hydrofoil service to Ándros, Mýkonos, Páros, Tínos, Sýros, Íos, Rafína, Amorgós, Thíra and Anáfi.

One of the island's best beaches, Agía Ánna, on a quiet day

from Amorgós and the other Cyclades. **Kéros▶** is the important site of ancient Karos, but the island is now uninhabited. Tiny **Áno Koufonísi▶▶** has only one village and lovely beaches such as Fínikas and Bóri with underwater caves to explore. **Káto Koufonísi** is barely inhabited, apart from its goat herds, but it has some splendid secluded beaches. On **Schoinoússa▶▶** it is only a short walk from Mirsíni, the harbour, to the capital with its medieval fortress. The nearest beach to the capital is Tsigourí. Mesaría is a small resort on the north coast.

Irákleia▶▶▶ is an idyllic islet with a fishing harbour (Ágios Geórgios) and a village up in the hills. The large sandy beach at Livádi is excellent but Fínikas beach is even better, with trees and bushes along the shore and clear turquoise water. **Donoússa▶▶**, even more remote, is the island of silence with one village, about 50 houses and fine sandy beaches nearby. It can also be the island of hunger—fresh food and water are sometimes scarce.

Beaches

The best beaches on the island are south of Náxos Town, easily accessible by bus, daily boat or walking. Ágios Giórgios and Ágios Prokópios are long sandy bays with a few hotels and campsites, while Agía Anna is the island's busiest beach with facilities and a nudist beach nearby. Farther south is the excellent 5km-long (3-mile) beach of Pláka with fine sand, popular with campers, but usually almost empty at its southern end. Even better and easier to reach by road, are Mikrí Vígla and Kastráki, which has brilliant water and pure white sand, an ideal beach for children. The last stop on the bus route is Pyrgakía, not as beautiful but more remote.

The beaches near Moutsoúna—little bays fringed with trees and here and there a little chapel on a rock—are usually completely deserted. Apóllon, on the northern tip of the island, has a good beach, but the *meltemi* winds can make life unpleasant. Avram Beach is magnificent and has a lovely taverna; Amýti and Pachiá Ámnos are more deserted, like most of the beaches in this part of the island.

Walk

Ágioi Apóstoloi and Potamiá

A walk through some of the most fertile land on Náxos, taking in some famous but quite hidden sights, including a *kouros* in someone's orchard and the 9th-century church of Ágios Mámas (8–10km/5–6 miles; allow about 5–6 hours).

Regular buses from Náxos Town pass the village of Ágioi Apóstoloi (see the map on page 122). From the church at Ágioi Apóstoloi continue 200m (220 yards) south, where a path goes along the slope overlooking the Melanés valley. As the path becomes unclear, follow the red markers in a wide arc around the hill, looking out for a white chapel in the south.

At a crossroads, 300m (330 yards) farther on, follow the path to the east, cross the stream and continue to a cemented street, which leads from the main street to the *kouros*. At the end of the street, turn left under the trees and look for a sign to a garden, where a family will show you the well-

Lovely old churches like the Ágioi Apóstoloi are scattered all over the peaceful Tragéa region

preserved, 6th-century BC ***kouros***▶. There is another one nearby, both probably left in the quarry because they broke before they were finished.

Return to the cement road where a red-marked path leads uphill, with views of **Náxos-Zéfs (Mount Zas)** and a Venetian fortress. Follow the red markings to the cemetery and **church of Ágios Ioánnis** in Potamiá, then continue to Áno Potamiá, where there is a pleasant taverna, Pigis. Take Odós Ágios Ioánnis Theológou and then Odós Protopapadáki. At the end of the village, turn eastward and head downhill, to the river. Across the river, a paved path leads along the slope to Káto Potamiá.

In the village, by the church of Panagía, Odós Nikodimu descends back to the river. Cross the river and follow the green arrows, crossing another river towards the **church of Ágios Mámas**▶, set among orange trees. Pause to look at the frescoes here before continuing up above the church to a farm. Beyond the farm, behind a wall, there is a clearly marked path: follow it westwards to the asphalt road, along which pass buses for Náxos Town.

Drive

The Tragéa valley

Roads on Náxos are good and remote places can be reached by car (about 60km/37 miles; allow 5–6 hours).

Leave Náxos Town by the Apóllon road. After 1km (0.6 mile) turn right and later left to Galanádo. Farther on, to the left, is the church of **Ágios Mámas►** (see page 121). A while later, to the right, are Káto and Áno Sagkrí (see page 119), beyond which the road descends into the Tragéa valley and to Chalkí (see page 118).

Follow the sign to Filóti (right), turning left after another 300m (330 yards) for Kalóxylos, known for its pretty **church of Agía Triáda►**. Return to the main road and continue to Filóti (see page 119). Pass the chapel and the sign on the right to **Spiliá Za (Cave Zas)►**, reputedly the cave where Zeus was born.

After 6km (4 miles) Apeírados offers the possibility of lunch with a view (see page 118). Return to Filóti and beyond it, by a war memorial, turn right to Moní. Before Moní, on the right, is the **church of Panagía Drosianí►►** (see page 119). Go through Moní to Kinídaros, where there are spectacular marble quarries and good views out to sea. At Ágios Thalélaios follow the sign to the right and at the junction make another right turn for Náxos Town.

PÁROS

Páros provided the marble for some of the most beautiful classical statues, including the Venus de Mílo and the Winged Victory of Samothráki. It is also one of the most attractive Cycladic islands; towns like Páros, Náousa and Léfkes have managed to preserve their character despite attracting increasing numbers of tourists.

▶▶▶ Páros Town (Parikiá)   100B2

Beyond the busy commercial waterfront lies the well-preserved Cycladic old town. The narrow streets, lined with bars and shops, are completely overrun by visitors in summer but remain pretty and quiet for the rest of the year. Just beyond the centre is the interesting Byzantine cathedral of **Panagía Ekatondapilianí▶▶▶** (*Open* daily 7am–10pm, in summer. *Admission free*). Originally built in the 6th century, the church, whose name means 'Our Lady of the Hundred Doors', was rebuilt in the 10th century using fine Parian marble. Behind it is the small **Archaeological Museum▶▶** (*Open* Tue–Sun 9–3. *Admission charge*). Its exhibits include a good collection of sculpture and a fragment of the Parian Chronicle, which lists important political and social events in Greek history from the 16th to the 3rd centuries BC. It is through this document that we know the year of Homer's birth. South of the windmill are the remains of the 13th-century Venetian **kastro▶▶**. Marble fragments from ancient temples were used to build its fortified walls. On top of the *kástro* are the two superb churches of Ágios Konstandínos and Agía Eléni.

About an hour's walk from the town is the **monastery of Ágioi Anárgyroi▶**, a popular picnic spot for islanders. A two-hour walk will bring you to **Petaloúdes▶▶**, the 'Valley of the Butterflies' (*Open* Jun–Sep, Mon–Sat 9–8. *Admission charge*). As on Rhodes (see page 171), millions of Jersey tiger moths descend every summer on this walled oasis in the middle of a barren landscape. The route to Petaloúdes passes the 18th-century **convent of Christoú Dásos▶** (*Closed* noon–6pm, in summer). Men are not permitted inside, even though the convent contains the grave of the island's second patron saint, Ágios Arsénios.

Panagiá Ekatondapilianí

USEFUL NUMBER
Tourist information (near the windmill on the harbour, open daily 9.30–1) tel: 22840 22861; www.parosweb.gr
Tourist police tel: 22840 21673

OUR LADY OF THE HUNDRED DOORS
The cathedral was built in the 6th century by Isidore of Miletus and his pupil Ignatius. When it was finished it was of such beauty that, according to one story, the two architects started to fight on the roof. Both fell to their deaths. Another legend has it that there are only 99 doors and that the hundredth one referred to in the name will be found only when the Turks return Constantinople to the Christians.

Náousa harbour has some of the best and most atmospheric ouzeris *on the island*

DIVING OFF GOLDEN BEACH
The Aegean Diving School is no ordinary diving school; the founder is Peter Nicolaides, a professional diver and a biologist-oceanographer who worked on the *Calypso* with Jacques-Yves Cousteau, and who discovered and excavated several shipwrecks, including an early bronze period one, the earliest found to date. He offers diving trips for anybody interested in the history, archaeology and marine environment of the Aegean Sea, and a chance to participate in ongoing scientific experiments (tel: 22840 43347/69322 89649; www.aegeandiving.gr).

▶▶ **Antíparos** *100B2*

The island of Antíparos was once connected to Páros by a natural causeway, but visitors now have to take one of the many boats making day trips to the island to visit its beaches or famous cave. Many former devotees of relaxed Páros now stay on Antíparos which, despite the summer day trippers, is still a quiet backwater. Most of the 500 islanders live in the pleasant Cycladic village on the northern side of the island beneath a small Venetian **kástro**▶. There are several good beaches: Psaralidáki is a nudist beach just outside the village, but the small coves in Ágios Giórgios are far more pleasant and secluded. **Spílaio Stalaktitón**▶▶ (*Open* daily 10–3.30. *Admission charge*), the island's well-known cave, was known for its stalactites more than 2,000 years ago and has been attracting people to Antíparos ever since. (Two buses daily from the port.) There is electric lighting now and cement steps instead of ropes, but the 70m-deep (230ft) cave still retains its grandeur and some of its mystery.

▶▶▶ **Léfkes** *101C2*

Léfkes, the medieval capital where the population hid from raiding pirates, is still one of the most untouched towns on Páros. The lovely houses are set against the hill and the narrow marbled and cobblestoned streets are immaculately kept. There are a few traditional *kafeneía* and life here still seems very peaceful indeed. In nearby **Maráthi** are the ancient underground marble quarries from where marble was exported all over Europe: it was last used for Napoleon's tomb. **Prodrómos**, a charming farming village, formerly walled and still entered through a gateway, is named after the 17th-century **church of Ágios Ioánnis Prodrómos**▶. An equally attractive village, inland but not far from the resort of Píso Livádi, is **Márpissa**, its narrow alleys bordered by balconies full of flowers. Above stands a Venetian castle now occupied by the **monastery of Ágios Andónios**.

▶ **Náousa** *101C2*

Náousa may have succumbed to mass tourism in recent years, but its tiny, colourful fishing harbour is still a wonderfully picturesque place, with a choice of bars and tavernas for an early evening *oúzo* and a helping of freshly caught seafood *mezédes*. Near the harbour is a mostly

PARIAN MARBLE
Parian marble, used in so many classical statues, was particularly prized for its grainy, translucent quality. It is the closest of Greek marbles to the quality of Carrara marble. In some Athenian temples it was used for roof tiles in order to let in the light. It is unusual for quarries to be underground, but here the marble was hacked out of the mountain and brought up to the light by slaves. In the 19th century the French reopened the quarries to get marble for Napoleon's tomb, but today they are abandoned: the remaining marble is of poorer quality and the vein too deep to be economically viable.

125

submerged Venetian castle. Náousa's other 'sight' is the **Byzantine Museum**▶ (*Open* Tue, Thu, Sat–Sun 9–1.30, 7–9. *Admission free*) in the church of Ágios Nikólaos Mostratos, which has a good collection of icons.

Beaches
The best beaches near Páros Town are towards the south. Paraspóros is known for the remains of an Asklepion (therapy centre), while the better, sandy Agía Iríni has a taverna. Farther south, Poúnda, with all facilities, is very popular, while the large sandy cove and fishing harbour of Alykí is also fast becoming a major resort. From Alykí a dirt track leading to Dryós goes along several secluded and pleasant sandy coves, although Dryós is just a small pebble-stone beach overlooked by a modern tourist village. The beaches north of here are exposed to the strong *meltemi* winds, sometimes making them unpopular with sandcastle builders but a first choice for windsurfers. Chrysí Aktí, or Golden Beach, lives up to its name but is becoming more developed, while the once quiet Píso Livádi has become a full-blown resort. The island's best beaches, however, are on the north coast near Náousa. Kolimbítres, to the west, has beautiful sand, clear azure water and a lunar landscape with strange rock formations. Just a little farther along is the mainly nudist beach of Monastíri. To the north are found the clearest waters and good windsurfing. Langéri Beach is popular, but the trendiest beach is definitely Sánta Mária.

CONNECTIONS
Páros has ferry links with Antíparos, Piréas, Náxos, Thíra, Sýros, Tinos, Thessaloníki, Mýkonos, Sífnos, Sérifos, Amorgós, Crete, Rhodes, Ikaría, Sámos, Síkinos, Kós, Anáfi, Kárpathos, Koufonísi, Schoinoússa, Chálki, Donoússa, Folégandros, Fournoi, Irákleia, Kásos, Kastellórizo, Astypálaia, Skíathos, Pátmos, Leipsoi, Léros, Kálymnos, Nísyros, Tílos and Sými. There are hydrofoil and catamaran services to Mýkonos, Tínos, Ándros, Náxos, Rafína, Thíra, Íos, Sýros, Irákleia, Schoinoússa, Koufonísi and Anáfi.

There is still much of Páros that has escaped the effects of mass tourism

The Greeks loved both continuity and variety in art as elsewhere, so while Greek artists absorbed new ideas and influences, they also preserved all that was best in their tradition. The result is an extraordinary legacy that continues to fascinate and inspire.

Above: a fine plate made in Athens c520–510BC Below: a beautiful depiction of a lyre-player on a black-figure vase

126

Regional beginnings The first art in Greece was localized. In the 3rd millennium BC, the appearance in the Cyclades of idols of soft marble—elegant figures with minimal detail—coincided with the development of the trade in metal. As the power of the Cyclades declined, so their artistic style gave way to that of the Minoans from Crete, who took control of the Aegean around 1600BC. Frescoes, particularly those from Thíra, are among the most powerful Minoan creations, their everyday subjects, such as people, animals and leaves, animated and joyful. Great treasures have been found from the Mycenaeans who succeeded the Minoans, including jewellery, weapons, vases, pots and copper tripods, all of which suggest a shift in the attitude of their creators: where the Minoans were playful and celebratory, life for the Mycenaeans was clearly a struggle against nature.

Ceramic art The end of Mycenaean civilization brought another shift: Archaic art concentrated on terracotta vases and *kraters* (drinking vessels), with a new geometric style (900–700BC) in which images on stone and terracotta were contained within geometric patterns. In the 7th century BC, exotic creatures and plants from Egypt and the Near East appeared on vase decoration. Around this time, when the finest ceramics came from Corinth and mythological stories were the usual source for decoration, the technique of putting black figures against orange backgrounds was perfected. Late in the 6th century BC the tradition was turned on its head: the backgrounds became black and the figures red. A few decades later, new techniques allowed artists to paint against a white background.

WORLD WONDER
One of the Seven Wonders of the Ancient World, Phidias's statue of Zeus for the temple at Olympia is believed to have been about 12m (40ft) high. Sitting on a throne of ebony, ivory, gold and precious stones, it suffered from the Olympian climate. The ivory cracked in the 2nd century BC; the statue was struck by lightning during Julius Caesar's rule and reportedly ended up in Constantinople, where it was destroyed by fire in AD475.

Kouros in Vathí Museum, Sámos

Sculpture When the Greeks started building big temples in the 7th century BC, the need for statues in their sanctuaries gave a boost to large-scale marble sculpture. In the 6th century BC, two Samian artists, Rhoikos and Theodorus, learned to make hollow bronze statues. Whether stone, wood or metal, most art remained religious in function until the 4th century.

The finest sculptures from the Archaic period were *kouroi*, carvings of naked youths which show, in their increasing attention to detail, a growing understanding of human anatomy.

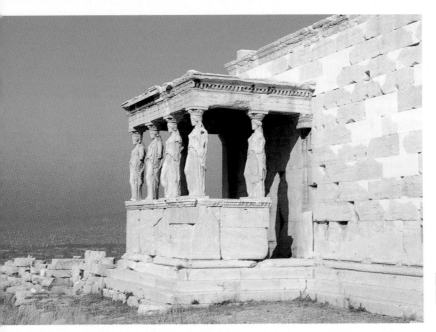

Kouroi were placed in sanctuaries to delight the gods or as funerary offerings. A rare series of female figures, *korai*, were dedicated to Athena at her temple on the Acropolis. Notable *kouroi* can be seen in the National Archaeological Museum in Athens, in the museum of Vathí on Sámos and in the quarry near Apóllon on Náxos.

Classical masters Some of the finest sculptures ever executed belong to the Classical period, whose artists created works that perfectly expressed both the grandeur and spirituality of the gods and, in breathtaking detail, the reality of the human form. Among the masters were Polykleitos and Phidias, the latter the creator of the chryselephantine statues of Olympian Zeus (one of the Wonders of the Ancient World) and of Athena in the Parthenón—both now lost—as well as of the Parthenón frieze. In the 4th century BC, artists such as Praxiteles concentrated increasingly on the expression of the moods and character of humans, making their sculpture less stylized and more lifelike.

Hellenism After Alexander the Great's conquest of the known world, the Greek market became increasingly cosmopolitan and Greek artists found themselves expected to satisfy demands for a variety of forms and styles, trends and influences and also found a new and very mixed market for their work. The tastes of the period were clearly different, more theatrical, with artists looking to thrill or charm the spectator. The 2nd-century BC Horse and Jockey of Artemision (National Archaeological Museum, Athens) exactly expresses the mood of the period in its dramatic sense of movement and in its perfectly executed forms of horse and boy rider (who is certainly not a native Greek).

The Parthenón has some of the finest art of Classical times

AGES OF GREEK SCULPTURE
Cycladic; Minoan; Mycenaean; Archaic; Classical; Hellenistic; Roman-Greek

NO SCUBA HERE
The Aegean looks so inviting in summer that it would seem to be a perfect place for scuba-diving. Too perfect, in fact, as the number of sculptures and other treasures recovered from the Aegean and now on display in Greek museums testifies. To stop people helping themselves to antiquities, the Greek government banned the use of scuba equipment in Greek waters (there are a few exceptions; see panel page 124). Among the masterpieces in the National Archaeological Museum in Athens that were recovered from the sea are the Boy of Marathon, the Poseidon of Artemision and the Youth from Antikýthira.

SÉRIFOS

Nothing ever seems to happen on Sérifos, which is what attracts more Athenians and foreigners every summer. Most islanders, meanwhile, remain hard at work on their farms and seemingly want little to do with visitors.

Sífnos is one of the best-kept secrets in the Cyclades

USEFUL NUMBERS
Tourist information (Sífnos harbour) tel: 22840 31977; www.sifnos.gr, which also provides a good brochure on walks on the island
Tourist information in Apollonía (Sífnos) tel: 22840 31333)

A GOOD WALK ON SÉRIFOS
A path leads from Sérifos Town to Kállitsos (allow at least an hour), from where it is another 3km (2 miles) to the striking monastery of Taxiarchón. This beautiful place is inhabited by a lone, happy monk, Makarios. An asphalt road leads back to the town, via the lovely villages of Galaní and Panagía, where you will find a 10th-century church.

▶▶▶ **Sérifos Town (Chóra)**   *100A2*
The island's capital, clinging to its rock, looks particularly spectacular when seen from the harbour. At the top of the ruinous **kástro**▶, a gleaming white church sticks to it like a melted ice-cream.

▶ **Livádi**   *100A2*
The harbour of Livádi, where most visitors stay, is set in an oasis of fields and orchards. An old long stairway, hand-hewn into the rock, goes up to Sérifos Town.

Beaches
Psilí Ámmos has a superb sandy beach with two popular tavernas. Nearer to Livádi is the beach of Livadáki, with fine sand, and the smaller (partly nudist) Karávi beach. West of Livádi is the old mining village of Koutalás, a small sandy beach at Ganema and, beyond, the peaceful beach of Megálo Livádi.

SÍFNOS

Sífnos, a favourite with young Greeks wanting to avoid the crowds on the other Cyclades, is one of the prettiest islands. Delightful walks meander through a landscape dotted with windmills, Venetian dovecotes and hundreds of chapels. Book ahead in summer, as rooms go quickly.

▶▶▶ **Apollonía**   *100B2*
Apollonía is an idyllic village, with lovely squares, belfries and flowers everywhere. On the main square is the **Folk Museum**▶ (tel: 22840 33730. *Open* Tue–Sun 10–2, 7.30–10.30, in summer). The church of **Panagía Ouranoforía**▶ was built over (and incorporates fragments of) the 7th-century BC Temple of Apollo. Nearby **Artemón**▶▶ has elegant mansions and fine churches. The

17th-century **church of Ágios Geórgios**► has a collection of icons while the multi-domed **church of Kochí**►► was built over a temple of Artemis. The harbour of Kamáres, down below, is where most of the visitor facilities are.

►► Kástro 100B2

Kástro, the ancient and medieval capital, has maintained its character and its picturesque streets with old houses and 17th-century churches. Higher up in the village is a small **archaeological museum**► (*Open* Tue–Sun 9–3. *Admission free*).

►► Vathý 100B2

Although remote, Vathý is an excellent base for beaches and walks to the nearby monasteries of Firágia, Ágios Andréas, Chrysopigí and Panayía Vounoú. There is even a tiny monastery of the Archangel Gabriel on the quay.

Beaches

Platýs Gialós is a long stretch of fine sand, clear calm water and sunbathers. Fáros is quieter with excellent beaches nearby, including naturist Glifó and Chrysopigí where the monastery rents out cells.

SÍKINOS

Síkinos is a sleepy island with only one town, from where you can walk (or take a mule) to most beaches.

►► Síkinos Town (Kástro-Chóra) 100A1

Boats go to the harbour of Aloprónoia. From there an erratic bus service goes up to Síkinos Town, which consists of the simple village (Chóra) and the medieval *kástro*, its 18th-century houses still packed within the fortified walls. The town is overlooked by the ruins of the **Monastery of Zoödóchou Pigís**. An hour's walk away at **Episkopí**, an ancient temple or Roman tomb was incorporated in a 7th-century church known as the **Iroön**►►. **Palaiokástro**► is the site of an ancient fortress.

Beaches

Ágios Pandelímonas is easily the nicest and certainly the most sheltered beach, an hour's walk from the harbour. Towards the north are the beaches of Ágios Nikólaos and Ágios Geórgios.

CONNECTIONS
From Sérifos and Sífnos ferries operate to Piréas, Páros, Kýthnos, Kímolos, Sýros, Mílos, Folégandros, Síkinos, Íos, Thíra, Mýkonos, Sýros and Crete. There are high-speed links with Piréas, Sífnos, Kýthnos and Mílos.
Ferries from Síkinos serve Piréas, Folégandros, Íos, Páros, Thíra, Sérifos, Sífnos, Náxos, Kímolos, Sýros, Kýthnos and Mílos.

THE SIFNOS CUISINE
Sífnos is known for producing the best olive oil and the best chefs in Greece. The chefs are in such demand that most of them leave the island, but happily there is still some good food to be had. The island's most famous dish is *revithada*, a simple stew made with chick peas, olive oil and bay leaves, baked in the oven. Sífnos also produces some unique cheeses including fresh *xinomizithra*, similar to a ricotta, and *gilomeno*, a hard, mature goat's cheese with a strong taste.

FAMOUS POTTERY
As if good cooking were not enough, Sífnos is also famous throughout Greece for its ceramics. There are still several workshops making simple, inexpensive grey and red clay pottery for daily use, although some do more elaborate work with folk motifs.

Almost every single corner of Sífnos is pleasing to the eye

Below the Catholic Cathedral of Ágios Giórgos is the intricate and fascinating medieval quarter of Áno Sýros

SÝROS

Sýros, the administrative capital of the Cyclades, sees relatively few foreign tourists apart from ferry travellers in the process of changing boats in its busy port. Without a tourist economy, the island has remained very Greek, supporting itself from its traditional businesses of shipping, agriculture and the production of *loukoúmia* (Turkish delight). Sýros is as good a place as any in the Cyclades for visitors who want to experience the flavour of workaday Greek life. Buses and bicycle-rental outlets make this an easy island to explore. Distances are manageable, with nowhere very far from the sea.

►►► Ermoúpoli and Áno Sýros   *100B3*

Either by day in the dazzling sunlight or at night when wonderfully illuminated, the twin cities of Ermoúpoli and Áno Sýros, built on neighbouring hills, entrance the visitor upon entering the harbour. Ermoúpoli, 'City of Hermes', founded by refugees in 1824, quickly became the most important harbour in Greece after the War of Independence. These refugees were Eastern Orthodox while most of the islanders were Roman Catholic, but the two communities lived, and continue to live, side by side, each on its own hill: to the left, as you sail in, Catholic Áno Sýros and to the right, Orthodox Vrondádo.

Ferries and hydrofoils dock at the busy waterfront of Ermoúpoli, where the large neoclassical mansions are slowly crumbling. Just inland is the grand Plateía Miaoúli, paved with marble, where islanders drink their coffee or early evening *oúzo* on elegant terraces under palm trees. This is a good place to sit and watch the nightly *volta*, where locals stroll up and down, often dressed up, meeting friends and enjoying the cool of the evening. The square is dominated by the imposing, neoclassical **Town Hall**. To its left is the **Archaeological Museum►►** (tel: 22810 88487. *Open* Tue–Sun 8.30–3. *Admission free*),with a small collection of early Cycladic, Hellenistic and Roman sculpture. Beyond the museum is the **Apollon Theatre►**, a 19th-century scaled-down copy of the famous La Scala in Milan.

USEFUL NUMBERS

Sýros does not have an official tourist office, but the travel agents in the port are quite helpful. Gaviotis Tours tel: 22810 86244
Teamwork (tel: 22810 83400;
www.teamwork.gr
Port Authority tel: 22810 88888

SYRIAN DELIGHTS

On the quayside and even on the ferries, various hawkers sell *loukoúmia* (Turkish delight) and delicious *chalvadópita* (a sugary confection), for which the island is famous. *Loukoúmia* comes in different flavours: mastic, almond, rosewater and mint.

The next square up with the world's first **Monument to an Unknown Warrior**, is the heart of Vaporía, where wealthy shipowners built mansions in a French style. Uphill from the Platea Miaoúli, stairs climb to the Orthodox quarter of **Vrondádo▶▶**, topped by the church of **Anástasi▶▶**. Just outside the centre is the fascinating **Industrial Museum of Ermoúpoli** (Odós Papandréos, tel: 22810 84764. *Open* Wed–Mon 10–2, Thu–Sun 6–9 in summer, also 10–2, 6–9 Wed, Sat–Sun in winter. *Admission charge*) in an old factory, which reveals all about the island's shipbuilding history.

Áno Sýros▶▶▶, on the taller hill, was Sýros's medieval capital, founded by the Venetians. There are several Catholic churches below the **Cathedral of Ágios Giórgios▶**, one of the oldest Catholic churches on Sýros, founded in the early 13th century and rebuilt in the 1830s. Nearby is the 16th-century **monastery of the Capuchins▶▶** with magnificent views over Ermoúpoli and the island. Áno Sýros can be reached by a steep stairway from Ermoúpoli or by bus. On a small square nearby stands the statue of *rébétiko* singer Markos Vamvarakis, who was born in this neighbourhood. A little museum is dedicated to his memory (*Open* daily 10.30–1, 7–10, in summer).

▶ Poseidonía
100B3

Poseidonía, also known under its Venetian name Dellagrazia, is the favourite summer resort of the Syrians. It still has some flamboyant neoclassical villas surrounded by beautiful gardens, now often up for rent. The exclusive Possidonia Club established itself here in 1913. The entire southern part of the island is taken up by vineyards and by greenhouses producing vegetables for export to Athens.

Beaches

Few beaches on the more accessible Greek Islands have escaped development and Sýros is no exception. However, it has escaped the worst excesses of the tourist boom and there are still pleasant bays and coves to be found.

Kiní is a charming resort with summer villas and a good beach. For more isolation head farther north to the lovely sandy beaches of Delfíni, Varvaroússa and Grámmata, surrounded by rocks. South of Kiní is the bay of Galissás. Near-by is the more solitary nudist beach of Arméos. Within walking distance of Poseidonía are some good sandy beaches; Agatopés, empty Komitó and lovely Ambéla. Mégas Gialós has a long beach with pebbles.

CONNECTIONS
Sýros has ferry links with Piréas, Tínos, Mýkonos, Náxos, Páros, Íos, Amorgós, Astypálaia, Thíra, Koufonísi, Rhodes, Schoinoússa, Sámos, Chálki, Crete, Donoússa, Irákleia, Kárpathos, Kásos, Kéa, Kímolos, Kós, Kýthnos, Mílos, Rafina, Sérifos, Sífnos, Ándros, Folégandros, Ikaría, Kastellórizo, Síkinos, Patmos, Leípsoi, Léros, Nísyros, Tílos and Sými. High-speed services and catamarans operate in summer to Piréas, Rafina, Páros, Mýkonos, Tínos, Náxos, Íos, Thíra, Amorgós and some of the other Cyclades.

131

The grand buildings in Ermoúpoli are a reminder of its days as an important port

Wine has been produced in Greece for over 4,000 years—a considerable tradition—and yet most visitors expect to find only retsina and Demestica. Reasons for this lie in recent history, but a remedy has already been applied: winemaking has been transformed and Greek wines are now worthy of their tradition.

GOOD QUALITY WINES FROM THE ISLANDS

Several islands produce superior quality wines. In the Ionian Islands, Cephalonia produces a dry white and a sweet red wine with the robola grape. In the Aegean, Lemnos has both sweet (Muscat) and dry white wine, while Samos only produces a dry white. Paros produces a dry red from Mandelaria and Monemvasia grapes, and Thíra produces a dry white. On Rhodos the vineyards are cultivated on northern slopes of the Mount Attaviros and produce dry wines, both red and white. With its mild winters and hot summers, Crete produces a large variety of quality wines.

THE RETSINA TASTE

Retsina owes its distinctive flavour to the addition of resin. The amount of resin that can now be added to white wine is governed by law. Until recently it was hard to imagine a meal in a traditional Greek taverna without the iconic blue or orange aluminium carafe of retsina, but now retsina is drunk more by visitors than Greeks! In southern Greece it is losing market share to cheap white and red wines, and in the north there is the less resinated Malamatina retsina that has little in common with the original. Upmarket Greek wine producers are struggling to promote quality Greek wines, as most people still think of cheap retsina when they think about Greek wine.

From Homer to home-leavers Anyone who has read Homer's epics will know how central winemaking was to ancient Greek culture. A meal was not complete without wine, with drops being poured as a libation to the gods. At Vathípetro on Crete a wine press has been found dating back to the 16th century BC, while the Archaeological Museum of Thásos holds several 4th-century BC artefacts from winemakers, including *appellation* stamps and a tablet laying out winemaking laws. Winemaking was a profitable business under the Byzantines, but the Turks did not encourage it and only the Greek Orthodox Church kept the traditions alive. In the 1950s the movement away from countryside and vineyards, to cities or overseas, led to a drop in the quality of wine.

New Greek wines The situation improved in the late 1960s, and in 1971 *appellation* laws were brought into force. Ten years later, when Greece joined the EU, subsidies helped to modernize wineries. At the same time, Australian and American winemakers were forcing French growers to change their style; Greek winemakers have now brought in a number of overseas oenologists to help them blend their wines.

Choosing Greek wine The best wines are usually from small producers. Recommended for general drinking are the Muscat from the Samos Cooperative (tel: 22410 29111); the dry white Boutari (www.boutari.gr) from Irákleio, which goes perfectly with herbs and seafood; the Sigalas from Thíra, an organic white and red from vineyard which is reputedly one of the oldest in Europe (tel: 22860 71644; www.sigalas-wine.gr); and Gentilini from Kefallonía (www.gentilini.gr). For sparkling white try the Emery from Rhodes (tel: 210 6844336; www.emery.gr).

THÍRA (SANTORÍNI)

Thíra, also known as Devil's Island, offers one of the most appealing natural spectacles in the entire Mediterranean. Visitors arriving by boat sail into the flooded crater (caldera) of its volcano to find two dazzling white Cycladic towns dramatically perched high on the rim. The island is unique, but as most visitors list it as one of their favourites, it has also become heavily developed and in season gets very crowded.

►►► Thíra (Fíra)   101C1

Painstakingly rebuilt after the serious 1956 earthquake, the island's capital, in its spectacular setting, never fails to impress. However, the toll that tourism has taken on the town is easily felt. Many terraces with views over the caldera have been turned into bars or *kafeneía*, and a drink to watch the sunset over the caldera is far from cheap. Most of the narrow streets are taken over by expensive jewellery shops, trendy boutiques and bars playing Euro-pop. A young crowd is being attracted to Thíra in increasing numbers and nightlife is getting livelier. Some of the old atmosphere can be detected in the quieter area past the **Archaeological Museum►** (*Open* Tue–Sun 8.30–3. *Admission charge*), which has stunning and free views of the amazing caldera. The museum has a good collection of Cycladic and Hellenistic sculpture, and some artefacts from Akrotíri. More interesting is the new **Prehistoric Museum►►** (opposite the bus station, tel: 22860 23217. *Open* Tue–Sun 8.30–7.30. *Admission charge*), with finds from the Akrotíri excavations, including some of the beautiful frescoes which have been returned from the Athens Museum. Nearby is the **Megaron Gyzi Museum►►** (*Open* Mon–Sat 10.30–1 and 5–8, Sun 10.30–4.30. *Admission charge*), in a lovely 17th-century mansion, with old maps, costumes and photographs of a Thíra that is no more.

Most ferries dock at Athiniós, south of Thíra, while excursion boats and cruise ships usually call at Skála Thirás from where some 600 steps or a cable car climb steeply up to the sparkling white capital.

Continued on pages 136–137.

If you are looking for peace and quiet on Thíra, head straight for Oía, on the northern tip of the island

133

USEFUL NUMBER
Port Authority
tel: 22860 22239;
www.santorini.net

EARLY EVENING STROLL
To escape the sunset madness of Thíra's bars, head north along the footpath on the island's spine to Imerovígli, the old Catholic quarter. The views over Thíra and the volcano are stunning and some of the houses have been elegantly restored. The last sunlight softens up this hard landscape and adds to its appeal and its sense of mystery. Take a flashlight for returning after dark, since the edge of the cliff is surprisingly nearby and it's a very long way down to the bottom.

Drive

Thíra in a day

Thíra is a small island with good roads. The countryside, with its vineyards and views over the caldera, offers a welcome change from the over-commercialized capital (about 50km/31 miles; allow 6–8 hours).

Drive out of Thíra following signs for the airport and after 5km (3 miles) follow signs to Akrotíri and go through **Megalochóri**▶▶. Beyond it, on the right, is a signpost for the **Boutari Winery** (see panel on page 137). About 2km (1.2 miles) on, follow the sign to the right for Akrotíri. From this part of the road the views over the **caldera** and Thíra island are superb. Continue through the village of Akrotíri, then follow signs to the archaeological site of **ancient**

Akrotíri▶▶▶ (see page 136). Just down the road from the site is a small beach of red, white and black pebbles, pleasant for a swim.

Return through Megalochóri, then follow the road to the right to the beautiful village of **Pýrgos**▶▶ (see page 137). From the main square in Pýrgos you can make a detour to the **monastery of Profítis Ilías**▶ (see page 137), the road winding up the hill with wonderful views. Return to Pýrgos and follow signs for Episkopí, continuing through Episkopí and Kamári, then following signs to **Archaía Thíra** (see page 136).

Return to Thíra by the same route. Drive through the main street in Thíra, take a left at **Imerovígli**▶▶ to enjoy the views and return to the main road. The road farther north is the best part of the drive, with the caldera on one side and a fertile valley down below on the other side.

Be sure to get to **Oía** (see pages 136–137) before sunset and have a well-deserved drink on one of the cliffside terraces before returning by the same route to Thíra.

'Larger than Libya and Asia put together...the island of Atlantis...was swallowed up by the sea and disappeared.' So wrote the Greek philosopher Plato (c428–347BC), lamenting the loss of an island and the passing of a golden age. Since then, there has been much speculation as to where this magical place might have been.

The legend of Atlantis Plato describes Atlantis as a rich, sophisticated place that had been given to Poseidon, god of the sea, at the sharing out of the Earth. At the centre of the city of Atlantis there was a palace and a temple dedicated to Poseidon, decorated with silver and surrounded by a golden wall. Atlantis, initially a utopia, became corrupt and aggressive and finally disappeared into the sea, reclaimed by Poseidon.

The search for Atlantis Ever since Plato's description of the place, scholars and adventurers have speculated on the whereabouts of this lost realm. When Columbus reached the Americas, some people believed that he had found Atlantis. Since then, Atlantis has been variously identified with Sweden, Brazil, a submerged landmass near the Bahamas and the Atlantic Ocean off Africa.

Thíra's claim Frescoes, pots and other artefacts have proved the connection between Thíra and Minoan Crete and obvious parallels can be drawn between the Minoans and the inhabitants of Atlantis. Both were wealthy and sophisticated and both worshipped the bull, sacred to Poseidon. According to Plato's account of the matter, the Egyptian priests told Solon (c640–c559BC), the Athenian poet and ruler, that Atlantis was destroyed 9,000 years before their time. Some scholars believe that they meant 900 years; if so, the destruction of Atlantis would have occurred around 1450–1550BC, the time of the disastrous volcanic eruption on Thíra. Crete's Minoan civilization collapsed at around the same time. So could Thíra, or even Crete, be Atlantis?

Plato is explicit that Atlantis lay *beyond* the Pillars of Hercules, the Straits of Gibraltar, and therefore out in the Atlantic Ocean. This seems to favour the New World theories of Atlantis's whereabouts, but (fortunately, perhaps) the mystery seems likely to remain unsolved.

PLATO'S SOURCE
Plato, the first author to write about the legend, claimed that the story of Atlantis was true and had been told to Solon by priests of Saïs, in Egypt. Since Plato published his account, more than 2,000 books have been written on the subject, most accepting his statements as true.

135

The legend of Atlantis continues to fascinate the world: a clip from the film The Warlords of Atlantis

THE GARDENS OF THE HESPERIDES
The Gardens of the Hesperides were, according to Greek mythology, the home of the Hesperides, a group of nymphs. The gardens were to be found on an island in the ocean far to the west and on them grew a tree which belonged to the goddess Hera and bore golden apples. The nymphs, aided by a dragon called Ladon, were responsible for the tree. The eleventh labour of Hercules was to kill the dragon and take the apples, which he did. Was this magic isle part of Atlantis, perhaps?

Cyclades

Continued from page 133.

▶▶▶ Akrotíri
101C1

Currently undergoing repairs following roof collapse
Regular buses from Thíra
Professor Spyridon Marinatos started excavating this site in 1967, hoping to find that the eruption of Thíra's volcano precipitated the downfall of Minoan civilization on Crete. Instead he discovered a large and well-preserved Minoan city, destroyed by a massive volcanic eruption in 1625BC. The area of 1 hectare (2.5 acres) has now been roofed and is one of the most exciting archaeological sites in the Cyclades. The superb frescoes from the two- and three-storey houses are in the National Archaeological Museum in Athens and much of the Cretan pottery is in Thíra's museum. Walking around Akrotíri's streets, lined with *píthoi* (huge storage pots), it is easy to visualize what life in this town must have been like. Peering through windows into houses, one almost expects to find women preparing dinner for the family.

136

Walking the streets of Minoan Akrotíri

THE ATTRACTION OF THIRA
'I found it a fantastic spot. Picturesque, or romantic, is too mild a term; the cliff-scenery and the colours of the sea and land made one catch one's breath. Under a bleak northern sky it would be a horrific kind of place; drenched in the glittering light of May it was fabulously beautiful... Santorin is surely a vision which can disappoint nobody.'
Norman Douglas, *Looking Back* (1933)

▶▶ Archaía Thíra (Ancient Thíra)
101C1

Open: Tue–Sun 8.30–2.30. Admission charge
Regular buses from Thíra to Périssa, then a steep walk, expensive taxi or a donkey ride up to the site
Arkhéa Thíra was the island's ancient capital, inhabited from the 9th century BC onwards. Most of the ruins visible today are Ptolemaic, with temples dedicated to Egyptian gods and to Dionysos and Apollo. The impressive remains of the *agora* and the theatre command dazzling views of the sea straight below. Some houses and temples have kept their mosaics.

▶▶▶ Oía (Ía)
101C1

Although it is well known as the most beautiful place on the island, Oía has preserved most of its character and its peacefulness. Its white houses, built virtually on top of each other, appear to hang on to the cliff; some of them are even built into it. Although there are many rooms and cave dwellings for rent, the place rarely feels overrun, except sometimes towards the end of the day when busloads from Thíra and Kamári come to watch the sunset. On the little headland is a ruined fort and below it the remains of a basilica. In the other direction, a rough footpath towards Imerovígli offers some of the island's most memorable views (especially on the way back towards Oía). About 200 steps lead down from Oía to the tiny fishing harbour of Ammoúdi, which has several tavernas and some good bathing nearby. Some ferries dock at Arméni, the other beach near Oía. There is also a winery at Oía (see panel).

▶▶ Pýrgos   *101C1*

Pýrgos is one of the oldest villages on Thíra, with a cluster of traditional houses, a Venetian fort and Byzantine walls. A small road leads to the island's highest point (566m/ 1,856ft), where the 18th-century **monastery of Profítis Ilías▶** shares the remote hilltop with several large communications antennas. The monastery, in a lovely garden, has a small museum of religious objects and folklore items (*Open* Wed–Sun 5–10am, 5–7pm; currently closed).

▶▶ Thirasía   *101C1*

An excursion to the dark islets opposite Thíra gives a clearer idea of the volcano. Like Thíra itself, they form the edges of the now mostly submerged crater. Thirasía, which was part of Thíra until the 3rd century BC, has three small hamlets with a few tavernas and plenty of peace and quiet. The nearby islets of Paleá and Néa Kaméni are still volcanically active.

Beaches

Thíra is not the best place in the Cyclades to look for a secluded beach. Buses from Thíra bus station pass close to most of the island's beaches, so that wherever you go you are unlikely to be alone. The volcanic black sand gets unbearably hot on summer afternoons, so beach footwear is recommended.

The nearest beach to Thíra is Monólithos, but Kamári has a longer and cleaner beach, although it is now a package-tour resort. Périssa beach is a little less crowded but also less well kept. Oía has two small but average beaches, Ammoúdi, with a small harbour and Arméni, which has a fish taverna.

Kamári's black pebble beach was long ago discovered by package tourism. It is Thíra's most popular destination

TICKETS
A single ticket (€7) is valid for the Prehistoric Museum and the Archaeological Museum in Thíra and Akrotíri and Ancient Thíra.

GOOD WINE ON THIRA
Thíra has always been renowned for its wines, especially its rather sweet white wine. The volcanic soil is good for growing grapes, but the vines are kept short and basket-shaped to protect them from strong winds and the dry climate. Boutari, one of Greece's biggest wine producers, has a winery just outside Megalochóri, producing several excellent white wines and offering daily tastings. For a more specialized tasting, islander Paris Sigalas has set up a small winery in Oía, using only grapes from the northern part of the island, which produce a different kind of wine.

There are two great earthquake 'belts' in the world: one in the Pacific Ocean, another in the Mediterranean, running through the Greek Islands into Asia Minor. Even since 1900 parts of Greece have been shattered by earthquakes.

KOS'S DOUBLE BLOW
There is a certain satisfaction in the history of earthquakes on Kós for, while the ancient city was brought down by an earthquake in AD554, the earthquake that devastated the medieval and modern city in 1933 allowed archaeologists to expose the ancient site, which is still visible in the centre of the rebuilt town today.

SEEING IS BELIEVING
If you want more evidence of the extent of the 1953 earthquake that ripped the Ionian islands apart, visit Kefalloniá's Historical and Cultural Museum (see page 184). On Zákynthos, visit the Solomós Museum (see page 198) where you can buy N. A. Varviani's book with photographs of Zákynthos before, during and after the quake.

Pýrgos, one of the oldest settlements on the islands, is still scarred by the 1956 earthquake

Recent earthquakes When Thíra was levelled around 1450BC, the ancients thought it was the work of the god 'Earth-Shaker'. Nowadays we know differently, but that does not stop it from happening. In September 1986, the mainland town of Kalamáta was destroyed and many of its 42,000 inhabitants lost their homes and livelihood. In September 1999, a serious earthquake hit Athens leaving 139 dead and over 100,000 homeless, and in 2003 one hit the island of Lefkada causing injuries.

The islands The Greek islands have been just as vulnerable as the mainland and you are likely to find evidence of a long history of earthquakes. Archaeologists have confirmed that on several occasions the Minoans on Crete suffered from earthquakes. The Colossus of Rhodes, one of the Seven Wonders of the Ancient World, stood for only 65 years before being brought to its knees by an earthquake in 225BC. In this century, even little Kastellórizo was shattered by an earthquake in 1927.

The Ionian tragedy The Ionian islands seem particularly susceptible to earthquakes. Archaeologists hoping to uncover traces of Odysseus's palace on Itháki are hindered by the damage from previous quakes which has shuffled the stones around beneath the earth. In 1948 a quake destroyed Lefkáda Town. When it was rebuilt, the bell towers were made of iron, which is more likely to withstand another earthquake (and less likely to cause damage if they fall) and houses were mostly limited to two storeys, the upper ones built of corrugated iron or wood. The most damaging earthquake of modern times happened across the Ionian Islands in August 1953: most of the towns on Zákynthos and Kefalloniá were levelled by it.

The elaborate Tinian dovecotes are strewn all over the island's striking countryside

USEFUL NUMBERS
Port police
tel: 22830 22348
Windmills Travel (on the quay) tel: 22830 23398;
www.windmillstravel.com
www.tinos.biz

TÍNOS

Tínos is often characterized as the island of pilgrimage, but many visitors come for the beauty of its countryside, a rolling, fertile land filled with 60 villages, 1,200 white chapels and about 600 typical Tinian dovecotes. This is an ideal island for hikers.

►► Tínos Town   *100B3*

The island capital is dominated by the neoclassical **church of Panagía Evangelístria►►** (*Open* daily 7am–8pm), the main attraction for thousands of pilgrims. Streets leading up to it from the harbour are lined with stalls of religious paraphernalia. A huge staircase leads to the atmospheric marble church, which has several galleries and a famous icon of the Virgin, covered in gold offerings. Found in 1823 by a local nun, whose dream of a buried icon turned out to be true, the icon is the focus of special celebrations on 25 March and 15 August, when sick people from all over Greece make pilgrimages to Tínos in the hope of a miraculous cure. Also worth a visit in Tínos Town is the **Archaeological Museum►** (tel: 22830 22670. *Open* Tue–Sun 8.30–3. *Admission charge*), which houses finds from the Sanctuary of Poseidon and Amphitrite.

►►► Exómpourgo   *100B3*

Both the ancient acropolis and the medieval capital were on the summit of Mount Exóbourgo, now best reached from the steps in nearby **Xínara**. Xínara is the seat of the Roman Catholic Bishopric and, apart from Tripótamos which is deeply Orthodox (and has very striking buildings), most of the neighbouring villages are Catholic. The area offers plenty of opportunities for long walks to remote villages and monasteries, of which there are many.

►►► Pýrgos   *100B4*

The artisans of this beautiful village are famous for their fine marble work. Sculptors can still be seen at work here and local marble is much in evidence, paving the streets as well as embellishing buildings. Pýrgos has a famous school of sculpture, a museum dedicated to local sculptors and next door another small museum of the 19th-century sculptor Halepas. Below Pýrgos, the harbour of Pánormos has a crowded beach, while the nearby Kardianí village has one of the island's most striking settings.

Beaches

Northwest of Tínos town is Kiónia, site of the Sanctuary of Poseidon and Amphitrite. Eastwards, Pórto has two sandy beaches while Lychnaftía is usually less crowded than Ágios Fókas and Livádi·nearer to town.

CONNECTIONS
Tínos is connected by ferry with Piréas, Rafína, Mýkonos, Sýros, Ándros, Náxos, Páros, Crete and Skíathos. Summer catamarans and hydrofoil services run to Mýkonos, Náxos, Páros, Thíra, Sýros, Rafína, Íos and Piréas.

139

Pýrgos's artisans are known throughout Greece for their intricate marble ornamentation

Reminders of religious life are never far away in Greece. All over the islands, inhospitable hilltops and secluded valleys provide often spectacular settings for monasteries. Priests mingle with villagers in kafeneía and on buses. In times of need, Greeks make pilgrimages to pray before specific icons or shrines.

THE ANCIENTS LIVE ON

It is tempting to see the Greek reverence for icons as a continuing of pagan practices, where offerings were made to images of the gods. In some cases it is more than tempting: after the last pagan temples were shut down in AD392, the image of the goddess Demeter at Eleusis was replaced by that of a Christian saint, Dimitra. The saint's story was very similar to that of the ancient goddess; both lost a daughter and, after much searching, had her restored.

140

Right: the walls of even the most derelict churches and monasteries are often covered in stunning frescoes
Below: all Greek monks belong to the same order

An everyday religion Religion lies at the heart of Greeks. When fleets go out to fish or the olives are ready to harvest, prayers are offered and a procession may be gathered together. When something in life requires exceptional intercession, Greeks make a pilgrimage.

Saints, icons and relics In ancient Greece every settlement had its shrine and every city its grand temples. Today every modern Greek community has its icons and shrines. Icons often miraculously appear or, as on Tínos (see page 139), are found by a pious person, guided by a dream. Greek Orthodox worshippers believe that during Communion saints inhabit their icons: it is to icons and relics that people will turn in times of need.

The Greek Orthodox Church has a wealth of relics. Some are kept hidden, like the part of the nail from the

Holy Cross, formerly kept at Mount Athos, which was miraculously transported to Archangélou monastery on Thásos by the Archangel Michael. Others become the focus of public celebrations, like the relics of St. Spiridon which are paraded through the streets of Corfu Town four times a year to commemorate the saint saving the city from the threat of plague or war.

Miraculous powers The icon of the Virgin at Tínos (see page 139) is held to have the power to heal and throughout Greece, individual saints are credited with the skill to deal with specific problems. A typical case is that of the icon of St. John the Theologian on Mílos: when the community was threatened by pirates and took refuge in the church, the saint protected them by turning the church door into impenetrable iron.

The monastic order Greek monasticism traces its origins to the 4th century when, after periods of persecution under Decius and under the Emperor Diocletian, Christians responded by leaving the community to live in remote places. Greeks have no different monastic orders: monks all wear the same habit, recite the same liturgy and follow a single tradition. Monks are laymen, not clerics, their main goals being not to teach, to convert, or to do good work in the community, but to remove themselves from the community, to escape the trials and temptations of society and to come closer to God. Still, there are differences in the way they go about this. Some monks are *cœnobitic*, living in a community, under an abbot, sharing work, meals and services; others are *idiorrhythmic*, literally 'going their own way', living apart from each other during the week, coming together as a community only on Sundays and holidays. The most extreme monastics are anchorites, who take the idea of living apart literally and will not see other humans for weeks, months, or even years at a time.

Greece's monastic centres The remote peninsula of Mount Athos, on the northern mainland, towers both literally and metaphorically over all other monasteries in Greece. An autonomous republic within Greece, this haven of the reclusive life includes 20 monasteries.

   Throughout the islands there are monasteries of great age and importance. The monasteries and convents of St. John on Pátmos (1088), Néa Moní on Chíos (1042), Archangélou on Thásos (established in 1974 on a 12th-century site), and Tóplou (1365) and Arkádi (11th-century) both on Crete, are all highly respected.

TRADITION OF PILGRIMAGE
There is a long tradition in Greece of making pilgrimages to places with sacred connections. One of the most important centres of pilgrimage in antiquity was the supposed birthplace of Zeus in the Idean Cave. Among the rich and famous who made the journey, Pythagoras visited the cave and Plato wrote about the pilgrimage route in *The Laws*.

141

Every year the Panagía Evangelístria in Tínos draws thousands of pilgrims, many of whom crawl up the long flight of steps on their knees

Somehow the island of Pátmos has managed to resist the damage done by package tourism, even though it is very welcoming to all visitors

THE DODECANESE The farthest-flung of Greece's islands, the Dodecanese cling to the Turkish coast and were only officially united with Greece in 1948. For most of their recorded history, the islands have had to face up to invasion. As a result, their archaeology and architecture are as varied as the landscape.

THE ANCIENT ISLANDS Early and lucrative trading links existed between the Dodecanese and the nearby coast of Asia Minor. In the era of city-states, both Rhodes and Kós enjoyed prominence. When the Persian threat disappeared, after the Persians' defeat at the Battle of Salamis (480BC), the Dodecanese flourished. Such was their prestige that Ptolemy I claimed them on the death of Alexander the Great. By 164BC, Rhodes was sufficiently powerful to negotiate an independent treaty with Rome.

A SPECIAL PLACE FOR CHRISTIANS St. Paul is believed to have visited the Dodecanese and, according to tradition,

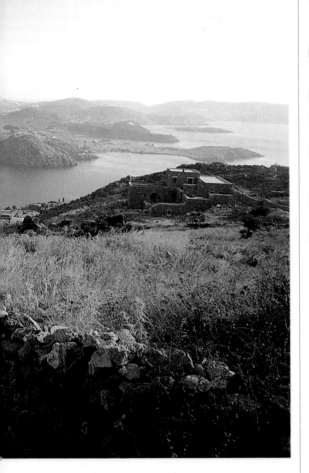

the islands had another part to play in the spread of Christianity when St. John the Theologian was exiled from Asia Minor to Pátmos, where he received his Revelation. The founding in 1088 of a monastery in honour of St. John has ensured that the island is still treated with reverence.

CENTURIES OF OCCUPATION Their remoteness made the Dodecanese a suitable stopping place for Crusaders on their way to the Holy Land and several of the islands experienced the Christian form of savagery which led, in 1204, to the sacking of Constantinople by Crusaders. The islands then became the war booty of the Genoese nobility, one of whom traded Rhodes to the Knights Hospitallers of St. John after the Holy Land fell to the Turks at the end of the 13th century. But as the Turks' power in the region grew, so did their hold over the islands and by the time the Knights of St. John finally abandoned Rhodes in 1522, all the Dodecanese were under the Sultan's control.

The Dodecanese
Astypálaia
(ΑΣΤΥΠΑΛΑΙΑ)
Chálki (ΧΑΛΚΗ)
Kálymnos
(ΚΑΛΥΜΝΟΣ)
Kárpathos
(ΚΑΡΠΑΘΟΣ)
Kastellórizo (Megisti)
(ΜΕΓΙΣΤΗ)
Kós (ΚΩΣ)
Léros (ΛΕΡΟΣ)
Leipsoí (ΛΕΙΨΟΙ)
Nísyros (ΝΙΣΨΡΟΣ)
Pátmos (ΠΑΤΜΟΣ)
Ródos (Rhodes)
(ΡΟΔΟΣ)
Sými (ΣΥΜΗ)
Tílos (ΤΙΛΟΣ)

Dodecanese

144

*The old traditions still
prevail in some mountain
villages on Kárpathos*

ITALIAN OCCUPATION The Turks held the Dodecanese for almost four centuries but eventually lost them in the Italo-Turkish war (1911–12). Italy cherished these possessions and Mussolini ordered the construction of grand public buildings throughout the Dodecanese (most obviously in Rhodes Town) as well as the excavation and sometimes the reconstruction of buildings from earlier periods. But while this civic activity was welcome after more than a century of Turkish neglect, the accompanying cultural scheme, whereby the islanders were forbidden to speak Greek or follow the Orthodox rites, made the occupation particularly bitter. The British fought the Italians out of the

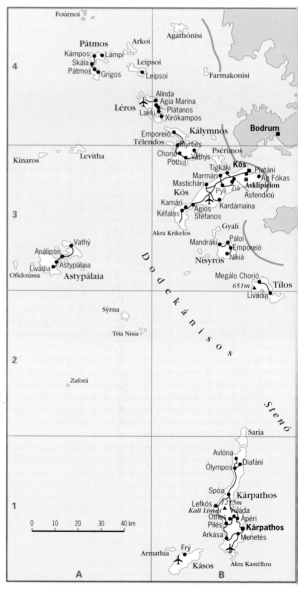

islands during 1944 and 1945 and on 7th March 1948, they were formally returned to Greece.

LOCAL CHARACTERISTICS If the islands share a history and a geographical location close to Turkey, they differ widely in their landscapes. Pátmos is rocky with volcanic soil, Léros's valleys are abundantly fertile, while Rhodes is blessed with a great variety of landscape, flora and fauna. Some of the Dodecanese have undergone extraordinary changes in the past few decades as mass tourism, particularly on Kós and Rhodes, has changed the look of some islands as well as the customs of their inhabitants.

A MISNOMER
'Dodeca' means 'twelve' but there are in fact 14 inhabited islands in the group. They were given their name in 1908, when 11 of them, along with Ikária, protested when the Turkish government took away privileges, including tax exemptions granted by the 16th-century Sultan Suleiman.

BEST BEACHES
● The sandy cove beneath Líndos (Rhodes)—out of season!
● Tsampíka (Rhodes' east coast)
● Psili Ammos (southern Pátmos)
● Kéfalos (southern Kós)

145

The villagers of Ólympos on Kárpathos were only recently introduced to the idea of mass tourism

146

ASTYPÁLAIA

This most westerly island of the Dodecanese is shaped like
a butterfly, with a narrow isthmus a mere 100m (330ft)
wide connecting its two wings.

►►► Astypálaia Town (Chóra)   144A3

Ferries dock at the harbour of Gialós with its Italianate
waterfront. As the steep road goes up to the capital, the
whitewashed, Cycladic-looking houses become older and
more derelict. The town is crowned by an impressive 14th-
century **kástro**, built on the site of the old acropolis by the
Venetian Quirini family, whose arms are on display above
the entrance. Still called the Palazzo Quirini-Stampalia,
the fortress contains a fine collection of Venetian art. Two
churches survive inside the ruined shell.

► Análipsis (Maltezána)   144A3

Análipsis is a small fishing harbour surrounded by olive
groves. Nearby are some well-preserved Roman baths
with fine mosaic floors.

►► Vathý   144A3

In winter, ferries dock in the attractive harbour of this
remote and peaceful fishing village if the winds are too
strong at Gialós.

Beaches

Livádia's beach is adequate; nearby Tzanáki is a quieter
nudist beach and Ágios Konstantínos is a lovely cove
surrounded by orchards. On the isthmus Sténo offers the
best bathing. The beaches round Análipsis are fine and
often empty.

CHÁLKI

Less than 300 people remain on this tiny island, most of
the population having moved to nearby Rhodes or emigrated abroad. Designated by UNESCO as the 'isle of
peace and friendship', it still offers a relaxing escape from
Rhodes, although tourism is developing slowly.

►► Chálki Town (Emporeió)   145C2

The sea captains' mansions on the waterfront of the small
harbour have been almost all restored, often by Chalkiots
now living in Florida. The clock tower in the harbour was
also a present from across the ocean. The now mostly
ruined old settlement of Chorio is a 35-minute walk up the
hill. Chalkiots ascend to Chorio on 14 August for the
Festival of Virgin Mary, when the beautiful church is
opened. The ruins of the Kastro, a medieval castle of the
Knights of St John on the smaller hill near Emporeió, commands spectacular views. The walk across the island
(8km/5 miles) from Chorio to the monastery Ágios
Ioánnis, with views of the sea on both sides, is superb.

Beaches

Chálki's only sandy beach is Póndamos, west of Emborió.
For superb views, walk from here to the deserted village of
Chorió, with its hilltop Crusader castle and church, Ágios
Nikólaos, which has Byzantine frescoes. Elsewhere are
many peaceful shingle coves, reached by boat or on foot.

KÁLYMNOS

To compensate for the decline of the natural sponge industry (see page 148), Kalymniots have built up Greece's largest fishing fleet and have opened their doors to tourism.

▶ Póthia
144B3

Most islanders live in Póthia, a lively and sometimes extremely noisy commercial centre. The houses are bright and colourful, a symbol of the resistance against the Italian occupation. The **Archaeological Museum▶▶** (tel: 22430 23113. *Open* Tue–Sun 9–2. *Admission charge.* Guided tours only), a stunning mansion owned by a local sponge magnate, has a strange collection of archaeological finds and personal memorabilia. The **Astor Sponge Workshop▶▶** (*Open* daily in summer, 10–10) is one of the better sponge factories, which shows every stage in the preparation of sponges.

▶▶ Chorió
144B3

The old capital is watched over by two ruined castles, which offer fine views over the island. There is a group of Hellenistic graves and the remains of a temple of Apollo in the nearby village of Dámos. The church of Christos of Jerusalem was built with stones that came originally from a Hellenistic temple.

▶▶ Vathýs
144B3

A long, narrow and sheltered inlet of the sea reaches into this long, lush valley of fruit trees, making for pleasant walking country dotted with well-kept villages and several early churches.

Beaches

The beaches at Myrtiés and Massoúri are often very crowded, but from Myrtiés frequent boats cross to the islet of Télendos, which has a castle, a monastery and good beaches. Emporeió's fine beaches, in the far northwest, are seldom overrun. South of Póthia, Vlihada Bay has an attractive sandy beach; boats go to the beautiful caves of Skaliá and Kéfalos.

The imposing Castle of the Knights of St. John overlooking the old capital of Chorió, Kálymnos

THE CUBES OF KÁLYMNOS
'In Kálymnos the infant's paint-box has been at work again on the milky slopes of the mountain. Carefully, laboriously it has squared in a church-yard, a monastery and lower down repeated the motif: a church, a monastery, a town; then, simply for the sake of appropriateness, a harbour with a shelf of bright craft at anchor and the most brilliant, the most devastatingly brilliant houses.'
Lawrence Durrell, *Reflections on a Marine Venus* (1953)

CONNECTIONS
Kálymnos has ferry links with Kós, Léros, Pátmos, Rhodes, Piréas, Sámos, Nísyros, Tílos, Astypálaia, Kastellórizo, Sými, Agathónisi, Leipsoí, Crete, Kásos and Kárpathos. Summer hydrofoil and catamaran services go to Kós, Rhodes, Pátmos, Sámos, Léros, Leipsoí and Sými.

Fifty years ago, sponges were one of Greece's most sought-after commodities, but growing demand and sudden blight has led to the catastrophic depletion of sponge beds around the islands. The remaining sponges will need very careful management indeed if the industry is to survive.

LIBYAN SPONGES
When the beds near Kálymnos failed to satisfy demand for natural sponges, divers began looking elsewhere in the region. As sponges thrive in clean water, the search in the Mediterranean became increasingly frantic. The sea off Libya was the exception and Kálymniot divers regularly sailed south until Libya's Colonel Qaddafi banned them.

THE LAST DIVE
'The younger generation, they won't see sponges; all of them are dying in the shallow waters of Greece, Turkey and Egypt.'
Lefteris Kampourakis, Kalymniot sponge diver.

SPONGES IN HOMER
The ancient Greeks knew the properties of sponges. Homer provides useful insights: in the *Iliad*, the god Hephaistos cleans himself with a sponge, while in the *Odyssey*, servants in the palace of Odysseus use sponges to wipe tables. Sponges were also used by warriors to make shields more comfortable.

Few natural sponges come from Kálymnos now

The life of a sponge Sponges are multicelled living organisms, shaped like vases and supported by tiny spines. Growing together in beds, in large colonies, sponges survive on organisms carried in the water that is filtered through their porous walls. When dried and with the living matter removed, sponges remain malleable, absorbent and tough, making them sought after for both domestic and industrial use.

From the sea to the bathroom Sponges need treatment to reach the state in which we like to use them in our bathrooms. Black when first brought from the seabed, they are purged of impurities and rinsed in saltwater tanks. Sponges for home use are then bleached to lighter shades which many foreign users seem to prefer.

The two most sought-after varieties of sponge are the honeycomb, mainly used for the bath, and the cup, preferred for industrial use. The cheaper unbleached sponges are for cleaning while the smooth ones with fine pores are for cosmetic use.

Sponge divers Of all the islands, it was Kálymnos that grew rich from sponges: from the 1880s its economy was dominated by the trade. The sponge trade peaked in the 1950s, when Kálymnos exported over 5 million sponges a year, but by 1985, the whole of Greece produced only 2.5 million sponges. By 1988 the number had fallen to one million as a blight decimated eastern Mediterranean sponge beds. They have not recovered and little more than 100 Kalymniots now dive, the others having changed profession or moved abroad.

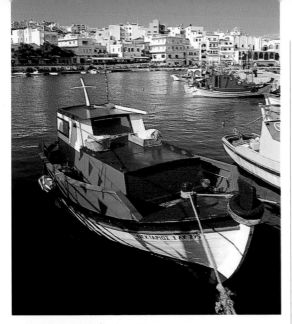

Pigádia's colourful fishing harbour is surrounded by lively cafés and places with rooms for rent

KÁRPATHOS

Isolated Kárpathos, a large and mountainous island, fiercely guarded its age-old traditions and its peace and quiet. That was until recently, but the island is slowly changing. Lawrence Durrell called it 'an ideal hideaway' and American Karpathians who have been returning each summer agreed. Increasingly, their influence is being felt as new roads are laid, charter flights land more frequently and new hotels appear. The visitor looking for unspoiled village life may be disappointed, but the natural beauty of the superb beaches and the interior remains, thanks largely to the island's rugged terrain and often hair-raising roads, especially in the remoter north.

▶ Kárpathos Town (Pigádia)   *144B1*
Almost completely modern, Kárpathos Town has no 'sights', but its small sleepy fishing harbour is a pleasant enough place to while away an evening. The town beyond the waterfront has many bars and restaurants. One of the older surviving houses, beside the church, is now a traditional *kafeneío* with good live music in the evening.

▶▶▶ Apéri   *144B1*
Apéri is the largest of a series of attractive villages dramatically set in the hills of central Kárpathos. The others are Voláda, Pilés and, prettiest of all, Óthos.

▶▶ Arkása   *144B1*
Arkása has been developed for package tourism in recent years and has lost a lot of its charm, but it has retained some Venetian buildings. Near the town are the remains of the ancient capital **Arkessia▶**, where mosaic floors from several Byzantine churches can be seen. From **Finíki▶**, 2km (1.2 miles) away, a small fishing harbour with a tiny beach, it is a steep climb to the striking village of **Menetés▶▶**, which contains some old houses and a small folklore museum.

USEFUL NUMBER·
Tourist information (Pigádia)
tel: 22450 23835 (summer only)
www.karpathos.com
www.karpathos.org

KÁSOS
The 1,500 inhabitants left on the barren neighbouring island of Kásos mostly live in the five villages clustered on the north side of the island. From Emborió, the port, it is a 10-minute walk to the capital, Frý. The place has little to offer the visitor apart from small but good beaches, total peace and rural calm in the many groves and gardens.

In 1824 the Egyptian troops of Ibrahim Pasha killed most of the men on the island and enslaved the women and their children. Strangely enough there was later a voluntary emigration to Egypt where Kasiots helped to build the Suez Canal.

*Apéri is the wealthiest of
the hillside villages:
nearly everyone has spent
some time in North
America to make money*

▶▶ Lefkós (Paralía Lefkoú)   144B1

Lefkós, a beautifully situated resort on the west coast with
excellent beaches, is still quite unspoiled. The only problem is getting there: buses are few and far between and it
is a long way by bicycle.

▶▶▶ Ólympos   144B1

The traditional village of Ólympos is one of the most popular day trips from Kárpathos Town; however, the road to it
is rather long and most people prefer to take a boat to the
harbour of Diafáni and from there take a bus or walk (see
page 151). There are some hotels and rooms to rent if you
wish to stay overnight. The influx of visitors has seriously
taken its toll on Ólympos and a lot of the traditions are
being kept for the sake of the holidaymakers, but it remains
a lovely village, clinging to its steep hilltop site and offering
breathtaking views. A family runs a small cafeteria near
their windmill, where they grind the flour they use to make
excellent *loukoumádes* (honey puffs) and cheese and
spinach pastries. Nearby is a small folklore museum,
which is just a traditionally furnished room.

Beaches
Most of Kárpathos's splendid beaches are accessible only
by boat from Kárpathos Town. To the north of the town,
within easy walking distance, is Vrontis Bay, a long stretch
of white sand. Amopí, 8km (5 miles) south, has a fine
sandy beach, crowded at times and a more secluded pebbly beach, the only place on the island where nudism is
(unofficially) allowed. There are several beautiful beaches
in Lefkós, but they can be crowded. Boats go every morning to Apélla, a fine beach with clear water and a rocky
background. It can also be reached by road. Kýra Panagía
is a lovely sand and pebble beach overlooked by the village of Mertonas and surrounded by pine forest. Also on
the east coast is the fine sandy beach of Ágios Nikólaos.

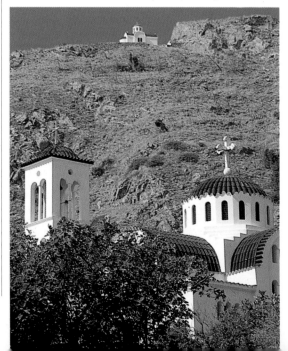

Walk

Diafáni to Ólympos

Every travel agent in Kárpathos Town advertises the boat trip to Diafáni and a visit by bus to Ólympos. The bus ride is an experience, but the walk through the village of Avlóna is unforgettable. If you do not like climbing, take the bus up and walk back downhill, taking enough to drink. Wear a hat and good walking shoes (about 11km/7 miles; allow 4 hours).

Boats leave Kárpathos Town at 8.30 and return at 4.30 from Diafáni. The walk starts at Diafáni waterfront; walk northwards and then follow the path between the houses. Ignore the signpost after a few metres to Vanandá (right) and stay in the valley, passing Hotel Sunrise. Walk through the wood and, after 500m (545 yards), veer left, uphill, with good views over Diafáni. About 3km (2 miles) from Diafáni continue straight where a dirt track goes right to Vanandá. Approximately 700m (765 yards) from here, turn right onto an old road with red markings. There is a final view of Diafáni and Vanandá and then there are only mountains and the serpentine road ahead of you.

After another 2km (1.2 miles), in a valley with fields surrounded by old walls, a donkey track comes in from the right, from Vanandá. Ignore this, taking instead the left-hand path which leads to **Avlóna**, an age-old agricultural community. Heading southeast at the edge of the village, a small road runs through the fields and, after 600m (655 yards), makes a sharp bend to the right. Walk straight on to join the old road again.

About 1.5km (1 mile) from Avlóna, a paved donkey path leads to the pretty

Ólympos is run by women as most of the men emigrate to work outside the village, only returning on holidays

church of **Ágios Konstantínos**. Suddenly the village of Ólympos comes into sight; the road from here is one of the island's most beautiful.

Some 50m (55 yards) beyond the church turn left and look out for a small winding path on the right that goes down into the valley, joining the road. Follow the road south through the valley, amid lovely fields and gardens, towards the delightful old village of **Ólympos**▶▶▶ (see page 150).

A GREEK BASTION

Until she died in 1982, Despoina Achladiou, the 'Lady of Rho', daily raised the Greek flag on the islet of Rhó, close to the Turkish coast near Kastellórizo. Now Kastellórizo itself is being disputed, with some people claiming that the island will revert to Turkey if the Greek population dwindles to less than 200. Whatever the truth, the number of inhabitants now seems stabilized at around 200. In 1996 the Greek government vigorously opposed Turkish moves on the island. On the other hand, necessity forces the islanders to deal with the Turkish mainland: although food is brought to the island from Rhodes, the boat service can be so unreliable that most Fridays a 'shopping party' crosses to Kaş to visit the market.

CONNECTIONS

Kastellórizo has ferry links with Rhodes, Kálymnos, Páros, Náxos, Nísyros, Tílos, Sýros and Piréas. Day trips operate from Kaş in nearby Turkey.

The sweeping sandy bay of Kamári on Kós, with modern whitewashed buildings backing the beach

USEFUL NUMBERS
Port Authority
tel: 22460 49270
Papoutsis Travel
tel: 22460 70830;
www.papoutsistravel.gr

KASTELLÓRIZO (MEGÍSTI)

Kastellórizo, one of the smallest of the Dodecanese islands, is far closer to the Turkish mainland town of Kaş than to its nearest Greek neighbour, the island of Rhodes, which is more than 100km (62 miles) away. Less than 100 years ago there were over 16,000 inhabitants, but today the permanent population is down to about 200 people. Emigration has been largely responsible: there are now over 30,000 Australians of 'Kassie' descent.

▶▶▶ Kastellórizo Town   145D1

Kastellórizo thrived by transporting goods between the Turkish mainland and Greece, but the trade went into decline when the Italians captured the island in 1912 and stopped completely after Anatolian Greeks were expelled in 1923. In 1943 it was occupied by the British, who blew up more than 2,000 houses when they were forced by the Germans to leave.

Most people live in Kastellórizo Town, which feels distinctively Asian. The attractive waterfront, still much visited by passing yachts, has red-tile roofed mansions with balconies and coloured doors, but just beyond this, the houses look desolate and abandoned.

The **museum▶** (*Open* Tue–Sun 7–2.30. *Admission free*) in the ruined Castle of the Knights has an eclectic collection of Byzantine ephemera and frescoes from local churches. The mosque has now been turned into a folklore museum. Restaurants lining the quay serve excellent seafood. A short walk up from the port lie the remains of the Doric city of Palaiokástro; the views from here are truly stunning.

Beaches

Kastellórizo has no beaches and the sea near the town is often infested with sea urchins. Boats make excursions to Perastá to visit the astonishing 'blue grotto', which is hung with stalactites.

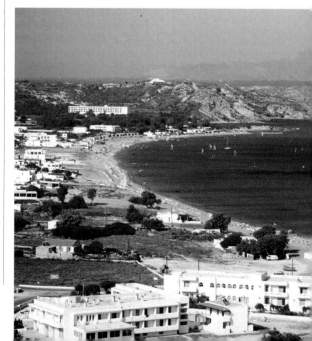

KÓS

Kós has to be the number one choice in the Dodecanese for sun, beaches, nightlife and fun. Avoid it if you long for the Greece of quiet individual experiences, although there are still some lovely corners on the island and Kós's friendly people make it well worth a short visit.

▶▶▶ Kós Town   144B3

Kós Town is a strange mixture. Beach tourism, complete with a lively nightlife, shares the town centre with Hellenistic and Roman archaeological sites. To escape the crowds in summer, wake early and explore while others recover from their long night on the town.

Approaching Kós harbour, the first striking sight is the imposing 15th-century **Castle of the Knights**▶▶ (tel: 22420 27927. *Open* Tue–Sun 8–2.30. *Admission charge*). A walk on the walls offers splendid views over the town, and the interior is littered with fragments of ancient columns and statues. The 18th-century Turkish **Mosque of Hatzi Hasan** in Plateía Lózia is partly occupied by souvenir shops and nearby is the Hippocrates Plane Tree. The old Turkish bazaar, now filled with tacky souvenir shops, lacks authenticity. The **Archaeological Museum**▶▶ (Plateía Eleftherías. *Open* Tue–Sun 8–2.30. *Admission charge*) has lovely mosaic floors and elegant statues from Roman town houses. The **Agora**▶ has a 4th-century stoa and the ruins of a Temple of Aphrodite. The **Casa Romana**▶▶ (Odós Grigouriou. *Open* Tue–Sun 8.30–3. *Admission charge*) is a complete Roman villa restored by the Italians in the 1930s.

Farther down the road at the well-kept Roman **Odeum**▶, a statue thought to be of Hippocrates was found. Across the road is the site known as the **Western Excavation**▶▶, whose ruins include a **Nymphaeum** with superb mosaic floors, the colonnade of a gymnasium, and some Roman and early Christian houses, the best of which is the **House of Europa**.

Most visitors to Kós prefer the vibrant nightlife to the ancient sites

THE HIPPOCRATES TREE

In Platía Lózia is the famous Hippocrates Tree, a plane tree under which Hippocrates is said to have taught. The tree may well be one of Europe's oldest, but not old enough to have been here since the time of Hippocrates.

TOURIST INFORMATION

The tourist office in Kós Town offers free maps, a magazine about what is on in town and a list of doctors (Odós Vas. Georgiou 1, tel: 22420 24460; www.kosinfo.gr. *Open* May–Oct Mon–Fri 8–2.30, 3–10, Sat 9–2).

Cycle ride

The island of Kós is dedicated to Hippocrates, even though there is little evidence of his existence. The healthiest and most pleasant way to get around Kós is to cycle. Bicycles can be rented in town. This trip (approximately 25km/15 miles) will take most of a day, with time for a swim. In summer take sunscreen, hat and water. (Note that the optional detour to Asfendioú demands fitness and a mountain bicycle; see below.)

Start from the **Hippocrates Tree▶** (see panel on page 153) in Plateía Lózia, between the Castle and the Roman Agora. Turn right along Aktí Miaoúli and right again at the tourist office into Odós Ippokrátous, passing the modern Hippocrates Hospital (No. 32). In the **Archaeological Museum▶▶** on Plateía Eleftherías (see page 153) is the statue of Hippocrates and a well-preserved

In the footsteps of Hippocrates

The tree may not have been around in Hippocrates's time, but its maturity certainly demands respect

mosaic depicting him welcoming Asklepios to Kós. Take Odós Vassiléos Pávlou, then at the end of the street turn right into Odós Grigoriou and continue to the circle with flags where a signpost points right to the Asklepion (Asklípieio; about 4km/2.5 miles). Continue under pine and fig trees to the village of **Platáni▶** (see page 157). Beyond the village the road climbs gently. At the little traffic island, continue straight ahead along the lane that leads to the **Asklepion▶▶▶** where Hippocrates' techniques were applied (see page 156). From here you can try out his recommendation of fresh clean air by cycling a further 10km (6 miles) through pine forests to the villages of **Asfendioú▶▶** (see page 156). (The road is steep; try it only if you have a mountain bicycle and are fit.) Alternatively, return to Platáni where a road to the left leads to the main coastal road and beyond it to the beautiful beaches just past **Tigkáki** (about 12km/7.5 miles). Reward yourself with a cooling swim before riding back to Kós Town.

The priest-doctors of the Ancient Egyptians claimed to have invented medicine and that may be true, but it was from Hippocrates and the priests of the Asklepion that western medicine and its code of practice evolved.

Asklepios The Greeks believed that Asklepios, god of medicine, was a son of Apollo and Coronis. His daughter was Hygieia, goddess of health. Asklepios's main cult centre and temple was in the Peloponnese, at Epídavros, where patients initially received prescriptions in the form of a dream as they slept in the temple. Those who were cured later offered a sacrifice at the temple, traditionally a cockerel. The god is often shown as a bearded man, with a stick with a snake curling round it, a symbol now sometimes used to denote a pharmacy.

Hippocrates Born on Kós around 460BC, Hippocrates became the most famous physician of antiquity. Many surviving texts on medical subjects are credited to him, but there is some doubt over the authorship of most of them. Certainly, he classified the medical knowledge of his time. Unlike priests at the Asklepion in Epídauros, Hippocrates sought to treat the sick by using drugs, infusions and other therapies and he understood the importance of diet, climate and living conditions in maintaining good health. He believed that most diseases were carried in the four fluids or humours of the body: blood, phlegm, black bile and yellow bile. How much of this was his own thinking and how much was wisdom imported from Egypt or elsewhere is unknown. The practice was carried on by hereditary temple priests, called Asklepiadai, who claimed descent from the god himself.

After Hippocrates The riches of the Asklepion on Kós and the Sanctuary at Epidávros suggest that the cult continued to grow after Hippocrates's death, reaching its peak during Ptolemaic and Roman times, when both sites functioned as spas for the healthy and sanitariums for the sick. The reputation of Asklepios and of Hippocrates was such that when Rome was suffering from a particularly savage epidemic in 293BC, Asklepios's serpent was sent for to work a cure.

THE HIPPOCRATIC OATH
Although many of the great number of writings ascribed to Hippocrates are disputed, the Hippocratic Oath is usually credited to him. In it, he expresses the ethical doctrine of physicians which remains in use today. Part of the oath states: 'I will use treatment or help the sick according to my ability and judgement, but never with a view to injury and wrong-doing. Neither will I administer a poison to any body when asked to do so. Similarly I will not give to a woman a pessary to cause abortion. Into whatever houses I enter, I will enter to help the sick and I will abstain from all intentional wrong-doing or harm. And whatever I shall see or hear in the course of my profession in my intercourse with men, if it be what should not be published abroad, I will never divulge.'

A CURE TOO MANY
According to mythology, Asklepios went too far with his cures and brought a man back from the dead. For daring the gods, Zeus struck him down with a thunderbolt and Apollo turned him into a constellation, the Serpentaria.

Hippocrates, the Father of Medicine, who established a medical code still in use today

The temple dedicated to Apollo the Healer in the Asklipeío

CONNECTIONS
Kós is well served by inter-island ferries. There are links with Rhodes, Kálymnos, Nísyros, Léros, Pátmos, Piréas, Sými, Tílos, Kastellórizo, Náxos, Páros, Leipsoí, Astypálaia, Thessaloníki, Chálki, Kárpathos, Crete, Sýros, Mýkonos, Tínos, Ándros, Rafina and Cyprus.
In summer there are frequent hydrofoils and catamarans to Rhodes, Ikaría, Pátmos, Nísyros, Kálymnos, Léros, Sámos and Bodrum (Turkey).

▶▶ Asfendioú   144B3

The villages clustered on the slopes of Mount Díkeos, known as the Asfendioú, offer a welcome cooling breeze in summer. This is definitely the most Greek part of Kós, though some of the more accessible villages see their fair share of visitors. Buses go to Pylí, from where a dirt track crosses the island's only forest to the other villages. A steep walk away from Pylí is the old town **Palaiopíli▶▶**, where an amazing ruined castle sits on top of a rocky pinnacle. Crumbling stone walls and little abandoned churches stand among drifts of wild plants and the views over mountain and sea are magnificent. **Evangelístria▶** has lovely houses and a good taverna while nearby **Asómati** has picturesque whitewashed houses. **Ziá▶▶**, more developed with some excellent tavernas, is a spectacular place to watch the sunset.

▶▶▶ Asklipeío (The Asklepion)   144B3

4km (2.5 miles) from Kós Town, past Platáni (tel: 22420 28763). Open Tue–Sun 8–6 (earlier in winter). Admission charge. Frequent buses and the Tourist Bus from Kós Town

The Asklepion was a religious centre, with temples dedicated to Apollo the Healer and his son Asklepios and also a medical resort with a medical school, a treatment centre and a museum of anatomy and pathology. Although the Asklepion was built after Hippocrates' death, it was undoubtedly based on his theories and methods. The three wide terraces seen at the Asklepion today were built after the 4th century BC and most of the buildings are Hellenistic or Roman. The lowest terrace, just beyond the Roman baths, was once the medical school, the museum and the hospital. The middle terrace has an altar dedicated to Apollo the Healer, with an elegant 4th-century BC Ionic temple to the right and a less impressive Roman-Corinthian version to the left. An imposing ceremonial stairway leads to the highest terrace, crowned with the huge 2nd-century BC Doric Temple of Asklepios, where the Hippocratic Oath is still sworn today. Along the exterior wall there are two subterranean chambers with a statue of Venus, where it was believed that venereal diseases were treated.

▶ Kamári   144B3

This fishing harbour boasts some good beaches and is rapidly developing into a package-tour resort. Nearby, at **Ágios Stéfanos▶▶**, are two very early Byzantine churches with well-preserved mosaic floors and some columns, probably built on the site of a Classical temple.

▶ Kardámaina   144B3

A stone's throw from the airport, Kardámaina is the second largest and fastest growing resort on Kós. There is nothing left of the old fishing village, but a beach packed during the day (and often at night) and continuous nightlife attract young people from all over Europe.

▶▶ Kéfalos   144B3

Kéfalos, at the end of the bus line on Kós's southwestern peninsula, has its fair share of bungalows and summer houses but still tends to be less hectic than the other resorts. Nearby, the remains of a Hellenistic temple and a theatre were probably part of ancient Astypálaia, the earliest capital of Kós.

▶ Mastichári   144B3

Another fishing village recently turned resort, Mastichári is more relaxed than Kardámaina. Boats leave from here for the islands of Psérimos and Kálymnos.

▶ Platáni   144B3

Platáni is a bi-ethnic village where Greek Orthodox seem to live rather peacefully with a Muslim minority of Turkish descent. It is a popular lunch stop on the way back from the Asklepion and, apart from some Turkish-style houses and an Ottoman fountain, its main attractions are the Turkish–Greek restaurants under the plane trees.

▶ Psérimos   144B3

Almost equidistant between Kós and Kálymnos is the small island of Psérimos. Day trips from both islands are popular and a few lucky visitors can stay overnight in one of Psérimos's guest houses. There are no cars on this idyllic island and the main settlement consists of a mere 30 or so houses. The main sandy beach is just in front of the village and there are other, pebbly, beaches nearby.

Beaches

Most people visit Kós for its superb beaches even though these become very crowded in summer. The beaches nearest Kós Town are narrow and absolutely packed. To the west are Lámpi and, 9km (5.5 miles) on, Tigkáki, equally crowded, while Marmári is slightly calmer, with good windsurfing. Eastwards, the good pebble and sand beaches are lined with big beach hotels. Brós Thermá, 5km (3 miles) past the last bus stop at Ágios Fókas, is more isolated and has black sand and hot springs. Mastichári, on the north coast, is a fast-developing resort with sandy beaches. The

157

Most independent travellers avoid Kós as there is not much left to discover

It has no superb beaches, but Léros is becoming increasingly popular

EXCURSIONS TO TURKEY
In summer there are usually daily boats to Bodrum from Kós Town. Information and tickets from Exas Travel, near the harbour (tel: 22420 28545) for the latest information on boats and regulations, which change frequently.

CONNECTIONS
There are ferries from Léros to Kós, Rhodes, Piréas, Kálymnos, Tínos, Pátmos, Agathónisi, Leipsoí, Sámos, Tílos, Sými, Páros, Sýros and Náxos. In summer, hydrofoils and catamarans go to Kós, Pátmos, Kálymnos, Sámos, Ikaría and Leipsoí and boats serve Leipsoí and Kálymnos.

From Leipsoí, ferries go to Pátmos, Agathónisi, Kálymnos, Léros, Piréas and Sámos. There are hydrofoil and catamaran services to Léros, Rhodes, Kálymnos, Kós, Pátmos, Sámos and Ikaría and summer boats to Pátmos and Léros.

fine beaches at Kardámaina, in the south, are lined with hotel complexes. The most beautiful beaches on the island are Paradise Beach (an often crowded stretch of sand between dramatic cliffs), Ágios Stéfanos (the site of a Club Med complex) and Kamári. There are still deserted beaches on the southern tip of the island, beyond Kéfalos, but it can be quite an adventure to reach them.

LÉROS

Léros, with its deeply indented coastline, somehow still feels more Italian than Greek. The island has quite a reputation among Greeks, to whom it is best known for its prisons and mental hospitals. It is definitely the island for those who like a laid-back atmosphere, with beautiful beaches, a green interior and good tavernas.

▶▶ Plátanos   *144B4*

The inland capital of the island is a busy market town with some attractive 19th-century mansions. Above the town towers the *kástro*, built by the Byzantines, restored by the Knights of St. John and later by the Venetians. The small museum of local finds and craft items, in the Castle of Pandeli, is worth a visit (tel: 22470 23211. *Open* daily 8–1 and 5–8.30. *Admission charge*).

▶▶ Lakkí   *144B4*

Lakkí, the main harbour, is a surreal sight with crumbling fascist art-deco buildings and empty broad avenues. Boats usually arrive in Xirókampos, a little fishing port nearby.

Beaches
The main resort, Alínda, has a good gravel beach, which gets crowded in summer. Vromólithos is nicer, with a sand and gravel beach and forested hills behind. The nearest beach to Plátanos is Agía Marína, which has tavernas open in season.

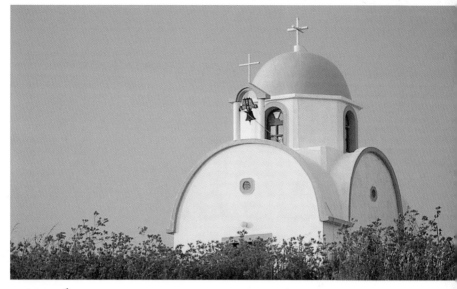

LEIPSOÍ

Leipsoí gets more visitors now than ever, since it became a port of call for ferries between the Cyclades and the Dodecanese, but it is still a good place to do nothing more than swim, walk, eat and relax.

▶▶▶ Leipsoí   144A4

Leipsoí, the only village on the island, has cube-shaped houses painted in bright colours and is crowned by a blue-domed church. There are several good tavernas, rooms for rent and lively *kafeneía* on the fine harbour front. As there are few cars there is often little to do other than walk, but it takes only two hours to cross the island.

Beaches

To the west of the town is Liéndou, but Katsadía is more pleasant, with sandy coves and an excellent taverna in summer. Less than an hour's walk away is Platýs Gialós, a sheltered sandy bay on the north coast.

A blue-domed church is part of Leipsoí's charm

USEFUL NUMBER

Tourist Information (Lakkí harbour) tel: 22470 22937
Port Police (Leipsoí) tel: 22470 41133
Tourist Information (Leipsoí village) tel: 22470 41185

ROBINSON CRUSOE ISLANDS

There are a few tiny islands near Leipsoí which can sometimes be reached from there, or more often by boat from Pátmos. Arkoí has about 25 inhabitants and a few rooms for rent. Maráthi has some lovely empty beaches and tavernas rent rooms here, but boats are very erratic. Agathónisi has two villages and a guest house providing lunch and dinner. The population makes a living from goat herding and fishing.

The sheltered and undeveloped bay at Platýs Gialós

The sunken crater of Nísyros volcano is like a dramatic grey and brown moonscape

ST. JOHN THE DIVINE
The Roman emperor Domitian, who banished John the Theologian to Pátmos in AD95, made the island famous forever. The only mention in the *Book of Revelation* of the saint's stay on Pátmos is: 'I dwelled in an island which is called Pátmos, as to preach the word of God and have faith in the martyrdom suffered by Jesus Christ.' A writer named Prochorus, who claimed to have been St. John's disciple but is now considered to have lived a few centuries later, wrote the eventful *Travels and Miracles of St. John*, both filled with fantastic stories and adventures.

CONNECTIONS
Nísyros has ferry links with Kós, Rhodes, Kálymnos, Sými, Kastellórizo, Tílos, Piréas, Astypálaia, Páros, Náxos, Sýros, Léros and Leipsoí. A summer hydrofoil and catamaran service runs to Kós, Rhodes, Tílos and Sými.

NÍSYROS

Day-trippers from Kós invade the island to visit its volcano, but drinking water is scarce, so Nísyros cannot support large numbers of visitors. However, it manages very well without the dubious benefits of mass tourism, deriving its prosperity from its rich volcanic soil and from the quarrying of pumice and gypsum on the neighbouring islet of Gyalí.

▶▶▶ Mandráki   144B3

Mandráki is a jewel of a harbour with fine whitewashed houses and brightly coloured wooden balconies. The narrow streets are overlooked by two castles: the highest, *Palaíokastro*▶▶ is a stunning 6th-century BC Doric bastion with thick Cyclopean walls. Below it, the Knights' Castle contains the **monastery of Panagía Spilianí**▶▶ (tel: 22420 31125. *Open* daily 10–3. *Donation welcome*), its much-venerated icon of the Virgin usually covered with gold and silver offerings. A house nearby has been converted into the **Historical and Popular Museum**▶.

▶▶▶ Nikiá   144B3

Nikiá is set dramatically on the rim of the volcanic crater, while the nearby **monastery of Ágios Ioánnis Theológos**▶ offers another spectacular angle. Neighbouring Emporeió was abandoned until foreigners and Athenians started restoring the old houses. From Nikiá a path descends to the crater floor, where there is still volcanic activity, occasional bubbles are seen and the sulphurous smell is often overpowering. Subterranean rumbling noises, according to legend, are the groans of the giant Polyvotis, who was crushed when Poseidon threw at him a huge lump of rock wrenched from the island of Kós.

Beaches
The town beach is not very pleasant, but nearby Hohláki beach, covered in volcanic stones, has clear water. Farther east, the spa of Loutrá has hot mineral springs which are reputed to have healing properties for sufferers from rheumatism and arthritis. Just beyond it, White Beach is often crowded with guests from the adjoining hotel. The best beach is Páloi, with a wonderful taverna.

CONVENTS

In addition to the monasteries, the Chóra has over 40 churches and convents in and around the town. Try to see the 17th-century Convent of Zoodóchos Pigí (tel: 22470 31991.*Open* daily 8–12 and 4–7; chanted Mass Thu 5pm), which has some excellent frescos. The Convent of the Evangelismos is signposted to the west of the town and is open daily 9–11am.

CONNECTIONS

Ferry services from Pátmos operate to Piréas, Léros, Kálymnos, Leipsoí, Rhodes, Sámos, Kós, Léros, Ikaría, Agathónisi, Lésvos, Thessaloníki, Crete, Sými, Tílos and Rafína. Hydrofoils and catamarans go to Ikaría, Léros, Kálymnos, Kós, Sámos and Leipsoí in summer, when excursion boats also serve Sámos, Leipsoí, Kós, Arkoí and Maráthi.

The Treasury of the Monastery of St. John contains the most important monastic collection in Greece after the one at Mount Áthos

PÁTMOS

This unique and beautiful island has managed to keep a happy balance between maintaining its old religious and monastic traditions and welcoming the 'considerate' kind of visitor. It is a sacred island where, according to tradition, St. John the Divine had the revelation described in the Bible's *Book of Revelation*. Its other attractions are beautiful beaches and a lively social scene.

▶▶▶ Pátmos Town (Chóra)   *144A4*

The houses and monasteries of the island capital loom dramatically from their steep cliff over Skála, the harbour. A bus travels between the two several times a day but the walk up is much more spectacular, either along the road or up the old cobbled path. Many of the wonderful old houses in Pátmos Town have been restored by residents, who fiercely guard the tranquillity of the place. The town looks compact but contains no fewer than 40 churches and monasteries in its narrow alleys. The most famous is undoubtedly the **monastery of St. John**▶▶▶ (tel: 22470 31223. *Open* Sun, Tue, Thu 8.30–1.30 and 4–6; other days morning only. *Admission free*, moderate entrance fee for museum/treasury). Founded in 1088 by the monk Christodoulos, the monastery was built as a fortress to protect it from pirates. Although much of it is closed to the public, there is still plenty to see. The outer narthex has striking 17th-century frescoes depicting the life of St. John. The refectory has a long stone table with spaces for storing plates and cutlery and there is a bakery, part of the original building. The museum/treasury dis-

plays part of the monastery's rich collection of icons, manuscripts and religious artefacts. Halfway between Skála and Pátmos Town, the **monastery of the Apocalypse**▶▶ (*Open* as for the monastery of St. John, see above. *Admission free*) is built around the cave where the saint is said to have heard God's voice.

THE COLOSSAL LEGEND
The Colossus—the leg-
endary bronze statue,
more than 30m (98ft)
high, which was one of
the Seven Wonders of the
Ancient World—was a
symbol of Rhodes' wealth
and power. The sculptor
Chares is said to have
worked on it for 12 years
before killing himself in
despair after discovering
that some of his calcula-
tions were wrong. The
work was completed
around 292BC by another
sculptor, Laches. The
statue stood in place for
only 65 years before it
was brought down by an
earthquake. The pieces
lay on the ground for hundreds of years before they
were taken away to Syria
where they were probably
melted down. At the
harbour entrance two
columns with a stag and
a doe mark the place
where the Colossus is
believed to have stood.

▶▶ Skála   144A4

Unlike Pátmos Town, hanging above the harbour halfway
to heaven, Skála, Pátmos's port of arrival, seems to be
devoted to the more worldly of pleasures. In July and
August the town is overrun by scantily dressed day-trippers, but for the rest of the year an air of sophistication
pervades the simple waterfront cafés, where well-heeled
visitors and long-time residents sip coffee. Most visitors
head for the beaches or make their way to the monastery.

Beaches
Pátmos has excellent beaches. The town beach is sandy but
unexceptional and boats go to the better beaches further
away. Méloi, the next beach along (15 minutes' walk), has
a good taverna and is pleasant but quite crowded. More
secluded is the sandy cove of Agriolivádo, while its neighbour, Kámpos Beach, is the most developed on the island.
Lámpi in the north is one of the most beautiful beaches,
famous for its multicolored stones. On the other side of
Skála, Grígos, reached by bus, gets crowded, but from
there a 30-minute walk crosses the island to Psilí Ámmos,
a splendid sandy beach which has an area where nudism
is tolerated. Many residents prefer the (often windy)
beaches of Léfkes, in the northwest, for their isolation and
rough beauty.

RÓDOS (RHODES)

Excellent beaches, rich history and a wonderful climate
have made Rhodes one of the most popular Greek islands.
Most visitors come for the sea and the sun, but the historic
monuments reward close inspection and the countryside
inland, away from the often commercialized resorts, can
be truly entrancing.

▶▶▶ Rhodes Town   163C4

Rhodes Town is divided into two main areas, the Old and
the New Town. The much bigger New Town, which surrounds the medieval town, is a mainly residential area
with many hotels, especially near the town beach and the
yacht harbour, Mantráki, whose entrance was famously
(but briefly) spanned by the enormous Colossus of Rhodes
(see panel). **Monte Smith▶**, to the southwest of the New
Town, is the site of the 5th-century BC Hellenistic acropolis, with a restored theatre, a stadium and a few columns of
the Temple of Apollo. It is a popular place for joggers. In
the stunning Villa Nestoridis on Plateía Haritos is the
Museum of Contemporary Greek Art▶▶▶ (tel: 22410
43780. *Open* Tue–Sun 9–2, also Fri 5–8. *Admission charge*),
with more than 1,000 work (not all on display) of the major
Greek artists of the 20th century.

The most exciting sights are in the Old Town, an historic
monument in its own right and designated by UNESCO as
a World Heritage site. The easiest way to enter this
medieval maze for the first time is from Mantráki Harbour
through **Pýli Eleftherías (Liberty Gate)**, which leads to
Plateía Sýmis.

The excellent **Mouseío Archaiologikó (Archaeological
Museum)▶▶** (Plateía Mouseío, tel: 22410 27657. *Open*
Tue–Sun 8.30–2.30. *Admission charge*) offers a chance to see
the Knights' Hospital, in which it is housed. The collection

consists mainly of Hellenistic sculpture including a striking statue of Aphrodite, some fine funeral steles and 5th- and 6th-century pottery. Close by, in Plateía Argyrokástrou, is the **Decorative Arts Collection**▶ (*Open Tue–Sun 8.30–3. Admission charge*), which displays woodwork, furniture and tiles from old houses. The **Mouseío Vizantinó (Byzantine Museum)**▶▶ (Plateía Mouseío. *Open Tue–Sun 8.30–2.30. Admission charge*), in the grand 11th-century Knights' Cathedral, has a superb collection of icons from the 5th to the 18th centuries; evocative medieval religious music is played in the background.

The heavily restored **Odós Ippotón (Street of the Knights)**▶▶▶ leads from **Plateía Mouseío (Museum Square)** to the Palace. This lovely cobbled street is lined with the Inns of the medieval Order of the Knights of St. John which functioned as clubs and meeting places and were divided by languages ('Tongues') or countries (see panel).

On top of the hill is the **Paláti Ippotón (Palace of the Grand Masters)**▶▶▶ (*Open Tue–Sun 8–7. Admission charge; free Sun in winter*). The original 14th-century palace, a wonder of medieval architecture, stood until the

ODOS IPPOTÓN (STREET OF THE KNIGHTS)
Starting from Plateía Mouseío, the inn next to the museum shop was the Spanish House. Beyond it stands the 16th-century Inn of the Order of the Tongue of Italy. Opposite was the Inn of England, destroyed and rebuilt several times. The French Language Institute is housed in the Inn of France, built in 1492. Past the arch over the street, on the right, is the Inn of the Tongue of Provence, while facing opposite is the Inn of the Tongue of Spain.

HE WALLS

Rhodes Town's
ent fortified walls
nly be gained by tak-
an organized walking
tour. These depart from
the entrance to the Paláti
Ippotón (Palace of the
Grand Masters) on
Tuesdays and Saturdays
at 2.45. The walls are
5km (3 miles) long, but
the walk is only 1.5km (1
mile) and takes about 90
minutes. The Knights
worked on these walls for
many years and in some
places they are 12m
(40ft) thick. Each stretch
was called a curtain and it
was up to every different
Tongue (see page 163) to
defend its curtain.

*One of the most
picturesque streets in
Rhodes Old Town, the
beautifully restored Street
of the Knights*

SON ET LUMIÈRE
The history of Rhodes at
the time of the Knights is
told in an interesting
'Íchos kai Fos' (sound
and light) show which
takes place in the
Municipal Park on Plateía
Riminí. The show, in sev-
eral languages, has two
or three performances
nightly from May to
October. For more infor-
mation check the board
outside or call
the box office (tel:
22410 21922;
www.hellenicfestival.gr).

19th century, when it was first damaged by the earthquake in 1851 and, five years later, ruined by an explosion. The Italians started to restore it in 1939 as a summer palace for Mussolini and King Victor Emmanuel III, but not without removing most of its character. The first floor, a series of rather dull state rooms, contains fine mosaics from Kós and some good Renaissance furniture. The superb ground-floor exhibits explain the importance of Rhodes throughout its 2,400 years of history.

There is evidence all over the Old Town of the Ottoman occupation, which started in 1522 and lasted over 300 years. **Odós Sokrátous**, now very much geared to the souvenir shopper, formed the heart of the Turkish bazaar. No. 76 is still a lovely Turkish-style coffee-house where men play *tavli* (backgammon).

At the end of Sokrátous is the stripy **Tzamí Suleïman (Suleiman Mosque)** with, opposite, the **Tourkikí Vivliothíki (Turkish Library)**. There are mosques and masjids all over town (see Walk opposite), some of them still used by the Turkish-speaking minority.

The 16th-century **Bánio (Turkish Bath)▶▶** was once con-sidered one of the finest in the East (Plateía Ariónos. *Open* Mon–Fri 10–5, Sat 8–5, but check times for men/women. *Admission charge.* Take your own soap and towels). Damaged during World War II, it has been restored and is now in use again. The eastern part of the Old Town once had a flourishing **Jewish Quarter▶▶**, with the fine **Kahal Shalom Synagogue▶▶** just off Plateía Martyrón Evraïón (Square of the Jewish Martyrs).

Walk

Rhodes Old Town

This walk meanders through narrow arched lanes and past attractive squares with little chapels, mosques and even a synagogue. Although not all the monuments will be open, the best time to do the walk is late afternoon, when the light softens the colours and a breeze cools the town (allow 2 to 3 hours).

Walk south from Plateía Sýmis and turn right onto **Odós Ippotón** (**Street of the Knights**)▶▶▶. Walk up past the **Paláti Ippotón** (**Palace of the Grand Masters**)▶▶▶ into the bazaar area and turn left onto the tree-lined Odós Orféos. To the left is the **Roloï** (**Clock Tower**)▶ and to the right, at No. 44, is the interesting 18th-century **Tourkikí Vivliothíki**

(**Turkish Library**)▶▶ with rare editions of the Koran and finely illustrated manuscripts. Just past the library, by the pink **mosque, Tzamí Suleïman**▶, turn right onto Odós Ippodámou. Turn right again after the 15th-century **church of Agía Paraskeví**▶ (on the right), to see the elegant minaret of the mosque **Tzamí Hamza Bey**▶. Return to Ippodámou and go straight ahead via Odós Archeláou to Plateía Ariónos and another mosque. Turn left onto Odós Androníkou, then right at Taverna Nisyros and into the alleyway, immediately left, going to Plateía Dorioús. Past the fountain turn left onto Plateía Aíschylou and left again between two tavernas towards the **mosque, Tzamí Ibrahim**▶. To the right Odós Pythagorá goes under a beautiful arch, then turns left past walled gardens and vines. At Odós Perikléous turn left, follow the bend in the street to Odós Symíou, then turn left again onto Odós Dosiádou with the **Synagogue**▶▶ on the left. At the end of the street turn left towards Plateía Martyrón Evraïon.

Dodecanese

RHODIAN SPECIALITIES

Rhodes is definitely the gastronomic centre of the Dodecanese, with a cuisine that has always been influenced by the East. Franks, Turks, Jews and Armenians all made an impact and Rhodian food often seems closer to Middle Eastern cuisine than to the Greek kitchen. Among the island's specialities are fish baked with *tahini* (sesame paste) sauce and a *pilaf* with seafood. A few restaurants serve a wide variety of fresh seafood: molluscs, mussels and even oysters, especially those from Kastellórizo.

The Monastery of Filérimos, used by Suleïman the Magnificent as his base for the take-over of the island

▶ Archángelos   163C2

This large, pleasant village, overlooked by a crumbling fortress, was until recently hidden by its citrus orchards; it now risks disappearing under the weight of package tourism. The two churches of Archángelos Gavriél and Archángelos Michaíl are beautiful and the church of **Ágios Theodóros** has 14th-century frescoes. Nearby are **Charáki**, a quieter fishing harbour and the ruins of **Feráklos**, once one of the strongest castles on Rhodes.

▶▶ Asklipeío   163B2

This hill village once had a school for the followers of Asklepios, but there are no Classical remains. Instead, the 11th-century **church of Koímisis Theotókou▶▶** contains some remarkable and well-preserved 17th-century frescoes, unusual in that they are like cartoon-strip versions of Old Testament stories, extending all over the church.

▶▶ Eleoússa   163B3

The monastery of Eleoússa, on the slopes of the Profítis Ilías ridge, has been taken over by the military, but happily the nearby **church of Ágios Nikólaos Fountoúki▶▶** (St. Nicholas of the Hazelnuts) is still open to the public. This Byzantine church, in the shape of a perfect Greek cross, has fine Cretan-style frescoes from the 13th to the 15th centuries. Surrounded by lovely pine woods and commanding great views, it is a favourite weekend picnic spot for locals. Several dirt tracks lead to the summit of Profítis Ilías, where an almost-abandoned Italian summer station lies hidden in the forest. It is possible to stay at the chalet hotel Elafos, about as close as you can get to Switzerland in the islands.

▶▶ Empónas   163B3

Empónas is a quiet traditional village in the heart of the wine-producing region of western Rhodes. A two-hour trail leads to the summit of the island's highest peak, Mount Attávyros (1,215m/3,985ft), from where the views stretch (on a clear day) as far as Crete. The village is also known for its fine folk dances: in summer, daily folk-dance tours arrive from Rhodes Town.

▶▶▶ Eptá Pigés (Seven Springs)   163C3

Open: Apr–Nov daily 9–6. Admission charge
Buses: Rhodes Town–Kolýmpia, several daily
This lovely oasis, one of the island's most popular beauty spots, can be reached by a fine 3km (2-mile) walk from Kolýmpia. There is a small man-made lake for a cool swim and a good taverna overlooking the stream.

▶ Faliráki   163C3

Faliráki has what many people want from Rhodes: a long sandy beach, every imaginable watersport facility and a nonstop exuberant nightlife. It is consequently very popular with the younger crowds. In summer the nightlife can be unbearable for those not participating, and in recent years some of the behaviour has even turned criminal. Nostalgics will find nearby **Kalithéa▶** more to their taste. The Italians built this spa town in the 1920s in pure Hollywood style. Today it is dilapidated and almost completely abandoned.

▶▶ Ialyssós 163C3

Open: Tue–Sun 8–5. Admission charge
Tourist developments on the approach to Ialyssós do little to honour the past of this once important city, one of the three powerful city-states (with Líndos and Kameíros) which together founded, in 408BC, a new common capital, Rhodes. Very little remains of the Classical site at Ialyssós, but the view over Rhodes harbour and the sea to the north, south and west explains its strategic importance. The Knights, who began their invasion of the island here, built the Church of Our Lady of Filérimos as a military bastion, beside and on top of the vestiges of a 3rd-century BC **Temple of Athena▶**. On the walk down from the temple there is a fine 4th-century BC fountain. The Italians built their **monastery of Filérimos▶** on the same site.

Kameíros (below) united in the 5th century BC with Líndos and Ialyssós to found the powerful state of Rhodes

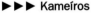

▶▶▶ Kameíros 163B3

Open: Tue–Sun 8–5 (8.30–3 in winter). Admission charge
Two morning buses from Bus Station, Rhodes Town
One of the best-preserved Classical Greek towns, set on a beautiful hillside above the sea, Kameíros lay forgotten under the dust until it was rediscovered in 1859. Once a large and important city, tracing its origins back into pre-historic times, the site was inhabited until the 4th century, when it was abandoned; this has undoubtedly contributed to its remarkable state of preservation.

The upper part of the site was probably used for religious rituals and the two water basins that supplied the city are still visible. The lower valley has clearly distinguishable foundations of houses, streets, temples and an *agora*, which give a good impression of what the city must have looked like.

Finds from Kameíros are on display in the Archaeological Museum in Rhodes Town (see page 162) and also in London's British Museum.

WINE ON RHODES
The house of Emery, one of the leading winemakers on Rhodes, produce their much appreciated Villare wine in Empónas, the island's main wine-growing area. Most vineyards are exclusively planted with the Athiri grape, which is indigenous to the area and has proved difficult to transplant. The Emery Winery at Empónas offers free tasting as well as an opportunity to purchase direct from the producer (tel: 22460 41208; www.emery.gr. *Open* Mon–Fri until 3pm).

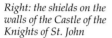

For 200 years, the Knights of St. John ruled Rhodes as their private domain, making its name famous throughout the Mediterranean for the strength of its defences and the advancement of its society, and making its harbour one of the most important gateways to the East.

Right: the shields on the walls of the Castle of the Knights of St. John

MAINTAINING ORDER
Five years after losing Rhodes to the Turks, the Knights were given Malta by the Emperor Charles V. When Malta was taken by Napoleon Bonaparte in 1798, the Knights practically ceased to exist. They have, however, survived in Rome in much reduced circumstances and in Britain, mainly as the St. John Ambulance Association which has a charter to carry out ambulance and other charitable work, not so very different from the original hospital duties the Knights carried out in 11th-century Jerusalem.

One of the gates into the walled medieval city of Rhodes

The Order of St. John In 1099, when the Crusaders captured Jerusalem from the Seljuk Turks, the Knights Hospitallers of St. John, originally a militaristic, religious order, became responsible for running the city's hospital for sick Christian pilgrims. In 1290, after 200 turbulent years, the Crusaders were finally forced out of the Holy Land. The Knights Hospitallers fought to the end but when Acre fell to the Mamluks from Cairo, even the Knights were obliged to flee. In 1309 they captured the city of Rhodes and, soon after, some neighbouring islands. Until 1522 they controlled what was to all intents and purposes, an independent state.

The order of the Order The most obvious characteristic of the Order was its rigid hierarchy. Members of the lowest level of the Order were known as sergeants. The sons of freemen, they helped the Knights to run and defend their small empire and to look after the sick and needy. Above them were the Chaplains—the priests of the Order—and higher still were the Knights, drawn from the ranks of Europe's aristocracy and responsible for all administrative and military matters.

The Knights' Tongues Members of the Order were divided according to nationality as well as rank. There were seven 'Tongues' (referring to the languages spoken) at the outset: Provence, Auvergne, France, Italy, Aragon, England and Germany. Castile was admitted in the 15th century. The leaders of the Tongues sat on the Council, headed by the Grand Master. As supreme ruler of Rhodes, elected for life, he held great power, for the Order controlled not only Rhodes and most of the Dodecanese but also large estates across Europe.

Life on Rhodes Under the Knights, Rhodes became rich, shipping and trading imported perfumes, spices, wool and silk, oil and wine as well the island's products, mostly sugar and soap. The Knights also looked after transport and their fleet protected the sea passages as well as carrying merchandise. Rhodes under the Knights was also an important conduit for knowledge and culture: everything from the study of history to the painting of icons was encouraged.

The siege Rhodes thrived for as long as the Knights controlled the sea passages essential for trade, but throughout the 15th century the shadow of the Turks grew longer. After 1453, when Constantinople fell to the Turks, the Knights hurriedly strengthened their own fortifications. After many smaller skirmishes and attacks, on 23 May 1480, a Turkish fleet of 170 ships sailed to Rhodes, 100,000 soldiers disembarked and the city was besieged. After many fights, some within the fortifications, the Knights inflicted such losses on the Turks that the siege was lifted on 17 August and for some years the Knights were left alone. On 26 June 1522, a Turkish army of 100,000 again besieged the city. This time the Knights were less prepared: inside the town were fewer than 7,500 soldiers, only 290 of them Knights. The fighting was lengthy and bloody, but the Knights finally admitted defeat and negotiated a surrender with the Turkish Sultan Suleïman. On 1 January 1523, the Grand Master, the Knights and up to 5,000 islanders sailed out of Rhodes and into history.

The Knights' legacy There is no escaping the Knights, either in Rhodes Town or elsewhere: the great stone forts, churches and palaces are reminders of one of the island's most glorious periods. In the museums, collections of icons, manuscripts and other objects, for daily use and for special rituals, are an equally eloquent testimony to the Knights' cultural legacy.

The splendid courtyard in the Palace of the Grand Masters, reconstructed by the Italians as a summer home for Mussolini

THE KNIGHTS AND THE JEWS
Whatever social benefits the Order brought to Rhodes (and there were many), justice for minorities was not one of them. Subjugated from the beginning of the reign of the Knights, Jews were always considered a problem and on 9 January 1502 an edict was issued by the Order to provide a solution: Jews must either be baptized or leave the island within 40 days.

CHOOSING THE MASTER
When a Grand Master died, a commander was chosen by the Order. He had the right to name 13 electors, who then met to choose the new Grand Master.

Damp has damaged the 14th- and 15th-century frescoes in the monastery of Láerma, but they are still exquisite

ANCIENT LÍNDOS
Archaeologists have found remains showing that Líndos was already inhabited in the 3rd millennium BC. The city's importance grew as it became richer from its many colonies, the most important of which were Parthenope (Naples) and Gela in Sicily, founded in the 7th century BC. It was the only city on Rhodes with natural twin harbours. Cleobulos, its 6th-century BC ruler, was so enlightened that he was considered to be one of the Seven Sages, respected by all Greeks. After Rhodes Town gained importance, Líndos remained a religious centre and St. Paul is said to have stopped here on his way to Rome.

▶▶ **Kritiniá**   *163A3*

Near the quiet village of Kritiniá, founded by Cretans, towers an impressive fortress built by the Knights. On closer inspection, the **kástro** is only a shell but still worth a visit as its masonry is quite intact and the fantastic views explain its strategic importance. Not far away is the striking village of **Siána** in the middle of the forest, famous for its local alcoholic brew called *souma* and for its sage honey. **Monólithos**, the main village in the area, takes its name from the 250m-high (820ft) single rock on which a Crusader castle is dramatically perched.

▶▶ **Láerma**   *163B2*

The **church of Ágios Giórgios**▶ in Láerma has some 14th-century frescoes, but it is for the **Thári monastery**▶▶ that most visitors make their way here. This is the oldest monastery on the island, although its community was only recently reestablished, by a few monks from Pátmos. The fine frescoes can be hard to make out, but they date from the 14th and 15th centuries. The monastery is said to have been founded after a princess, who had been kidnapped by pirates, had a visitation from the Archangel Gabriel. The princess promised the archangel that if he helped her out of her predicament, she would build as many monasteries in his honour as her gold ring, thrown from her hand, would make circles. As the princess lost her ring soon after being freed, her family built only this one monastery.

▶▶▶ **Líndos**   *163C2*

Líndos, Rhodes's second tourist attraction and the jewel in its crown, offers a unique view into the island's long history. Although the town's stunning beauty is protected as a National Monument, a lot of its atmosphere has been lost to commercialism—in summer it gets very crowded. The town has a Byzantine **church of Panagía Líndou**▶▶, with fine 18th-century frescoes and elegant well-preserved merchants' houses from the 15th to the 18th centuries, many of them restored for renting out to tourists.

Líndos was the most important of the three ancient cities of Rhodes and visitors still head first for the ancient **acropolis**▶▶▶ and the **Knights' castle**▶▶▶ (tel: 22440 31258. *Open* Tue–Sun 8–6, in summer; 8.30–2.45, in winter. *Admission charge*). All castles should look like this—imposing and impregnable, perched on a perfect rock and dwarfing the town in its shadow. The path leading up to the castle is lined with souvenir stalls and women selling handicrafts, but near the top is a podium carved in the rock which once supported a statue of a priest of Poseidon.

Farther on is a stoa of Athena Lindia, the patroness of the ancient city. Higher up, inside the fortress, the small 4th-century BC **Temple of Athena** is under scaffolding. The Knights recognized the excellent strategic position of the acropolis and built their citadel over it.

▶▶ Petaloúdes (Valley of the Butterflies)   *163C3*

Open: May–Sep daily 8.30–sunset. Admission charge
Morning buses from West Side bus station, Rhodes New Town
Visitors continue to flock to this thickly forested gorge covered with pine and storax trees. The resin of the storax tree, which smells like vanilla and is used to make frankincense, attracts millions of Quadrina 'butterflies'— actually Jersey tiger moths *(Panaxia quadripunctaria)*—to the valley in summer. The population of these black-and-white moths has seriously declined in recent years: the poor creatures are continually disturbed by hordes of visitors clapping their hands to make them fly up in a cloud exposing their red upper wing sections, so they can take that special souvenir photograph.

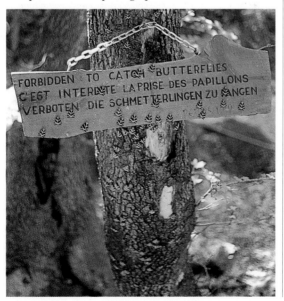

LÍNDOS POTTERY
Líndos is famous for its fine pottery, characterized by flower motifs in red against a green background. One legend has it that, seeing the city did not have a pottery, a Grand Master of the Knights captured a ship with Persian potters on board, and forced them to work in Líndos. Others believe that the plates are now merely copies of pottery that came from the Anatolian mainland. Whatever the truth of the story, some of the plates are truly exquisite.

171

REFLECTIONS ON RHODES
'In Rhodes the days drop as softly as fruit from trees. Some belong to the dazzling ages of Cleobolus and the tyrants, some to the gloomy Tiberius, some to the Crusaders. They follow each other in scales and modes too quickly almost to be captured in the nets of form.'
Lawrence Durrell, *Reflections on a Marine Venus* (London, 1953)

Petaloúdes is a popular family excursion and often nicknamed 'the Valley of the Tour Buses'

Drive

The stunning view over the Castle of Monólithos and the bay

The Knights' castles

This is a drive from Rhodes Town along the less-visited west coast to sites associated with the Knights of St. John. The route offers great coastal views, spectacular inland scenery and opportunities for bathing and sightseeing. (See the map on page 163. Up to around 200km (125 miles); allow a whole day.)

Leave Rhodes Town from Mantráki harbour and head south for **Ialyssós**►► (9km/5.5 miles, see page 167). Follow signs left to **Filérimos**► (5km/3 miles), a hilltop (267m/875ft) with wonderful views, ancient ruins, a Knights' church and a monastery. Return to Ialyssós and turn left, following the coast for 25km (15.5 miles) to Kaméíros. Turn left at the sign for **Ancient Kameíros**►►► (see page 167). Head south for 13km (8 miles), passing several exposed gravel beaches. Ignore the sign for 'Johnny's to the Beach' to reach the new access road to **Kritiniá Castle**►► (see page 170), a fine ruin with excellent views. Continue on the main road to Kritiniá (3.5km/2 miles) and follow signs for Empónas, then (3.5km/2 miles) for Siána on an older road through pine-clad hills. Some 5km (3 miles) later, a sign to **Glyfáda** beach gives no warning that it is 6km (4 miles) away, mostly on dirt track. The beach is minimal, but there is a 13th-century tower and an old-style taverna.

From the main road, continue to **Siána** (7km/4 miles), a quiet hill village noted for its sage honey sold by the roadside) and on to **Monólithos**► (5km/3 miles), whose ruined castle is built on a rock high above the sea, with views, on a clear day, to Chálki.

From here, either retrace the coast road back to Rhodes Town or continue south to Apolakkiá and cross to the east coast, making time to visit **Líndos**►►► (see pages 170–171), **Archángelos**► and Feráklos (see page 166).

▶ Tsampíka 163C3

The beach at Tsampíka is wonderful, but Greek visitors usually come here for the **Tsampíka monastery▶**. The small white Byzantine church comes alive on 8 September when women climb up to it, barefoot or on their knees, to pray for fertility. If their prayers are answered, the child may be called Tsambíkos or Tsambíka.

Go early if you want to be sure of a towel space on the long and sandy Rhodes Town beach

173

Beaches

Rhodes has excellent beaches and clean water. The sheltered east coast is the most popular, while the west offers good windsurfing. Between Rhodes Town and Líndos the coast is well developed and often crowded; most beaches are easily accessible by car or moped and often also by bus from either town. The beach of Rhodes Town is a large sandy stretch but becomes completely packed in the summer months, as does the beach in Faliráki, which draws a younger crowd. The best spot to swim near here is Ladikó, with its pebble beach. Tsampíka has an excellent beach which draws a lot of sunbathers but has no development going on. Agía Agáthi beach near Charáki is a small, secluded sandy beach which is lovely even in summer.

The sandy beach at Líndos always seems crowded and even the nearby coves, which are generally more pleasant, attract crowds. The coast south of Líndos might belong to a different island, its beaches more deserted, wilder and more beautiful. Gennádio is a long pebble beach with deserted stretches, while Plimíri is an attractive sheltered sandy bay. Ágios Geórgios has excellent bathing and fine sand but is difficult to reach. Akra (Cape) Prasonísi, practically an island, is a paradise for windsurfers and a lovely spot to camp.

There are fewer beaches on the west coast and they are usually very windy, with rocks rather than sand. The villages west of Rhodes Town were the first to be developed for package tourism: the coast here is completely built up and tends to attract an older clientele than the other resorts on the island. Monólithos and Apolakkiá, in the south, have good and secluded pebble beaches but the sea can often get rough.

CONNECTIONS

Rhodes has ferry services to Piréas, Kós, Kálymnos, Sými, Pátmos, Léros, Nísyros, Páros, Náxos, Tílos, Sýros, Crete, Kárpathos, Kásos, Kasteilórizo, Thíra, Chálki, Astypálaia, Mílos, Mýkonos, Folégandros, Tínos, Sífnos, Sérifos, Leipsoí, Síkinos, Thessaloníki, Cyprus and Haifa (Israel). Excursion boats go to Sými and Marmaris (Turkey) and in summer there are hydrofoil and catamaran services to Kós, Kálymnos, Sými, Nísyros, Léros, Kastellórizo, Pátmos, Tílos and Marmaris (Turkey).

USEFUL NUMBERS
Symi Tours (for tourist information)
tel: 22460 71307;
www.symivisitor.com
Tilos Travel (for tourist information)
tel: 22460 44294;
www.tilostravel.co.uk

POSTCARD SÝMI
The traditional well-kept houses of Sými are featured on many Greek postcards. The Sýmians are proud of their many ornate churches and grand mansions, proof of the island's prosperity at the end of the 19th century. Sými is under the same archaeological decree as Pátmos and Líndos, by which the restoration of old buildings and the construction of new ones is carefully regulated. Developers, together with foreign tour operators, have restored some old houses and the island is now popular with wealthy Athenians and smaller tour groups trying to avoid the crowds.

SÝMI
This small and rugged island just off the Turkish coast has a lot to offer independent travellers: well-preserved villages, good beaches and, most of all, a peaceful countryside with good walking trails.

▶▶ Sými Town   145C3
The island's capital is, like many other port towns, divided in two: Gialós, the harbour and port of arrival and Chorió, the older town on top of the hill. Once the excursion boats have left Gialós the town becomes a tranquil place again, with several beautiful neoclassical mansions and a few shipbuilding yards, reminders of Sými's illustrious past, as a prosperous trading and sponge-fishing port. Recent years have seen many buildings restored and a thriving tourist industry established. The **Naval Museum▶** (*Open* Tue–Sun 10–2. *Admission charge*) in the port has some great wooden models of the ships that used to be built here.

Two huge stairways, the Kalí Stráta and Kataráktes, go up to Chorió, whose attractive houses are almost Cycladic in style. The **museum▶▶** (*Open* Tue–Sun 10–2. *Admission charge*), housed in one of the old mansions, has good exhibits from medieval Sými and frescoes from local churches. On top of the village is the **Castle of the Knights▶**, built over the ancient acropolis and the lovely **church of the Panagía▶▶** (*Open* only during services, 7–8am daily and Sun morning), which has the best frescoes on the island.

▶▶▶ Taxiárchis Michaíl
Panormítis Monastery   145C3
The principal 'sight' for visitors to Sými (and usually the first stop for excursion boats) is the vast **Panormítis monastery▶** (*Open* daily 9–2 and 4–8). Very few of its treasures survived the pillaging of World War II, but the courtyard, a galleried cloister, is the most appealing part. Rooms are available for those who want to stay overnight

Until the beginning of the 20th century, when the Kalymniots took over the sponge diving, Sými Town was wealthier and bigger than Rhodes Town

ELEPHANTS ON AN ISLAND
Archaeologists working on Tílos found a burial pit near Livádia containing the bones of what is believed to have been a herd of small mammoths (some of the bones are in the small museum in Megálo Chorió). Local historians find in this the proof that all of these small Dodecanese islands were attached to the Anatolian mainland in pre-history.

WALKS ON SÝMI
There are lots of lovely walks on Sými: the one from Gialós to Kefálos passes five monasteries. A dirt road past the monastery of Panormítis leads to the monastery of Ágioi Anárgyroi and then past a hill to Ágios Ioánnis Theológos. From there a path goes to Ágios Filomónos and on to Ágios Emiliános near Kefálos (allow 6 hours to walk there and back).

An English guide organizes walking tours locally. For more information contact Sými Tours (see USEFUL NUMBERS, opposite or check the symi visitor website).

CONNECTIONS
Sými and Tílos have ferry links with each other and also with Rhodes, Kós, Kálymnos, Nísyros, Kastellórizo, Léros, Pátmos, Leipsoí, Páros and Piréas. In addition, Sými has ferries to Crete, Sámos and Arkói, while Tílos is linked with Sýros and Náxos. In summer, hydrofoil and catamaran services operate between the two islands and go from both to Rhodes, Kálymnos, Kós and Nísyros.

(only one monk is now in residence). The small museum has an eclectic collection of exhibits, from a stuffed koala bear to models of ships.

Beaches
The nearest swimming to Sými Town is at the rocky beach of Nós or, slightly farther away but more attractive, the pebble beach of Emporeió. On the other side of the town is Sými's only sandy beach, at Ágios Nikólaos, which has a taverna. More secluded but beautiful coves in the south, like Maratoúnda, Nanoú and Ágios Giórgios Dissálona, can only be reached by taxi-boats or after a serious hike. The best beach, accessible only on foot, is Ágios Vassílios.

TÍLOS
Tílos, the least visited of the Dodecanese, is a small, remote and delightful island, the perfect place to get away from it all. The fertile landscape, crisscrossed by many old mule tracks, makes Tílos a pleasure for walkers.

▶ Livádia   144B2
Livádia, Tílos's minuscule harbour, has a few tavernas, hotels and rooms for rent. The only road on the island leads from here to Megálo Chorió, 7km (4 miles) away, but the bus is erratic. The road passes **Mikró Chorió**, the remains of a ghost village abandoned in the 1950s.

Megálo Chorió   144B3
Megálo Chorió, the island's second village, has the interesting **church of Taxiárchi Michaílis**, preserving a wall of the classical temple over which it was built. A Venetian castle looms very high on a rock over the town.

Beaches
Livádia has a long rocky beach; also good are Erestos, lost in orchards and gardens and the isolated Pláka.

THE IONIAN ISLANDS The Ionian Islands run down the western coast of Greece with Corfu (Kérkyra), in the north, facing Albania, and Kýthira, the most southerly, some distance away from the others, off the Peloponnese. Known to Greeks as the Eptanísi (seven islands), after the principal islands (Corfu, Paxoí, Lefkáda, Kefalloniá, Itháki, Zákynthos and Kýthira), the Ionians, with the exception of Kýthira, are united by a common history and culture. Since they stand in the southern Adriatic, in many of their towns everything from architecture to food has been influenced by the Italians. Heavier rainfall makes the islands green and fertile, and agriculture still plays its part in island life, along with fishing and transport. Tourism, of course, has an increasingly large role; several islands, most noticeably Corfu and Zákynthos, have become major international tourist destinations.

MYTHOLOGY AND EARLY HISTORY The Ionian Islands have a rich history, with early Kefallonian remains dating back to prehistoric times. The islands' earliest chronicle is

The Ionian Islands
Itháki (ΙΘΑΚΗ)
Kefalloniá
   (ΚΕΦΑΛΟΝΙΑ)
Kérkyra (Corfu)
   (ΚΕΡΚΨΡΑ)
Kýthira (ΚΥΘΗΡΑ)
Lefkáda (ΛΕΦΚΑΔΑ)
Paxoí (ΠΑΞΟΙ) and
   Antipaxoí
   (ΑΝΤΙΠΑΞΟΙ)
Zákynthos (Zánte)
   (ΖΑΚΨΝΘΟΣ)

BEST BEACHES
● Cove below the Arethoúsa Fountain (Itháki)
● Mírtos (Kefalloniá)
● Myrtiótissa (Corfu)
● Porto Katsíki (Lefkáda)
● Porto Róma (Zákynthos)
● Antipaxoí

178

INTER-ISLAND CONNECTIONS
Because so many visitors arrive on direct charter flights or on ferries from Italy, it can be frustratingly difficult to move between the islands, so island hopping, especially out of season, often involves delays and doubling-back or travelling via a mainland port.

Pages 176–177: the pure transparent water and the secluded bays of Palaiokastrítsa on Corfu are as attractive as ever
Page 176: Kýthira's unspoiled beauty and Greek atmosphere are enough of a reason for a visit

Right: a tiny islet near Corfu's airport

Homer's *Odyssey*, based on the life of Odysseus, a 12th-century BC ruler of Itháki. Odysseus, according to the poet, went to fight against Troy with men from Itháki and Kefalloniá. Corfu was the home of the renowned King Alcinoös, while Kýthira is claimed as the place where the goddess of love, Aphrodite, rose from the waves. There are remains from the Mycenaean (Bronze Age) period (*c*1600–1100BC) at sites and in museums scattered throughout the islands.

The Ionians' next prominent moment came in 664BC, when galleys from Corinth and Corfu fought the first recorded sea battle. In the 5th century BC, fighting that started between these two adversaries spread to include Athens and Sparta in the Peloponnesian Wars, at the end of which Athens's power was fatally diminished. In 31BC the islanders witnessed another great moment in history, when Octavian (thereafter the Emperor Augustus) defeated the fleets of Mark Antony and Cleopatra at Actium, just north of Lefkáda.

The rule of Venice From the end of the Roman era to the 13th century AD, the Ionian Islands fell under Byzantine rule. When Constantinople fell to the Fourth Crusaders, the islands came under Venetian control, although the Italian Orsini family initially held only the islands of Kefalloniá, Lefkáda, Itháki, and Zákynthos. Corfu suffered under the Greek Despots of Epirus until 1386, when the Venetians took the island by force. The Venetians remained in control of the Eptanísi for more than four centuries and made a vital contribution to the character of the islands. The fact that they were only briefly under Turkish control also distinguishes the Ionians from other islands in the Greek seas.

The Ionian state At the beginning of the 19th century the three 'Great Powers'—Britain, France and Russia—took an interest in the Ionian Islands. Napoleon Bonaparte assumed control of them when he conquered Venice in 1797, and a treaty between Russia and Turkey bundled the islands into a short-lived republic in 1799. By 1815 the British had captured all of the islands and created an independent state under British protection and 'guided' by a British High Commissioner, based in Corfu Town. As much of the rest of Greece won its independence, so the

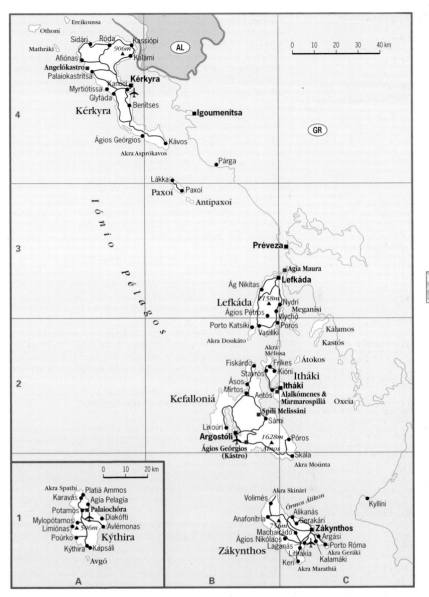

Ionian islanders struggled to be free. In 1864 the British finally agreed to unite the islands with the Greek state.

An Ionian character Of all the features that set the Ionian Islands apart from the rest of Greece, the landscape and architecture are probably the most noticeable. The lushness of the islands and their abundance of olives, fruits and flowers contrasts with many islands in the Aegean. Within the region, the music of Zákynthos, in particular its ballads or *arékias*, the earthquake-proof houses of Lefkáda, the Homeric traditions of the Ithakans and the cosmopolitan inheritance of Corfu are all distinctive.

THE IONIAN INHERITANCE
The word 'Ionian' has many applications. It is applied to one of the three orders of Greek architecture; to a mode in ancient Greek music regarded as soft or gentle; to a school of philosophy, founded by Thales of Miletus; and to a measure in poetic verse.

USEFUL NUMBER
Port Authority (Itháki
Town) tel: 26740 32209;
www.ithacagreece.com

**WHERE HAVE ALL THE
PEOPLE GONE?**
In 1939, over 15,000 peo-
ple lived on Itháki; there
are now around 3,000.
Mass emigration, particu-
larly after the war and the
1953 earthquake, has left
some villages, like Exoghí
and Anoghí, almost aban-
doned. But Ithakan exiles
(12,000 in Melbourne,
2,500 in Johannesburg)
maintain an interest in
their homeland and send
money to keep up houses
and churches.

ITHAKI
'...Keep Ithaka always in
your mind.
Arriving there is what
you're destined for.
But don't hurry the jour-
ney at all.
Better if it lasts for years,
so you're old by the time
you reach the island,
wealthy with all you've
gained on the way,
not expecting Ithaka to
make you rich.
Ithaka gave you the mar-
vellous journey.
Without her you wouldn't
have set out.
She has nothing left to
give you now.
And if you find her poor,
Ithaka won't have fooled
you.
Wise as you will have
become, so full of experience,
you'll have understood by
then what these Ithakas
mean.'
From Constantine Cavafy,
'Ithaka' (1911).

CONNECTIONS
Itháki has ferry links with
Kefalloniá and Pátra (from
Itháki Town) and with
Lefkáda and Kefalloniá
(from Fríkes and Píso
Aetrós respectively).

ITHÁKI

Rocky severe Itháki, Homer called it. The probable homeland of the hero Odysseus is a rugged island of two
distinct peninsulas joined by a narrow, hilly isthmus.
Some visitors come here in search of Odysseus and yachts-
men arrive to seek out its many coves and harbours, but
Itháki has been spared the worst excesses of the tourist
industry, as seen on nearby Zákynthos.

▶▶ Itháki Town (Váthi)   179C2

Badly damaged in the 1953 earthquake, the island's capital
has retained few mementoes of its past, but it is splendidly
sited on a huge, sheltered bay entirely enclosed by hills
and is still a place of some elegance.
  Of most interest is the **Archaeological Museum▶▶**
(Odós Kallinikó 30, tel: 26740 32200. *Open* Tue–Sun 8.30–3.
Admission charge), where finds from local digs include
items from Epáno Aetós and Polí Bay. Odysseus-seekers
should look at item No. 814, a bronze statue of the heroic
wanderer.

▶▶ Alalkómenes   179B2

The famous 19th-century German archaeologist Heinrich
Schliemann (see pages 86–87) came to the slopes of Mount
Aetós after finding Troy and believed this to be the site of
Odysseus' palace, but the British School in Athens dug in
the 1930s and could find nothing to support the theory.
Archaeologists resumed digging in 1984 and have since
found evidence of an important settlement going back to
1400BC, but none of the 250,000 artefacts so far uncovered
mention Odysseus.

▶ Marmarospiliá (Cave of the Nymphs)   179B2

Currently closed for excavation
Local legend claims this cave, half an hour's walk from the
capital, was the hiding place for Odysseus' treasure. It was
certainly an ancient shrine, as suggested by the 60cm-high
(24in) base on which a cult statue once stood and by the
hole in the roof, claimed to be a chimney for the smoke
from sacrificial burnt offerings.

▶ Stavrós   179B2

The main town in the north of the island has a small but
excellent **Archaeological Museum▶▶** (*Open* Tue–Sun
9.30–2.30. *Admission free*) showing objects from excavations at nearby Polí Bay and Pelikáta, another possible site
for Odysseus' palace, which fits Homer's description
'between three mountains and overlooking three seas.' On
display is a terracotta mask engraved 'Dedicated to
Odysseus', one of the few pieces of archaeological evidence for a connection between Odysseus and Itháki, his
reputed home.

Beaches

The sandy and pebble beach at Filiátro is accessible
by boat from Itháki. The cove below the Arethoúsa
Fountain (see Walk opposite) is idyllic. In the north,
Polí Bay has rocky swimming, but access is easier (and
there are more facilities) at Fríkes and Kióni, both
attractively situated little ports with a few low-key tourist
developments.

Walk

Walk across the south of Itháki to the **Arethoúsa Fountain►►**, where Odysseus met his swineherd Eumaus. The English poet Lord Byron thought that this walk alone was worth the journey to Itháki. There are no facilities *en route*, so take food, water and suitable clothing (approximately 6km/4 miles; allow 2 hours).

The road to the Arethoúsa Fountain is signposted on the waterfront in Itháki Town, near the Yacht Club. The town is soon left behind as the dirt road leads into a valley of olive groves. After 15 minutes or so the road splits, but the Arethoúsa path is still signposted. It is easy to imagine

The Arethoúsa Fountain

Odysseus or Telemachus hurrying into town along a path like this, between vines, olive and fig trees. Another 40 minutes of gentle climbing gives wonderful views back to Itháki's bay. Then a signposted track leads down the hill to the sea. The Arethoúsa Fountain, as Homer describes it, beneath the rock of Korax (the Raven), gives some shade and, usually, clean water. Continue down the path to the lovely cove below for a welcome swim.

181

Walk

Sites associated with Odysseus are the theme of this walk in northern Itháki, crossing the island from east to west (5.5km/3.5 miles; allow 2 hours).

Leaving Fríkes waterfront at the northern end, a road leads up the fertile valley to Láchos. At the next village, Platrithias, a right turn after the playground leads to the (unmarked) archaeological site known locally as 'Homer's School' (although there is no evidence that Homer visited Itháki). The most easily identified ruins belong to the Byzantine church of St. Athanasius.

Continuing along the main road towards Stavrós, another right turn leads 2km (1.2 miles) up to Exogí, a remote village with excellent views from its bell tower. Further on the main road, a left turn on Odós Aredátis leads to Stavrós' **Archaeological Museum►►** while the next left turn leads to the ongoing excavations at Pelikáta (see under Stavrós, opposite). A few minutes further brings you to **Stavrós►** (shops and cafés) and another road back downhill to Fríkes.

Fríkes to Stavrós

Top right: follow the Odysseus trail!
Above: the small port of Fríkes on the northeastern coast

Of all the great stories that have survived from antiquity, Homer's Odyssey *is among the most popular. While the* Iliad *tells us much about Greek warfare, the* Odyssey *provides an insight into Greek society. And as if that were not enough, it is also a great story.*

182

ODYSSEUS ON ITHAKI
'My home is Ithaca, that bright conspicuous isle, with Mount Neriton rising clear out of the quivering forests. Round it lie many islands clustering close, Dulichion and Samê and woody Zacynthos. My island lies low, last of all in the sea to westwards, the others away towards the dawn and the rising sun. It is rough, but a nurse of good lads; I tell you there is no sweeter sight any man can see than his own country.'
Homer, *Odyssey* Book IX

Homer, whose epics continue to confuse scholars: are they fact or fiction?

Odysseus In the *Iliad* (see pages 240–241), Homer describes the events of the Trojan War, in which an alliance of Greeks, among them Odysseus, the king of Itháki, set out to avenge the kidnapping of Helen by the Trojan prince Paris. Odysseus, Homer tells us, is 'never at a loss' and it is he who devises the wooden horse, which ultimately leads to the downfall of Troy. After Troy is sacked, the army disperses. But Odysseus' trials are not over yet, for he blinds a Cyclops, the son of the sea god Poseidon and the god is determined to punish him.

Travels and homecoming Poseidon is determined that Odysseus shall not reach his home. After wandering for many years throughout the Mediterranean (some say he even crossed the Atlantic), Odysseus is trapped on an island (perhaps Corfu) by the nymph Calypso until his ally, the goddess Athena, forces the great god Zeus to intervene and Odysseus is released. But Poseidon has not finished with him. Next there is shipwreck and seduction, while at Odysseus' palace on Itháki his faithful wife Penelope is being courted by 108 eligible men from the islands: while she stalls, they slowly eat away at Odysseus' wealth. But with Athena's help Odysseus does return home, bringing with him enough treasure to restore the family's fortunes. Arriving in his house in disguise, Odysseus and his son Telemachus take their revenge on Penelope's suitors, killing every one of them.

Homer Little is known about the poet called Homer, but this has not deterred speculation ever since the 2nd-century Greek historian Herodotus wrote Homer's biography. Homer is believed to have lived around 800BC, 400 years after Odysseus. Where he came from is not known, though several islands, including Itháki and Chíos, now claim him. His name is said to mean 'cannot see', from which comes the tradition that he was a blind poet. Not that his eyes would have helped him in telling the story, for in Homer's time epics like this were consigned to memory. It would not have been written down until several centuries after his death, perhaps in Alexandria or another centre of learning.

But is it true? Unlike the story of the *Iliad*, which is supported to some extent by excavations at Troy, the story of Odysseus' 20-year journey home is not borne out by archaeology. He is believed to have reached Itháki in 1174BC, but so far, although artefacts bearing the name of Odysseus have been found, suggesting that he was worshipped on Itháki long after his death, no physical evidence has yet been uncovered to prove the events that Homer describes. Professor Sarantis Symeonoglou of Washington University, St. Louis, Missouri, who has been digging on Itháki since 1984, explains it like this: 'There are those who believe Homer—and believe that this [Itháki] is the island he was talking about—and there are those who think it's all a myth. I believe in it. Of course I do....'

In the absence of proof... Until more tangible evidence for Odysseus' story comes to light, we only have Homer's text, as it has come down to us, to go by. Although there are inconsistencies and inaccuracies in describing the island—for instance, he calls Itháki the most exposed of its group of islands, whereas it is sheltered behind Kefalloniá—some experts point out that Homer was a storyteller, not a conscientious historian. Still, his description of the location of Odysseus' palace is exact enough, beneath three peaks and within sight of three seas, and both Alalkómenes near Váthi and Pelikáta near Stavrós fit that description.

CAVE OF NYMPHS
'[Here] is a beautiful dusky cave, sacred to the nymphs who are called Naiads. In the cave are great bowls and two-handled jars of stone and in these the bees hive their honey. There are also tall poles of stone like the beams of a loom, where the nymphs weave webs of sea-purple wonderful to behold...'
Homer, *Odyssey* Book VIII

183

Left: a precious early edition of Homer's masterpiece, the Odyssey

Below: Imprisoned by the Cyclops Polyphemus, Odysseus plies him with wine to get him drunk so he can engineer his escape

The west coast of Kefalloniá

USEFUL NUMBERS (ARGOSTÓLI)
Tourist information (by ferry docks, open Mon–Fri 8–2.30, in summer) tel: 26710 22248; www.kefalonia-greece.biz www.kefallonia.net.gr

KEFALLONIAN WINES
Notable among Kefalloniá's often excellent wines are those made by Nicholas Cosmetatos, whose family have been on the island for many centuries. His best-known wines are Gentilini and Gentilini Fumé.

THE RICHES OF NATURE
As well as thyme-scented honey, quince jelly and rabbit stew, Kefalloniá is famous for its ewe's milk feta cheese, which is put to good use in the local speciality *riganata*, where it is mixed with bread, oil and oregano.

KEFALLONIÁ

The 1953 earthquake hit Kefalloniá, the largest of the Ionian Islands, particularly badly, devastating most of the towns and villages and reducing to rubble many beautiful Venetian buildings. Their modern replacements may sometimes lack character, but it could partly be this—and partly the infrequency of international flights—that has saved the island from mass tourism. As a result, it has preserved much of its beauty and its people (despite their reputation for being insular) can be more welcoming than those of the more frequently visited islands. Kefalloniá is a great place for walking: many Greeks come here in spring and autumn to do just that. A free leaflet, *Trails of Kefalloniá*, is widely available from the island's hotels and tourist agencies.

▶ Argostóli 179B2

Kefalloniá's main town was almost completely destroyed by the 1953 earthquake, but was rebuilt more or less according to the same plan. For more insight into 19th-century life on the island visit the **Historical and Cultural Museum▶▶▶** (tel: 26710 28835. *Open* Mon–Sat 9–2. *Admission charge*) at the Corgialénios Library (corner of Rokkoy Vérgoti and Ilia Zérvou). As well as costumes and antiques, there are photographs of Kefalloniá before and just after the earthquake. The **Archaeological Museum▶** on Odós R. Vergotí (*Open* Tue–Sun 8.30–3. *Admission charge*) has a good collection of finds from the island. For a look at modern life take an excursion to Argostóli's beach resort, Lássi, which has a good but crowded beach: unless you are staying there, a glimpse may be enough.

▶▶▶ Ásos 179B2

The ancient Greeks built a stronghold on this rocky promontory, joined to the island by a small causeway and successive conquerors have added to it. The present castle, so spectacular when seen from the approach road, is

Venetian, built in the 16th century, its ruined interior converted into a park. The drive to Ásos, particularly the section from Angónas onwards, is among the most beautiful on the islands.

►►► Fiskárdo   179B2
A lovely fishing town which escaped relatively undamaged from the 1953 earthquake, Fiskárdo is one of Kefalloniá's main tourist attractions, so hotels and restaurants are more expensive. Still, it is worth making the trip north to see the 18th-century houses and to imagine how the rest of the island must have looked before the disaster.

►► Kástro (Ágios Geórgios)   179B2
The Venetian capital of Kefalloniá, with its looming castle of Ágios Geórgios, was a sizeable town until it was wrecked by a 17th-century earthquake. Its ruins still look good and the English poet Lord Byron is said to have waxed lyrical about the views from the castle (*Open* Tue–Sat 8–8, Sun 8–2, Jun–Oct. *Admission charge*), which was built over an earlier Byzantine fort. Under British rule, the terrible dungeons beneath the inner fort were used as a prison for Kefallonians of liberal persuasion.

To the southeast of Kástro, Lourdas has an excellent sandy beach backed by lovely walking country. Archipelagos, an environmental protection organization supported by the World Wide Fund for Nature, has laid out a beautiful and environmentally friendly trail along the coast here, involving about two hours of easy walking.

►► Sámi   179B2
The east-coast town of Samí, the island's main port, was also flattened by the earthquake. It's a working port, but the waterfront's many cafés and restaurants cater mainly for tourists. The town's main claim to fame is that it was used as a location in the film *Captain Corelli's Mandolin*. Samí works well as a centre for visiting the nearby Drogaráti and Melissáni caves. In the hills immediately above the modern port lie the ruins of ancient Sámi, the capital in Homer's time, destroyed by the Romans after a long siege. From Karavomílos beach, 2km (1.2 miles) north of Sámi, boats leave for the **Spiliá Melissáni (Melissáni cave)►►** (*Open* daily 8–8; 10–4 in winter. *Admission charge*). Here an underground saltwater lake is fed by water from the other side of the island near Argostóli. A hole in the cave roof lets in sunlight which brings out beautiful shades of blue and violet from the water. A short ride from Sámi is the equally extraordinary **Drogaráti cave►►** (*Open* daily summer only 8–8), with yellow and orange stalactites. One of its chambers has excellent acoustics and was used for concerts, most famously one given by the diva Maria Callas.

Beaches
Kefalloniá has many wonderful beaches. Best of all is the dramatic, white-stone Mírtos, with clean white sand and turquoise waters. Farther north, Ásos is picturesque. Andisámos is quiet; the more developed Plátis Giálos, Póros and Skála in the south are still enjoyable, while sandy Potomákia beach, near Skála, is a breeding ground for loggerhead turtles, so access is forbidden at night.

In Markópoulo, locals claim that on 15 August, the Assumption of the Virgin, small, non-poisonous snakes with crosses on their heads slither towards the church

CONNECTIONS
Ferries run all year round from Argostóli and Póros to Kyllíni (Peloponnese), from Sámi to Itháki and Pátra and from Fiskárdo to Itháki and Lefkáda. There are additional summer sailings from Sámi to Paxoí, Igoumenítsa (Epirus) and Ancona (Italy) and from Pessáda and Argostóli to Zákynthnos. Hydrofoils link Póros with Itháki, Zákynthos and Pátra and there are summer services to Corfu, Paxoí and Lefkáda.

USEFUL NUMBER
Tourist Police
tel: 26610 30265;
www.kerkyra.gr
www.corfuonline.gr

KÉRKYRA (CORFU)

According to mythology, the sea god Poseidon fell in love with Corcyra, a daughter of the river-god Asopos and brought her to this island, which then took her name. Homer credited the islanders with being among the most civilized in the world, a view based on the story that, 3,000 years ago, when his hero Odysseus was washed up on the island, he received wonderful hospitality. In the last century the writers Lawrence and Gerald Durrell recorded a similar warmth among the islanders. Blessed with fertile land, an idyllic coastline and some fascinating architecture, Corfu is still a beautiful island, but rapid development means you must now choose your spot carefully.

The two forts of Corfu Town

PUBLISHED INFORMATION
Look for *The Corfiot* and the *Ionian Times*, both English-language papers.

ÁGIOS SPIRÍDON CELEBRATIONS
There are large celebrations at the church four times a year when the saint's relics are taken in procession around the city: on Orthodox Holy Saturday (to commemorate his help in averting a famine), on Palm Sunday and the first Sunday in November (to commemorate an end to plagues in 1629 and 1673) and on 11 August (to celebrate the defeat of a Turkish attack in 1716).

▶ ▶ ▶ **Kérkyra (Corfu Town)**   *187C4*

To understand Corfu history, step away from the arcades of Odós E. Voulgaréos or Odós N. Theotóki and head for the wonderfully atmospheric **Old Town**▶ ▶ ▶, known as the Campiello. You could be forgiven for thinking yourself in Italy. It is full of fascinating narrow streets and lanes, often linked by stone stairways, and the houses, now with peeling plaster, date from the Venetian period. The **church of Ágios Spirídon**▶ ▶, Corfu's patron saint, is cool and dark, full of shadows and incense, and is still a place of pilgrimage to this day. The remains of the saint, a 4th-century Bishop of Cyprus, were smuggled to Corfu from Istanbul, and are now contained in a silver-coated casket, to the right of the altar. The elaborate 17th-century **town hall**▶ ▶ (not open) enhances the sloping main square of the old town, where some of Corfu's most elegant restaurants are to be found.

It was the Venetians who created the **Spianada**▶ ▶ ▶ (Esplanade), the large open area which covered one third of the town's area, but the British developed it during the occupation. A reminder of that period can be seen in the cricket grounds and the bandstand of the **Maitland Rotunda**. The Frenchman De Lesseps, father of the engineer of the Suez Canal, built the arcaded Maitland area, with its elegant cafés, all still exuding an air of Parisian chic.

Continued on page 189.

From culture to cooking, many aspects of life in the Ionian Islands have been influenced by the country that faces the islands across the Adriatic. Not surprisingly, four centuries of Venetian rule have also left their mark on these islands and on their people.

THE NOBLE GRAPE
The Comoútos family were given the title of count by the Venetians, perhaps in appreciation of their wine. Their Zákynthos winery, founded in 1638 and still family-run, is now the oldest in production in Greece. While many Ionian wineries have closed in recent years, the Comoútos have improved the range and the style of their products.

188

IONIAN MURDERERS
'In habit they imitate the Italians, but transcend them in their revenges and infinitely lesse civill. They will threaten to kill a Merchant that will not buy their Commodities and make more conscience to breake a Fast, than to commit a Murther...He is weary of his life that hath a difference with any of them and will walke abroad after day-light.' George Sandys, an English traveller on Zákynthos (1610)

Venetian rule When Constantinople fell to the Crusaders in 1204, the Ionian Islands were given to various noble Venetian families to control. Corfu, however, was ruled by the Greek despots of Epirus. After the Venetians moved on Corfu, in 1386, they ruled all the Ionian Islands directly until the arrival of Napoleon Bonaparte in 1797.

The look Many Venetian buildings survive, but there were many more before 1953, when the islands were hit by disastrous earthquakes. Zákynthos Town was, until then, regarded as even more exceptional than Corfu Town. Still, churches, *kastri* and town houses survive throughout the Ionian Islands with an occasional coat of arms or Catholic motif as a reminder of the builder.

The sound Not having been colonized by the Turks, the Ionian islanders have an Italian-influenced musical tradition unique in Greece. *Kantádes* and the particular form known on Zákynthos as *arékias*, are ballads played on guitar and mandolin, with lyrics of a political, topical, or extremely personal (and sometimes sexual) nature being improvised.

The taste of Italy Traditional Ionian cooking shows Italian influence and is all the better for it, as in the Corfiot dish *pastitsatha*, which combines veal and pasta, or *mandolato*, a nougat from Zákynthos. The islanders also owe the quality of their wines, some of which are highly regarded, to the influence of the Italians.

The most atmospheric part of Corfu Town is Campiello, with its tiny alleyways and Venetian houses

Continued from page 186.

Beyond the bandstand is a statue of **Ioánnis Kapodístrias**, first president of modern Greece. At the top of the Spianada is the finest building of the British period, the neoclassical **palace of St. Michael and St. George**▶▶ (not open), former residence of the High Commissioner and seat of the Ionian Senate. It is partly occupied by a **Museum of Asian Art** (*Open* Tue–Sun 8.30–3. *Admission charge*). Next door is the **Municial Art Gallery**▶▶ (*Open* Tue–Sun 9–7. *Admission charge*) with a fine collection of Byzantine icons and works by local painters.

There was a fortified settlement on Cape Sidaro in ancient times but it was the Venetians who built the impressive **Old Fortress**▶▶▶ (*Open* daily 8.30–7, in summer; 8.30–3, in winter. *Admission charge*), which has wonderful views from its highest point. The fort's British-built Church of St. George is now used as an exhibition centre and a nearby café serves refreshments.

Following the road past the British palace, Odós Arseníou rounds the headland towards the new port. Steps off it lead to the **Antivouniotissa Byzantine Museum**▶▶▶ (*Open* Tue–Sun 9–3. *Admission charge*), a collection of rare icons housed in a late 15th-century church with an extraordinary carved-wood ceiling.

The modern port is dominated by the **New Fortress**▶▶ (*Open* daily 9–9. *Admission charge*), also built by the Venetians and now used as a base by the Greek navy.

The **Archaeological Museum**▶▶, to the south of the Spianada (5 Odós Vraila. *Open* Tue–Sun 8.30–3. *Admission charge*), has some spectacular antiquities including the famous Gorgon Pediment, found near Kanóni, a 7th-century BC stone lion, a clay head of Artemis (6th–5th century BC) and a 1st-century BC marble head of the poet Meander.

▶ Achileío (Achilleion Palace)   187B3

A must if you love kitsch, the palace was built in 1890 for the Empress Elizabeth of Austria, popularly known as 'Sissi'. Her enthusiasm for Homer led her to fill the place with second-rate neoclassical sculpture. The gardens, however, are beautiful. The palace is open as a museum by day (*Open* daily 9–7, in summer; 9–2.30, rest of year. *Admission charge*) and becomes a casino at night.

The Austrian Empress 'Sissi' named the Achileío (above) after her hero Achilles, whom she identified with her son Rudolph

CYCLING
An alternative to hiring a car or motorcycle is to cycle on Corfu. Several companies rent bicycles to help escape the crowds and explore the island.

COLONIAL TASTE
The ghosts of Corfu's colonial past seem to congregate around the Spianada, especially when cricket is being played. To enjoy the experience to the full, sit at one of the tables under the mature trees and order a *tzntzi* (ginger beer), a tasty relic of the days of British occupation.

MON REPOS PALACE
Prince Philip, the Duke of Edinburgh, was born in this villa, the former residence of the British Commissioner for the Ionian Islands. It now houses the Palaeopolis Museum (Kanoni Peninsula, *open* Tue–Sun 8.30–7.30, in summer; until 3, in winter; *Admission charge*), with a mixed collection of botanical, historical and archaeological interest.

Ionian Islands

DURRELL'S KALAMI HOUSE

'A white house set like a dice on a rock already venerable with the scars of wind and water. The hill runs clear up into the sky behind it, so that the cypresses and olives overhang this room in which I sit and write. We are upon a bare promontory with its beautiful clean surface of metamorphic stone covered in olive and ilex: in the shape of a *mons pubis*. This is become our unregretted home. A world. Corcyra.'
Lawrence Durrell, *Prospero's Cell* (London, 1945/1962)

190

As you often see in Greece, the summit of Mount Pantokrátoras is graced with a lovely church

CORFU CLICHÉ

One of the most familiar images of Corfu is of the two islets off the south of Kanóni, on one of which stands the Vlachérne Convent, linked to the mainland by a causeway, while on the other the 12th-century church of the Pantokrator is surrounded by greenery (and, in season, by visitors).

OLIVES

There are 3 to 4 million olive trees on Corfu, covering 30 per cent of the island. Corfiots have cultivated the olive for 5,000 years, but do so by letting the olives fall to the ground naturally. They also do not prune their trees. The result is that they have some of the largest trees in Greece.

▶▶▶ Ermónes, Myrtiótissa, and Glyfáda   *187A4/B4*

A rival to Palaiokastrítsa as a possible site for King Alcinoös' palace (see panel opposite), cliffside Ermónes has a pebble beach and notoriously cold water due to nearby streams. Myrtiótissa beach, accessible only on foot, is one of the island's most beautiful and secluded. Glyfáda is something less of a secret. Its wonderful beach caused a rush of construction, making it one of the island's larger resorts.

▶▶▶ Kalámi and Kouloúra   *187C5*

Kalámi is a must for Lawrence Durrell fans, for this is where he lived, as described in his book *Prospero's Cell* (see panel). Durrell's 'white house' is now rented out to visitors and has a taverna downstairs (tel: 26630 91040). The neighbouring cove of Kouloúra, thick with cypress and palm trees, has a pebble beach and great views of Albania. Most of this stretch of coast is beautiful but less developed than elsewhere and has clear water.

▶▶ Kanóni   *187B3*

The ancient settlement was based on the peninsula south of Corfu Town, but little remains. Some 3km (2 miles) from the town, **Mon Repos Palace▶▶** was built by British High Commissioner Sir Frederick Adam in 1831 and was at one time used as a retreat by the Greek royal family (*Open* daily 8–7. *Admission free.* See page 189). Opposite the palace gate is the site of the ancient *agora*. Nearby is one of Corfu's more interesting Byzantine churches, the 11th-century **Ágios Iassonos and Sosipáter▶▶**.

▶ Kassiópi 187C5

The pretty harbour at Kassiópi is used to invasion. Julius Caesar landed here in 31BC, Venetians later destroyed the fort and then the Turks came and massacred the population in 1537. Now the fishing community has been transformed into a resort town, though it has kept some of its village atmosphere. Remains of the Byzantine fortress stand on the hill behind the resort. There is swimming in the town, but the pebble beaches are a walk away.

▶ Kávos 187C1

No place to get away from it all, Kávos has become one of Greece's rave centres, suiting those who want to dance all night and sleep on the beach all day, without seeing Greece.

Close by, near Ákra (Cape) Asprókavos, the southernmost point of the island, lies the fortified **monastery of Arkoudíllas▶**, surrounded by beautiful landscape.

▶▶ Mount Pantokrátoras 187C5

Various rough tracks approach Corfu's highest mountain (906m/2,971ft): from the north, a road leads to Perítheia, a remote, partly deserted village, lovely in spring when blossom covers the trees. From the east coast, tracks leave from Kouloúra and Nisáki. The easiest way up is the track from the windswept inland village of Strinýlas. The view from the top (on a clear day) is stunning evidence of why Corfu is called the emerald island.

▶▶▶ Palaiokastrítsa 187A5

Tradition sets the ancient palace of King Alcinoös here, though no remains have been found. One of the most beautiful bays on Corfu (discovered by visitors long ago), Palaiokastrítsa has developed into a major resort. Off season, however, it makes a good base, offering excellent watersports facilities, including a rare chance to scuba-dive. **Theotókos monastery▶▶** (*Open* daily 7–1 and 3–8. *Admission free*), out on the edge of the bay, deserves a visit.

Palaiokastrítsa has been identified with Homer's Scheria, where Nausica took Odysseus to the palace of her father

KING ALCINOÖS' PALACE
'Round the courtyard, walls of bronze ran this way and that way...and upon them was a coping of blue enamel; golden doors and silver door-posts stood on a threshhold of bronze, with silver lintel and golden crowlatch. Golden and silver dogs were on either side, which Hephaistos had made by his clever brain to guard the mansion of proud Alcinoös...Within the hall were seats fixed along the wall on both sides, from the threshold right to the inner-end; and spread over these were soft coverings of fine-spun stuff which the women had made. There the leaders of the Phaiacians used to sit, eating and drinking, for they had plenty which never failed.'
Homer, *Odyssey* Book VII

Founded around 1225 and reconstructed in the 18th century, it has a good display of rare icons.

To the north, **Angelókastro▶▶** is a 13th-century castle built by the Byzantine despot Michael Angelos II. The fort looks formidable up on its rock—a half-hour walk from the nearest road—and proved so on many occasions. From Palaiokastrítsa you can rent small boats or canoes to explore the nearby caves and grottoes.

▶ Sidári
187A6

A lively town with shallow water and soft sand, Sidári is understandably popular as a family resort, but beautiful it is not. Hotels, shops and house rentals abound, but the main natural attraction is the sea-eroded rock formation, famous for its **Canal d'Amour**, a passage through which it is possible to swim and about which there are several traditions ensuring eternal love.

Beaches

Looking for an idyllic, empty stretch of sand on Corfu during the summer is a hopeless task, but the island does have some wonderful beaches. The northern half of the island is more developed: north from Corfu Town, developments are shoulder to shoulder for some distance. The north coast, from Kassiópi to the other side of Sidári, has a string of family-orientated resorts with sandy beaches and good bathing, but the land is largely featureless. Ágios Geórgios, in the northwest, is a large and lovely sandy bay, around which package tourism has created a village.

CONNECTIONS
Corfu Town has ferry links with Igoumenítsa, Pátra, Kefalloniá, Paxoí and Syvota; also with Italy (various parts).
There are summer hydrofoil and catamaran services to Paxoí, Lefkáda, Itháki and Kefalloniá. Excursion boats also run, in season, to the offshore islets of Ereíkoussa, Othoní and Mathráki.
Buses run to Athens (under 12 hours) from the terminal on Odós Solomoú in Corfu Town.
International ferries go to Brindisi, Bari and Venezia in Italy.

Tourism has taken over the stunning bay of Palaiokastrítsa in a big way

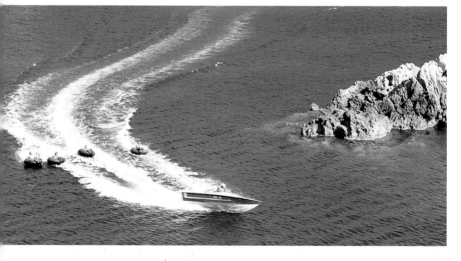

Palaiokastrítsa is the next in a string of excellent sandy beaches, including Glyfáda and Ágios Górdis, but they can be windy. Palaiokastrítsa has good watersports facilities. Ágios Geórgios, farther south (increasingly referred to as St. George South to distinguish it from the northern bay of the same name), has a fine beach backed by a vast array of package hotels. The east coast, which is more sheltered, has a medley of villages, resorts and mostly mediocre beaches which have been hideously developed, even to the end of the airport runway.

Drive

Palaiokastrítsa and Ágios Geórgios

A drive through the hills and cultivated valleys of northwestern Corfu, passing traditional villages and offering wonderful coastal and rural views. (About 40km/25 miles; allow 2 to 3 hours. See the map on page 187. The rough track between Prinýlas and Vístonas is not suitable for mopeds and bicycles.)

The road to Lákones climbs steeply out of **Palaiokastrítsa▶▶▶**, a beautiful bay with a number of hotels and restaurants. The hillside is covered with olive trees to Lákones. Beyond the picturesque village are several restaurants and tavernas competing for the best **views of Palaiokastrítsa▶▶▶**. Some 2km (1.2 miles) farther, in Makrádes, a right turn leads inland. Above the village is a fertile plain with vines and roadside shrines; 5km (3 miles) from Makrádes, ignore the left turn to Alimatádes and continue for 3km (2 miles) to the junction at

A view of the Byzantine fortress of Angelókastro, near Palaiokastrítsa. A path leads up to it from Krini

Troumbetás. Ignoring the road to Corfu Town, turn left towards Sidári and shortly follow signs right for a 2km (1.2-mile) detour to **Chorepískopoi▶▶**, as traditional as any village on Corfu can be. Back on the main road, follow signs to Págoi, along a **country road▶▶▶** through the villages of Arkadádes and Vatoníes. In **Págoi▶▶**, where you may see women wearing traditional costume and, in summer, herbs in their hair, veer right at the church. Immediately, there are signs to the sandy bay of **Ágios Geórgios▶▶**. If you have time, stop at the **Fisherman's Taverna** (tel: 69425 85550) at Ágios Geórgios for a delicious seafood lunch. Returning to the road out of Págoi, continue to Prinýlas, from where Palaiokastrítsa is signposted. The road beyond Prinýlas is unsurfaced but has **wonderful views▶▶▶** of Ágios Geórgios and Graviá island, said to be the ship that took Odysseus to Itháki, turned to stone by Poseidon. Turn right in Vístonas; return through Makrádes and Lákones to Palaiokastrítsa. (Alternatively take the left turn, east of Lákones, onto the main road for Corfu Town.)

Walk down the steep slopes of many an island village and you could well hear the tapping of typewriter keys as another foreign writer sets out to emulate Lawrence Durrell and Henry Miller. Whether it is because of their fecundity, their rich vein of history or their easy living, the Ionian Islands have seen their fair share of foreign writers and none more so than Corfu.

Above: the writer, Samuel Clemens (Mark Twain)

BYRON'S ISLANDS

'The isles of Greece, the isles of Greece!
Where burning Sappho loved and sung.
Where grew the arts of war and peace
Where Delos rose and Phoebus sprung!
Eternal summer gilds them yet,
But all, except their sun, is set.'
Lord Byron, from *Don Juan* (written 1811)

194

FURTHER READING

Gerald Durrell, *My Family and Other Animals* (London, 1956)
Lawrence Durrell, *Prospero's Cell* (London, 1945)
Gustave Flaubert, *Letters, 1830–57* (London, 1954)
Edward Lear, *Selected Letters* (London, 1988)
Henry Miller, *The Colossus of Maroussi* (London, 1942)

Lawrence Durrell (below) lived in The White House, Kalámi (above right), less isolated now than when he described it in Prospero's Cell

Earlier travellers The most famous of all foreign writers to visit Greece must surely be the British poet, Lord Byron, not because he wrote most beautifully about it—most of his writings in Greece were notes and letters—but because he came to help the Greeks fight for their independence in the 1820s and died of fever (and the local doctors' attempts to cure it) in 1824 at Missolonghi in western Greece. After Greek independence, as a result of the rest of the Mediterranean being pacified after the Napoleonic campaigns, there was a flow of inquisitive writers visiting the Greek Islands as part of a grander tour: Herman Melville, Mark Twain, Edward Lear and William Thackeray were among them.

The 20th century During the last century, the names of three foreign writers in particular have been linked with Corfu. Gerald Durrell described his childhood on the island in *My Family and Other Animals*, giving a unique and often comical insight into Corfu wildlife and creating some entertaining pen-portraits of local people he knew. His elder brother Lawrence wrote *Prospero's Cell*, a beautiful evocation of northern Corfu, after he had been evacuated before the Nazi invasion in World War II. The American novelist Henry Miller recorded his visit to Lawrence Durrell before the war in *The Colossus of Maroussi*. But not everyone was passionate about Corfu: Evelyn Waugh, passing through in 1927, found it 'a very clean and rather attractive town' which reminded him of Brighton.

Sailing is the ideal way to discover and enjoy Kýthira's splendid and isolated beaches

USEFUL NUMBER
Kythira Travel (Chóra)
tel: 27360 31490

CONNECTIONS
Ferry services run (weather permitting) from Diakófti to Piréas and to Monemvasia and Neápoli (southern Peloponnese). Hydrofoils operate to Piréas in summer.

KÝTHIRA

Out on its own off the southern coast of the Peloponnese, nearer to Crete than to the other Ionian Islands, Kýthira shared Venetian and subsequently British occupation with the Ionians. In antiquity, the Phoenicians and Minoans had bases here. After massive emigration in the 1950s (many islanders now live in Australia), Kýthira is quiet and in some places even abandoned, attracting Athenians and foreigners to its fine beaches.

▶▶ Kýthira Town (Chóra) *179A1*

The island capital is a quiet place with wonderful views over its port, Kapsáli and the islet of Avgó, reputed birthplace of Aphrodite. The nearby fort, **Kástro tis Chóra▶**, was built by Venetians in the 13th century and restored later, hence the inscription of 1503. The small museum (*Open* Tue–Sun 8.45–3. *Admission free*) has evidence of the island's various occupiers. Below the *kástro*, **Kapsáli**—popular with yachts rounding the Peloponnese—is Kýthira's most visitor-orientated village.

▶▶ Potamós *179A1*

The largest settlement on the island is quiet and has some accommodation to rent. To the east lies **Palaiochóra▶▶** or Ágios Dimítrios, the medieval town. Built on a strong site, invisible from the sea, it was a flourishing fortress-town in 1500, with 72 churches and a population swelled from the fall of Mýstra, a Byzantine city in the Peloponnese. In 1537 the Turkish admiral Barbarossa destroyed the fort, killing thousands and capturing 7,000 islanders.

▶▶ Mylopótamos *179A1*

This beautiful village near the west coast is set in a lush valley near a ruined **Venetian fortress▶**. A half-hour walk leads to the cave of Agía Sophía (*Open* summer only, Mon–Fri 3–8, Sat–Sun 11–5. *Admission charge*). Formerly used as a church, it has stalactites and stalagmites and a chamber where, locals say, Aphrodite slept.

Beaches

Kýthira has a number of sandy beaches, good if it is not too windy. Kapsáli has pebbles and sand and is busy in summer. Diakófti is a beautiful strip of sand, Platiá Ammos in the north is served by a summer taverna, while sandy Limiónas on the west coast is quiet but hard to reach.

Detail, the Venetian kástro

DROIT DE SEIGNEUR
In the 13th and 14th centuries there was a custom at Palaiochóra that new brides must first sleep with the local ruler. When a young man of noble Venetian descent objected, the ruler agreed to waive his rights if the young man would throw himself off a nearby cliff. The young man accepted, but when he jumped he took the ruler with him. Both men died and the custom was dropped.

LEFKÁDA

Lefkáda, connected to the mainland by a causeway, hardly feels like an island. Its towns, which have been badly damaged by earthquakes, are unspectacular but there are excellent beaches and, particularly in the south, dramatically beautiful scenery.

A series of fortresses is proof that Lefkáda was long an important strategic base

►► Lefkáda Town   179B3

Along the causeway is the impressive **Fortress of Agia Mavra►►►** (*Open* Tue–Sun 9–1), built by Giovanni Orsini in the 13th century, with great views from the top. In the town is the **Archaeological Museum►►** (see panel) and the **Icon Museum►►**, on (Odós Rontogianni. *Open* Tue–Sat 8.30–1.30; also 6–8.15 Tue and Thu. *Admission free*), with a marvellous collection of post Byzantine icons.

► Nydrí   179C3

German archaeologist Wilhelm Dörpfeld claimed, in the early 20th century, that Nydrí, not Itháki, was the site of Odysseus' palace, his evidence being some Bronze Age tombs he had found nearby. His theory was never accepted, but his statue still stands on the quay at Nydrí. From this growing resort, there is a wonderful view of several green, offshore islets including Skórpios, famous as the playground of Jackie Kennedy and Aristotle Onassis (landing is forbidden) and Meganísi, a short ferry ride away but retaining a surprising atmosphere of the real, agricultural Greece.

►► Ákra Doukáto (Cape Lefkádas)   179B2

Lefkáda's southernmost point is a thin and dramatic ribbon of rock, high above the sea, where, according to tradition, unrequited love could be cured by throwing yourself off the 72m-high (236ft) cliff. The most famous casualty was the great poet Sappho, rejected by the boatman Phaon. She is said to have died by jumping (the place is known as Sappho's Leap), although it is likely that she died a more natural death in Sicily. A lonely and spectacular spot. Bring poetry.

Beaches

Windsurfers enjoy the high rollers at Vasilikí, while sand-and-pebble Póros beach is beautiful and quiet. A dirt road leads to Pórto Katsíki, one of Greece's most spectacular beaches, the white stones giving the water an extraordinary brilliance, but there are currents and high waves. Farther north, Ágios Nikítas has access to an expanse of pebble and sand at Mílos beach.

USEFUL NUMBER
Borsalino Travel (Nydrí)
tel: 26450 92528;
www.lefkas.net

LEFKÁDA TOWN
Lefkáda Town's small, modern Archaeological Museum is on Odos Fanermomenis. If you continue in this direction by car you will climb up to the Faneromeni Monastery, a peaceful retreat with great views over the town, and a small museum and chapel, both worth seeing.

CONNECTIONS
Ferry services operate from Nydrí to Kefalloniá and Itháki and also to Meganísi and other islets.

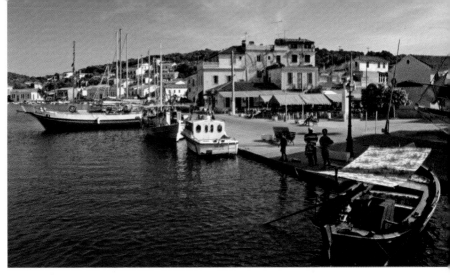

PAXOÍ

Lacking an airport and with a shortage of water, tiny Paxoí has kept mass tourism at bay. With an excellent hotel, a range of rental properties, a good anchorage and a gently rolling interior dominated by olive trees, it is one of the most relaxed and charming Ionian islands.

▶▶ Gáïos (Paxoí Town)   *179B3*

The main pleasure in this mostly car-free town is strolling around or visiting the islet of **Ágios Nikólaos**▶▶, with its windmill and a ruined 15th-century Venetian fort. Behind it lies another islet, **Panagía**▶, whose monastery is a popular place of pilgrimage for 15 August celebrations.

▶▶ Lákka   *179B4*

The island's main road runs to Lákka. The pretty, enclosed harbour has been taken over by apartment- and villa-rental companies, but it is a quiet and pleasant place.

▶▶ Longós (Loggós)

Paxoí's third small town clusters round a tiny harbour, where there are several excellent restaurants.

▶▶ West-coast caves   *179B3*

Paxoí's caves, famous even in antiquity—Homer mentions one, Ipparándi, as being covered in gold—make a good excursion by boat from Gáïos or Lákka. Kastanída and Ortholíthos are the most extraordinary.

▶▶ Antipaxoí   *179B3*

A short boat ride from Gáïos, Antipaxoí has few hotels but is a welcome day trip from Paxoí. While Paxoí is famous for its olives, Antipaxoí produces powerful wine. Agrapídia, the main settlement, is the anchorage. The island has fine, sandy beaches.

Beaches

Paxoí's beaches are mostly pebble or rock. The Paxos Beach Hotel has the best swimming cove in Gáïos, while Kaki Lagada, north of the town, has good bathing. Orkós, off the Lákka–Longós road, is worth the excursion.

The waterfront at Gáïos, on Paxoí

USEFUL NUMBERS
Port Authority (Gáïos)
tel: 26620 31259
Information and accommo-
dation: Paxos Magic
Holidays, tel: 26620
32269;
www.paxosmagic.com
www.paxos-greece.com

Life on Paxoí revolves around its olive groves

CONNECTIONS
Paxoí has ferry links with Corfu, Párga, Igoumenítsa and Antipaxoí. A summer hydrofoil service operates to Corfu.

USEFUL NUMBER
Tourist Police (on water-front, open daily 7.30am–9.30pm)
tel: 26950 27367
www.zanteweb.gr
www.justzante.co.uk

DIONYSIOS SOLOMOS
Born into a Hellenized Venetian family and educated in Italy, Solomós began writing verse in Italian but then became the first poet to use the demotic Greek language and Greek legends, and this at a time when Greece was fighting for its independence. He dedicated poems to the independence fighters and to the British Lord Byron, who died while helping them and his *Ode to Liberty* was used as the Greek national anthem.

CONNECTIONS
Zákynthos has ferry links with Kyllíni (Peloponnese) and Kefalloniá. There is also a summer hydrofoil service to Kefalloniá, and to Brindisi in Italy.

Loggerhead turtle

ZÁKYNTHOS (ZÁNTE)

If you are looking for streets lined with disco-bars and beaches thick with comatose bodies sleeping off hangovers, then Zákynthos in high season (especially the south of the island) is for you. Otherwise, come in spring or autumn to enjoy the island's other considerable attractions, which include spectacular landscapes, several unspoiled villages, beautiful sandy beaches and, especially in spring, the blossoms that earned it the label 'the flower of the East'. Whatever your reasons for coming, make time to appreciate the plight of the island's special wildlife, particularly the threatened loggerhead turtle (see panel opposite) and the rare Mediterranean monk seal, which return to the island to breed.

►► Zákynthos Town   179B1

The Venetians prided themselves on Zákynthos Town, but the 1953 earthquake brought it all crashing down. Many houses were rebuilt in an Italianate style, most successfully around **Plateía Solómou►►**, a grand open space fronting the water, surrounded by the 16th-century church of Ágios Nikólaos Molou and the **Byzantine Museum►►** (*Open daily 9–1 and 5–9. Admission charge*). Among ornaments salvaged from ruined churches are the 1681 iconostasis of the Church of the Pantokrátor and the walls of the 17th-century church of Ágios Andréas with their frescoes of Judgement, Heaven and Hell. There is also a collection of icons and a model of the town before 1953.

In the neighbouring square, the **Solomós Museum►►** (Plateía Ágios Márkou. *Open daily 9–2. Admission charge*) is dedicated to local poet Dionysios Solomós (1798–1857) and his brother. On display are memorabilia of their lives and times, the most bizarre being part of the tree under which Solomós composed his great works of May 1823. The beautiful Byzantine church of Kyrias ton Angelou (Odós Archiepiskópou Kokkiní), reconstructed after the earthquake, is closed, but the waterfront **cathedral of Ágios Dionysios►** (*Open daily 9–8*) survived the earthquake and has a profusion of frescoes and a silver reliquary for the saint's bones.

A steep climb above the town, the walls of the **Venetian kástro►►** (*Open daily 8–7.30, in summer; 8–2, in winter. Admission charge*) survived the 1953 earthquake, unlike the buildings inside, now replaced with a park commanding excellent views over the beautiful bay.

►► Ákra Skinári (Cape Skinári) 179C1

Between the northern cape of Zákynthos and the port of Ágios Nikólaos, the **Blue Caves►►** make a popular excursion. The combination of diffused light, rock and water makes the sea in the caves appear a brilliant blue.

► Laganás 179C1

If Zákynthos Town goes quiet at night it is because the noisy ones have come to this exploding and brash resort for dancing, drinking and sex. Even if the barman has just poured a bottle of vodka down your throat (they do), remember that the beach belongs to the loggerhead turtles at night; it is forbidden to go on it after dark (see panel).

►► Machairádo 179B1

A place of pilgrimage, Machairádo is one of the most interesting inland villages for its **church of Agía Maura**, a survivor of the 1953 earthquake. Ornately decorated, its wall and ceiling painted with biblical themes, it is accompanied by its separate bell tower, another happy survivor. .

►► Volimés 179B1

This rather sprawling village in the northwest of the island is known for its handicrafts and local produce, often enthusiastically marketed to visitors. Several kilometres to the south is the monastery of **Anafonítria**, an earthquake survivor which has retained some of its frescoes. A well-advertised tourist attraction nearby is the **wreck of a ship**, smashed off the inhospitable west coast and now mostly buried in sand. It can be seen from the cliffs above and is often combined, on boat excursions from Ágios Nikólaos and elsewhere, with a visit to the Blue Caves (see Ákra Skinári, above). In summer, with your own transport (mopeds are not suitable), drive to Pórto Vrómi, on a bay near the wreck and take a boat from there, making time to eat at Uncle Yanni's Cantina on your return.

Beaches

Zákynthos's beaches can be overrun in the summer. Pórto Róma, south of Zákynthos Town, has good gentle bathing and a good taverna. Gerákas can be quieter but is also a nesting ground for loggerhead turtles, as are the next two beaches, smaller pebble-and-sand Kalamáki and the many kilometres hemmed in by hotels at Laganás. Órmos Álikon (Álikon Bay) in the northeast has a long sandy beach on which are the unexciting resorts of Alikanás and Alikés.

NOMAPXIA ZAKYNΘOY PREFECTURE OF ZAKYNTHOS

ΠΡΟΣΤΑΤΕΥΟΜΕΝΟΣ ΒΙΟΤΟΠΟΣ ΘΑΛΑΣΣΙΑΣ ΧΕΛΩΝΑΣ
PROTECTED SEA-TURTLE NESTING BEACH

ΣΤΟ ΧΩΡΟ ΑΥΤΟ ΓΕΝΝΟΥΝ ΟΙ ΘΑΛΑΣΣΙΕΣ ΧΕΛΩΝΕΣ ΤΑ ΑΥΤΑ ΤΟΥΣ
SEA TURTLES USE THIS BEACH AS A NESTING AREA

ΑΠΑΓΟΡΕΥΕΤΑΙ Η ΚΑΤΑΣΚΗΝΩΣΗ ΚΑΙ Η ΔΙΑΜΟΝΗ ΣΤΗΝ ΠΑΡΑΛΙΑ ΜΕΤΑ ΤΗ ΔΥΣΗ
ΤΟΥ ΗΛΙΟΥ ΓΙΑΤΙ Ο ΘΟΡΥΒΟΣ ΚΑΙ ΤΑ ΦΩΤΑ ΔΙΑΚΟΠΤΟΥΝ ΤΗΝ ΩΟΤΟΚΙΑ

IT IS STRICTLY PROHIBITED TO CAMP OR REMAIN ON THE BEACH
AFTER SUN-SET AS ANY LIGHT OR NOISE PREVENTS NESTING

Thásos is popular with northern Greeks for its excellent sandy beaches

NORTHERN AND EASTERN AEGEAN Unlike the Cyclades or the Ionian Islands, the islands in this group have no common identity. Sometimes separated into the Northern Aegean (Límnos, Samothráki and Thásos) and the Eastern Sporades (Chíos, Ikaría, Lésvos, and Sámos), they cling like barnacles to the Turkish coast. Sometimes hard to reach and spartan in accommodation, they offer visitors who make the effort a wonderful range of possibilities, from antiquities on Samothráki to a genteel resort atmosphere on Thásos, from the volcanic drama of Chíos to the lush countryside and unspoiled villages of Lésvos.

EARLY HISTORY In antiquity, visitors came to Thásos and Límnos for gold, stone and wine, and for theatre, while everyone from emperors to pious citizens visited Samothráki to take part in the sacred mysteries connected with its Great Gods. But of these islands, Sámos and Lésvos were most renowned in the ancient world. When the Greek historian Herodotus visited Sámos he thought that the defences of the city of King Polycrates (6th century BC), the water tunnel that fed them and the nearby temple to Hera (the Heraion) were among the greatest architectural achievements of the Greeks. Lésvos's claim to fame was more literary and cultural. The third largest Greek island, with a wealth assured by its fertility, it was the homeland of Terpander (the father of Greek music) and of the lyrical poets Arion, Alcaeus and, of course, the famous Sappho, while in its schools the great Aristotle and Epicurus came to teach. There is still a hint of this cultural achievement about the island, a touch of pride in the islanders' character, especially in the main town of Mytilíni, home to several modern painters and writers.

ITALIAN AND TURK Like so many other islands, those of the Northern and Eastern Aegean came under Venetian or Genoese influence in the 13th century after the fall of Byzantium, but, being so close to the Turkish mainland, many were quickly retaken by the Turks. The Genoese Gattilusi family held Thásos and Samothráki throughout

The Northern and Eastern Aegean Islands

Chíos (ΧΙΟΣ)
Ikaría (ΙΚΑΡΙΑ)
Lésvos (ΛΕΣΒΟΣ)
Límnos (ΛΗΜΝΟΣ)
Sámos (ΣΑΜΟΣ)
Samothráki (ΣΑΜΟΘΡΑΚΙ)
Thásos (ΘΑΣΟΣ)

the 14th and 15th centuries, but Límnos, at the mouth of
the Dardanelles and the shipping lane to Constantinople
(Istanbul) and Asia, was not so secure. The fate of Límnos
became a gauge of Turkish power and it was only in 1912,
after the Balkan War, that the Greeks finally won it back,
along with Lésvos, Sámos and Chíos, held by the Turks
since the 15th and 16th centuries.

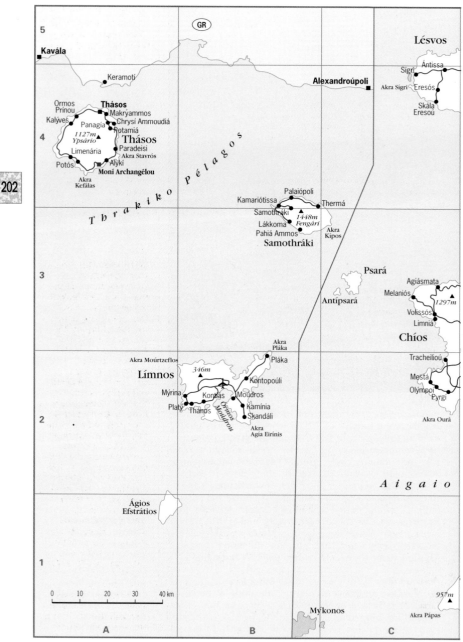

GREEK WARINESS The islands are too close to Turkey not to be an issue; Sámos is only 3km (2 miles) from the Turkish mainland. There were still sizeable Turkish communities on these islands until the exchange of citizens in 1924. The Greeks remain wary of Turkish intentions and Límnos continues to be a place of contention, with the Turks calling for the large Greek garrison to be removed.

►►► REGION HIGHLIGHTS

Agiássos
see pages 208–209
Mastic villages
see pages 204–205
Míthymna (Mólivos)
see page 212
Néa Moní see page 205
Palaiópoli see page 216
Sanctuary of the Great Gods (Samothráki see page 216

203

BEST BEACHES
● Empóreio (Chíos)
● Aktí Mýrina (Límnos)
● Alykí and Paradise (Thásos)
● Tzamadoú (Sámos)
● Livádia (Ikaría)

INTER-ISLAND TRAVEL
Improvements in sea communications mean that it is at last feasible to hop through these islands in a single trip without taking months over it, as Ptolemy or Anthony and Cleopatra would have done. However, although in summer frequent boats and hydrofoils connect the islands, the distances between them make it necessary to think carefully about your itinerary. If travelling from the mainland, note that the port of Keramóti is closer than Kavála to 'Megas Alexandros' (Alexander the Great) Airport and to Thásos island. An unreliable hydrofoil service connects Samothráki to Límnos in the summer, otherwise it is a long boat ride from Kavála or a hydrofoil from Alexandroúpol. Connections, however, made from Límnos down through the other islands are both more frequent and more reliable.

The sticky sweet smell of mastic resin still pervades the air in villages where mastic is cultivated

CHÍOS

The economy of Chíos depends much more on its shipowners, on mastic production and on citrus groves than on tourism. Although there are a few tour groups, the island has most to offer the more adventurous traveller.

USEFUL NUMBER
Tourist information (Odós Kanari 18, Chíos Town. *Open* daily 7am–10pm, May–Oct; Mon–Fri 7–4, Nov–Apr)
tel: 22710 44389
www.chios.com
www.chiosnet.gr

THE MASSACRE OF CHIOS
The year 1822 is hard to forget in Chíos. In 1821 the Chiots joined the people from Sámos in the War of Independence, but in 1822 the Turks, in revenge, massacred more than 25,000 Chiots, enslaved about 50,000 and destroyed many religious monuments. During the year of 1822, the island's population fell from 120,000 to around 30,000. The massacre, depicted in all its horror in *The Massacre of Chios* by the painter Eugene Delacroix, caused an uproar in Europe and won great sympathy for the Greek cause. The original painting is in the Louvre, in Paris, but there is a copy in the Argenti Museum in Chíos Town.

▶▶ Chíos Town   203D3

Chíos, the capital and port, is a lively commercial centre that has not compromised itself for tourism. Beyond the ferry landing is a busy bazaar, very Asian in atmosphere, where everything from mastic and metal cheese-cupboards to live animals is on sale. The **Philip Argenti Museum▶▶** (2 Odós Kórai. *Open* Mon–Fri 8–2, Sat 8–12.30, also Fri 5–7.30pm. *Admission charge*) houses an amazing collection of local folkloric costumes, maps and family paintings. The **Byzantine Museum▶** in the old Mecidiye Mosque (Plateía Plastíra. Closed for restoration at time of writing) has lots of 14th- and 15th-century sculpture. The small **Archaeological Museum▶** (Odós Mihalon 10. *Open* Tue–Sun 8.30–3. *Admission charge*) has artefacts from local excavations. Just outside the town is the **Kámpos**, settled in the 14th century by the Genoese aristocracy who built magnificent villas in the middle of olive and citrus groves. Many made way for the airport or fell into ruin, but a few have been beautifully restored, the most famous being the Villa Argenti which offers the most exclusive (and expensive) hotels on these islands.

Just outside the suburb of Vrontádos, in an olive grove, is the 'Stone of Homer' where the great poet supposedly composed his famous epics.

▶ Kardámyla   203D3

Káto Kardámyla, the island's second town, set in a fertile plain, is a welcome sight after 'Homer's Crags', the rugged mountains of the north. There is little to interest visitors beyond some excellent beaches.

▶▶▶ Mastikochoriá (mastic villages)   202C2

Traditionally used in many products from varnish to chewing gum, the resin of the mastic tree (a relative of the pistachio) was the basis of much of Chíos's early prosperity. The mastic business in this part of the island was profitable until the discovery of petroleum-based products and now most of the mastic trees have made way for olives and apricots. The medieval villages, however, preserve their unique character. **Pyrgí▶▶** is famous for its houses elaborately decorated with *sgraffito*, geometric patterns in white and grey paint. The cathedral is of little interest, but the 12th-century church of Ágioi Apóstoloi (*Open* Tue–Thu and Sat 10–1), in the corner of the square, is a gem. **Olýmpoi▶▶**, the least pretty of the villages, is still worth a visit for its old town. **Mestá▶▶▶**, the finest, is a walled-in village with dark streets which often feel like underground tunnels built by ants. The main square has some excellent tavernas serving local specialities.

▶▶▶ Néa Moní   203D3

Néa Moní (*Open* daily 8.30–1 and 4–8. *Admission charge*), one of the most famous Greek Orthodox buildings in all Greece, was founded in 1042 by the Emperor Constantine Monomachos after three hermits discovered a miraculous icon of the Virgin. The setting is superb, but reminders of a troubled past are close at hand: beyond the main gate, an

ossuary contains the bones of the victims of a savage Turkish attack in 1822. The church suffered from Turkish ransacking and a later earthquake, but happily some magnificent mosaics have survived. Before 1822 the monastery supported over 600 monks, but only a handful of nuns are in residence today.

▶▶ Volissós   202C3

Most of Volissós's older inhabitants live in new houses around the main square, but their old stone houses, dramatically set beneath the crumbling Byzantine castle, have been mostly restored. Traditions have been well preserved in Volissós; the local baker, who can never make enough bread, still bakes on olive wood. The nearby port of Limniá has a few good fish tavernas.

Beaches

Near Chíos Town are the sandy beach at the resort of Karfás and two lovely pebble beaches at Vrontádos. Emporeió's black-stone beach, on the south coast, has good snorkelling. The best beach in the north is Nagós—not the crowded main black-sand beach but the small beaches beyond it. There are good white-pebble coves near Tracheilioú and below Volissós.

WOMEN'S AGRICULTURAL-TOURIST COOPERATIVE
This women's cooperative offers visitors the opportunity to stay with local families, in simple houses in the mastic villages and share their lives and work. It operates in four villages—Armolia, Pyrgí, Olympoi and Mestá—and now has 63 rooms, all with private bathrooms, or bathrooms shared between two rooms. For reservations tel: 22710 72496. Breakfast and homemade meals are available.

Axe-clefts in children's skulls are a painful reminder of the brutality of 1822

LIVE THE VILLAGE LIFE
Old stone houses are being restored on Chíos, particularly in the lovely mastic village of Mestá and in Volissós. Some of these are being done by and for local people, but others are available for rent and make wonderful places to stay if you want to get a feel for village life. Many are decorated with traditional old furniture, to give them an authentic look. In Mestá you can make reservations through Dimitris Pipidis (tel: 22710 76319), or in Volissós with Argyris Angelou (tel: 22740 21421). In Kámpos there is an award-winning organic farm with beautiful rooms at Perleas Mansion (tel: 22710 32217; www.perleas.gr).

CONNECTIONS
Chíos has ferry links with Piréas, Lésvos, Sámos, Léros, Thessaloníki, Kós, Kavála, Límnos, Rhodes, Oinoússes, Ikaría and Cesme (Turkey). Hydrofoil services operate to Piréas, Sámos, Ikaría, Pátmos, Foúrnoi and Lésvos.

Drive

To the mastic villages

Cross the island to explore the mastic-growing country of the southwest, with its well-preserved villages. (Approximately 55km/34 miles to Mestá; allow all day, with a good lunch stop.)

Leave Chíos Town on the road for the airport, following signs for Nénita and Kallimasiá and passing through the Kámpos (see page 204). Follow the sign for Kalamotí, heading uphill. About 3km (2 miles) farther on, pass windmills and the monastery of Ágía Miná. Continue through Kallimasiá, following a sign (right) by the church to Tholopotámi and after 3km (2 miles) drive between the windmills to the right, back towards Chíos. Go through Vavíloi and shortly a small yellow sign in Greek leads to a dirt track on the right, which leads through an olive grove to the amazing 13th-century **church of Panagía Krína**►►► with splendid wall paintings. Return to the main road at Vavíloi and follow signs for Pyrgí. The road winds through olive and mastic groves, past the first mastic village of **Armólia**, famous for its pottery. After 16km (10 miles), reach **Pyrgí**►► (see page 205). The main road leads on to the other mastic villages of **Olýmpoi**►► and **Mestá**►►►, a good lunch stop. Either return the same way or continue along the scenic west coast to Elínta, where the road cuts inland to Chíos Town, passing the lovely villages of **Anávatos**► and **Avgónima**► and the monastery of **Néa Moní**►►► (see page 205).

IKARÍA

The prosaic explanation of Ikaría's name is that it comes from the Phoenician word for fish. Locals prefer to link it with the famous legend of Icarus, whose home-made waxen wings melted when he flew too near the sun. The island (which some claim to be wing-shaped) is not exceptionally beautiful, but it does offer an increasingly rare commodity: peace and quiet. Roads are rough and public transport is minimal, but the bus ride from Évdilos to Ágios Kírykos is spectacular.

► Ágios Kírykos
203D1

The waterfront, with its tree-shaded cafés, provides the greatest excitement in Ágios Kírykos, but even in summer it remains a sleepy fishing town. The small **Archaeological Museum►** (near the hospital. *Open* Tue–Wed, Fri–Sun 10–3, in summer. *Admission free*) has local finds. The radioactive springs in Thérma are a strange sight: while patients bathe in the thermal springs, their partners sip coffee by the side. The hot springs at nearby Thérma Lefkádas, boiling up in a seawater pool formed by volcanic rocks, are more attractive.

► Évdilos
203D1

After the empty, rugged landscape of the interior, Évdilos can appear to be a lively place, but it is a very relaxed resort. In nearby Kámpos is the site of ancient Oinon (*Open* daily. *Admission free*), once Ikaría's main town, and the charming 11th-century church of Agía Iríni.

► Armenistís
203D1

The island's two best sandy beaches, Livádi and Messakhtí, are within walking distance of this fishing village, now the island's main resort. In Nás, 4km (2.5 miles) farther, are the ruins of the temple of Artemis Tavropoleio, overlooked by a small hippie community. The older residents in the nearby village of Christós still speak an ancient Homeric dialect.

► Foúrnoi
203D1

The island of Foúrnoi, a popular Sunday lunch excursion from Ágios Kírykos, offers the opportunity for a walk or an afternoon swim. Most people stay in the port or walk to the small village of Kámbi, 15 minutes away.

One of the more secluded coves on the splendid Livádi beach

USEFUL NUMBER
Tourist Police
tel: 22750 22207
www.island-ikaria.com

CONNECTIONS
Ikaría has ferry links with Piréas, Sámos (Vathí or Pythagóreio), Páros, Pátmos, Náxos, Foúrnoi, Mýkonos and Sýros. Hydrofoil services operate in summer to Pátmos, Piréas, Páros, Naxos, Lésvos, Sámos, Chíos, Foúrnoi, Leípsoi, Léros, Kálymnos and Kós and summer boat services also run to Foúrnoi.

USEFUL NUMBERS
Tourist information
(Plateía Sappho, on the
waterfront, Mytilíni) tel:
22510 44165 and (Odós
Aristarchou 6) tel: 22510
42511
www.lesvosonline.gr
www.lesvos.com

POETRY AND MUSIC
Lésvos, always a prosperous island, has since antiquity been a haven for artists and poets. In the 7th century BC Terpander, the father of Greek music, lived in Ántissa and the poet Arion, from Mólivos, wrote for the first time personal poetry instead of long epics. Both of them inspired the two great poets of the next century, Sappho from Eresós and Alcaeus from Mytilíni. In the 4th century BC the famous School of Philosophy was founded where Aristotle and Epicurus often lectured. Poetry is still alive at the *Vallia* in Agiássos where, every year on the Monday before Shrove Tuesday, villagers try to outdo each other in exchanging satirical verse.

The north coast of Lésvos has some pretty bays and harbours, including Skála Sikaminéas

LÉSVOS

Lésvos is the third largest Greek island after Crete and Évvoia. Although it is rapidly replacing its traditional industries—olives, *oúzo*, fishing and shipbuilding—with tourism, it still has lots of Greek character, unspoiled villages, good beaches and lovely countryside for hiking.

▶▶ Mytilíni   203D4

Mytilíni, the capital and main harbour, has a bustling waterfront with plenty of sophisticated cafés and *ouzerí*. The modern city is built on the ruins of ancient Mytilíni, of which only the large Hellenistic theatre has survived. A huge 6th-century *kástro*, repaired by the Genoese in 1373, divides the two harbours. Despite the modern character of the town, its busy Old Market still has the feel of a bazaar. The impressive **Archaeological Museum▶▶▶** (Noemvriou 8. *Open* Tue–Sun 8.30–3. *Admission charge*) has wonderful mosaics from the Hellenistic period The old building of the Port Authority houses a small **Folklore Museum▶** (*Open* Tue–Sun 8.30–3. *Admission free*) with costumes, embroidery and other crafts from the islands.

Just south of town, past many of its grand old mansions, is the **Thériade Museum▶▶▶** (Odós Alice Thériade, Variá, tel: 22510 23372. *Open* Tue–Sun 9–2 and 5–8. *Admission charge*). This collection of book illustrations by Picasso, Chagall, Matisse and others, published by the Lésvos-born art critic Elefteriades (better known under his French name Thériade), is delightful and unexpected. Next door is the **Theophilos Museum** (*Open* Tue–Sun 9–2 and 6–8, in summer. *Admission charge*) with an extensive collection of works by the native primitive painter Theophilos.

▶▶▶ Agiássos   203D4

This charming village in the foothills of Mount Ólympos makes an enjoyable day excursion. The stalls in the bazaar filled with religious and kitsch souvenirs are aimed at the many Greek tourists. The village has maintained its

The capital of Lésvos, Mytilíni is a lively town, with a bustling port

At the foot of Mount Lepétimnos

A long but easy walk through some inviting villages overlooked by Mount Lepétimnos, with good views over the surrounding countryside. The route follows one of several signposted trails laid out by the Mytilíni tourist office (21km/13 miles; allow most of a day. Buses leave Mytilíni every morning around 8 or 9 for Kallóni and Mólivos. A bus returns from Mantamádos at 4.30).

Start at the spring on the road from Kallóni to Mólivos, just before the junction to Stypsí. Follow the signpost to Stypsí, taking the paved road into the heart of the village. There are a few tavernas on the way and good views over the sea. Walk through Stypsí's main street, with its lively *kafeneía* and tiny old shops.

Follow the sign in the centre for Mantamádos, along a dirt track past a little church. From the road there are fine views over the abundant valley of Kallóni, with its orchards. A drinking fountain, after half an hour, announces the peaceful village of Ipsilométoro, with its *kafeneía* in the shade of the trees and a minaret but no mosque. The road leads on to the scenic village of Pelópi which is built around a ravine and is very lush. Its mosque has now been turned into a warehouse. The road continues to Kápi, a small village with cobbled streets, from where you continue to nearby Mantamádos. This lovely village is famous for its pottery and its huge monastery of the Archangel Michael (*Open* daily 6am–10pm, in summer, 6.30am–7pm, in winter). Believers offer tin slippers full of money to the eerie 'black icon' of the archangel, because they believe that he often wears out his shoes while fulfilling the wishes of his devotees.

special atmosphere along with its grey stone houses with Ottoman balconies, its noisy *kafeneía* and its quaint butchers' shops which sell, among other things, a local cheese in goatskin. The church of the Panagía Vrefokratoússa provides plenty of interest before a good lunch in one of the tavernas.

▶ Eresós   202C4

Famous as the birthplace of Sappho, Eresós and its nearby beach resort Skála Eresoú have become fully developed because of the wonderful beach. Between here and Sígri, little remains of the Petrified Forest (*Open* daily 8–4), but the Turkish castle at Sígri, near the island's most westerly point, is still standing and open to visitors.

CONNECTIONS
Lésvos has ferry links with Piréas, Chíos, Límnos, Kavála, Thessaloníki, Sámos, Pátmos and Ayvalik (Turkey). Summer hydrofoil services run to Sámos, Chíos and Pátmos and less frequently to Kavála and Límnos.

The Greeks invented poetry and their political security created an environment in which a poetic tradition flourished. Literature students around the world study the early Greeks today, but some modern Greek poets find this legacy more of a hindrance than a help.

Memorial stone to British poet Rupert Brooke on Skíros

Origins of poetry There is little evidence today of

Greece's once-thriving oral tradition, but storytellers everywhere know that it is easier to remember lines that are sprung with a rhythm. Perhaps it was from the simple need for an aid to memory that poetry developed. The origins of written poetry are lost, although Homer is usually placed at the beginning, with his *Iliad* and *Odyssey*. Even if he did compose those epic poems—and their authorship is in doubt—their content was the product of a long-established oral tradition.

210

SOME MODERN GREEK POETS
Constantine Cavafis
Odysseus Elytis (Nobel prize-winner)
Níkos Kazantzákis (Nobel nomination)
Takis Papatsonis
Yannis Ritsos (Nobel nomination)
Angelos Sikelianos (Nobel nomination)
George Seferis (Nobel prize-winner)

SAPPHIC LOVE
'...—so sobbing, many times, she left me
and she said this [to me]
'My god! what awful things are happening to us:
Sappho, I swear I am leaving you against my will.'
And I replied to her in these words:
'Go with a light heart and with memories
of me, for you know how we cherished you.'
Sappho, from Fragment No. 94

Establishing the tradition The earliest surviving poems took as their subject the behaviour and attitudes of men faced with the often incomprehensible activities of the gods. Hesiod (c8th century BC) continued this didactic tradition in his *Theogony*, which explained the creation of the world and recounted the history of the gods. His *Works and Days*, however, praised honest labour, attacked corrupt judges and gave a vivid picture of village life. Of the early poets, Sappho (c7th century BC) stands out, although she is almost as well known now for her lifestyle and sexual preferences as for her poetry. As a lyrical poet she is believed to have led a female literary

The poetess Sappho had a school of poetry on Lésvos

circle in her native Mytilíni (Lésvos). Not everyone admired her poetry, some of which was said to be very erotic and addressed to women; her work was burned and, of the original nine volumes, only fragments survive.

Change of content As Greek society evolved, so poets focused increasingly on the activities of their contemporaries. Their popularity hardly suffered: Pindar (c520–c440BC), probably the finest of ancient Greece's lyric poets, was composing celebratory odes from an early age for victorious athletes at the Olympic Games—poems that the 17th-century British poet Dryden was quite happy to imitate more than 2,000 years later.

In the 5th and 4th centuries BC, the public imagination was caught by dramatists like Aeschylus, Sophocles and Euripides (see pages 218–219) and by the great historian Herodotus, who created the first prose masterpiece in Greek. By the time cultural pre-eminence passed to Alexandria in Egypt, poets were looking back fondly to the glory days of Greek poetry.

A language problem With the rise of Greek nationalism in the late 18th century, poets were faced with the problem of having to choose between Greek as spoken by farmers and islanders (demotic) and the official and literary language known as *katharévousa*, a simplified version of classical Greek. Controversy raged throughout the 19th century and the Greek government fell in 1901 after the New Testament was translated into demotic. The move away from the élitism of *katharévousa* was inevitable— the Alexandrian-Greek Constantine Cavafis was writing his great works in demotic early in the 20th century—but the controversy rumbled on: in 1963 the Nobel laureate George Seferis called *katharévousa* 'some kind of Esperanto masquerading as [Greek].'

A perennial subject Some of Cavafis's poems take their subjects from ancient Greek history and myth. This shows up one of the ironies of Greek poetry: myths and symbols of ancient Greece, the subject matter of the first poets, still form part of the raw material of poetry today. Two recent Nobel prize-winning poets have been Greek: Odysseus Elytis, who wrote primarily about the natural world and George Seferis, who revisited ancient myths.

A famous episode in Homer's Iliad: *Hector saved from Achilles by the god Apollo*

THE WEIGHT OF TRADITION
'In a land which has produced so many master-pieces in architecture, sculpture and literature, the Greek creative temperament has constantly to struggle against the crushing precedents set by its ancestors. For some, the Parthenon is not so much a symbol of the glorious past as an overbearing weight that suffocates inspiration and stunts expression.'
Kimon Friar, *Modern Greek Poetry* (Athens, 1993)

THE *EROTOKRÍTOS*
The masterpiece of Greek literature during the Turkish occupation was an epic poem called the *Erotokrítos*. Written on Crete around 1646 by Vincenzo Kornaros, it tells of the love between a princess and a commoner. Written in the Cretan vernacular rather than the more literary *katharévousa*, the *Erotokrítos* became as important a Greek heritage as the Parthenón.

HOT SPRINGS

Lésvos has several mineral springs that have been used since ancient times. The baths on the beach in Eftaloú near Míthymna should not be missed. There is a choice between the communal old bathhouse, or the new one where you get your own tub, but both are recommended for skin problems, arthritis, rheumatism, hypertension and other ailments. The largest springs on the island are in Therma Yera, 5km (3 miles) west of Mytilini, with a temperature of 39.7°C (103.4°F), and some of Europe's hottest springs are in Polichnitos, with a temperature of 87.6°C (189.6°F).

The pretty town of Mólivos has been declared a protected monument, but lost part of its character during restoration

▶ ▶ ▶ Míthymna (Mólivos)   203D5

It is easy to see why many visitors to Lésvos choose to stay in this lovely old town on the north coast of the island. The dramatically situated medieval *chora*, with its Macedonian-style houses and delightful streets, was declared a protected monument, so has been spared new development. Above the *chora* towers an impressive Genoese-Byzantine *kástro*▶ (*Open* Tue–Sun 9–7. *Admission charge*), where the island's most prestigious cultural events take place. The views are especially stunning towards sunset, sometimes extending as far as Mount Áthnos, rising from the sea in the far distance, with the Turkish coast much closer at hand. From the top of the town it is a pleasant walk, through cobbled, vine-covered streets, down to the fishing harbour and its choice of tavernas.

To the east of Mólivos, beyond the developing resort of Eftaloú, are the pretty village of Sykamineá and the island's most attractive fishing harbour, Skála Sykaminéas, with some excellent restaurants.

▶ Plomári   203D4

Known to produce the best *oúzo* on Lésvos, this relaxed resort with its scenic fishing harbour is especially popular with Scandinavian visitors.

Beaches

Peaceful, unspoiled beaches can still be found on Lésvos. Pétra has a good sandy beach, but it is noisy and crowded in season. The beaches are quieter farther west; Ambélia has a long bay with a sandy beach. Between Míthymna (Mólivos) and Skála Sykaminéas there are many little pebble-stone bays, one of the nicest being at Eftaloú. Ágios Isídoros is the best beach in the south, with pebbles and good bathing. The long sandy beach of Vatera is also very good, but in places really crowded. Skála Eresoú beach has good dark sand and is also very popular.

LÍMNOS

Its position near the entrance to the Dardanelles has long guaranteed Límnos great strategic value; it was from here that the World War I Gallipoli campaign was launched. Greek troops are still among the island's most frequent visitors and archaeologists also come here to explore the ancient sites. For the rest, Límnos has some good beaches, a wonderful resort hotel and one of the Aegean's most atmospheric ports.

▶▶ Mýrina 202B2

The main town on Límnos is literally divided in two by a ruined *kástro*. Built by 14th-century Venetians over the temple of Artemis and rebuilt under Turkish occupation, the *kástro* offers excellent views over the sea and island. Running around the *kástro*, from the port to the beach, is a lively shopping street with a distinctly eastern feel to it. This is where Limniotes stroll in the evening.

On this street, opposite the beach, finds from the island's three ancient sites are housed in a Turkish mansion, the **Límnos Archaeological Museum▶** (*Open* daily 9–3. *Admission charge*). Among the well-presented chronological displays, the 6th- to 8th-century BC vases from Kabeirion and grave goods from Hephaistia are outstanding.

▶ Moúdros 202B2

Central Límnos arches around the bay of Moúdros (Órmos Moúdrou), one of the finest natural harbours in the Aegean. This was the starting point for the 1915 Anglo–French attack on Gallipoli, intended to force Turkey out of World War I, which left about 36,000 Commonwealth soldiers dead: the **Commonwealth War Cemetery**, just outside unexciting Moúdros Town, contains the graves of 887 of them, most of whom died in the base hospitals around the bay. Sikh and Muslim casualties are buried at the side of the cemetery.

Beaches

Límnos has some good sandy beaches. Mýrina has an excellent large public beach to the north of the *kástro*; beyond it is the private beach of the wonderful Ákti Mýrina Hotel. Out of town, the villages of Platý and Thános overlook fine sandy beaches, which are usually less crowded than Mýrina.

USEFUL NUMBERS
Port Police
tel: 22540 22225
Theodoros Petrides Travel
tel: 22540 22039;
www.petridestravel.gr

Mýrina may be provincial (Greeks call it boring), but it's a pleasant place to spend an afternoon

A LÍMNIOT HEROINE
In 1475, after the fall of Byzantium, the victorious Turkish general landed on Límnos with an army carried in 300 ships. The Venetian garrison fought bravely but were outnumbered and talking of surrender when a Límniot girl called Maroula picked up the sword and shield of her dying father and rushed at the Turkish forces. The invaders fled, the fortress was saved (for a while) and Maroula was rewarded by a dowry and her choice of Venice's young aristocrats.

CONNECTIONS
Límnos has ferry links with Kavála, Piréas, Lésvos, Thessaloníki, Chíos and Ágios Efstrátios; in summer with Sámos, Samothráki, Pátmos and the Sporades.

213

The Allied military cemetery in Moúdros commemorates the 36,000 Allied soldiers who died here in 1915

Vourliótes, in the hills near Kokkári

SÁMOS

Lush and green Sámos was once the wealthiest island in the Aegean, where the arts and sciences flourished. Its coastal resorts become more popular every summer, but the interior remains comparatively untrodden.

▶ Sámos Town (Vathí) *203E1*

With its perfect horseshoe-shaped harbour, this is the main port and provincial capital. It has a busy pedestrianized bazaar area and some good neoclassical mansions. The excellent **Archaeological Museum▶▶▶** (Plateía Ágios Spyridónos, behind the little park. *Open* Tue–Sun 8.30–2.30. *Admission charge*) is the town's main attraction. The old wing has griffin-heads, for which 7th-century BC Sámos was famous; other exhibits show foreign influences on local artwork. The new wing was specially constructed to house a magnificent 5m-high (16ft) *kouros*, the largest free-standing statue known from ancient Greece. Picturesque old Vathí, on the slopes behind the modern town, is worth a visit.

▶ Karlovási *203E1*

Karlovási, the island's second town and port, is little more than a cluster of four small villages. Limáni, the port itself, has hotels and a waterfront lined with terraces and tavernas. Meséo and Paleó are residential areas with a few friendly *ouzerí*, while Néo is only a wasteland.

▶▶ Kokkári *203E1*

Once a quaint fishing village, Kokkári has good beaches which attract the crowds. For some island atmosphere, head for the nearby hills where good walking trails link villages in a countryside of cypresses, orchards and pine forests. The most atmospheric villages are Vourliótes, a maze of narrow streets with a pretty central square, and Manolátes with its flowering gardens.

▶ Mytilinioí *203E1*

Mytilinioí has a pleasant main square with some old *kafeneía* and a disorganized **Palaeontological Museum▶** (tel: 22730 52055. *Open* Mon–Fri 10–2. *Admission charge*).

▶▶ Pythagóreio

Sámos's ancient capital, Pythagóreio, was built by the 6th-century BC autocrat Polycrates; and his two great engineering projects, which astonished the ancient world, are still more or less visible: the ancient port, exactly where the harbour and jetty are today and the amazing **Efpalinion Tunnel▶▶** (*Open* Tue–Sun 8.30–2.30. *Admission charge*). This 1km-long (0.6-mile) aqueduct was cut through the mountain to bring water to ancient Sámos.

The **Roman baths▶** (*Open* Tue–Sun 8.30–2.30. *Admission free*) are less impressive and the **Archaeological Collection▶** (*Open* Tue–Sun 9–2.30. *Admission free*) is small. Far more interesting is the **Temple of Hera▶▶▶** (*Open* Tue–Sun 8.30–2.30. *Admission charge*) at nearby Iréon, a huge shrine dedicated to the Mother Goddess. Although only foundations and a re-erected column have survived, they do give an impression of how important this temple once must have been.

▶ Votsalákia (Kampos)

Votsalákia has a long beach backed by a sprawling resort. If the beach gets too crowded, or for a change of scene, try climbing Kerketéfs (Mount Kérkis) for some fabulous views. Neighbouring Marathókampos, dramatically built on a hillside, overlooks its port, Órmos Marathókampou. Tavernas in villages like Vourliótes often serve local specialities which are worth trying out: *tirópita*, cheese pastries made with fresh goat's milk; *revithokefthédes*, fried chick-pea balls; and syrupy *moskháto*, a white dessert wine.

Beaches

Good beaches can be found almost all around the coast, but you will need to choose carefully to avoid the crowds, especially in high season. The best beach near Sámos Town is at Kalámi. The good sandy beaches past Logothetis castle are used by several big hotel complexes. Near Kokkári, Tzamadoú beach has good bathing, with nude sunbathing at the west end. There are excellent beaches on the unspoiled coast past Karlovási. Potámi is lovely, with sand and pebbles and is a pleasant walk away from Karlovási. A further one-hour walk leads to Megálo Seïtáni, a wildly beautiful beach. Votsalákia is a rapidly growing resort with a good but crowded beach; Psilí Ámmos, 3km (2 miles) away and one of two beaches on the island to share this name, is quieter.

CONNECTIONS
Sámos has ferry links with Piréas, Ikaría, Foúrnoi, Chíos, Kálymnos, Pátmos, Páros, Náxos, Leipsoí, Sýros, Agathónisi, Léros, Lésvos, Mýkonos and Límnos. Hydrofoils run in summer to Pátmos, Kós, Léros, Kálymnos, Ikaría, Chíos, Leipsoí and Lésvos. Excursion boats go to Kusadasi (Turkey) in the summer.

The crescent-shaped Tzamadoú beach features on almost every poster of Sámos

HERODOTUS ON SAMOS
'I have written somewhat at length concerning the Samians, because they have the three greatest constructions of all the Greeks: first a channel with two mouths dug beneath a mountain a hundred and fifty fathoms high...The architect of this channel was Megarian, Eupalinos son of Naustrophos. This is one of the three and the second is a breakwater in the sea around the harbour, twenty fathoms in depth. Their third construction is the greatest of all known temples, of which the first master-builder was Rhoikos son of Phileus, a Samian.'
Herodotus, *The Histories* (London, 1972)

SAMOTHRÁKI

Samothráki is dominated by mountains and lashed for much of the year by fierce winds and high seas. It was the site of one of the ancient world's most enduring rituals, the 'mysteries' at the Sanctuary of the Great Gods. The sanctuary's ruins are among the most impressive to be found in the Greek islands.

USEFUL NUMBER
Port Police
tel: 25510 41305;
www.samothraki.com

The Hieron, in the sanctuary of the Great Gods, is all that is left of a large Doric temple from the 4th century BC

WORLD MUSIC FESTIVAL
Towards the end of July Samothráki is home to the World Music Festival (www.samothrakifestival. com) with a good programme of world music, reggae and blues, as well as a focus on green issues, as it is organized in cooperation with Greenpeace.

SOLVING THE MYSTERIES
No writer in antiquity dared record exactly what went on at the sanctuary, but the Samothráki mysteries were based on the worship of the Great Gods—the Great Mother, a lesser male figure called Kadmilos and the Kabeiroi. The first stage of initiation involved a ritual based on the cycle of life and rebirth, while higher initiation required purification and then a baptism with animal's blood. Samothráki's Great Gods were later assimilated with gods in the Greek pantheon, so the Great Mother became Demeter, Kadmilos became Hermes and the Kabeiroi became the Dioscuri—the twins Castor and Pollux (Gemini in the constellation).

CONNECTIONS
Samothráki has ferry links with Kavála, Alexandroúpoli and Límnos, which can also be reached by hydrofoil in summer.

▶▶ Samothráki Town (Chóra)   202B3

There is nothing in particular to see in the island capital, but its quiet alleys, clinging attractively to their hillside, are the best place to stroll or have lunch if the weather forces you off the coast.

▶▶ Thermá (Loutrá)   202B4

The road along Samothráki's rough and rugged north coast towards Thermá gives no hint of what is to come: the little spa is a place of soft beauty. The air is inspiring, sunlight filters through aged trees and sulphur-rich springs fill the therapeutic baths (tel: 22510 98229. *Open* daily 6–11 and 5–7, Jun–Sep. *Admission charge*).

▶▶▶ Palaiópoli   202B4

Philip of Macedonia and the Roman emperor Hadrian went straight to the sanctuary, but lesser mortals should start at the **museum**▶▶ (*Open* Tue–Sun 8.30–3. *Admission charge*). Here, objects like the 3rd-century terracotta Eros, a dancing-girl frieze and a cast of the famous Winged Nike (Victory), the original of which is in the Louvre in Paris (see panel opposite), help to give the place a human proportion. A path leads to the clearly marked **Sanctuary of the Great Gods**▶▶▶ (*Open* Tue–Sun 8.30–8.30. *Admission* same ticket as museum), where the Arsinoeion, named after the wife of Ptolemy of Egypt, is Greece's largest ancient rotunda. Most impressive are the re-erected columns and architrave of the Hieron. Above here stood the fountain and statue of Nike; below is the wild sea and all around there is an extraordinary atmosphere of power and desolation.

Beaches

Kamariótissa's stone beach, in the northwest, is very exposed. Much better is Thermá (Loutrá) with sand and stone. In the south, the large sandy beaches at Pachiá Ámmos and Kípos require private transport.

THÁSOS

A short hop from the mainland, Thásos is a popular resort island with Greek and foreign holidaymakers. Small and hilly, with good beaches and important antiquities, its character has been transformed by tourism.

▶▶ Thásos Town (Liménas)　　　　202A4

The beauty of the capital is assured by the surrounding pine-covered hills, by its pretty port and by its antiquities. The **Agora▶▶**, fenced off but often open, covered with mostly Roman ruins and shaded by trees, makes a wonderful, peaceful retreat from the tourist shops. Nearby is an excellent Archaeological Museum (*Open* Tue–Sun 9–3. *Admission charge*) and a Greek Theatre which has fabulous views. The acropolis is topped by a **fort▶▶**, originally built in the 5th century BC and enlarged over the centuries. The **ancient walls▶▶** repay closer inspection.

▶ Moní Archangélou　　　　202A4

The original 12th-century church here was built by an ascetic who had a vision of St. Michael; the icon of St. Michael and the natural spring were credited with healing powers. The spring has dried up, but the church is still a popular sight. The convent was established in 1974.

Beaches

Thásos has excellent sandy beaches with good bathing, especially on the east and south coasts. Chrysí Ammoudiá is convenient from Thásos Town, but Paradise Beach, farther south, is worth the extra effort. Alykí is in a beautiful cove but is impossibly crowded in high season. Potós is the best beach near Limenária.

217

USEFUL NUMBERS
Tourist Police
(on the waterfront)
tel: 25930 23111 (open daily 8am–10pm)
www.gothassos.com

FLYING NAILS
Among the treasures to be found in the Moní Archangélou is what is claimed to be part of a nail from the Holy Cross. Previously held on Mount Áthos, the nail miraculously appeared one day at the Thásos convent, reportedly carried there by St. Michael himself.

CONNECTIONS
Thásos has ferry links with Kavála (from Órmos Prínou and Thásos Town) and Keramotí (from Thásos Town). There are hydrofoils to Kavála in the summer season.

The acropolis of ancient Thásos was converted into a medieval fortress, first by the Venetians in 1204 and a hundred years later by the Genoese

Before the Ancient Greeks there was no theatre; some would claim that there has been little theatrical innovation since then. Exploding out of the extraordinary celebrations for Dionysos at the time of Athens' greatest power, wealth and prestige, theatre quickly developed into the exchange between actors and audience that we continue to enjoy today.

The mask of a tragic actor from Piréas, 4th century BC

218

AESCHYLUS' EGG
Tradition has it that the great poet Aeschylus, who was bald in his old age, was killed at the age of 69 when an eagle mistook his head for a rock and dropped a tortoise on it from some height.

ANCIENT THEATRES TODAY
Only the foundations of Athens' Theatre of Dionysos are now visible, but elsewhere in the country fine examples of early Greek auditoriums have survived. One of the most spectacular theatres built in Ancient Greece was at Epídavros. It is still known for its extraordinary acoustics. The popularity of the works of Sophocles, Euripides and their rivals is clear from the fact that this theatre could seat up to 13,000 spectators. Set in thick pine woods, it was hidden for many centuries, but since 1955 Epídavros has been the venue for a summer theatre festival. There are similar theatre festivals at several other places, including Thásos.

The birth of Tragedy Tragedy, strangely enough, has its origins in the most carefree of all Greek festivals, the Dionysia, a time of orgiastic celebration. It was at the Dionysia in Athens in 536BC that Thespis first put in front of the festival audience an actor and a chorus. The success of his venture can be gauged by the popularity of tragedies at subsequent festivals.

Aeschylus' revolution Aeschylus (525–456BC), the first great tragic poet, went against tradition by putting several actors on stage at the same time, creating drama between them and by giving the chorus more of a background role. He is believed to have composed more than 80 plays, although only seven survive, the most famous being *The Persians*, about the the Greek victory at Salamis and the *Oresteia*, a trilogy of plays about Orestes, who avenged the murder of his father Agamemnon.

Human failings At the festival of 468BC, Aeschylus found himself competing with a younger poet by the name of Sophocles, who won the laurels that year and became the Athenians' favourite. Sophocles (496–406BC) stands out as the master of Greek tragedy. Where the characters of Aeschylus are doomed from their opening lines, Sophocles' characters are plausible human beings who bring tragedy on themselves. They are brilliantly drawn, with all their human desires and failings. As a dramatist, Sophocles also understood that he could move his audience with pathos, as is obvious in his masterpieces, *Antigone*, still popular today and *Oedipus Rex*, on which Aristotle based his poetic theory and from which Freud named the Oedipus complex.

The development of the theatre In the 6th century BC, when Thespis was putting on his tragedies, 'theatres' were little more than open spaces in front of the tent in which actors and chorus prepared themselves for the performance. By the 5th century BC, a more permanent theatre was evolving in Athens to meet the demands of this changing art form; a stone auditorium on the side of the Acropolis, near the temple of Dionysos, was finally completed around 330BC. It could seat more than 20,000 people. (All that can be seen today are its foundations.) As dramas became more complicated and as audiences became larger, so the design of theatres needed to be changed, until the stage was raised, the orchestra sunk and the place began to look like something that we would recognize as a theatre.

Having a laugh One of the reasons for the growing popularity of theatre was the advent of a poet called Aristophanes (*c*448–*c*380BC), who abandoned the familiar legends about heroes and gods and instead staged satires about contemporary issues and characters. In one of them, *The Frogs*, he has Euripides (see panel) and Aeschylus competing against each other for the tragic prize in the afterworld—and so comedy was born out of tragedy.

The legacy When the Romans conquered Greece they maintained the theatres and Roman poets and playwrights continued Greek traditions. Virgil's *Aeneid* traces the founding of Rome back to a character Homer mentions at the sack of Troy. However, the fall of the Roman Empire brought an end to classical theatre. Plays were not performed again in Europe until the 15th century, initially accompanying religious festivals, as in early Greece. The texts of some early Greek plays survive and are now performed at theatres throughout the world.

The renowned Hellenistic theatre of ancient Thásos

THE THIRD GREAT TRAGEDIAN

The third of the great Attic tragic poets, Euripides (*c*480–406BC), brought to tragedy his gift for plot development. Although not as popular in his lifetime as his contemporary Sophocles—it is significant that he died outside his native land, in Macedonia—his work increased in popularity after his death. Of the 90 or so dramas that he wrote, 18 have survived, more than the surviving works of both Aeschylus and Sophocles together.

ARISTOPHANES' HUMOUR

In his comedy *Wasps*, Aristophanes showed that no subject was taboo in his theatre. A character called Xanthias has the following lines:
'Like that prostitute I visited yesterday at midday, When I told her to get on top, she got mad at me And asked if I wanted to set up a tyranny like Hippias.'

Classical artists often represented theatre scenes on ceramics

The Saronic Islands

The Saronic Islands
Aígina (ΑΙΓΙΝΑ)
Póros (ΠΟΡΟΣ)
Salamína
  (ΣΑΛΑΜΙΝΑ)
Spétses (ΣΠΕΤΣΕΣ)
Ýdra (ΨΔΡΑ)

Pages 220–221: the Póros Strait, so lyrically described in Henry Miller's The Colossus of Maroussi

THE SARONIC ISLANDS Sitting just south of Athens and its busy port, Piréas, the islands in the Saronic Gulf were among the first to be visited by pleasure-seekers. But although some of them have become almost a commuter belt for Athenians, the five main islands in this group have maintained some of their character and offer plenty of opportunities within reach of the capital.

WAR AND PEACE Although the islands are so close to the mainland, their history has been dominated by the sea. Ýdra was uninhabited in antiquity, but Salamína, Aígina and Póros (known as the island of Poseidon) were home to important seafaring communities. Salamína is famous for the sea battle that took place in 480BC off the narrow strait between it and the mainland, when the much smaller Greek navy outmanouvred the ships of the Persian King Xerxes. Neighbouring Aígina sent 30 ships to join the Greek fleet, an indication of its strength. The islanders were renowned for their skill at sea; ships from Aígina traded throughout the Mediterranean and the island was

222

Tiers of white-walled, red-tiled mansions around the idyllic horse-shoe harbour of Ýdra

BEST BEACHES
The Saronic Islands are not the best place to go for that idyllic seaside vacation since their beaches tend to be crowded with both Athenians and foreign visitors. However, the best of the lot is at Ágioi Anárgyroi on Spétses.

wealthy and powerful. But 50 years after the Persian defeat, the people of Aígina made the mistake of siding with the Spartans against Athens; after the Spartan defeat, Aígina was destroyed. The rest is history: Athens had all the glory, the Saronic Islands lived in her shadow, but Aígina's Temple of Aphaia serves as a reminder of just how grand the island was in the 5th century BC.

MODERN HISTORY During the War of Independence against the Turks, the Spétsian heroine Laskarína Bouboulína saved her native island in dramatic fashion (see panel on page 229). Aígina's past glory was recalled a few years later when Ioánnis Kapodístrias was sworn in as first governor of the free Greek state in Aígina's cathedral. The island's main town acted briefly as the first state capital and the first modern drachma was minted there.

LANDSCAPES AND FARMING The islands in the Saronic Gulf might be rocky, with poor volcanic soil, but they do support agriculture and, in some places, an abundance of wildlife. Aígina is the most fertile and its pistachio crop is so renowned that it has given the nut its Greek name, *aíginas*. Ýdra's fine houses are known for their gardens, while Spétses is famous for its woods of Aleppo pine.

CHOOSING YOUR SEASON Because of the number of Athenians who stay there and the even greater number of day-trippers, some Saronic Island ports have a cosmopolitan air, with the sort of cafés, restaurants and expensive boutiques that you would expect to see in Mýkonos. In summer, as elsewhere, beaches are crowded and discos noisy. So if island life and archaeology are what you are looking for then consider visiting off season. The sea may be too cold or rough for bathing, but the views will be unobstructed and you might have the privilege of hearing the islanders speaking their native language—a mix of old Albanian and Greek—instead of *kafeneía* English.

MYTHOLOGICAL ISLANDS
According to mythology the first king of Aígina was Aeacus, offspring of the liaison between Zeus and Aígina. Aeacus had three sons, Peleus, Telemon and his favourite, Phocos. When Phocos was killed by his jealous brothers, the latter were exiled, Peleus to Thessaly and Telemon to Salamina, where they proceeded to establish their dynasties. Peleus' son Achilles and Telemon's son Ajax were among the greatest warriors of the Trojan war.

223

THE ISLANDS IN A DAY
The Saronic Islands are known as the 'offshore islands' because of their proximity to Athens. They are close enough for it to be possible to visit an island for the day and be back in the city by nightfall. Athenian travel agents also offer a one-day cruise, usually to three of the islands; Aígina, Ýdra and Póros.

HENRY MILLER ON ÝDRA
'Hydra is a rock which rises out of the sea like a huge loaf of petrified bread. It is the bread turned to stone which the artist receives as reward for his labours when he first catches sight of the promised land.'
Henry Miller, *The Colossus of Maroussi* (London, 1942)

A GOOD ESCAPE
The small island of Agkístri, only a short boat ride away from Aígina and the latest to be included in travel brochures, still offers some authentic island life, especially off season. The main town Skála is already overbuilt, but Mílos still has an attractive village centre with a good beach close by.

224

CONNECTIONS
Aígina has ferry links with Piréas, Méthana, Póros, Ýdra, Spétses, Agkístri, Ermióni and Portochéli. Hydrofoil services operate to most of these places and one-day cruises to Póros, Ýdra and Spétses are also offered by local travel agents.

The Temple of Aphaia is one of the best preserved in Greece

AÍGINA

Athenians often regard Aígina as their nearest clean beach. Many visitors come only to visit the Temple of Aphaia.

▶▶ Aígina Town 223B3

Aígina harbour is always busy with hydrofoils, fishermen and the boats bringing fresh produce from the mainland. North of the port stands the *Kolóna*, a lone column from the ruined **Temple of Apollo▶** (*Open* Tue–Sun 8.30–3. *Admission charge*). The town has some grand houses from the brief period, in the 19th century, when it was the first capital of Greece.

An Archaeological Museum (*Open* Tue–Sun 8.30–3. *Admission charge*) exhibits the island finds that have not been removed to Athens. It was built on the site of what was the very first Archaeological Museum in Greece.

▶▶▶ Naós Afaía (Temple of Aphaia) 223B3

Tel: 22970 32398. Open: Mon–Fri 8–7 (5pm closing in winter), Sat, Sun and public holidays 8–3. Admission charge
Regular buses from Aígina Town and Agía Marína
This Doric temple, the best-preserved Classical temple in the Greek Islands, was built around 490BC, on the site of a more ancient cult place. It was dedicated to the Cretan nymph Aphaia, who was connected with Artemis and was worshipped as the protector of women. The temple's pediments, depicting the battles of Troy, were found intact but were removed to Munich.

▶ Pérdika 223B3

This quiet fishing village, overlooking the island of Moní, is renowned for its waterfront fish tavernas. Daily boats leave here for the small island of Moní, mainly a nature reserve but with some bays for bathing.

Beaches
The best places to swim include the small beach near the Kolóna (near Aígina Town), in west-coast Marathóna, or on Moní islet.

Cycle ride

To the Temple of Aphaia (Naós Afaía)

A steep ride, either by motorcycle or by bicycle for the more energetic, takes you from the present capital Aígina to the old capital Palaiochóri and from the modern monastery of Ágios Nektários to the ancient site of worship, Naós Afaía (Temple of Aphaia) (12km/7.5 miles each way; allow half a day. Bicycle and motorcycle hire agencies line the waterfront, but shop around since prices can vary).

Leave the waterfront in Aígina Town, going away from the ferry landing, passing the Hotel Brown and then taking the second street to the left, at the Hotel Miranda. Follow signposts for Agía Marína and, uphill, take the second street on the right. The road winds through pistachio orchards, past pretty villas and small villages. Turn right at the end of the road. About 5km (3 miles) from Aígina, on the left, you will see the monastery of Ágios Nektários. The enormous church, dominating the landscape, houses the tomb of a bishop from Aígina who died in 1920 and was canonized in 1967. Pass the signpost for Ágios Nektários and continue for 500m (545 yards) to the deserted old island capital of Palaiochóri, an extraordinary place where only 20 of the supposed original 365 churches and monasteries remain. A few are open in the morning.

Returning to the main road, turn left towards the pretty village of Mesagrós in the middle of vineyards and pine woods, whose products are combined to make excellent local retsina. Go past the churchyard taking the straight (slightly towards the left) road for Agía Marína and soon the **Temple of Aphaia** (see page 224) will come into sight, towering over the landscape and offering an interesting stop with magnificent views over the island. Make the return to Aígina Town by the same route.

The modern church of Ágios Nektários is dedicated to a rather controversial saint, only recently canonized

Many visitors to the Greek Islands expect to encounter mosquitoes or butterflies and to find some fish or squid on their plates, but few take time to find out about the islands' rich and varied wildlife. Sadly the visitors themselves are unwittingly one of the biggest threats to a fragile wildlife environment which is home to a number of endangered species.

A southern festoon, one of the most striking butterflies to be seen in the islands

WILDLIFE REHABILITATION

Aígina has one of the most successful animal rehabilitation centres in Greece. The Hellenic Wildlife Rehabilitation Centre, 10km (6 miles) southeast of Aígina Town, near Pahia Rahi, cares for thousands of animals every year. It looks after wild animals hurt during the hunting season, but also stray cats and dogs from the cities. Where possible the animals are released after recovery (tel: 22970 28367. *Open* daily 10–7; www.ekpaz.gr/index-en.html). Donations are welcome

FOREST FIRES

Every summer many hectares of Greek forests are destroyed by fires, sometimes started accidentally but too often lit on purpose by shepherds wanting more grazing, or by developers with their eye on another stretch of land. Repeated fires result in a barren, desert-like scrubland which, without ground cover, is very vulnerable to erosion. Wildlife also suffers in fires, as amphibians and reptiles rarely move fast enough to escape the flames and birds are asphyxiated by the smoke.

The hoopoe

Marine life Mainland Greece has its fair share of nature reserves and wildlife sanctuaries, but it is the marine life around the islands that is most under threat. The Northern Sporades have been chosen for the first (and long overdue) National Marine Park, where several endangered creatures including the Mediterranean monk seal will find protection. Of special interest are the loggerhead turtles, still quite numerous but seriously threatened by tourism. Playful dolphins often follow yachts and ferries, but sharks are seldom spotted near the islands' coasts. The Greek seas, like other parts of the Mediterranean, are heavily overfished and their fish stocks are decreasing.

Birdwatching in the islands The Greek Islands and Crete in particular, are fascinating for birdwatchers, who can see both resident Mediterranean species and, primarily from mid-March to mid-May, migratory birds on their way from East Africa and the Nile to Northern Europe, from where they return south in the autumn. In the mountains it is common to find rock nuthatches, buzzards, smaller eagles, alpine choughs and griffon vultures. With some luck it is possible to spot a rare vulture found mainly on the plateaus of Crete, the lammergeier. Near the coast you will see several species of egret and heron, black-winged stilts and marsh harriers. Outside villages and in the hills, swallows, nightingales, crows, crag martins, kestrels, tiny Scops owls, golden orioles and lovely black and white hoopoes can also be seen.

226

Insects Most people would probably rather not encounter insects on their holiday, but they can be beautiful and fascinating to watch. Even if you do not see them, the noisy presence of grasshoppers and cicadas will not go unnoticed. A great variety of beetles, flies, mosquitoes and wasps all make their home here, but probably the most beautiful of Greece's insects are the butterflies, especially visible in spring and summer. Crete, again, has some very colourful species such as the southern festoon with red, yellow and black zigzags; big bright yellow Cleopatras; and tiny green hairstreaks.

Reptiles Lizards of various species are found everywhere but they can be shy, darting away as you approach. However, look for them basking among the stones of ancient sites in the midday sun. The almost fluorescent Balkan green lizard, which can grow up to 50cm (20in) long, is quite common and unmistakable. In the Dodecanese and northern Cyclades it is possible to find the brown-greyish, iguana-like agama or Rhodes dragon and Crete is one of the few places in Europe where chameleons can be spotted. At night, geckoes come out to devour mosquitoes. Of several species of snake, only the cat snake is poisonous.

Mammals Comparatively few mammals are found in the islands but there are some endemic species especially in Crete, such as the Cretan spiny mouse and the island's mascot, the rare kri-kri or wild goat, now surviving mainly in nature reserves on deserted islets. Skýros has a rare variety of small wild horse, and monk seals can sometimes be spotted around Alónnisos (see page 236). Most islands are home to smaller mammals, such as hares, badgers, weasels, mice, rats and bats.

Threats Fish stocks are limited in the seas around the islands and until recently fishermen often killed the monk seals, which sometimes damaged their nets while looking for food. Pollution from fast-growing industries and forest fires is another danger as well as the undoubted threat from the large number of visitors, causing pollution and habitat loss as coast and countryside are lost to development. The most well-publicized example is the plight of the loggerhead turtles on Zákynthos (see panel on page 199). The tourist industry has grown very quickly and protecting the environment from its more undesirable consequences has often been ignored until it was too late to prevent damage.

A bee-eater

227

ARCHIPELAGOS
Archipelagos Aigaiou is a private non-profit environmental organization, which does research and protects the marine environment of the eastern Aegean. It is based on the island of Ikaría and has another base on Arki. It works together with universities all over Europe as well as with local people, to develop a programme of sustainable conservation (tel: 22750 71503; www.archipelago.gr). Another group, also by the name of Archipelagos, based in Argostóli on Kefalloniá (tel: 26710 24565) works in the Ionian Islands, and is concerned with the endangered monk seal and marine pollution. Both are working to have as many areas as possible designated as protected national parks.

The Balkan green lizard

USEFUL NUMBERS
Askeli Travel (for information and tickets on
Póros) tel: 22980 24900
Tourist Police (Póros)
tel: 22980 22256
www.poros.gr
www.poros-island.com
Alasia (for information
and tickets on Spétses)
tel: 22980 74098
Tourist Police (Spétses)
tel: 22980 73100
www.spetsesdirect.com
www.salamina.gr

THE STRAIT OF PÓROS
'If there is one dream
which I like above all others it is that of sailing on
land. Coming into Póros
gives the illusion of the
deep dream. Suddenly the
land converges on all
sides and the boat is
squeezed into a narrow
strait from which there
seems to be no
egress...To sail slowly
through the streets of
Póros is to recapture the
joy of passing through
the neck of the womb. It
is a joy too deep to be
remembered.'
Henry Miller, *The
Colossus of Maroussi*
(London, 1942)

THE BATTLE OF SALAMIS
On the stretch of water
between the mainland and
the bleak town of
Paloúkia, a battle took
place which changed the
course of European
history. In 480BC the
Persian fleet under King
Xerxes, who was already
occupying Attica, was all
set for victory over the
Athenians and
Peloponnesians who had
retreated to the waters
near Salamína. The Greek
fleet was outnumbered by
about two to one, but
thanks to the Athenian
strategist Themistocles,
the Persian fleet was outmanouvred and forced to
retreat.

PÓROS

Póros, separated from the mainland only by a 350m-wide
(1,150ft) strait, is in fact two islands: Sferiá, a small,
crowded island occupied almost entirely by the bustle of
Póros Town and the larger and until recently much wilder
Kalávria. Both Póros and the nearby mainland town of
Galatás have opened their doors to package tourism. Most
of the hotels are on Kalávria, but Póros Town has plenty of
more basic accommodation and a wide choice of places to
eat, both on the busy quayside and up in the town.

▶▶ Póros Town   223B2
Looking across to the mainland, Póros Town has a lively
and atmospheric waterfront—a good place to linger over a
meal or a drink, or simply watch the world go by. There is
a small **Archaeological Museum▶** (*Open* Tue–Sun 8.30–3.
Admission free) and a blue-domed clocktower from where
there are fine views over the mountains and sea. The
Greek Navy has a training college on the north side of
the town, evidence of the island's long and continuing
maritime tradition.

▶▶ Galatás   223B2
Galatás is a fast-developing mainland resort across the
strait from Póros, with two good beaches, Pláka and Alíki.
The **Limonódassos**, just beyond Alíki, is a vast lemon
grove with more than 30,000 trees and a taverna serving
fresh lemonade. From Galatás it is possible to travel by bus
to the renowned ancient theatre at Epidavros and other
mainland sites.

▶▶ Kalávria   223B2
On a longer visit to Póros, it is worth crossing the bridge to
Kalávria, though not, perhaps, for its beaches. Up in the
hills, well away from the ranks of seaside hotels, there are
some fine views over the sea and the Peloponnese. Places
to visit include a ruined 6th-century BC **Temple of
Poseidon** and the abandoned 18th-century monastery of
Zoodóchos Pigí▶ (*Open* sunrise–1.30 and 4.30–sunset).

Beaches
Kanáli has the best beach, but an admission fee is charged
to all who wish to use it. Farther down Askéli Bay there is
good bathing, but even more hotels are under construction here.

SALAMÍNA

Salamína sees few tourists, as its beaches are too close to
the pollution of Athens and Piréas to be recommended.
The island is remembered historically for the Battle of
Salamis, a momentous victory by Athens over the Persians
in 480BC (see panel).

▶ Salamína Town (Kouloúri)   223B4
Most people live here in the island's capital, a sprawl of
concrete buildings. There are no facilities for visitors and
nowhere to stay, but there is a good bus system to the villages. Bus No. 8 passes near the **monastery of Panágia
Faneroméni▶**, whose two churches have good 18th- and
19th-century wall paintings.

▶ **Aiánteio** *223B4*

This cosy village has a small pebble beach. The charming Hotel Gabriel is owned by Mr. Tzimas, an enthusiastic poet and journalist, who often recites his work.

▶ **Paloúkia** *223B4*

Paloúkia is the port of arrival and an important military base, but there is nothing worth staying for.

▶▶ **Selínia** *223B4*

Selínia is a summer resort popular with Greeks. There are several daily ferry connections to Piréas. The waterfront is quite pleasing and has a few tavernas.

SPÉTSES

Group tourism has reached Spétses, the farthest from Athens of the Saronic Islands, but away from the main town and the noise of the mopeds, there are still cool Aleppo pine forests and some fine beaches away from the crowds. There are few cars on Spetses; only locally owned ones are allowed, but the number of motorbikes and scooters makes up for this. If you don't fancy a scooter then a mountain bike is perfect to explore the island, and it is small enough for walking to be a pleasant option. There are a few buses in summer, but the service is erratic out of season.

▶▶ **Spétses Town** *223A1*

On summer days the port (Dápia—a name often used to refer to the town itself) is mobbed by hordes of day-trippers, so locals and resident visitors tend to emerge only in the early evening, after they have gone. The **Spétses Museum▶** (tel: 22980 72994. *Open* Tue–Sun 8.30–2. *Admission charge*), in the beautiful Hadziyánnis Mexís mansion (follow signposts from the waterfront), has a small collection of local costumes, memorabilia from the War of Independence and the bones of the local heroine Laskarína Bouboulína. Her statue, dressed in baggy pirate trousers, stands to the west of the new harbour. The

A few boatyards on Spétses still build sturdy kaíki, a familiar sight in the islands' harbours

229

CONNECTIONS
The easiest way to reach Salamína is by ferry from Pérama (near Piréas) to Paloúkia. Póros and Spétses have ferry links with each other and with Piréas, Aígina, Ýdra, Ermióni, Portochéli and Méthana. Hydrofoils operate to Piréas and the other Saronic Islands (except Salamína).

LA BOUBOULÍNA
In 1821, Laskarína Bouboulína led the uprising of Spétses against the Turks with her own fleet and army. Considered the local Jeanne d'Arc, she is remembered for her courage, having lost two husbands in pirate raids and subsequently losing two sons during the War of Independence. Accounts of her bravery include the story of her placing hats on bushes along the shore, to make the Turks think that soldiers were hiding there.

Laskarína Bouboulína overlooking the comings and goings of ferries in Spétses' harbour

230

Laskarína Bouboulína House▶▶ is now a private museum (*Open* Tue–Sun 9–9, in summer. *Admission charge*).

On the same square is the grand, slightly crumbling villa of the island's benefactor, Sotírios Anárgiros (see panel on page 231). Nearby on the waterfront is the impressive Possidonion Hotel. A 20-minute walk towards the east past some fine villas leads to the old harbour, Palaió Limáni, still with a boatyard and some good fish tavernas. Watching over all the activity is the old cathedral of Ágios Nikólaos, from whose clocktower the Greek flag was raised in April 1821, heralding Spétses' entrance into the War of Independence.

Beaches

Boat trips run to the bigger beaches in summer, so do not expect to have a beach all to yourself. West of Spétses Town are some hidden coves and pleasant beaches with tavernas, particularly Vrelloú and Zogeriá. Agía Paraskeví is a pretty beach with a little church, but Ágioi Anárgyroi is definitely the finest of all, a long bay with fine sand which fills up quickly in summer. Heading east, Agía Marína has good bathing and a taverna.

Walk

Spétses' pine forests

A walk along part of the road that rings Spétses island, built by the millionaire Sotírios Anárgiros to reveal its beauty, tranquillity and wonderful beaches. Instead of completing the circle on the road, return by climbing through the pine forests at the centre of the island (approximately 6km/4 miles; allow a whole day, including stops for bathing).

Start from Spétses Town, head west past the Possidonion and Spétses hotels. The imposing Anárgiros College soon appears on the left. The road winds on through pine trees, with views below of wonderfully clear coves and rocky sunbathing spots, to reach Vrelloú. The beach here (though sometimes litter-strewn) is pleasant and there are some good coves suitable for bathing.

Return to the road and walk on to Zogeriá, which has lovely coves, trees for shade and a few small tavernas. Off the road as it continues towards Agía Paraskeví there are larger coves for bathing, worth the long walk down small paths. Agía Paraskeví has a small, easily accessible beach with a white chapel. On the hill above is the Villa Yasemia, which appears in John Fowles's *The Magus* (see panel on page 231).

Farther on, the road suddenly reaches a residential area and the fine sandy beach of Ágioi Anárgyroi. This is a popular lunch spot and the beach is a good place to rest before heading inland. Walk to the main road and turn left. After about 200m (220 yards), past the villas on the right, look for a small path heading uphill. Beyond here directions are difficult to give, but at the top of the hill keep to the path that veers to the right. The pine forests are slowly recovering from the fires that destroyed them between 1990 and 2000, so the vistas are not always clear, but if you get lost you can always orientate yourself by following the direction of the boats heading for the new harbour. Depending on the path you have taken, you will arrive back in town either at the Spétses Hotel or farther on at the Lazaros Taverna.

ÝDRA

Wild rocky shores and one of the most beautiful and sophisticated harbours in the Aegean mean that Ýdra Town is completely overrun in summer. But as there is no transport apart from donkeys and boats, few visitors venture beyond the edge of the town.

►►► Ýdra Town   223B1

Arriving in Ýdra is truly magnificent; savour the view of the town descending dramatically into the perfect crescent-shaped harbour. The waterfront has many fine mansions, built by 19th-century shipbuilders and sea captains One grand building, off Odós Lignou, is the 18th-century **Lazaros Koundoriotis Mansion►►** (*Open* Tue–Sun 9–4. *Admission charge*) with period furniture. The **Byzantine Museum►►** (entrance under the clocktower. *Open* Tue–Sun 10–5, in summer. *Admission charge*), in the Monastery of Panagía Mitropóleos, has an icon collection.

►► Monasteries   223B1

Paths lead from the town to isolated monasteries inland. About an hour uphill are the **convent of Agía Evpraxía►** and the **monastery of Profítis Ilías►** and, farther away, the **monastery of Agía Triáda►**, where women are not admitted. The views alone justify the climb.

Beaches

Mandráki is the island's only real beach, with pebbles A path west of the harbour leads to a small, popular, pebbly beach just before Kamíni and, farther on, to Kastéllo, another pebble beach. The south coast has beautiful coves for bathing, such as Bísti and Ágios Nikólaos, most easily reached by boat from Ydra Town.

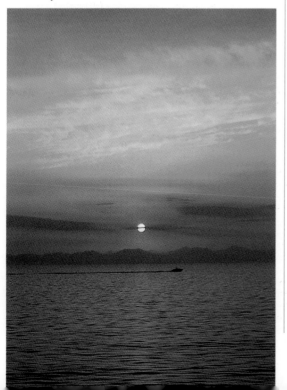

USEFUL NUMBER
Tourist Police (Ýdra)
tel: 22980 52205
www.hydra-island.com

THE GOOD MILLIONAIRE
Sotírios Anárgiros, a 19th-century native adventurer who made his fortune in America, came back to make Spétses the island of his dreams. He built a circular road around the island, dug wells and planted the pine forests that enhance Spétses today. He founded the Anárgiros College, for children of rich families from all over Greece (and the novelist John Fowles, who taught here, see below).

231

DIVING IN HYDRA
Diving around Ýdra's rock is increasingly popular. Hydra Divers offers a wide range of diving trips as well as equipment rental (tel: 22980 53900; www.divingteam.gr).

Once the daytrippers leave, Ýdra town regains its delightful mixture of peace and joie-de-vivre

CONNECTIONS
Both ferries and hydrofoils link Ýdra with Piréas and the other Saronic Islands.

THE MAGUS
The English writer John Fowles lived for a while on Spétses, while teaching English at the Anárgiros College. His famous novel *The Magus* was set on the island and both the Possidonion Hotel and the college are mentioned. On top of the hill near Agía Paraskeví is the Villa Yasemia, where the late Alkis Botassis resided. He prided himself on having inspired Fowles to write *The Magus*.

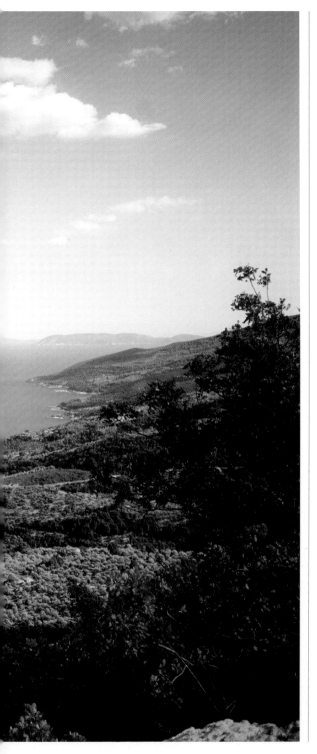

The Sporades and Évvoia

The Sporades and Évvoia

Alónnisos
 (ΑΛΟΝΝΗΣΟΣ)
Skíathos (ΣΚΙΑΘΟΣ)
Skópelos
 (ΣΚΟΠΕΛΟΣ)
Skýros (ΣΚΥΡΟΣ)
Évvoia (EYBOIA)

▶▶▶ REGION HIGHLIGHTS

Glóssa see *page 238*
Kástro *see page 237*
Skópelos *see page 238*

Pages 232–233: The rugged green coastline typical of the Sporades; Skíathos lies in the distance

Below: the landscape of southern Évvoia

THE SPORADES AND ÉVVOIA The Sporades are aptly named. The 'scattered ones' lie off the eastern coast of Thessaly and, perhaps because of their location, were overlooked by foreign fun-seekers. The Greeks have long preferred them for their great beaches, clean water and wooded hills. Now, direct charter flights have transformed Skíathos and Skópelos and are changing the face of Alónnisos and Skýros. Even so, there is still plenty of scope to get away from it all and if the Sporades seem too busy, nearby Évvoia beckons.

SPORADIC MYTHS The Minoans from Crete colonized the Sporades around the 16th century BC and brought with them the olive tree and the vine, which the islanders soon learned to cultivate with skill: wine from ancient Alónnisos was traded throughout the region. The islands were later settled by the Dolopians, seafaring Mycenaeans. Among them was Peleus, whose son, the great Achilles, led the Dolopian warriors in the Trojan

234

War. Skýros, especially, is rich in mythology from this period, for this was where Achilles' mother hid him to stop him going to Troy, where it had been prophesied that he would die. As another prophecy had announced that the Achaeans would not win at Troy without Achilles, he went to fight. During his stay on Skýros, he fathered a son, Neoptolemus, out of a liaison with King Lycomedes' daughter. After Achilles' glorious death, another prophecy announced that the Greeks would not win at Troy until Neoptolemus was fighting with them: Troy fell after his arrival on the scene.

BEST BEACHES
● Koukounariés and Banana beaches (Skíathos)
● Lalaria beach (Skíathos)
● Magaziá and Mólos (Skýros)
● Kokkinókastro (Alónnisos)

THESEUS' REVENGE When Theseus, the king of Athens who had killed the minotaur in Knosós (see panel on page 85), arrived on Skýros, King Lycomedes, fearing for his throne, killed the hero. The incident was without consequence for several centuries, until 476BC, when the oracle at Delphi insisted that Theseus' bones must be returned to Athens. An army was then sent, the islanders were made slaves and the other islands in the group, including Évvoia, were colonized. The hero's bones were then reinterred in his city. From Athens to Rome, Byzantium and Venice, the Sporades knew many masters, but, thanks finally to Turkish indolence, after the pirate Barbarossa had sacked the islands, they managed to retain their individual identity.

THE FIRST GREEKS
It was from Évvoia that the Greeks got their name, for one of the tribes from the island was known as the Graeci. Under the Roman occupation, all people of the area began to be referred to as the Graeci, or Greeks.

ISLAND LANDSCAPES There is great variety in the look of the islands. Alónnisos is the most remote, untamed and the least developed, and its waters are now the cleanest in the Aegean, having been declared a national marine park. Its mountainous interior provides excellent if demanding walking.

On Skíathos, other visitors are never far away, even in the hills, but the island has some of Greece's finest beaches. There are beautiful walks through hilly farmland on Skópelos, which still earns more from olives than from visitors. This island is also noted for its plums, pears and almonds, but at sea level it is getting harder to avoid the developments. Skýros has a greater variety, with barren mountains in the south and gentle walking through pine-clad hills and fertile valleys in the north.

THE FERTILE ISLAND Évvoia is the second largest Greek island, separated from the mainland by a narrow channel and near enough to the capital for Athenians to come just to eat, but its fields, hills and villages are a world away from the city's noise and pollution. Although the main town, Chalkída, is industrial, the rugged northeast, the mountainous centre, the open farmlands and the hidden coves make Évvoia one of the most fascinating islands to explore. This one, perhaps more than any, needs time.

Cats are a familiar sight on Alónnisos

USEFUL NUMBERS
Police (Alónnisos)
tel: 24240 65205
Alónnisos Travel (for tickets, excursions and general information)
tel: 24240 65188
www.alonissos.com

THE MONK SEAL
The Mediterranean monk seal is near extinction. There are only about 400 left, of which 40 live around Alónnisos. Until the waters were declared a national marine park in 1992, the seals were being killed by fishermen because they can damage their nets. The Hellenic Society for the Protection of the Monk Seal in Stení Vála on Alónnisos has won strong local support. Little by little, seal pups from a seal crèche in Holland are being released into the park. But in spite of growing numbers, there is still little chance of seeing the seals, as they often hide in sea caves. If you do spot them, try not to get any closer as they are easily scared away from their habitat.

ALÓNNISOS

This mountainous island, the quietest and most remote of the Sporades, is a paradise for walkers. Although the island suffered badly in the 1965 earthquake, there is plenty to discover if you have time and energy to spare: large areas are accessible only on foot, as roads on Alónnisos are few. Shops on the waterfront in Patitíri sell the excellent walking guide *Alonisos on Foot: A Walking & Swimming Guide*, by Bente Keller and Elias Tsoukanas.

▶ Patitíri   235B3
Most islanders live in Patitíri, a concrete development with a few waterfront bars and tavernas. A bus (or a 30-minute walk) goes up to the picturesque **Palaiá Alónnisos▶▶**. Abandoned in the 1960s, following earthquake damage, the old village with its narrow, cobbled streets is coming to life again as its houses are being restored for the summer by Athenians, British and Germans.

▶▶ Stení Vála   235B3
This is a small, tranquil village with nearby pebbly beaches. There are some rooms for rent, a campsite and a few restaurants.

▶▶ Nearby islets   235B3/C3
In summer there are daily excursions to neighbouring islets. Peristéra has fine sandy beaches which are often empty. Kyrá Panagía, home to a few wild goats, has good sandy beaches and two empty monasteries. Gioúra, a reserve for wild goats, claims to have the cave where the Cyclops imprisoned Odysseus. Pipéri is a reserve for monk seals (see panel), and visitors are now banned.

Beaches
The best beaches, most of which are on the more sheltered east coast, are reached by boat. Chrysí Miliá, crowded in summer, has pine trees and a taverna. Kokkinókastro has a lovely pebbly beach, remains of ancient Ikos and a taverna. Stení Vála has good pebble beaches and Ágios Dímitrios, farther up the coast, is often empty. In the south of the island is Vithísma, a good sand and pebble beach, as well as Vrisítsa, on the west coast.

235B3

The best view of lively Skíathos Town is from a distance. Close up, the centre of town looks very tourist-orientated and soulless

SKÍATHOS (Skiáthos)

With the best beaches in the Sporades, if not in all Greece, Skíathos gets very crowded in summer. Although this is no longer the place to find the 'real Greece', a walk inland soon reveals the island's striking nature.

►► Skíathos Town   235B3

What was left of Skíathos Town after World War II has been taken over by the tourist trade. More bars and tavernas open every year and even the Boúrtzi fortress now has a bar. The **Papadiamántis House►** (off Plateía Papadiamántis, near the harbour. *Open* Tue–Sun 9.30–1 and 5–8. *Admission charge*), now a museum, is filled with memorabilia of the native author who wrote about customs and traditions on the islands.

►►► Kástro   235B3

The sight of this 16th-century village is a great reward after the two-hour walk from the harbour. Abandoned in 1830 when the inhabitants moved to the main town after Greek independence, most houses fell into the sea and only three churches have survived, some with original frescoes. It remains a charming site.

►► Monasteries   235B3

A paved road off the road to the airport leads to the lovely **Evangelístria monastery►►** (tel: 24270 22012. *Open* daily 8–9. *Admission free*). A small track leads farther to the uninhabited but beautifully situated **monastery of Ágios Charálampos►**, from where it is possible to reach Kástro. Before Evangelístria, a signpost points the way to the 15th-century **Panagía tis Kehrias**, believed to be the oldest monastery on the island.

Beaches

Some say Koukounariés is the best beach in Greece—it's certainly one of the most crowded. The nearby Banana Beach is the island's trendiest. Vromólimnos is a lovely big sandy bay. Paths lead to Mandráki and Elia, less packed, even in summer. Lalaria beach, accessible only by boat, is dramatically surrounded by steep cliffs. To avoid the crowds you could head for the islet of Tsougriá.

USEFUL NUMBER
Tourist Police
tel: 24270 23172
www.skiathosinfo.com

237

WONDROUS CAVES
Some of the many spectacular caves in Skíathos's rugged rocky coastline can be visited by boat from the town. The most beautiful and most accessible are Spíliáa Káminari and the caves near Laláría beach: Skotiní, Glázia and Hálkini.

CONNECTIONS
Alónnisos and Skíathos are connected by ferry to each other and to Skópelos, Vólos and Ágios Konstantínos. Alónnisos also has ferry links with Kými (Évvoia), while from Skíathos ferries run to Oreoí (Évvoia), Tínos, Mýkonos, Páros, Thíra, Crete and Skýros. Both islands have hydrofoil links with Ágios Konstantínos, Vólos, Skópelos, Oreoí, Skýros and Thessaloníki and with each other. From Alónnisos, hydrofoils also run to Kými and from Skíathos to Chalkída and Aidipsoú (Évvoia).

Climb up through the back streets of Skópelos Town for lovely views

OLIVE TREES
Olives, not tourism, are
the main source of
income on Skópelos. In
November most of the
islanders get ready for
the picking season. Many
stay in the *kahlevi*, shel-
ters originally built for the
olive season, now often
restored as rural homes.
During the harvest,
tourists are forgotten and
the talk in town is all
about how big and how
plentiful the olives will be
and how much oil they
will yield. Once
harvested, the olives are
taken to the refinery, just
off the waterfront, where
olive oil is produced for
local use.

CONNECTIONS
Skópelos has ferry links
with Skíathos, Vólos,
Ágios Konstantínos,
Alónnisos, Oreoí or Kými
(Évvoia) and
Thessaloníki. Hydrofoil
services operate to
Alónnisos, Ágios
Konstantínos, Skíathos,
Vólos, Thessaloníki,
Skýros and Chalkída or
Oreoí (Évvoia).

SKÓPELOS

Skópelos's coastline is rugged, with steep cliffs and rocky
bays, while its interior is lush, with olive groves and fruit
orchards. The resorts are growing steadily, but Skópelos
still has a traditional feel and offers a welcome escape
from its crowded neighbour Skíathos.

▶▶▶ Skópelos   235B3
The waterfront in Skópelos Town is where most visitors
congregate. A walk through the streets behind, winding
up to the ruined Venetian *kástro*, will reveal the true character of the pretty town. There are supposedly 123
churches in the town and three monasteries stand just outside it (see Walk opposite). A small **Folklore Museum▶**
(Odós Hatzistamati. *Open* daily 10–10, in summer.
Admission charge) illustrates the old ways of the island.

▶▶▶ Glóssa   235B3
Skópelos's second town, Glóssa has a more traditional
feel. Perched high above the fishing harbour of Loutráki, it
is a charming Greek town with a few guest houses, some
kafeneía and fantastic sea views. A pleasant walk east leads
to the rather ugly **monastery of Ágios Ioánnis**, set on a rock
above a small cove with good bathing.

Beaches
The beach in Skópelos is sandy but far from clean.
Stáfylos, a 40-minute walk away, is quite rocky and very
popular. Pánormos is a crowded resort, but the pebble
beach between there and Miliá, facing the islet of Dasía, is
one of the best, with pines coming down to the beach.
Sáres, reached by boat from Skópelos, is pleasant and not
too crowded.

Walk

From Skópelos Town

A quiet walk through olive groves to two monasteries perched on the hills overlooking the town (approximately 5km/3 miles; allow 2 hours for the monastery of Evangelístria, or a good half-day for both monasteries). Take enough water and food for a picnic if you are planning the half-day trip. In summer start early to avoid motorcycles and midday heat.

Walk along the harbour front and the bay, past the row of hotels towards the hills opposite the town. At the end of the bay follow the paved road uphill through the olive groves.

At the Taverna Dilina the road forks and there are signs, left to the monastery of Evangelístria and right to Metamórfosis and Pródromos monasteries. Turn left and follow the dirt road, passing a fountain under two enormous sycamore trees, from which the local people get their drinking water.

Walk up 11 steep bends, or cut through on the even steeper goat paths, to the former monastery of **Evangelístria**►► (*Open* daily 8–1 and 4–7), which has stunning views over Skópelos Town. The monastery, now a convent rebuilt in 1712, has a gold-plated altar screen and a lovely 15th-century icon. The nuns make craft items which they sell to visitors. From here, either walk back down to town, or go as far as the Taverna Dilina and then walk uphill towards Metamórfosis. The more adventurous can follow the goat tracks from Evangelístria (ask the nuns for directions). The 16th-century monastery of **Metamórfosis**► is closed up for most of the year, but some monks from Mount Áthos stay there each August to celebrate the big annual *panagía*.

From Metamórfosis, either walk back down the road, or continue up the hill from the monastery and at the next bend take the small track along the rocks, which offers some magnificent views on the way back into Skópelos Town.

Bronze of Homer

The Iliad, *the oldest surviving work of Greek literature, tells of the war between the Greeks and the Trojans. While many of the events described in its 15,693 lines remain a matter of legend without historical evidence, Homer's evocation of the mighty warriors brings alive one of the ages of ancient civilization. Alexander the Great took the book with him when he set out to conquer the known world.*

PARIS

Also known as Alexandros, Paris is blamed by Homer for providing the cause for the Trojan War—the abduction of Helen—and thereby bringing about the downfall of his people and their city. Before this, he was famous for having been obliged to judge the beauty of Aphrodite, Hera and Athena; he chose Aphrodite, who promised him the most beautiful woman in the world: Helen. After the death of Hector, it was Paris who killed Achilles with an arrow in his heel.

ACHILLES

When Achilles' mother Thetis heard that her son was fated to die at Troy, she disguised him as a girl and hid him in the *kástro* of Skýros Town, the probable site of King Lycomedes' palace. When Odysseus came looking for Achilles, he brought gifts of jewellery, dresses and a sword. On leaving, Odysseus raised the alarm and while the ladies grabbed the jewellery and ran, Achilles instinctively seized the sword. Achilles became the most brilliant and feared of the Greek warriors, but for all his divine protection, he still died young.

The Trojan War Excavations at Truva in Turkey, close to Límnos, have uncovered what might be the fabled city of Troy, which once controlled the waterway between the Black Sea (and Asia) and the Mediterranean. Beyond that, there is very little evidence to authenticate the events of the Trojan War, believed to have taken place in the 12th century BC.

Homer's Trojan War Homer probably lived in the 8th century BC, over 300 years after the Trojan War. As most of his information about the war came from earlier tales and legends, historical accuracy was neither possible nor of interest, although the world he described would have been very real to him and his audience. The war, as he tells it, started when Paris, Prince of Troy, abducted Helen, wife of Menelaus of Sparta. Menelaus' brother, Agamemnon, the most powerful Greek ruler, collected an army of heroes and warriors, Achilles and Odysseus among them, and laid siege to Troy. The siege lasted 10 years and even then Troy's defences were only breached by Greek trickery: warriors hid in a massive wooden horse, presented to the Trojans as a gift, from which derives the saying, 'Beware of Greeks bearing gifts'.

The story of the *Iliad* Homer's companion work, the *Odyssey*, for all its suffering, is a comedy with a happy ending. The *Iliad* is a tragedy, ending in death and heartbreak beneath the negligent gaze of the gods, busy enjoying themselves up on Mount Olympus. And yet in telling the story, Homer makes us laugh, complain and feel elation before the tears roll. His interest is not in relating the events of the Trojan War: his story begins and ends during the 10th year of the siege and concerns a quarrel between Agamemnon and Achilles over a girl. As a result of Agamemnon taking the girl, Achilles withdraws his warriors from the Greek ranks. The Trojans take advantage of this rift and almost drive the Greeks into the sea. In response, Achilles allows his men to fight under the command of his friend Patroclus. The counter-attack is successful, but Patroclus is killed by Hector, King Priam's son and bravest of the Trojans. Seeking revenge, Achilles rejoins the war and kills Hector, dragging his corpse around the walls of Troy tied to his chariot. The Trojans pay a ransom to recover Hector's body, King Priam gives him a solemn burial and the *Iliad* ends with the line: 'Such were the funeral rites for Hector, tamer of horses'.

The islands and the *Iliad* The Greek Islands play an important part in the *Iliad* and their heroes are often mentioned. The most famous, and the main character in the *Odyssey*, is Odysseus, prince of Itháki (see pages 182–183). Others are the Abantes from Évvoia, with their long hair and ash spears, the proud-hearted men of Rhodes who filled nine ships, warriors from Aígina, from 'Crete of the Hundred Towns' as Homer calls it, from Kós, Kárpathos and a number of other islands.

Achilles dragging the corpse of brave Hector round the walls of Troy

241

HECTOR
Hector is one of Homer's most moving characters. The eldest son of King Priam and Queen Hecuba, brother of Paris, whose abducting of Helen was the primary cause of the war, Hector is described as the ideal hero—brave as a warrior, tender as a husband and father, attentive as a son. In earlier stories about the Trojan War, Paris was presented as the Trojan general, but Homer appears to have promoted Hector, finding in him the qualities that made him the equal of the leader of the Greeks, Achilles.

An entrance through the 'Cyclopean' walls of Gergis at the site of ancient Troy

Sporades

Isolated and far from Athens, Skýros has retained its traditions

242

DANCING WITH THE GOATS
Skýros is renowned for its traditional festivals, the most intriguing being the Carnival, held seven weeks before Easter, at which a 'goat dance' is performed. Géros, the main character, wears a goatskin mask and dances with strings of sheeps' bells attached to his costume. The second figure is a transvestite, while the third—the Frangi —is a figure dressed up as a foreigner.

TRIS BOUKÉS
The English poet Rupert Brooke, who died near Skýros in 1915 from blood poisoning on a ship bound for Gallipoli, knew the island only vaguely. Even so, he became something of a local hero and was buried in Tris Boukés, one of Skýros's most atmospheric spots. Only a year before he died, he wrote, somewhat prophetically, the famous lines:
'If I should die, think only this of me
That there's some corner of a foreign field
That is forever England...'
Tris Boukés can be reached on foot, or by boat from Linariá or Kalamítsa, or by taxi.
www.rupertbrookeonsky-ros.com

SKÝROS

Skýros is one of the most interesting islands to visit if traditional island life appeals to you. There is a theory that it was once two islands; the enormous difference between the green and hilly north and the barren mountainous south gives it credibility.

▶▶ **Skýros Town**   *235C2*

The island's capital is built like an amphitheatre at the foot of the **kástro**▶ (*Admission free*), a mostly Byzantine fortress covering the site of the ancient acropolis. There is a good walk up to the *kástro*, past traditional whitewashed cubist houses; there is little to see once you reach the top, but the great views over the town compensate for this. At the northern end of the town is a bronze **statue of 'Immortal Poetry'**▶, a memorial to the young English poet Rupert Brooke who is buried under an olive tree in Tris Boukés, at the southern end of the island (see panel). The **Archaeological Museum**▶ (*Open* Tue–Sun 8.30–3. *Admission charge*), below Brooke's memorial, has a small collection of objects from local excavations. More interesting is the nearby **Faltaitz Museum**▶▶▶ (*Open* daily 10–2 and 6–9. *Admission charge*), founded by the charming sociologist, artist and poet Manos Faltaitz in his family home to display his collection of local embroideries, pottery, carved woodwork, costumes and fine old photographs. One display is devoted to the island's famous spring Carnival and its extraordinary 'goat dance' (see panel).

▶ **Linariá**   *235C2*

Linariá, little more than the harbour across the island from Skýros Town, is where ferries dock. In the summer, boats visit the caves of Gerania and Pentekáli as well as the islet of Skyropoúla, where wild ponies roam.

Beaches

Called 'paradise' by the locals, the pebble beach at Ágios Fokás north of Linariá does come pretty near to deserving the name and it is probably almost as difficult to reach as its heavenly namesake; access is only by boat or a tricky hike. The sandy beach between Magaziá and Mólos, north

19th-century Skyrian embroidery on a bridal bedcover, with snakes for the newly-weds' protection

CONNECTIONS
Skýros has ferry links with Kými (Évvoia), Mýkonos, Páros, Thíra, Crete and Tínos. Hydrofoil services operate to Alónnisos, Skíathos, Skópelos and Vólos. (Regular buses link Kými with Athens.)

of Skýros Town, is now a resort, but is still good. Ahíli, south of the town, was an excellent beach until the new marina was built there. Atsítsa, across the island from Skýros Town, is a lovely bay with rocks and pine trees, though beaches on the west coast tend not to be very clean.

WILD HORSES OF SKÝROS
Skýros has a unique breed of very small horse, believed by some to be related to the Shetland pony and much like the horses depicted on the Parthenón frieze. On 15 August there is a children's race, near Magaziá, when competitors ride tame horses.

243

ÉVVOIA

The second largest Greek island, after Crete, Évvoia remains one of Greece's great unknowns. Although it sometimes seems like an extension of the mainland to which it is connected by bridge, Évvoia is an island with a rich, independent history. It is very fertile and the relatively prosperous islanders have so far done little to encourage tourism.

▶ Chalkída (Chalkís)　　　235B2

The heavily industrialized capital of Évvoia is also its biggest town, with more than 54,000 inhabitants. It has little going for it at first sight, but it is the scene of one of the liveliest evening promenades in the islands and it has excellent fish restaurants on the waterfront, to which Athenians will drive for the evening.

It is said that Aristotle threw himself in the water here in frustration at his inability to explain the flow of currents in the narrow **Évripos Channel**, which separates Évvoia from the mainland. Even today people stare in amazement at the current: some days it fails to change direction at all, while on others it changes up to 14 times. Not surprisingly, the Évripos (whose name means 'swift current') has always been a notoriously difficult passage for boats. the present **Évripos Bridge**, dating from 1962, replaced a Venetian structure called Negroponte (black bridge), which had a fort halfway across (see panel). Previous bridges were built by the Boeotians (*c*410BC) and the Emperor Justinian (6th century AD).

Near the bridge, in the old Ottoman quarter, is a fine 15th-century mosque, the church of Agía Paraskeví and the scattered remains of the *kástro*. This neighbourhood is still inhabited by some Turks, a few gypsies and a small Jewish community.

The **Archaeological Museum▶** (Odós Venizélou 13. *Open* Tue–Sun 8.30–3. *Admission charge*) houses a small collection of artefacts, most of them from ancient Erétria.

A TRAVELLER'S VIEW
'Khalkis was the showpiece of the Venetian Aegean and in old prints it is drawn bristling with towers and turrets, surrounded entirely by moat and sea-wall and tightstacked upon the water's edge. Its site remains extraordinary. The Euripos is one of the world's enigmas...The Venetians built actually on top of the channel, in the middle of a double drawbridge, a fortified tower that marked their imperial frontier. It was a romantic, Rhenish-looking construction, if we are to believe the old pictures and so remarkable was the place, so suggestive the movements of waters beneath it, that local rumour held it to be an enchanted castle, guarded by fairies or demons.'
Jan Morris, *The Venetian Empire: A Sea Voyage* (London, 1980)

THE NOEL-BAKER ESTATE

On the outskirts of Prokópi is an estate owned by the Noel family, who are descendants of the English poet Lord Byron. The house, in its lovely surroundings, is used as a centre for all kinds of residential holiday courses, from powerboat training to creative writing (tel: 29740 62100; www.candili.co.uk)

MOUNT DÍRFYS

If the busy town ambience or the summer heat gets too much, head west from Kými or east from Chalkída for Évvoia's highest mountain, Mount Dírfys (1,743m/5,178ft). Buses from Chalkída go as far as the pretty village of Steni Dírfos, from where a trail leads up the mountain. Telephone the Hellenic Alpine Club (tel: 22210 25230) for more information and to make arrangements to stay overnight in their refuge.

MOUNTAIN HONEY

Prokópi is famous for its honey, which is widely sold in the village. In George Vassos's shop on the corner of the church square, it is possible to taste it before buying. Mr. Vassos speaks some English and will happily explain about the different local varieties such as thyme (the most expensive), orange-flower and pine tree.

▶▶ Erétria   235B1

A rival city to Chalkída in ancient times, Erétria is now a sprawling resort. As the modern town was built over the ruins of the ancient one, little has survived of Évvoia's most important classical site, though the ruins of a Doric temple of Apollo and part of the agora are easy enough to spot in the town centre. Of more interest in the northeastern corner of the town, behind the museum (*Open* Tue–Sun 8–3. *Admission charge*), is a Hellenistic theatre, with an underground passage from where a *deus ex machina* could suddenly appear on stage carrying a god. Also on the site is a 4th-century BC palace with a clay bath tub and a gymnasium.

▶ Kárystos   235C1

Kárystos is an unexceptional 19th-century town built over an earlier site. All that remains of the earlier fortifications is a 14th-century Venetian tower. On the hill above the town is the **Castello Rosso▶▶**, a huge medieval castle on the site of an ancient acropolis. The castle is ruined inside, apart from an Orthodox chapel, but has magnificent views over the town and sea. Kárystos waterfront, lined with bars and pleasant tavernas, livens up after dark when the entire population comes down for the *vólta* or promenade. There are lovely beaches nearby and good hiking in the hill villages around Óros Óchi (Mount Óchi; 1,398m/ 4,587ft), of which Míli and Grábia are the best. Marmári, the nearest town to Kárystos, is a scenic fishing harbour where many Athenians have built summer houses.

▶▶ Kými   235C2

Perched high on a rock, Kými is a pleasant, undistinguished town surrounded by vineyards, orchards and forest. The pretty **church of Panagía Koímisis▶**, whose blue domes rise out of a garden, has an important 7th-century icon of the Virgin with Child. At the bottom of the town, the **Folklore Museum▶** (*Open* Tue–Sun 10–1 and 5–8. *Admission charge*) has a vast collection of local costumes and old photographs of Kymians both in Kými and in the USA, where they have formed a large community. The town overlooks Paralía Kýmis, from where ferries and

Friendly nuns at the Moní Nikoláou Galatáki are proud of their spectacularly set convent

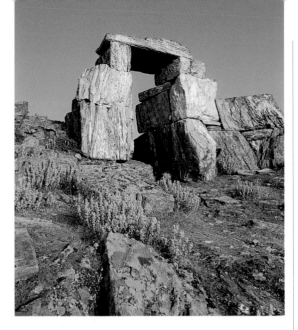

Legend has it that dragons moved these enormous blocks of masonry

WINE AND PINE
The retsina from fertile Évvoia is highly regarded everywhere in Greece. Retsina is a protected Greek speciality and no other country is allowed to make it commercially. It is not known if the ancients drank it for pleasure, but they certainly knew of the antiseptic properties of resin and used it as a disinfectant seal. It is possible that the origins of retsina can be traced to the need to preserve wine during transport. There is a popular belief that retsina gets its taste from pinewood barrels in which it is stored. In fact its unique flavour comes from the addition of a few pieces of Aleppo-pine resin during fermentation. Perhaps surprisingly, the largest consumers of retsina are visitors, not Greeks.

hydrofoils leave for the Sporades, especially Skýros. Nearby is **Moní tou Sotírou▶**, a 17th-century convent set in a lush garden (men not admitted).

▶▶ Límni   235A2
Límni, a small harbour where, legend claims, Zeus and Hera married, is a pleasing town with neoclassical houses and good beaches nearby. A little way south of the town, the 16th-century convent of **Moní Nikoláou Galatáki▶▶** is spectacularly set above the rocky shore, on the site of a classical temple of Poseidon. The tiny **Museum▶** (near the main square. *Open* Mon–Sat 9–1, Sat 10.30–1. *Admission charge*) has finds from local excavations.

▶▶ Loutrá Aidipsoú   235A2
The spa of Loutrá Aidipsoú has been known since antiquity for its therapeutic qualities. Fashionable and somewhat exclusive in the 19th century, it is now a boom town with over 100 hotels attracting crowds of mostly older Greeks. Loutrá is a long drive away from the capital, but can be reached by ferry from the mainland.

▶▶ Prokópi   235B2
At the foot of Mount Pixaria, in the middle of pine forests, is the village of Prokópi, famous for its honey and the huge **church of Ágios Ioánnis Róssos** which dominates the main square. Greek refugees from Turkey, who settled in Prokópi in 1923, brought with them the relics of their patron saint, St. John the Russian, a Russian soldier enslaved in Turkey, and built this church for him.

▶▶ Stýra   235C1
Néa (New) Stýra is a package resort, with a ferry connection to Rafína. Old Stýra, inland up the hill, is famous for its Drakóspita ('dragon houses'), strange towers built with enormous blocks which, according to legend, were carried here by dragons (if not by slaves).

It is the resin tapped from pine trees that adds the distinctive flavour to retsina wine

Sporades and Évvoia

The tower of the 14th-century Bourtzí is the only reminder of the once vast fortifications around Kárystos

CONNECTIONS
Trains run hourly from Stathmós Laríssis in Athens to the mainland side of the channel at Chalkída. Buses run regularly from Liossíon 260 terminal to Chalkída and Kými. Ferries link Kými with Skýros, Alónnisos and Ágios Ioánnis; Kárystos with Rafína; Erétria with Skále Oropoú; Loutrá Aidipsoú with Arkítsa; and Oreoí with Skíathos. Hydrofoil services operate between Chalkída and Loutrá Aidipsoú, Oreoí, Límni and (summer only) Skíathos and Skópelos; between Kárystos and Rafína, Mýkonos and Tínos; between Loutrá Aidipsoú and Skíathos; and in summer between Oreoí and Vólos, Skíathos, Skópelos and Alónnisos.

Psilí Ámmos beach, near Kárystos

Beaches

Évvoia is within easy reach of Athens and, although still not visited by many foreigners, it has become very popular with Athenians. Many of them have built summer villas along the coast, so on a summer weekend the best beaches can be crowded. Emptier beaches are here to be found, but are often accessible only on foot or after a long, slow drive. The nearest beach to Chalkída, Astéria, has a taverna and boats run from Astéria to the tiny islet of Tonnoíron which has a good beach, usually less crowded. Just below Moní Galatáki, outside Límni, is Glífa, one of the best beaches on this side of the island, with several long, clean bays of pebble and sand which can only be reached by footpaths. Angáli beach near Agía Ánna in the north is lovely but sometimes dirty, while the much smaller Ellinihá is cleaner and prettier. The beaches in the north, such as Pefkí and Oreoí, are nothing special. Stómio, near Kými, is a fine sandy beach near a river with good bathing, while the magnificent beach of Psilí Ámmos is sufficient reason to stay in Kárystos.

Drive

Northern Évvoia

Évvoia has lived off its agriculture for centuries; the north of the island is especially fertile. This drive from Chalkída to Límni goes through some magnificent scenery with impressive mountains, narrow ravines and pretty villages. (About 72km/48 miles one way; allow 4 hours. See the map on page 235. Most signposts on Évvoia are in Greek, so brush up on your Greek alphabet before setting off.)

Leave **Chalkída▶** by the main road that leads north out of the town past the central market, following signposts for Mantoúdi. The road first crosses saltmarshes and farmland and then, after about 5km (3 miles), passes the dull development of Néa Artáki. After 12km (7.5 miles), the road forks: take the right turn, towards **Psachná**, a pretty little market town with the Technical High School towering above it. From here follow signs for Prokópi. The road winds up through olive groves and pine forests, eventu-

ally giving splendid views over the island and the mainland. By the village of Néo Pagóntas (37km/23 miles) the scenery is positively alpine, but roadside shrines serve as reminders that this is not Austria. The landscape becomes even more dramatic, the road following a small river around steep rocks in a narrow ravine. Then the river broadens and there is flat farmland again. At **Prokópi▶▶** (see page 245) keep right, following signposts to Límni. There are several good picnic spots between here and the lively town of **Mantoúdi**. Drive through Mantoúdi, with its whitewashed houses and flower-filled gardens and follow signs for Strofyliá.

Kírindos▶, 4km (2.5 miles) farther on, has lovely summer villas in the middle of vineyards and cornfields, while nearby Paralía Kírindos has a few remains of 6th-century BC Kírindos, as well as a small beach.

Back on the main road, continue to **Strofyliá** whose houses have pretty gardens. Where the road forks, bear left through some quiet villages before returning to the main road, which suddenly descends towards **Límni▶▶** (see page 245).

Life still runs at a slow pace in the more remote parts of Évvoia

Ever since Zorba the Greek, *it has been tempting to think that all there is to Greek music is the sound of the bouzouki. But Greek music has a long and varied tradition and is an intriguing mix of east and west.*

ZORBA'S DANCE

'He threw himself into the dance, clapping his hands, leaping and pirouetting into the air, falling onto his knees, leaping again with his legs tucked up—it was as if he were made of rubber. He suddenly made tremendous bounds into the air, as if he wished to conquer the laws of nature and fly away. One felt that in this old body of his there was a soul struggling to carry away this flesh and cast itself like a meteor into the darkness.'
Níkos Kazantzákis,
Zorba the Greek
(London, 1959)

THE RISING EAST

'The modern Greek...when he begins to sing...breaks the crust of Greek logic; all at once the East, all darkness and mystery, rises up from deep within him.'
Níkos Kazantzákis

THE POWER OF SONG

Nicholas Gage, in *Hellas*, his excellent portrait of modern Greece, quotes the composer Manos Hadjidákis describing the feeling he had on first hearing *rembétika*: 'Dazed by the grandeur and depth of the melodic phrases, a stranger to them, young and without strength, I believed suddenly that the song I was listening to was my own, utterly my own story.'

Many Greeks, like Zorba, love spending the evening eating, drinking, singing and making music

The sound of the city First: the bouzouki. A bouzouki is a stringed instrument, like a lute, and is common throughout the region. The tradition seems to have come from Asia Minor, particularly Smyrna, earlier in the 20th century. When the Greeks of that area were expelled in 1923, they brought bouzouki music with them, as well as the more troubled sounds of *rembétika*. While bouzouki music has a certain insistent joy about it, *rembétika* is full of despair, its lyrics concentrating on broken hearts and brutal death. It is the music of urban repression and, since its birth in the tavernas and music cafés of the region's cities, it has developed into one of the most widespread and compelling of Greece's many musical styles.

Country music In contrast to the traditions of the city, country music is localized. On Crete, country music is played on a three-stringed fiddle with accompaniment from a lute-player. On Kárpathos, the bagpipes are still played. Zákynthos Town is proud of its Venetian-inspired *arekias*, whose lively and much repeated melodies are used as a background for improvized lyrics. Kazantzákis's Zorba played the *sandoúri*, a dulcimer, when he needed to express himself in music.

Music places Many Greek restaurateurs seem to believe that foreigners want only to hear the music of Míkis Theodorákis, link arms and throw plates. But Greece's musical tradition is both popular and varied: if you ask, you will often find more satisfying music to listen to. However, you will need to be in the right place at the right season, for Greek musicians tend to install themselves in Athens and Piréas in winter and then move with their audience to the islands for the summer.

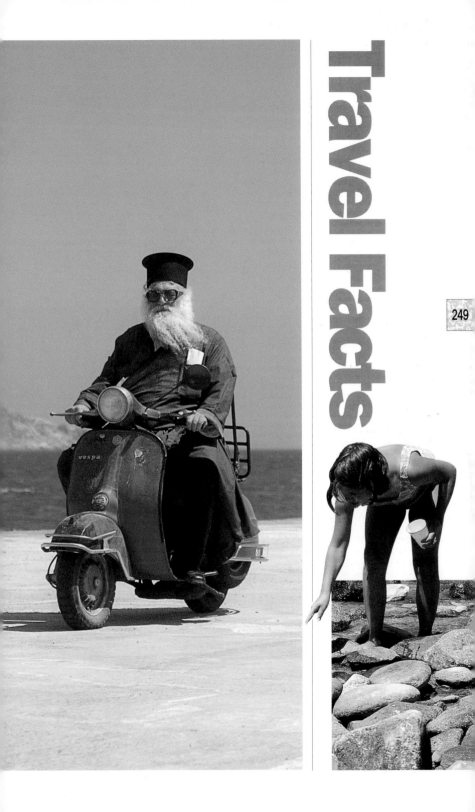

Arriving and departing

By air
There are daily scheduled flights to Athens from most European capitals as well as a daily direct flight to Thessaloníki from London Heathrow. From the USA the national carrier Olympic Airways offers daily flights. Delta also flies to Athens.

Olympic Airways offers the widest choice of scheduled flights, as well as connections from Athens to many islands. Domestic flights should be booked in advance, as they are in much demand, especially over weekends and around public holidays. From May to October the cheaper option is to take a charter flight either to Athens or direct to one of the major islands such as Mýkonos, Thíra, Rhodes, Crete, Corfu or Skíathos. If you plan to stay on one island, check out flight-and-hotel package offers from tour operators (see page 262). Any of the tour operators should be able to help with charter flights. There are also now several independent airlines operating in Greece, some of them offering good fares and regular inter-island and Athens services.

By sea
Regular car and passenger ferries operate between Ancona, Venice, Bari and Brindisi in Italy, and Igoumenítsa, Corfu and Pátra, some also calling at other Ionian islands. Less frequent ferries connect Trieste and Otranto to Igoumenítsa, Corfu and Pátra. It is necessary in summer to book ferry tickets in advance. Tickets are considerably cheaper out of season. Superfast ferries (www.superfast.com) operate from Ancona and Bari to Pátra and Igoumenítsa, and in summer there are high-speed catamaran services by Italian ferries (www.italianferries.it) from Brindisi to Corfu (just over 3 hours) and Paxoi (nearly 5 hours).

In summer, ferries, catamarans and hydrofoils run from the Dodecanese and northeastern Aegean islands to Turkey. The best connections are from Rhodes to Marmaris, by ferry or catamaran from Kos to Bodrum, and Samos to Kusadasi.

By train
Many young travellers arrive in Greece by train, using an InterRail or Eurail pass. Most people go through Italy and take a ferry from Bari, Ancona or Brindisi to Pátra (see **By sea**). The alternative is a train from Budapest via Sofia to Thessaloníki.

By bus
For those who believe that travel should still include suffering it is possible, in the good old 'hippie tradition', to take a bus from several European capitals to Athens, also via Italy. It is a long journey and, although considerably cheaper than the train, it is not the most reliable or comfortable way to travel.

By car
It is possible to drive to Greece and take car ferries to the islands, but if

you intend to go island-hopping it is probably easier and cheaper to rent a car locally. British visitors taking their own car should contact the Automobile Association (AA) in the UK for information (tel: 0870 2433 933). You will need an EU driving licence, vehicle registration documents and insurance. A green card is not necessary for EU citizens. US visitors bringing their own car will need an international driver's licence, vehicle registration documents and insurance.

Customs regulations
Travellers from outside the EU can bring in duty-free goods up to the current EU allowances for tobacco, alcohol, perfumes and gifts. It is forbidden to bring in plants with soil, bulbs, flowers or fruit, and pets must have a valid health and rabies inoculation certificate, issued between 6 days and 12 months (6 months for cats) before arrival. Exporting antiquities without a permit is a serious offence, as is drug-smuggling.

Passports and visas
EU nationals need a valid passport to enter Greece. Most non-EU Europeans and Australian, US, New Zealand and Canadian citizens will be issued on arrival with an entry visa permitting a stay of up to 90 days. There is no time limit for EU nationals, but they must report to the authorities every 6 or 12 months. A resident permit for 6 months can be obtained from the Aliens Bureau in Athens (tel: 210 646 8103 or check with your embassy). If you overstay your time, a hefty fine will be charged upon departure.

251

Hydrofoils are fast and reliable

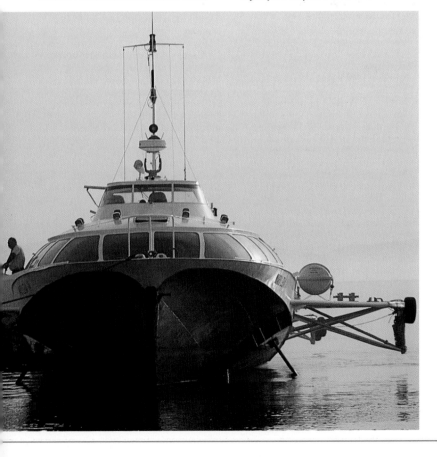

Essential facts

Climate and when to go

Greece has a generally mild Mediterranean climate. Most islands are far more pleasant out of season than during the busy weeks from late June to the end of August when the heat is intense and the crowds often unbearable. The islands are at their best at the beginning of June and in September, when the temperature is pleasant and most facilities are available. May and October are good too, but you may find establishments closed and ferry connections less frequent. Many island hotels and restaurants are closed from late October till Easter, especially in the more northerly islands. Out of season the evenings can still be cold, and few hotels have heating. The spring warms up slowly and even in May the sea can be cold. The traditional holiday month of August is best avoided if possible, as space is short in hotel rooms and on beaches.

What to take

In summer, take light cotton clothing and swimwear, as one is never far from a beach. A good protective sun-cream, a hat and comfortable sandals are essential. A pair of walking shoes never goes amiss. Always bring a sweater or a light jacket for those evenings when the *meltemi* blows, or for late-night ferries. Out of season bring warmer clothes as the nights can be damp and cold. Be modestly dressed (no shorts or vests) when visiting monasteries and chapels.

Smaller hotels lack soap and towels, and even bigger hotels often omit the shampoo. Colour-print film is widely available but is generally more expensive than in other countries. Slide film can be more difficult to find. A small flash-light can be useful for exploring archaeological sites and caves, and for a stroll on a moonless night.

National holidays

Although government offices and businesses close on national holidays, some shops and tourist sites remain open. There are also many local festivals, when some shops and businesses close.

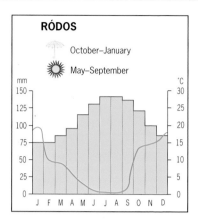

RÓDOS
October–January
May–September

1 January: New Year's Day
6 January: Epiphany
Lent Monday (precedes Shrove Tuesday)
25 March: Greek Independence Day
Good Friday, Easter Day and Easter Monday
1 May: May Day
15 August: Assumption of the Virgin
28 October: *Ochi* Day (celebrating Metaxas saying 'no' to Mussolini)
25 December: Christmas
26 December: Gathering of the Virgin (Sinaksis Theotokou)
(for religious festivals, see pages 20–21)

Time differences

Greek time is usually two hours ahead of GMT, seven hours ahead of Eastern Standard Time. Clocks in Greece go forward one hour at 4am on the last Sunday in March, and back one hour at 4am on the last Sunday in October.

Money matters

The monetary unit, the Euro (€), is circulated in coins of 1, 2, 5, 10, 20 and 50 cents and 1 and 2 Euros, and in notes of 5, 10, 20, 50, 100, 200 and 500 Euros. Most banks exchange foreign currency, as do most medium-priced and expensive hotels.

It is possible to exchange money in some post offices, which is handy on smaller islands which have no bank. On many islands there are also exchange offices which are open longer and often offer better rates (but

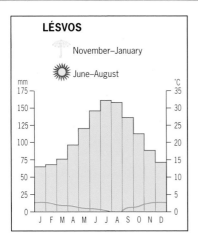

LÉSVOS

☂ November–January

☀ June–August

ZÁKYNTHOS

☂ November–January

☀ June–August

do check commission charges). Many exchange places now accept credit cards, and most cash dispensers will accept Visa and American Express cards for obtaining local currency; fewer take other cards. Travellers' cheques and Eurocheques can be cashed at hotels and banks. Exchange rates are published in newspapers. Some banks still demand to see your passport before changing money.

Travel insurance
In theory, all EU citizens can receive free medical treatment in Greece upon presenting an E111 form (available from most post offices in your home country). Unfortunately hospital staff will often make you pay,

leaving you to reclaim the money after your holiday. Travel insurance is often a more reliable option and is certainly indispensable for non-EU nationals. There are comprehensive travel policies which cover accidents, illness, delays, cancellation etc. In the case of medical care, keep all receipts and ask for a full medical report. In the event of loss or theft, you will need a police report giving details of the loss and stating how it happened. The police will issue a case number, which will allow the insurance company to follow up the case.

Exchange offices often offer better rates for foreign currency than banks, but charges may be high

Getting around

Domestic flights Olympic Airways (www.olympicairlines.com) and several domestic airlines connect Athens with many islands and also operate inter-island flights. During the summer season or around public holidays book seats as far ahead as possible as flights fill up quickly. Aegean Airlines (tel: 801 112 0000; www.aegeanair.com) is based in Crete and operates daily flights from Athens to the main islands.

In peak season delays are common, and flights can be cancelled due to bad weather. Domestic air tickets are non-refundable, but you can change your flight details.

Ferries and hydrofoils Hydrofoils and catamarans, which generally cost twice as much as ferries, are becoming more frequent in the summer and offer a fast and convenient service, but rough seas and high costs make it impossible for them to operate out of season. Ferries operate all year round to all inhabited Greek islands, although some smaller islands might only be served once a week. Timetables are published, but are not widely available, and tend to be unreliable anyway. There are several classes, the cheapest being Deck and

On smaller islands the only bus, out of season, is often the schoolbus, one in the morning and one late in the afternoon

the most expensive a private cabin. Food and drinks on ferries are often highly priced. Ferry and hydrofoil tickets can be bought in advance.

Buses Buses, operated by the privately owned KTEL company (www.ktel.org), are popular and cheap. Regular services link Athens to the main ports and even to Corfu. Long-distance tickets can usually be bought in advance; otherwise tickets are paid for on the bus. Even on the smallest islands a service will be provided, often by the school bus making a tour of the island and linking port and main town. If it is the school bus, be prepared to start early and to come back when classes are over. On larger islands, buses will also run from the main town in time to catch ferries.

Taxis Greek taxis are generally good value when they use the meter (obligatory only in towns), but tariffs double between midnight and 5am and out of town. Surcharges apply for large bags and for entering harbours or airports. Greek taxi drivers have a bad reputation: be sure that the correct rate is being applied and if you are riding without the meter, agree the fare per car before setting off. If you are dissatisfied, insist on your right to consult the Tourist Police.

Trains There are no trains on the islands but useful trains from Athens include services to Évvoia (almost hourly), Pátra (though the Athens bus service is more useful) and Kavála, for connections to the northeastern Aegean and Dodecanese islands.

Driving

Car rental Driving on the islands can be a great pleasure and renting a car will certainly open up the larger islands like Rhodes, Crete and Corfu. However, it can be an expensive and, if you break down, an infuriating

Rural scenery away from the coast rarely disappoints

experience. Before you start, a few things should be carefully considered.

There are two ways of going about car rental—through an international or a local agency. Of the international agencies (Avis, Holiday Autos etc) Hertz have the largest network. Telephone several companies to compare rates and get the best deal possible. Although prices are often higher than for renting from local firms, large agencies can at least offer peace of mind. They also usually have agents at international airports, so if you book ahead you can pick up your car on arrival. Local agencies are usually cheaper and you will often be served by the person who owns the cars. Out of season, it should be possible to talk down the rates of local agencies, something that can seldom be done with the international groups. However, local-agency cars

❏ Island driving can be different from driving elsewhere in Greece, especially in more remote places. In tourist centres the main problem might be traffic congestion and a shortage of parking places, obliging you to park in the sun while you are on the beach, for example. While island main roads are usually in good condition, remoter ones can be rutted, rarely have cat's eyes and are more often used by goats, men on donkeys and agricultural vehicles than by cars. It is wise to be off twisting mountain roads by nightfall. ❏

are often kept longer and some are not as well maintained, which can lead to problems: be sure you test the car before handing over money. The range of cars available for rent has been extended and on larger islands you will be offered everything from a basic Fiat Panda to an air-conditioned, new-model, top-of-the-range Mercedes. An international driving licence is not required for EU licence holders, but it can be useful if you get into difficulties. Most agencies will accept valid American, Australian and Canadian licences. Drivers must be at least 21 years of age (25 for some vehicles).

Breakdowns Whoever you rent from, be sure you know what to do if you break down or are involved in an accident (Greece has one of the highest accident rates in Europe). Proof of membership of the AA or RAC entitles you to free roadside assistance from ELPA, the Greek national breakdown service, which has centres on Crete and Corfu (dial 104 for service). Many agencies have agreements with ELPA's rivals, Hellas Service or Express Service, but it is essential that you have the agency's membership details when you telephone for the service, as their call-out charges for non-members are astronomical.

Freedom of the Greek roads The Greeks have embarked on a major road-improvement programme since

Hiring a car or scooter is recommended as public transport is limited on most islands

joining the European Union, and while this makes it easier to get around on the islands, it also makes it easier for people to drive faster. Wherever you are, be sure to keep an eye on your fuel tank, especially if you are running on lead-free fuel as not all filling stations will stock it.

Although some international fuel companies accept credit cards, many of the island filling stations are still run by local companies which will insist on payment in cash, so make sure you are carrying notes (bills).

Motorcycle and moped rental

Mopeds and motorcycles are usually readily available in tourist centres and can be an excellent and economical way of getting around. A wider range of motorcycles is available in more developed tourist centres and, with luck, you might even find a Harley-Davidson. Whatever you rent, be sure to check the machine before you rent for signs of previous damage and for faulty brakes. Although feeling the breeze in your hair may seem to go with the 'easy rider' image, helmets are recommended, even on mopeds, as accidents are not uncommon. Rates for rental can usually be talked down out of season.

Hitch-hiking

Public transport can be very erratic on some islands and hitching a short lift with a local is usually no problem as people are used to it, although taxi drivers might complain. Hitching can be a good way to meet some local people and try out a mouthful of Greek. Longer rides might be less easy but should not be a problem.

The media

International newspapers are widely available in Athens and at major resorts, sometimes on the day of publication, sometimes the following day. The *Athens News* and *Herald Tribune*, with its supplement, *Kathimerini*, are local English papesr with good listings, and several islands produce English-language newspapers

There is a wide variety of regional radio stations in almost every town, and the BBC World Service can be picked up on short-wave frequencies. The government-controlled TV station ET1 has news summaries in English (check papers for timing), and foreign soaps and films are broadcast in the original language with subtitles.

Post offices

258

Most post offices are open Monday–Friday 7.30–2, in larger cities often until 8pm and in the capital also during summer weekends, usually 8–2. Post offices will usually exchange money and travellers' cheques.

Air mail letters take over a week from the islands to Europe, and two weeks to North America; postcards are slower. The express service cuts the time by a few days. Poste restante should be addressed to the main post office of any larger town, with your name underlined. It is usually held for a month, and a passport is needed upon collection.

In Athens, Pátra, Irákleio, Corfu, Mýkonos, Rhodes, Thíra and Skíathos, American Express cheque- or card-holders can use the mail service in the Amex offices.

Telephone and fax

Although it is possible to telephone from any moderate or more expensive hotel, it is much cheaper to use a phone card in a telephone booth. Phone cards are available from OTE offices, newsagents and street kiosks, with 100, 200, 500 or 1,000 units. Local calls are cheap but long-distance calls are quite expensive.

For calls within Greece, cheap-rate times are 3–5pm, 9pm–8am and all weekend. Long-distance calls can also be made at OTE offices, as well as reverse-charge calls. Faxes can be sent from larger OTE offices and from some travel agents or hotels. To call abroad from Greece, dial 00 + country code (Australia 61, Canada and USA 1, Ireland 353, New Zealand 64, UK 44) + area code (minus initial 0) + number.

Language

The Greek alphabet

Alpha	A, α	a, as in rather
Beta	B, β	v, as in very
Gamma	Γ, γ	y, as in yes, before i or e; g, as in get, before o, a, ou
Delta	Δ, δ	th, as in that
Epsilon	E, ε	e, as in yes
Zita	Z, ζ	z
Eta	H, η	ee, as in meet
Theta	Θ, θ	th, as in thing
Iota	I, ι	i, as in lid
Kappa	K, κ	k
Lambda	Λ, λ	l
Mu	M, μ	m
Nu	N, ν	n
Xi	Ξ, ξ	ks
Omicron	O, o	o, as in pot
Pi	Π, π	p
Rho	P, ρ	rolling r
Sigma	Σ, σ (mid-word) ς (end of word)	s
Tau	T, τ	t
Upsilon	Y, υ	e, very similar to eta
Phi	Φ, φ	f
Chi	X, χ	h, as in loch
Psi	Ψ, ψ	ps, as in corpse
Omega	Ω, ω	o, as in bone

Pronunciation

αι	e, as in met
αυ	av/af
ει	ee, as in reed
ευ	ev/ef
ου	ou, as in tour
γγ	ng, as in angel
γκ	g, as in goat, at beginning of word; ng in the middle
μπ	b at beginning of word; mb in the middle
ντ	d at beginning of word; nd in the middle
σι	sh, as in shelter
τζ	j, as in Johnny

Numbers

1 énos, éna, mía	14 dhekatésseres
2 dío	20 íkosi
3 trís, tría	30 triánda
4 tésseres, téssera	40 saránda
5 pénde	50 penínda
6 éksi	60 eksínda
7 eptá	70 evdomínda
8 ohtó	80 oghónda
9 enéya	90 enenínda
10 dhéka	100 ekáto
11 endhéka	200 dhiakóssies
12 dódheka	1,000 hílies
13 dhekatrís	2,000 dhío hiliádes

Greetings

hello (informal)	yásas (yásu)
good morning	kaliméra
good evening	kalispéra
good night	kaliníkhta
goodbye	adío
please/you're welcome	parakaló
thank you (very much)	efharistó (párapolí)
okay, all right	endáksi
how are you?	ti kánis (ti káneteh)?
I'm fine	kalá ímeh

Essentials

yes (formal yes)	né (málista)
no	óchi

I don't understand	dhen katalavéno
how many?	póssi, pósses?
how much?	póso?
sorry	sighnómi
what can I do for you?	oríste?
be careful	ópa
take your time	sigá sigá
open	aniktó
closed	klistó
left	aristerá
right	dheksiá
far	makriá

Time

what time is it?	ti óra íne?
today	símera
yesterday	hthés
tomorrow	ávrio
now	tóra
later	argótera

Travel

airport	arothrómio
harbour	limáni
bus station	praktorío leoforíon
how far is it?	póso makriá íne?
where is...?	pou íne...?

Nudism is strictly forbidden on most islands, but some local authorities are tending to ignore it on more isolated beaches

Crime and the police

Greece is one of Europe's safest countries, with a relatively low crime rate. As you will notice, Greeks themselves often leave cars or houses unlocked or their bags unattended, but it is advisable to be reasonably careful.

Pickpocketing is increasingly common in crowded tourist areas in cities or resorts. Violent crime or rape is less common, but women travelling on their own can expect some minor harassment from the almost professional machos who operate in tourist resorts.

If you are involved in an incident, contact the Tourist Police or Police immediately: there is an office on every island and in every major town.

Embassies and consulates

Australia Odós D. Soutsoú 37, Athens (tel: 210 645 0405)
Canada Odós I. Gennadióu 4, Athens (tel: 210 727 3400)
Ireland Leóforos Vas. Sofias 60, Athens (tel: 210 723 2771)
New Zealand Odós Kifísias 268, Halandrí, Athens (tel: 210 687 4701)

United Kingdom Athens: Odós Ploutárchou 1 (tel: 210 723 6211); Irákleio: Odós Papa-Alexandroú 16 (tel: 2810 224012); Corfu: Odós Menekrátous 1 (tel: 26610 30055); Rhodes: Odós Lambraki 29 (tel: 22410 22005); Kós: Odós Annetos Laoumtzi 8 (tel: 22420 21549); Zakynthos: Odós Foskolos 5 (tel: 26950 22906).
United States of America Odós Vasilissís Sofías 91, Athens (tel: 210 721 2951)

Emergency telephone numbers

Ambulance–medical help	166
Police–emergencies	100
Fire	199
Road assistance	104
Tourist Police (in Athens only)	171

Lost property

Report losses to your hotel and to the local police station. Most larger bus and train stations have a lost property office. If you lose your papers or

The traditional taverna is a family-run affair, with mother or father usually behind the stove

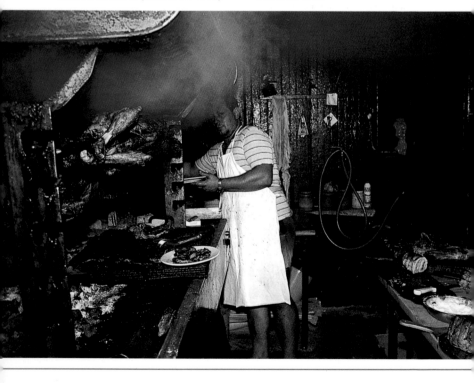

passport contact the police and your nearest embassy or consulate as soon as possible. If you lose travellers' cheques or credit cards, report the loss to the police and the issuing company immediately.

Health
There are no mandatory vaccination requirements but it is wise to be up to date with tetanus and polio immunizations. A typhoid-cholera booster is recommended. Tap water is safe in most places, but can be in short supply on drier, farther-flung islands. Bottled water is widely available.

For medical help in an emergency, telephone 166. If you are on an island with some tourist facilities, it is worth asking whether your hotel could contact an English-speaking doctor. The Tourist Police can also help with providing this information, as can your nearest consulate. Emergency treatment in state hospitals is free, but facilities can be pretty basic. Outpatient clinics (*iatreía*), which usually operate in the morning, are slightly better.

If you have travel insurance including medical cover, you may be able to use one of the more comfortable private hospitals. Keep the receipts of all bills and receipts for drugs. (See also page 253.)

Holiday hazards
More and more people visit the Greek Islands for sun and sex, both of which can be dangerous unless proper precautions are taken. One of the most common health problems suffered by visitors is sunstroke or over-exposure to the sun. Use a strong protective suncream, wear a hat, drink plenty of fluids and try to acclimatize gradually to the sun. Sex plays a major part in the holiday scene at some resorts, and here as well it is advisable to be prepared. Condoms are cheap and available everywhere at pharmacies, kiosks and supermarkets.

The sea can hide some dangers as well, such as sea urchins (on rocky shores) or jellyfish. Pharmacies sell remedies for stings. The spines of the urchins should be removed, with care, immediately.

Mosquitoes in Greece are nothing to worry about, but they can be irritating in the evenings. Repellents and electric devices are widely available. When sleeping or lying on the beach you may encounter sandflies, and when walking or climbing watch out for the odd snake or scorpion.

Hayfever sufferers should take precautions during the April to June pollen season.

Pharmacies
Pharmacists can usually help with minor ailments and it should be quite easy in the major resorts to find one who speaks English. A Greek pharmacy (*farmakeío*) can supply a wide range of drugs without a prescription. Pharmacies are usually closed in the evenings and on Saturday morning, but a notice should always be displayed outside showing the nearest one open.

261

Eating meals al fresco is one of the great joys of summer on the Greek Islands

Camping

The Panhellenic Camping Association publishes a yearly guide to all the official camp sites in Greece, available from GCA, 102 Odós Solonós, GR-10680 Athens (tel/fax: 210 362 1560; www.greececamping. org) or from tourist offices. The EOT runs some of the best organized sites. Most places offer hot showers, electricity, a restaurant and cooking facilities, and some also have a swimming pool. Greek camp sites accept people without tents, but you will need a sleeping bag—even summer nights can be chilly.

Some sites will add a government tax to the bill (often not mentioned on arrival), so be sure to check what is included in the price. Camp sites often insist on keeping passports. Free camping outside designated areas is strictly forbidden by a law which the police enforce more diligently every year.

Camping outside authorized campsites is illegal

Self-catering holidays

Houses, flats and self-contained studios are usually rented by the week or month. It can be a more pleasant and sometimes cheaper option than a hotel if there are several of you to share. Out of season it should be possible to find a house or flat on arrival on the island, at the ferry pier or in the nearby *kafeneía*, but in the summer season it makes sense to book ahead through a tour operator; many packages are available. Self-catering is becoming more and more common on the islands as it appeals to families.

Some specialist tour operators in the UK are:

Sunvil Holidays, Sunvil House, Upper Square, Old Isleworth, Middlesex TW7 7BJ (tel: 020 8568 4499; www.sunvil.co.uk).

Laskarina Holidays, Bolney Place, Cowfold Road, Bolney, West Sussex RH17 5QT (tel: 01444 880353; www.laskarina.co.uk). Specialists in remote and unspoiled Greek Islands.

The Best of Greece, Image House, Station Road, London N17 9LR (tel: 0871 423 5542; www.bestofgreece.co.uk).

Odyssey Holidays, 1 Torrington Park, North Finchley, London N12 9SU (tel: 0870 429 4141; www.odyssey holidays.com/Greece).

In the US try:

Cloud Tours Inc., 31–09 Newtown Avenue, Suite 311, Long Island City, NY 11102 (tel: 800/223-7880; www.cloudtours.com).

Abercrombie and Kent, 1520 Kensington Road, Oak Brook, IL 60521-2141 (tel: 800/554-7016; www.abercrombiekent.com).

Children

Greeks love children, so the islands are a good place for travelling with a family. You can take children everywhere, as the Greeks do, and expect hotels, restaurants and shops to be very welcoming. Children love the island life: beaches, ferries, sailing boats, the pedestrian streets of the old towns or *chóra*. Pushchairs can prove difficult to use in the steep, cobbled streets of these old towns, or on rough paths in the countryside, where a good backpack-seat is a better option. Except on the more remote islands, most necessities for babies and children are available from supermarkets or pharmacies, but do bring a total sunblock cream for children as this can be hard to find. A sun hat is also essential. When choosing a destination look out for shallow, sandy beaches, as pebble or rocky beaches are uncomfortable for the very young. Take warm clothes for the evening as it can be chilly even in summer.

Visitors with disabilities
Changing boats, visiting old towns or *chóras*, and walking around archaeological sites can be daunting for travellers with disabilities. Several package-tour operators, including Thomson and Horizon, will advise on suitable trips. For independent travellers, the following organizations offer advice and help: **National Tourist Organization of Greece** (see page 268); **RADAR** (12 City Forum, 250 City Road, London EC1V 8AF; tel: 020 7250 3222; www.radar.org.uk) publishes fact sheets and an annual guide to international travel for people with all kinds of disabilities; **Twin Peaks Press** (Box 129, Vancouver, WA 98666; tel: 206-694 2462) publishes a worldwide *Directory of Travel Agencies for the Disabled* and other useful books for people with

Children are guaranteed a warm welcome on their Greek holiday

disabilities, as do Mobility International USA, PO Box 10767, Eugene, OR 97440, USA (tel: 541-343 1284; www.miusa.org).

Electricity
Current is 220 volts AC throughout the country and the islands, with two-pin continental plugs.

Etiquette and local customs
Greeks, in a very Asian way, take their time with greetings and will often ask about the health of the entire extended family. It is considered rude to ask something without at least saying hello. Mastering the basic social graces, such as 'please' and 'thank you', in Greek, will always be appreciated (see page 259). When visiting a monastery or sacred chapel always dress modestly, which means covering up legs and arms. Apart from on the few official nudist beaches, nude bathing is illegal and some police are quite strict about it, especially on public beaches or near monasteries. Topless bathing has become acceptable on most of the islands, but use your discretion on beaches where the more traditional Greek families congregate.

CONVERSION CHARTS

FROM	TO	MULTIPLY BY
Inches	Centimetres	2.54
Centimetres	Inches	0.3937
Feet	Metres	0.3048
Metres	Feet	3.2810
Yards	Metres	0.9144
Metres	Yards	1.0940
Miles	Kilometres	1.6090
Kilometres	Miles	0.6214
Acres	Hectares	0.4047
Hectares	Acres	2.4710
Gallons	Litres	4.5460
Litres	Gallons	0.2200
Ounces	Grams	28.35
Grams	Ounces	0.0353
Pounds	Grams	453.6
Grams	Pounds	0.0022
Pounds	Kilograms	0.4536
Kilograms	Pounds	2.205
Tons	Tonnes	1.0160
Tonnes	Tons	0.9842

MEN'S SUITS

UK	36	38	40	42	44	46	48
Rest of Europe	46	48	50	52	54	56	58
US	36	38	40	42	44	46	48

DRESS SIZES

UK	8	10	12	14	16	18
France	36	38	40	42	44	46
Italy	38	40	42	44	46	48
Rest of Europe	34	36	38	40	42	44
US	6	8	10	12	14	16

MEN'S SHIRTS

UK	14	14.5	15	15.5	16	16.5	17
Rest of Europe	36	37	38	39/40	41	42	43
US	14	14.5	15	15.5	16	16.5	17

MEN'S SHOES

UK	7	7.5	8.5	9.5	10.5	11
Rest of Europe	41	42	43	44	45	46
US	8	8.5	9.5	10.5	11.5	12

WOMEN'S SHOES

UK	4.5	5	5.5	6	6.5	7
Rest of Europe	38	38	39	39	40	41
US	6	6.5	7	7.5	8	8.5

Maps

Free maps are usually available from tourist offices or local travel agencies. The most reliable maps are published by Athens-based publishers Road Editions (www.road.gr). Their maps cover the main islands in detail. Maps are available from good travel book-shops in the US, the UK and Greece, their bookshop in Athens or on-line. Road Bookstore Athens 9, Odós Ippokratou, Athens (tel: 210 3613242).

Opening times

It is hard to be precise about opening hours, especially for sites or museums, as the hours change from winter to summer, from early summer to peak season and, at some sites, according to the mood of the keeper. Opening times for individual sites are usually given in the A-Z section of this book, but changes occur frequently. Some sites and museums on the islands are closed all winter.

Government offices usually open from 8 until 2, although the rule is not to expect to get anything done after 1. In general, shops in the summer are open Monday to Saturday from 9 to 2.30 and on Tuesday, Thursday and Friday they reopen from 6 to 9 in the evening. In the winter businesses start later and close earlier. In major tourist resorts shops stay open all day and until late at night. Most shops close on national holidays (see page 252).

All state-run archaeological sites and museums are free on public holidays to all European Union nationals, which can mean a good saving. Student-card holders get a reduction of 50 per cent, and EU student-card holders may be admitted free.

Photography

There is usually no charge for taking photographs in museums, but an extra charge is levied for the use of tripods or video-cameras. Most brands of film are widely available, but slide films are expensive and hard to find.

Places of worship

There are Greek Orthodox churches and chapels on almost every street corner. The Muslim communities are very small now, but a few mosques in

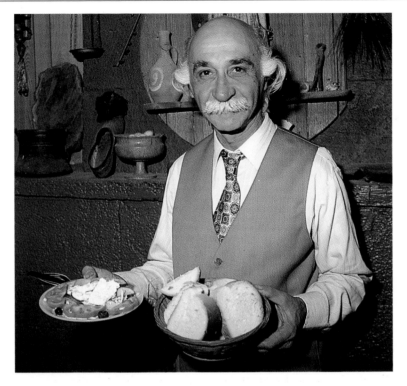

A simple Greek meal: choriátiki *or Greek salad and bread*

Rhodes Town and on Kós are still open for prayer. The Jewish community in the islands is almost non-existent, although there is still a synagogue in Rhodes and on Crete. There are some Catholic churches on Náxos, Tínos and Syros, remnants of the Venetian or Genoese occupation.

Student and youth travel
Students are well catered for on the islands, with budget food and accommodation, although prices are rising. Inter-Rail is a cheap way of getting to Greece, and camping and youth hostels offer cheap accommodation.

Tipping
A service charge is almost always included in restaurant bills but it is common to leave a small tip for the waiter. Taxi fares can be rounded up to the nearest convenient amount.

Toilets
The first thing you will notice in many Greek toilets is that paper should be dropped only in the appointed waste bin. Plumbing is seldom a strong point, and toilets easily get blocked. As public toilets tend to be fairly dirty, it is often better to use a toilet in a hotel or restaurant.

Watersports
Most major resorts offer windsurfing, water-skiing, pedaloes, jet-ski and paragliding. Prices to hire equipment are lower than in most other Mediterranean resorts. The islands are a wonderful place for sailing. It is possible to book tailor-made cruises or to charter boats

on arrival. The Hellenic Yachting Federation, Poseidonos 51, Moschato 183-44, Greece (tel: 210 940 4825; www.eio.gr) issues a brochure *Sailing the Greek Sea*, also available from tourist offices.

Until recently, diving in Greece was limited, mostly to prevent visitors finding or removing submerged archaeological treasures. Now the government is promoting it and several islands have good diving clubs. For more information contact the Hellenic Federation of Underwater Activities, Post Office of the Old West Air Terminal, Elliniko (tel: 210 981 9961) or www.greeka.com.

Women travellers

Greece has low rates of street crime, but it is a patriarchal society, which means that Greek women are usually less liberated than females elsewhere in Europe. Encouraged by past success, Greek men will often pursue foreign women in the hope of a liberating experience of their own, but a polite, firm refusal will usually deter them. If you do have difficulties with harassment, report them at once to the Tourist Police.

Women travelling on their own have become a common sight on the islands

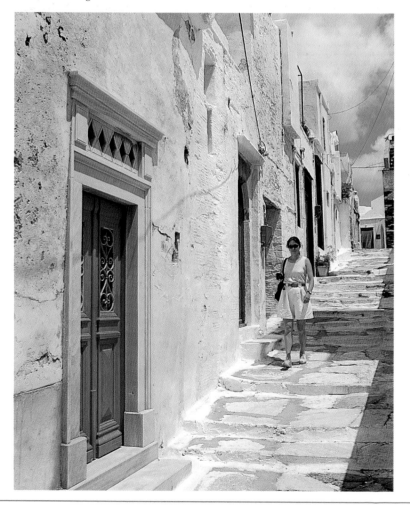

Greece in books

Archaeology and art
Mary Beard, *The Parthenon* (London, 2004).
John Boardman, *Greek Art* (London, 1989). A classic on the subject.
John Griffiths Pedley, *Greek Art and Archaeology* (US 2002).
Reynold Higgins, Minoan and *Mycenaean Art* (London, 1981). Well-illustrated exposé.
Curtis Runnels and Priscilla Murray, *Greece Before History: An Archaeological Companion and Guide* (London 2001).
Suzanne Slesin, *Greek Style* (London, 1993). Elegant and beautiful interiors from the mainland as well as from Corfu, Rhodes and other islands.

Biography
James Theodore Brent, *The Cyclades, or Life among the Insular Greeks* (London 2002). Excellent book about the Cyclades.
Nicholas Gage, *Eleni* (London, 1983). Moving story of a Greek-born American journalist who returns to his native Epirus and is condemned to death in 1948.
Andreas Papandreou, *Democracy at Gunpoint* (London 1973). Moving account by the late socialist Greek prime minister of the *coup d'etat* in 1967 by the colonels.
George Psychoundákis, *The Cretan Runner* (London, 1955). The story of the World War II invasion of Crete and the resistance, told by a message-runner for the British (translated by Patrick Leigh Fermor).

Foreign fiction about Greece
Louis de Bernières, *Captain Corelli's Mandolin* (London, 1994). Set during the Italian occupation of Kefalloniá.
John Fowles, *The Magus* (London, 1966). Acclaimed novel, inspired by Spétses in the 1950s.

Modern Greek fiction and poetry
Mary Bernard, *Sappho: A New Translation* (US 1959).
C. P. Cavafy, *Collected Poems* (London, 1968). A translation of all the work of the celebrated poet who spent most of his life in Alexandria, Egypt.
Nikos Kazantzákis, *Zorba the Greek* (London, 1961), *Report to Greco* (London, 1965), *Freedom and Death* (London, 1956) and *Christ Recrucified* (London, 1954). Just a few of the novels by the famous Cretan writer.
Kimon Friar (ed.), *Modern Greek Poetry* (Athens, 1993). A good anthology.
David Ricks (ed.), *Modern Greek Writing: An Anthology in English Translation* (London 2002).
George Seferis, *Collected Poems, 1924–1955* (London, 1967). Excellent works from the Nobel Prize-winning islander.

Specialized guides
Marc Dubin, *Trekking in Greece* (London, 1993). A good hiker's guide to both the mainland and the islands.
John Freely, *The Cyclades, Discovering the Greek Islands of the Aegean* (London, 2006).
Barry Unsworth, *Crete* (London 2004. (Lycabettus Press Guides in Athens produce a series of excellent guidebooks to the more visited islands. Páros and Pátmos are especially good.)

Travellers' tales
Gerald Durrell, *My Family and Other Animals* (London, 1969). Durrell recounts his childhood on Corfu and his adventures with the local fauna.
Lawrence Durrell, *Prospero's Cell* (London, 1945). Lovely account of the life the young writer led with his wife, Nancy, on Corfu, before World War II. *Reflections on a Marine Venus* (London, 1952). Durrell's experiences during the war on Rhodes and the other Dodecanese. *The Greek Islands* (London, 1978). A romantic vision of the islands as they are no more.
Rory MacLean, *Falling for Icarus: A Journey Among the Cretans* (London 2005). Compelling and humorous tale, with great insights in Cretan culture, of a man who wants to build an airplane.
Henry Miller, *The Colossus of Maroussi* (London, 1942). Miller at his happiest on Corfu and other islands.
Sofka Zinovieff, *Eurydice Street: A Place in Athens* (London, 2005). Evocative account of moving to Athens.
Sara Wheeler, *An Island Apart* (London, 1992). A traveller's account of Évvoia.

Tourist Offices

Abroad
The National Tourist Organization of Greece (NTOG, known in Greece as EOT) has offices in Austria, Belgium, Czech Republic, Denmark, Finland, France, Germany, Israel, Italy, Japan, the Netherlands, Spain, Sweden, Switzerland, Russia, the UK and the USA.
Australia 51 Pitt Street, Sydney NSW 2000 (tel: 00 612 9241 1663)
Canada 91 Scollard Street, Toronto, Ontario M5R 1GR (tel: 416/968-2220) 1170 Place du Frère André, Suite 300, Montréal, Québec H3B 3C6 (tel: 514/871-1535; fax: 514/871-1498)
United Kingdom 4 Conduit Street, London W1R 0DJ (tel: 020-7495 9300; www.gnto.co.uk)
USA Olympic Tower, 645 Fifth Avenue, New York, NY 10022 (tel: 212/421-5777; www.greektourism.com)

In Greece
The head office of the EOT is in Athens. There are EOT offices on several major islands (opening times vary, and often offices are closed in winter), as well as local municipality information booths. Where there is no official tourist information, a local travel agency dealing with ferry tickets, excursions and accommodation often assumes the role.

Sources of tourist information are listed in the A-Z sections of this book.

Main EOT offices are as follows:

Athína (Athens)
Greek National Tourist Organization (GNTO) administrative headquarters: Odós Tsokha 7 (tel: 210 870 7000; www.gnto.gr)
Odós Amerikís 2 (tel: 210 331 0692); Athens airport (tel: 210 353 0448); 26a Odós Iéoforos Amalias, Syntagma, opposite the National Garden (tel: 210 331 0392
Kavála Odós Ethnikis Anistasis 2 (tel: 2510 231653)
Kefalloniá Customs Pier, Argostóli (tel: 26710 22248)
Kérkyra (Corfu) Odós R. Vouleuton and I. Polyla, Corfu Town (tel: 26610 37520
Kós Vas Georgiou 1, Kós Town (tel: 22420 24460; www.kosinfo.gr)
Kríti (Crete) Odós Xanthídou 1, Irákleio (tel: 28210 246106); Megáron Panthéon, Odós Kriári 40, Chaniá (tel: 28210 92943); Odós S. Venizélou, Réthymno (tel: 28310 29148)
Lésvos Aristarkou 6, Mytilíni (tel: 22510 42512)
Piréas Zea Marina (tel: 210 413 5716)
Ródos (Rhodes) Odós Archiepiskópou and Odós Papagoú, Rhodes Town (tel: 22410 44330)
Sámos Odós 25 Martíou 4, Vathí (tel: 22730 28582)
Sýros Odós Thimaton Sperxeiou 11, Syros Town (tel: 22810 86725).

Some words of Greek will come in handy, and will be appreciated by local people

Hotels and Restaurants

HOTELS

A disturbing number of hotels has been constructed on the islands over the past few years, but it does mean that there is something for every budget. Most are aimed at package tourists and are booked in advance through travel agents; few of these have been included in this listing. Most of the hotels listed below were chosen for their good value, atmosphere and standards of cleanliness, and/or for their views. Relatively few cheaper hotels are included, because at the lower end of the market it is often better (and in Greece far more usual) to rent a room in a private house (*domatia*). We have not included specific room-rentals, as these change by the season. The best way to find a room is to ask the owners, many of whom usually meet incoming ferries in search of custom; failing that, tourist offices will usually be able to provide a list of available rooms.

Most Greek hotels fall into one of five categories—de luxe, A, B, C and D—but the ratings mean very little. Prices seldom include breakfast: few Greeks take a proper breakfast, so it is often the least interesting meal, even in more expensive hotels. If a room in the cheap or medium categories seems expensive, try bargaining, especially if the hotel is not full. Prices are very much lower out of season, but remember that, as there are few visitors on the islands in winter, many hotels close from October or November until Easter or even May. There are no fixed dates for opening: that depends on the weather and on the mood of the owners. On the other hand, during Easter and the peak months of July and, especially, August, it can be very difficult to find a room at all without booking in advance.

The *Greek Travel Pages* is Greece's monthly travel guide. It includes most hotels, with phone and fax numbers, as well as flight and ferry schedules. It is available from International Publications in Athens (tel: 210 324 7511; fax: 210 323 3384).

The hotels recommended below have been divided into three price categories:

(€) = budget
(€€) =moderate
(€€€) = expensive

ATHÍNA (ATHENS)

Acropolis House (€)
Odós Kodroú 6–8, Pláka tel: 21032 22344
This is a friendly family-run hotel in a restored 19th-century villa. It is very conveniently located, in a pedestrianized street on the edge of the Pláka district. Spotless rooms with more character than most, some with good views.
Athenian Inn (€€€)
Odós Cháritos 22, Kolonáki tel: 21072 38097
In a lovely residential area very near the city centre, this is a favourite with regular visitors to the capital. Small and cosy, with friendly service.

Fresh Hotel (€€€)
Odós Sofokleous 26 tel: 21052 4851;
www.freshhotel.gr
Located near Omonia Square and the market, this ultra contemporary designer hotel is perfect if you want to explore Athens by foot. The rooms are bright and colourful, and the rooftop restaurant has great views over the city.
Grande Bretagne (€€€)
Plateía Syntágmatos (Syntagma Square)
tel: 21032 30251; fax: 21032 28034
The city's oldest and most elegant hotel. Since the mid-19th century, royals and celebrities have occupied its suites, some with magnificent views of the Acropolis. Fun for a drink, or a meal at the excellent GB Corner.
Student and Travellers Inn (€)
Odós Kydathinaíon 18, Pláka tel: 21032 44808; www.studenttravellersinn.com
Simple, clean rooms and friendly service in a very central location. Front rooms are noisy.

KRÍTI (CRETE)

Irákleio
Atlantis (€€)
Odós Ygias 2 tel: 28102 29103;
www.theatlantishotel.gr
This large 5-star hotel, built in an attractive 1960s modern style, has been renovated and has all amenities. One of the best and most luxurious hotels in town.
Hotel Kronos (€)
Odós Sofokli Venizelou 2 tel: 28102 82240;
www.kronoshotel.gr
Inexpensive central option on the waterfront. Clean and comfortable, 32 rooms, bar and breakfast room.
Lato (€€–€€€)
Odós Epimenidoú 15 tel: 28102 28103;
.www.lato.gr
Stylish boutique hotel in contemporary toned-down colours, with spacious and comfortable rooms, almost all overlooking the waterfront and harbour.

Ágios Nikólaos
Mavrikiano Houses (€–€€)
Mavrikiano, Elounda tel: 28102 43714;
www.traditional-homes.gr
The owners have lovingly restored 10 old stone cottages, with a lot of atmosphere and all modern comforts, as a reaction against the concrete resorts so often seen on this beautiful island.
Palazzo (€€)
Kitroplatia Beach tel: 28410 25080;
www.palazzo-apartments.gr
Airy and spacious studio flats for two to four people, tastefully decorated and mostly overlooking the sea.
St. Nicolas Bay Hotel (€€€)
tel: 28410 25041; www.stnicolasbay.gr
Luxurious, well-equipped resort hotel with impressive service, 2km (1.2 miles) north of Ágios Nikólaos port, overlooking the town and islands in the bay. Three restaurants, several pools and a small private beach.

270

Chaniá

Casa Delfino (€€€)
Odós Theofánous 8 tel: 28210 87400;
www.casadelfino.com
Beautiful 17th-century Venetian mansion in
the Old Town converted into apartment
suites, some overlooking the old harbour. Many
of the rooms are split-level, with the bed on the
upper level, and all are tastefully decorated.
Close to the harbour but in a quiet, elegant
area.
Hotel Manos (€)
Odós Zambelioú 24 tel: 28210 94156;
www.manoshotel.gr
Old and popular waterfront hotel with cheap
and comfortable rooms overlooking the
picturesque harbour.
Theresa (€€)
Odós Angeloú 8 tel: 28210 92798
In an old house, rooms decorated with local
crafts and antiques. Nos. 1 and 4 have good
sea views, No. 3 for its style. Kitchen facilities
and a roof terrace are a bonus.

Réthymno

Palazzino di Corina (€€€)
Odós Dambergi 7–9 , next to the Venetian
fortress tel: 28310 21205; www.corina.gr
Fine boutique hotel in a superb Venetian mansion that has been restored to its former glory.
Spacious and attractive rooms with polished
wood or tiled floors and old-stone walls. Good
pool in the courtyard.
Veneto (€€–€€€)
Odós Epimenidoú 4 tel: 28310 56634;
www.veneto.gr
The oldest part of the building is a 14th-cen-
tury Dominican monastery, and the newer part
is 15th- to 16th-century Venetian, so this hotel
has a lot of wonderful details. The rooms are
simple but tastefully decorated and offer great
comfort.

Siteía

Arhontiko (€)
Odós Kondilákis 16 tel: 28430 28172
Spacious, friendly, wooden guest house with
orange and lemon trees in the courtyard.
El Greco (€€)
Odós Arkadioú 13 tel: 28430 23133
Well-run family hotel with 19 impeccable rooms
and superb views over the harbour.

THE CYCLADES

Amorgós

Aegiális (€€€)
Órmos Aigiális tel: 22850 73393;
www.amorgos-aegialis.com
A modern hotel with all facilities, a wonderful
pool and good views over the bay.
Hotel Ágios Géorgios (€€)
high part of Xylokératidi, near Katápola tel:
22850 71228; www.hotelagiosgeorgios.gr
Family-run hotel in white and blue with comfortable quiet rooms all with superb views.
Breakfast is served on the balcony and there's
a good restaurant.

Minoa (€€)
on the harbour square, Katápola tel: 22850
71480; www.travel-to-amorgos.com
Pleasant rooms in traditional-style hotel, but
can be noisy.

Anáfi

Several pensions offer rooms on the island, but
facilities are slowly improving.

Villa Appolon (€€)
Klisidi beach tel: 22860 61348;
www.apollonvilla.gr
Built like an amphitheatre against the rock,
the family-run Villa Apollon, overlooks the
beach and blue waters. On offer are Cycladic-
style, fully equipped studios and rooms.

Ándros

Chryssí Aktí (€€)
Batsí tel: 22820 41236;
www.hotel-chryssiakti.gr
The most popular hotel for its location, in the
city centre and across from the beach.
Advance reservation is recommended in summer.
Eleni Mansion (€€–€€€)
Odós Empirikou 9, Chorá tel: 22820 22270;
www.elenimansion.gr
Small hotel in the centre of Chorá, in a beautiful 19th-century neoclassical mansion, formerly
used as a hospital and then as a school. Stylish
rooms with all modern comforts, and very welcoming hosts.

Folégandros

Anemomylos (€€€)
on the edge of Folégandros Town tel; 22860
41309; www.anemomylosapartments.com
Fully equipped apartments built in traditional
style on the cliff's edge, with stunning views.
One is equipped for visitors with disabilities.
Fani-Venis (€€)
Folégandros Town tel: 22860 41282
Comfortable hotel in a neoclassical mansion,
with rooms overlooking the sea (summer only).
Odysseus (€€)
Folégandros Town tel: 22860 41276
Pleasant, friendly hotel, a long-time favourite
with visitors to Folégandros.

Íos

Homer's Inn (€€)
Gialós tel: 22860 91365; www.homersinn.net
Breakfast room actually overlooking the port;
others look out on the countryside. Swimming
pool and bar, but open summer only.
Íos Palace (€€€)
Mylopótamos tel: 22860 91224;
www.iospalacehotel.com
Modern, traditional-style hotel near the beach
with comfortable rooms overlooking the sea.

Kéa

Hotel Tzia Mas (€€)
Korissía tel: 22880 21305
The island's only motel, near the beach, fills up
quickly in summer, so reserve in advance.

Hotel Brillante Zoi (€€–€€€)
Korissía tel: 22880 22685;
www.hotelbrillante.gr
Charming hotel, close to the waterfront, which combines traditional architecture with elegant and cosy furniture. In summer breakfast is served in a lovely garden, in winter near the fireplace. Popular with Athenians at weekends.

Kímolos
Not many stay on Kímolos, but there are a few rooms for rent in Psáthi and Kímolos Town.

Kýthnos
Filoxenia (€–€€)
Chora tel: 22810 31644
The only place to stay in Chora, with studios for 2 or 3 people, in a house full of character.

Mílos
Panorama (€–€€)
Klíma tel: 22870 21623
Small seafront hotel with friendly service. Has its own taverna.
Vourakis (€€)
Apollónia tel: 22870 41111
Studios and rooms with pretty terraces in two houses, built in traditional Cycladic style, with a garden full of flowers. Open Aprril to mid-October.

272

Mýkonos
For rooms in Mýkonos in the summer, reserve well in advance, as room prices can treble. Mýkonos Accommodation Centre (Odós Enoplon Dinameon 10, 1st floor, tel: 22890 23408; www.mykonos-accommodation.com) can arrange accommodation for all budgets. On the arrival quay is the office for the Hoteliers Association of Mýkonos (tel: 22890 24540; www.mykonosgreece.com). No advance reservations but they will look for a room on arrival.

Apollo (€€)
Paralía, Mýkonos Town tel: 22890 22223
Small but long-established, in the heart of the fun. Ten spotless, good-value rooms with bath.
Cavo Tagoo (€€€)
past the new harbour, Mýkonos Town
tel: 22890 23692
Prize-winning Cycladic architecture, a uniquely friendly atmosphere, sharp service and wonderful views over Mýkonos Town and the Aegean make the Cavo Tagoo, in its hillside setting, one of Greece's most special hotels. Swimming pool. Highly recommended.
Delos (€€)
At the entrance to the city on a small beach
tel: 22890 22517; fax: 22890 22312
Spacious rooms in a small hotel, one of the oldest on the island, some with seaview. Open April to October.
Philippi (€€)
Odós N. Kalogerá 25, Mýkonos Town
tel: 22890 22294
A converted traditional house, central but quiet, with a charming garden, friendly service and spotless rooms.

Náxos
Anixis (€)
Kástro, Náxos Town tel: 22850 22112;
www.hotel-anixis.gr
There are 16 rooms, mostly en suite, in this simple but spotlessly clean little hotel, which is near the Venetian tower.
Castro Residence (€€)
Kastro, Chora tel: 22850 25201;
www.naxostownhotels.com
Two beautifully furnished apartments in the Venetian *kastro* at very reasonable prices.
Chateau Zevgoli (€€€)
Boúrgo Kástro, Náxos Town
tel: 22850 26123; www.chateau-zevgoli.gr
One of the island's most interesting hotels: 10 rooms, tastefully decorated, high up in the old town. Good views and great atmosphere.
Grotta (€€)
Grotta, Náxos Town tel: 22850 22201;
www.hotelgrotta.gr
Modern, Cycladic-style hotel, with sparkling clean rooms and great views over the sea and the *kástro*. The best mid-range hotel in town, within easy walking distance of the port.

Páros and Antíparos
Páros is absolutely packed during the summer months and it can be hard to find any accommodation at all. Make reservations in advance or take up an offer of a room at the ferry arrival. Remember that rooms north of Páros Town are often a long walk from the centre.

Artemis (€€)
At the end of the harbour, Antiparos
tel: 22840 61460; www.artemisantiparos.com
Cycladic architecture and comfortable air-conditioned rooms and studios, all with a balcony overlooking the harbour.
Astir of Paros (€€€)
on the beach, Náousa, Páros tel: 22840 51797; www.astirofparos.gr
One of the best deluxe hotels in Greece, with a large pool and a three-hole par-3 golf course. Spacious rooms with all facilities.
Eleftheria (€€)
Odós Livadia, Parikia, Paros tel: 22840 22047
Air-conditioned rooms with balcony in a lovely house, drowning in bougainvilleas. A good breakfast is served on the balcony. Calm and very friendly. Reservation essential. Open mid-April to mid-October.
Golden Beach (€€)
Chrysí Aktí (Golden Beach), on the east coast of Páros tel: 22840 41194;
www.goldenbeach.gr
Modern low-rise hotel with excellent service and good, balconied rooms overlooking the beach. Very popular with windsurfers.
Lefkes Village (€€–€€€)
Lefkes, Paros tel: 22840 41827;
www.lefkesvillage.gr
Designed like a small village with a big pool, an art gallery, a small museum and neo-classical houses, set in a large garden with cypresses, fruit trees, old olive trees and a vineyard. Great views over surrounding hills.

Mantalena (€)
Kástro, Antíparos tel: 22840 61206
Clean but simple rooms, with harbour views.
Sofia (€€)
Parikia, Paros tel: 22840 22085;
www.pensionsofia.com
A peaceful place in the heart of town, with
stunning Cycladic architecture, a colourful
garden and bright and cheerful rooms. Open
April to October.
Villa Giorgio (€€)
Pisso Livadi, Paros tel: 22840 41713
Very friendly hotel in a blue-and-white house on
the port, with bright rooms overlooking the sea.

Sérifos

Areti (€€)
Livádi tel: 22810 51479; fax: 22810 51547
A very enjoyable hotel, near the ferry landing,
built on a hill and with superb views.
Serifos Beach (€€)
Near the harbour, Livádi tel: 22810 51209;
www.serifos-gr.com
Bright and spacious air-conditioned rooms with
fridge and bathroom, and very friendly service.

Sífnos

Sífnos is very popular with young Athenians on
weekends, so book ahead.

Anthoussa (€€)
Apollonía tel: 22840 31431; fax: 22840
32207
Small and charming hotel with 10 rooms
around a courtyard. Excellent breakfast as the
hotel is above the bakery of the same owners.
Artemon (€€)
Ayiou Konstandinou 3 tel: 22840 31303
Lovely family hotel with rooms that overlook
fields rolling towards the sea.
Moní Chrysopigí (€)
near the beach of Apokoftó tel: 22840 71295
This 17th-century monastery rents out simple
cells in summer. Reserve well in advance.

Síkinos

Lucas (€–€€)
Alopronoia tel: 22860 51076
Cheerful rooms in a beautiful house just uphill
from the port, so with great views over the sea.
Porto Sikinos (€€€)
on the beach in Alorónoia (tel/fax: 22860
51220
The best accommodation available, a small
resort hotel with traditional-style rooms.

Sýros

Dolphin Bay Hotel (€€€)
on the beach at Galissás tel: 22810 42924;
fax: 22810 42843
The largest and most modern hotel on the
island, with all facilities, a large swimming pool
and lovely views. Family-orientated.
Omiros (€€)
Odós Omiroú 43, Ermoúpoli tel: 22810 84910;
fax: 22810 86266
Restored neoclassical mansion, with good
views over the lively harbour.

Villa Maria (€€–€€€)
42 Odós Hydra, Ermoúpoli tel: 22810 81561;
fax: 22810 86536
In a quiet area, 10 minutes walk from the centre, the Villa Maria offers spacious room in a
neoclassical mansion, all with views over the
town and surrounding islands.

Thíra

Hotels with a view over the caldera are expensive. Many of the cheaper rooms are in modern,
characterless house extensions, often a long
walk from town. Prices more than double in
summer and reservations are essential.

Artemis Villas (€€€)
Imerovigli tel: 22860 22712/22179;
www.artemisvillas.gr
Rooms, suites, studios and apartments in
gorgeous white Cycladic architecture, all com-
manding great views over the volcano and
turquoise waters. There is also a beautiful
swimming pool.
Atlantis (€€€)
Thíra Town tel: 22860 22232;
www.atlantishotel.gr
Luxurious hotel, built in the 1950s but now
very up-to-date. Spacious rooms, most with bal-
conies overlooking the town and the volcano.
Katikies (€€€)
Oía tel: 22860 71401
Small but stunning hotel built on a cliff over-
hanging the *caldera*.
Keti (€€)
Thíra Town tel: 22860 22324;
www.hotelketi.gr
Family-run hotel with just seven spacious
rooms, in traditional Greek style, and with
amazing views over the *caldera*. Good value.
Lauda (€€)
Oía tel: 22860 71204
Pleasant Cycladic-style rooms with superb
views over the caldera.
Perivolas Traditional Homes (€€€)
Oía tel: 22860 71308; www.perivolas.gr
Former cliff-face dwellings turned into simple
but tasteful suites with cooking facilities.
Stunning views, a cliff-top pool, a well-run café,
excellent buffet breakfast and a relaxed atmo-
sphere.

Tínos

Porto Tango (€€€)
Pórto Ágios Ioánnis tel: 22830 24411
Cycladic-style resort hotel with a large swim-
ming pool and big, comfortable rooms.
Posidion (€€)
Panalia waterfront, Tínos Town tel: 22830
23121; fax: 22830 25808
Charming old-world hotel with tiled floors, lace
curtains and a large balcony.
Poreades (€€)
Odós N. Foskolou 7, Tinos Town tel: 22830
23845; www.voreades.gr
Beautiful house with 12 bright and white bed-
rooms furnished in traditional style, most of
which have a veranda overlooking the harbour
and the city.

273

THE DODECANESE

Astypálaia

Australia (€–€€)
On the harbour tel: 22430 61275
Popular waterfront hotel with comfortable
rooms and a good taverna.
Paradissos (€)
on the harbour, Gialós tel: 22430 61224
Clean, comfortable rooms, recently
refurbished; some with sea views.

Chálki

Captain's House (€)
Chálki Town tel: 22410 45201
A lovely restored mansion with a few rooms
for rent. The management may be able to
help you to find a room elsewhere if the house
is full. Reservations in advance essential.

Kálymnos

Manolis (€)
Vathýs tel: 22430 31300
Lovely, well-equipped rooms in a blue and white
house with a flowery garden.
On the Rocks (€–€€)
*Télendos tel: 22430 48260;
http://otr.telendos.com*
Tiny but charming family-run pension with well-
kept rooms and very friendly welcome.
Panorama (€)
Amoudára, Póthia tel: 22430 23138
Worth its name, as this hotel was built on the
high centre of the town, overlooking the har-
bour. If you reserve in advance, someone will
come and pick you up.
Tatsis (€)
*Massouri tel: 22430 47887;
www.kalymnos-isl.gr*
Impeccable rooms and studios with a little
kitchen and a terrace overlooking Télendos.

Kárpathos

Aphrodite (€)
*near the restored windmill, Olymbos
tel: 22450 51307; fax: 22450 51454*
Perched on top of a cliff overhanging the sea,
this small hotel commands superb views.
Elias Rooms (€)
*Pigadia tel: 22450 22446;
www.eliasrooms.com*
Quiet and comfortable rooms with good views
over the town.
Karpathos (€–€€)
*Odós Dimokratías 25, Kárpathos Town
tel: 22450 22347*
Pleasant rooms and a central location.
Krinos (€€)
Léfkos tel: 22450 71410
Pleasant hotel facing the sea and set in a
pleasant garden. Offers good value; necessary
to reserve in advance.
Possirama Bay (€€–€€€)
*Vróntis beach tel: 22450 22916,
fax: 22450 22919*
A five-minute walk from Kárpathos Town. Quiet,
spotless, spacious apartments have balconies
overlooking the beach and the port.

Kásos

Anagennisis (€€)
on the waterfront in Frý tel: 22450 41495
Probably the best place to stay on Kásos. Run
by a Greek-American. Comfortable rooms, the
most expensive with harbour views.
Captain's House (€–€€)
Fry tel: 22450 42716
This fine house, with five bright, well-
appointed and traditionally furnished
apartments, offers some of the island's best
accommodation.

Kastellórizo (Megísti)

Kastellorizo Hotel-Apartments (€€)
*Waterfront tel: 22460 49044;
www.kastellorizohotel.gr*
Picturesque waterfront hotel with spotless
rooms overlooking the harbour. You can jump
in the water right outside the hotel.
Megistis (€€)
*harbour of Kastellórizo Town tel: 22460
49219*
Pleasant, cosy rooms overlooking the port.

Kós

Most hotels on Kós are used by package
companies and are often noisy.
Afendoulis (€€)
Odós Evripiloú 1, Kós Town tel: 22420 25321
Small, modern hotel with balconied rooms. One
of the few hotels which has not given in to
package tourism. Reserve in advance.
Pension Alexis (€)
*Odós Irodotoú and Omiroú 9, Kós Town
tel: 22420 28798*
Friendly central guest house. Good value.
To Kyma (€)
*Mastihari, in the street parallel to the beach
tel: 22420 59045; http://kyma.kosweb.com*
Comfortable rooms with balcony, some with sea
views. Also a communal kitchen for guests.

Leipsoí

Kalypso (€€)
Leipsoí tel/fax: 22470 41420
One of the few hotels on the island (but there
are quite a few cheaper rooms for rent). All
rooms have bathrooms.

Léros

Ara (€€)
Alinda tel: 22470 24140; www.hotelara.com
Several rooms, flats and apartments, all with
balcony and sea view, set around a swimming
pool.
Archontiko Angelou (€€)
*Alinda tel: 22470 22749; www.hotel-angelou-
leros.com*
Stunning 19th-century house set in a lush
garden, with large and airy rooms, traditionally
decorated. Very peaceful place.
Pension Margarita (€)
Vromolithos tel: 22470 22889
Small but cosy rooms with bathroom in a
friendly family-run pension. In summer breakfast is served on the terrace overlooking
the sea.

274

Nísyros
Romantzo (€)
by the ferry landing at Mandráki tel: 22420 31340
Clean rooms with good harbour views and a big shady terrace.
Porfiris (€€)
Mandráki tel: 22420 31376
Comfortable modern hotel with well-maintained rooms, gardens and a swimming pool.

Pátmos
Captain's House (€€)
Skála tel: 22470 31793
Lovely hotel overlooking the sea, with sparkling and bright rooms.
Eirini Traditional Houses (€€€)
Sapsila tel: 22470 32826; www.traditional.gr
Beautiful rooms and small cottages looking over Sapsila Bay, at the far side of the island.
Maroussa Kouva (€€)
near the main square, ask instructions from Vangelis Taverna, Chora tel: 22470 31026
Three double rooms in a wonderful house with sweeping views over the village. Communal kitchen and bathrooms.
Pension Avgerinos (€)
Skála tel/fax: 22470 32118
Lovely little family-run pension with sea views and large, spotless rooms.
Skala (€€–€€€)
Skála tel: 22470 32465
This quiet and welcoming hotel, drowning in bougainvillaea, is on Skála's increasingly busy waterfront. Excellent breakfast terrace and pool. Reserve in advance.
Villa Knossos (€€)
Skála tel: 22470 32189
Good-value hotel with 10 rooms in a villa overgrown with bougainvillaea. Just off the port.

Ródos (Rhodes)
For individual travellers the most atmospheric option is to stay in the Old Town. It is possible to rent rooms there through the tourist information office (tel: 22410 31900).
Apollo Guesthouse (€–€€)
Odós Omirou 28c, Rhodes Town tel: 22410 32003; www.apollo-touristhouse.com
Wonderful and charming pension with stylish and comfortable rooms in the old town.
Cavo d'Oro (€€)
Kisthiríou 15, Rhodes Town tel: 22410 36980; www.cavodoro.com
This 13th-century house has been sympathetically restored. Breakfast is served in the lovely courtyard.
Marco Polo Mansion (€€€)
Odós Agios Fanouriou 40–42, Old Rhodes Town tel: 22410 25562; www.marcopolomansion.web.com
Spectacular 16th-century Turkish house with several rooms decorated in a dramatic but very tasteful Oriental style. A delicious breakfast is served in a courtyard full of flowers. The best place to stay in town, but only if you are staying several days.

San Nikolis (€€–€€€)
Odós Ippodámou 61, Rhodes Old Town tel: 22410 34561; www.medievalcityhotel.com
Delightful hotel, in the most attractive area of the Old Town, with comfortable rooms, friendly service and great breakfasts.
Via Via (€€)
Odós Pythagora 45 tel: 22410 77027; www.hotel-via-via.com
Charming hotel in the heart of Rhodes with eight rooms all decorated individually.

Sými
Aliki (€€)
Yialós, Sými Town tel/fax: 22460 71665
The island's best, with elegant and comfortable rooms, some with excellent sea views. Advance reservations necessary.
Hotel Fiona (€€)
Chorió, Sými Town tel: 22460 72088; www.symivisitor.com
Bright rooms with good views, situated in the Old Town.

Tílos
Irini (€€)
Livádia tel: 22460 44293; www.tilosholidays.gr
Charming small hotel with beautiful gardens and helpful owners. Reserve in advance.

THE IONIAN ISLANDS

Itháki
Mentor (€€)
Itháki Town tel: 26740 32433; www.hotelmentor.gr
Most people's choice; spacious rooms overlooking the beautiful harbour. Open all year.
Perantzada 1811 Art Hotel (€€€)
Odós Odissea Androutsou 821, Vathi tel: 26740 23914; www.arthotel.gr/perantzada
Stylish hotel in a 19th-century neo-classical building in a stunning hilltop location. Modern furniture blends in perfectly with the traditional architecture.

Kefalloniá
Agnantia (€€€)
Tselentata, Fiskárdo tel: 26740 51801; www.agnantia.com
Smart hotel, 2km (1.2 miles) east of Fiskárdo, with luxury in traditional style.
Emelisse (€€€)
Emblissi Bay, Fiskardo tel: 26740 41200; www.arthotel.gr/emelisse
Set in a garden with majestic cedars and cypresses, this modern hotel offers airy and spacious rooms with modern furniture and contemporary Greek art work. Great views.
Linardos (€ €€)
Assos tel: 26740 51563; www.linardosapartments.gr
Simple and traditional rooms and studios overlooking the beautiful bay of Assos and small beach.

275

Melissani (€–€€)
just south of Sámi tel: 26740 22464
Backed by the hills, facing the sea, a calm
hotel with large balconies.

Kérkyra (Corfu)
Green House (€–€€)
Palaiokastrítsa tel: 26630 41311
A small and basic guest house in this popular
resort. Reserve well in advance.
Konstantinoupolis (€€)
Odós K. Zavitsianou 11 tel: 26610 48716;
www.konstantinoupolis.com.gr
Bright and airy rooms with balconies offering
great views over the sea and the town.
Levant (€€)
Pelekas tel: 030 661 94230
Large neoclassical mansion with 50 rooms, set
in a large garden with fine views.
Pelecas Country Club (€€€)
Pelekas tel: 26610 52239/52917;
www.country-club.gr
This vast 18th-century estate of 50 acres has
been converted into a luxury hotel with rooms,
apartments and bungalows, far away from the
lively west coast beaches.
Villa de Loulia (€€€)
Peroulades tel: 26630 95394;
www.villadeloulia.gr
Several large rooms in a stunning villa set in a
huge garden with swimming pool, in the quiet
and atmospheric village of Peroulades.
Zefiros (€€)
Paleokastrítsa tel: 26630 41088
Well-established family-run hotel with bright
rooms with seaviews.

Lefkáda
Ianos (€€)
Lefkada Marina tel: 25450 22217
Young, fun and contemporary atmosphere on
the waterfront with good-size rooms full of
eclectic furniture.
Pirofani (€€)
*Odós Dorpfeld, Lefkada Town tel: 26450
25844*
A bit noisy perhaps, but very good value rooms
in the centre of town.
Santa Maura (€€)
*Spyridónos Viánda 2, Lefkáda Town
tel: 26450 21308*
In the centre of town, can be noisy. Spacious
rooms, some with private bathroom.

Paxoí
Paxos Beach (€€€)
Paxoí Town tel: 26620 31211;
www.paxosbeachhotel.gr
The island's first and best, with simple rooms
and good beach, water sports and tennis.

Zákynthos
Archontiko Village (€€)
Katstari, near Alyikes tel: 26950 83080;
www.archontikovillage.com
Studios, rooms and villas on this gorgeous hill-
side resort with olive groves.
Good swimming pool.

Crystal Beach (€€€)
Kalamáki tel: 26950 42912
crystalbeachhotel@hotmail.com
Right on Kalamáki beach, very calm and quiet
for a Zákynthos beach hotel.
Palatino (€€–€€€)
*Kolokotróni 10 and Kólyva, Zákynthos Town
tel: 26750 27780; www.palatinohotel.gr*
A block back from the sea, this modern,
elegant city hotel has sea views and a good
bar. One of the quietest hotels in town.
Villa Tzogia (€€)
Kambi tel: 26950 94060; www.tzogia.gr
Studios, flats and a small house in beautifully
renovated traditional architecture, in the
unspoiled village of Kambi, overlooking the sea.

NORTHERN AND EASTERN AEGEAN ISLANDS

Chíos
Kardamyla (€€€)
Kardámyla tel: 22720 23353;
fax: 22720 23354
A quiet beach resort with good rooms
overlooking the Marmara bay. A range of water
sports are available.
Kyma (€€)
*Odós Evgenías Chandrís 1, Chíos Town
tel: 22710 44500*
Characterful hotel in a 1917 shipowner's villa.
Its rooms were completely modernized a while
ago and are now distinctly old-fashioned. Very
helpful manager. Excellent breakfasts.
Perleas Mansion (€€€)
Kámpos tel/fax: 22710 32217;
www.perleas.gr
Next to one of Greece's most expensive hotels,
surrounded by orange groves, this lovingly
restored mansion offers quiet, comfortable
rooms with antique furnishings.
Phaedra (€)
*Odós Livanós 13, Chíos Town
tel: 22710 41129*
Small hotel with clean rooms in an old mansion
run by young people.
Ta Petrina (€€)
Volissós tel: 22740 21128; www.tapetrina.gr
Wonderfully restored stone village houses in
this peaceful village near the beach.

Ikaría
Akti (€)
*on the waterfront in Ágios Kírykos tel: 22750
22694*
Simple but well-maintained rooms with views
over the bay from the garden.
Cavos Bay (€€–€€€)
Armenistís tel: 22750 71381;
www.cavosbay.com
Luxurious, quiet hotel set on a hillside.
Daidalos (€€)
Armenistís tel: 22750 71390;
www.360.gr/daidaloshotel-ikaria
Traditional-style, very airy hotel, in blue and
white, overlooking the bay. Good views, relaxed
atmosphere. This hotel tends to be popular with
Athenians.

Evdoxia (€€)
Évdilos tel: 22750 31502
Modern hotel with balconied rooms overlooking the harbour and the bay.

Lésvos
Blue Sea (€€)
Odós Kountourióto 91, Mytilíni tel: 22510 23994; fax: 22510 29656
Comfortable rooms, many with balconies overlooking the harbour.
Delfinia (€€€)
Mólivos tel: 22530 71315;
www.molyvoshotel.com
Pleasant resort hotel overlooking the town and harbour with simple rooms, swimming pool and sports facilities. Open all year.
Nassos Guest House (€)
Molivos tel: 22530 71432;
www.nassosguesthouse.com
Wonderful budget hotel in the centre of Molivos with spotless shared bathrooms and spectacular views over the village rooftops and the sea.
Sea Horse (€€)
near the beach at Mólivos tel: 22530 71320;
www.seahorse-hotel.com
Modern hotel below the old town with unfussy, clean rooms and friendly service.
Villa 1900 (€€)
Odós Vóstani 24, Mytilíni tel: 22530 23448
Small hotel in a restored *belle-époque* villa.

Límnos
Aktaion (€)
Odós Arvanitáki 2, Mýrina tel: 22540 22258
A two-storey hotel on the port, somewhat noisy and run down, but open all year.
Aktí Mýrina (€€€)
Mýrina tel: 22540 22681;
www.360.gr/aktimyrina.lemnos
One of the finest and most expensive hotels on the Greek Islands. Simple but spacious accommodation in bungalows, each with its own small private garden. Marvellous beach, several excellent restaurants and all water sports.

Sámos
Armonia Bay Hotel (€€–€€€)
Tsamadou Beach, Kokkari tel: 22730 92279
Small elegant hotel in a splendid setting, hidden in greenery and overlooking a stunning bay.
Avli (€)
Odós Aréos and Kaloméri, Sámos Town tel: 22730 22939
Wonderful hotel in an old monastery in the quiet back streets near the harbour.
Paradise (€€)
Odós Kanarí 21, Sámos Town tel: 22730 23911
Elegant hotel set in a lush garden with a swimming pool, away from the tourist hubbub, but still central.
Pythagoras (€)
Odós Kallystratou 12, Samos Town tel: 22730 28422; www.pythagorashotel.com
Welcoming budget hotel in a quiet part of town with clean and airy rooms, and a good taverna.

Samothráki
Aeolos (€€)
Kamariótissa tel: 22510 41595
Comfortable hotel, a short walk up from the port and waterfront restaurants. Quiet.
Kaviros (€€€)
Thermá tel: 22510 98277
Surrounded by lush greenery, only a short walk from cafés and restaurants and within easy reach of an attractive pebble beach.

Thásos
Thassos Inn (€€)
Panagía tel: 25930 61612; fax: 25930 61027
Pleasant hotel in a pine forest on the hillside, with rooms with balcony overlooking the village.

THE SARONIC ISLANDS

Aígina
Eginitiko Arhintiko (€€)
Odós Nikólaou and Thomáidou 1, Aígina Town tel: 22970 26716
This is a charming traditional guest house in a neoclassical house with tastefully decorated rooms around two flower-filled courtyards.
Moondy Bay (€€€)
5km (3 miles) south of Aígina Town tel: 22970 61622; fax: 22970 61147
Friendly resort hotel with frequent bus services into Aígina Town and Pérdika. Lovely gardens, with a good private beach and swimming pool.
Pension Rena (€€)
Parodos Ayias Irinis, Aígina Town tel: 22970 24760; fax: 22970 24244
Eight white and blue spotless rooms in the heart of town, and a wonderful breakfast.

Póros
Latsi (€–€€)
Odós Papadopoúlo 74, Póros Town tel: 22980 22392
Simple, slightly worn but clean rooms; balcony overlooking the Peloponnese. Good value.
Pavlou (€€)
Neório bay tel: 22980 22734
Pleasant and quiet hotel on Kalávria.
Villa Mimosa (€€)
Odós Monastiriou 7, near Askeli, Kalavria tel: 22980 24659
Spacious studios in a lovely villa with garden filled with flowers, and direct access to the beach. Open May to September.
Villa Tryfon (€–€€)
Just off Plateia Agios Giorgiou, Póros Town tel: 22980 22215
Very friendly hotel with airy rooms, some with sea view.

Salamína
Gabriel (€–€€)
Aiánteio tel: 210 466 2275
Definitely the best guest house on the island, with simple rooms.
Votsalakia (€)
Odós Themistokléous 64, Selinia tel: 210 467 1334
Pleasant, simple hotel with swimming pool.

Hotels and Restaurants

Spétses

Armata (€€€)
behind Possidonion hotel, Spetses Town
tel: 22980 72683; www.armatahotel.gr
Characterful boutique hotel with elegantly furnished rooms, a wonderful breakfast terrace in the garden and a good-size swimming pool.
Possidonion Hotel (€€–€€€)
Spétses Town tel: 22980 72308
Refurbished Edwardian hotel overlooking the waterfront. Once legendary for its wealthy and famous clientele.
Villa Christina (€€)
54m (60 yards) uphill from the ferry landing in Spétses Town tel: 22780 72218
Secluded hotel with comfortable and clean rooms around a courtyard.

Ýdra

Leto (€€€)
Off Odós Miaoúlis tel: 22980 53385; www.leto-hydra.gr
Charming hotel in a quiet back street, with comfortable rooms with shiny parquet floors. A delicious buffet breakfast is included in the price.
Orloff (€€)
Odós Rafália 9 tel: 22980 52564
Another tasteful renovation of a typical Hydriot mansion, with 10 differently designed rooms.
Pension Anna Kavalierou (€€)
Near the port tel: 22980 53066; www.pensionannahydra.gr
Friendly Anna receives her guests with open arms and homemade cakes. Comfortable rooms and good breakfast.

THE SPORADES AND ÉVVOIA

Alónnisos

Kavos (€€)
Off the main street, Alónissos Town tel: 24240 65216; www.kavoshotel.gr
Simple but well-kept rooms, all with balcony and great views over the harbour.
Liadromia (€€)
Patitíri tel: 24240 65521; fax: 24240 65096
A modern hotel overlooking the harbour, a few minutes' walk from tavernas and shops.
Paradise (€€)
Magnísias, adjacent to Patitíri tel: 24240 65130; www.paradise-hotel.gr
Lovely, family-run hotel built on the rocks, above the harbour and with sea views from many rooms. Great terrace.

Skíathos

Australia (€–€€)
Skíathos Town tel: 24270 22488
Popular hotel in a quiet street in the centre of town, offering good-value rooms with bathrooms and some studios.
Karafelas (€)
Odós Papadiamánti 59, Skíathos Town tel: 24270 21235
Pleasant little hotel with quiet rooms and garden and very friendly owners. Reserve in advance.

Meltemi (€€)
Skiáthos Town tel: 24270 22493; www.meltemiskiathos.com
Comfortable modern hotel, overlooking the yacht harbour. Reserve well in advance: this is a popular place even in spring and autumn.

Skópelos

Archontiko (€€)
Xánthou 1, Skópelos Town tel: 24240 22049
Well-situated guest house in a stylish mansion with comfortable rooms.
Drossia (€–€€)
Skópelos Town tel: 24240 22490
Built on top of the hill overlooking the town. The rooms are tidy and have excellent views.
Prince Stafylos (€€€)
Livádi tel: 24240 22775; www.prince-stafylos.gr
Lovely hotel, built like a country house within walking distance of the town. Swimming pool and perfumed garden. Advance reservations necessary. Recommended, despite being expensive.

Skýros

Angela (€€)
Mólos tel: 22220 91764
Spotless rooms, all with balconies.
Nefeli (€€)
Skýros Town tel: 22220 91964; www.skyros-nefeli.gr
Best choice in the town, modern but with Skyrian-style architecture and tastefully decorated bedrooms, most with lovely views. Reserve beforehand.
Skyros Palace (€€€)
Acheroúnes tel: 22220 91994; www.skiros-palace.gr
Big resort built in traditional style with a good swimming pool.

Évvoia

Eleonas (€€)
Roviés Evia 340 05 tel: 22270 71619; www.eleonashotel.com
Luxurious rooms in a villa set in a working olive grove within easy walking distance of the sea.
Kentrikon (€)
Odós A. Gotsioú, Chalkída tel: 22210 22375
Old-fashioned hotel near the Évripos bridge with clean but simple rooms.
Limni (€)
Límni tel: 22270 31316
Offering good value, this hotel has spotless rooms overlooking the quiet bay.
Thermae Sylla (€€€)
Odós Paraliakis 18, Loutrá Edipsoú tel: 22260 60100; www.thermaesylla.gr
Luxurious, well-designed hotel, reputed for the excellent spa treatments.
Vateri (€€)
Limni tel: 22270 32493
Several comfortable rooms and suites overlooking a trimmed lawn with colourful flowerbeds and further out the mountains and sea.

RESTAURANTS

On many islands, particularly the smaller ones, the choice of restaurants is limited to two or three on the waterfront. As space here is limited, we have only mentioned tavernas and restaurants that we think stand out, or ones that are more difficult to find. Telephone numbers are given only for establishments where advance reservations might be appropriate.

Greeks almost never look at the menu, preferring to ask the waiter what's cooking, because often the specialities or more interesting items are not written down. If you do not know the names of Greek dishes, and if you would like to see the prices, it may be sensible to look at the menu. If not, ask to have a look in the kitchen, and also take note of what your Greek neighbours are eating. Part of the pleasure of eating out in the islands is wandering around to find the place right for your mood. Remember that many restaurants are closed out of season, from October to March or April. The restaurants recommended below have been divided into three price categories:

(€) = budget
(€€) = moderate
(€€€) = expensive

ATHÍNA (ATHENS)

Karavitas (€–€€)
35 Odós Arktinou/4 Pausaniou, Pangrati
tel: 210 721 5155
This traditional taverna, with great atmosphere and delicious food, is very popular with locals. Book ahead.
Sigálas (€)
Plateía Monastiráki tel: 210 321 3036
Ancient taverna with boisterous atmosphere. Simple, cheap, good.
Socrates' Prison (€€)
Odós Mitséon 20, Koukáki tel: 210 922 3434
Atmospheric restaurant with good fresh Greek and more continental dishes.
Spondi (€€€)
Odós Pironos 5, Pangrati tel: 210 752 0658
Award-winning *haute cuisine* Mediterranean restaurant with excellent food, a stylish interior and a beautifully overgrown summer terrace.
To Kafineio (€€)
1 Odós Epicharmou, Monastiraki tel: 210 324 6916
This authentic restaurant is a rare find in the touristic area of Plaka, serving excellent *mezedes*, tucked away on a side street.

KRÍTI (CRETE)

Irákleio
Prassein Aloga (€€)
corner of Odós Chandakos & Cydonias
tel: 28102 83429
Tiny restaurant cum delicatessen with excellent Cretan-Mediterranean food, often inspired by age-old traditional recipes, but always served with an inventive twist.

Terzakis Ouzéri (€–€€)
Odós Marinéli 17, opposite Agios Dimitrios church tel: 28102 21444
Delightful *ouzeri* with a good variety of *mezédes* and grills, including some more unusual ones like sea urchins, snails and sheep testicles, all served with wine or *raki*.

Ágios Nikólaos
Itanos (€–€€)
Odós Kyproú 1 tel: 28410 25340
Huge taverna with tables on the pavement, serving well-prepared traditional Cretan specialities.
Pelagos (€€)
corner of Odós Koraká and Katecháki 10
tel: 28410 25737
Atmospheric taverna in an old villa, with fish specialities and an interesting menu. Dining also on the terrace.

Chaniá
Apostolis (€€–€€€)
Odós Aktí Enoseos 6 tel: 28210 43470
Excellent fish restaurant with views over the eastern harbour serving. Fish is sold by the weight and the seafood platters for two are delicious and good value.
Tamam (€€)
Odós Zambelioú 49 tel: 28210 58639
Very popular and good-value restaurant in part of an old *hammam*. Imaginative food.
To Karnagio (€–€€)
Platéia Katehakí 8 tel: 28210 53366
A favourite with locals for its delicious Cretan dishes and fresh seafood, served on a pleasant terrace in the harbour.

Réthymno
Avli (€€–€€€)
Xanthoudidou 22 tel: 28310 26213;
www.avli.com
Gourmet cooking of Cretan produce in a delightful sprawling Old Town setting.

Siteía
O Mixos (€–€€)
Kornarou 117 tel: 28430 22416
With a café on the waterfront and restaurant up the hill, this serves excellent Cretan food.

THE CYCLADES

Amorgós
Akrogiali (€–€€)
Katápola tel: 69772 51656
The most atmospheric of the tavernas, with good fresh Greek specialities.
Taverne Liotrivi (€–€€)
on the way up to Amorgós Town tel: 22850 71700
Excellent taverna with a deserved reputation for serving an inventive and fresh local cuisine.
Vitzentos (€€)
seafront, Xylokeratídi, Katápola
tel: 22850 71518
Very popular seafood restaurant with a more inventive menu than most.

Hotels and Restaurants

Andrós

O Tassos (€–€€)
Next to hotel Pighi Sariza, Apikia tel: 22820 22582
This taverna is popular with Greek families who come to eat the well-prepared, traditional local dishes, and enjoy the view from the terrace.
Ta Yialia (€€)
Yialia, on the road to Stémies tel: 22820 24650
Excellent fish taverna close to the beach.

Folégandros

Meltemi (€–€€)
in the harbour Karavostassi tel: 22860 41557
Popular with Greeks, despite the slow service, who come and eat a selection of good *mezédes*, while watching the boats come in and out.
O Kritikos (€€)
near the 3rd square, Chóra tel: 22860 41219
Typical taverna famous for its meat grills, which include delicious lamb, chicken and rabbit.

Íos

Elpis (€–€€)
on the neach, Mylopotas tel: 22860 91626
Very popular and well-established beach restaurant with good fish and meat grills run by twin brothers.
Lord Byron (€€)
near the main square, Chora tel: 22860 92125
Popular taverna with excellent food. Book ahead.
The Mills (€€–€€€)
top of Íos Town tel: 02860 91284
Wonderful Greek food. Try the excellent stuffed aubergine or the tender goat's meat.

Kýthnos

Gialos (€€)
on the beach, Mérichas tel: 22810 32277
Traditional taverna on the beach with good service, excellent fresh food and a shaded terrace.

Mílos

Ergyna (€–€€)
centre of Tripiti tel: 22870 22524
Inventive regional cuisine served on a terrace with views over the gulf. Reservations essential.
Zygos (€€)
Adámas (a five-minute walk east along the seafront, then follow sign for restaurant grill) tel: 22870 23120
Lovely view over town, good Greek fare and better value than in the port.

Mýkonos

Dilés (€€)
Platia Lakka, Mykonos Town tel: 22890 22120
Beautiful terrace with tables beside the pool, and excellent Greek food prepared with the freshest produce, using interesting mixtures of herbs. Recommended.
La Maison de Catherine (€€)
corner of Odós Gerasimou and Nikou, Mykonos Town tel: 22890 22169
Excellent traditional Greek food with a little twist, laid back but efficient service and beauti-

ful décor has made this restaurant an institution for locals and visitors.
O Kounélas (€€)
just off the harbour, Mykonos Town tel: 22890 28220
Simple fish restaurant where local families, and the old fishermen come to eat.

Náxos

Lucullus (€€)
Kastro, Naxos Town tel: 22850 22569
The oldest taverna in town is a sophisticated eatery serving well-prepared regional cuisine amid antique furniture. Book ahead.
Meze 2 (€)
Paralia, Naxos Town tel: 22850 26401
Excellent old-style *ouzéri* where the family cooks and serves a wide variety of excellent *mezedes*, particularly the fish and seafood.
O Apostolis (€–€€)
near the old market, on the way to Grotta Beach, Naxos Town tel: 22850 26777
A small taverna in a quiet street with simple but good Greek food.
Sto Liofago (€–€€)
Beach Mikri Vigla tel: 22850 75214
Well-established beach restaurant with excellent traditional Greek dishes.

Páros

Happy Green Cow (€)
Odós Ágora, Páros Town tel: 22840 24691
Delightful, tiny world cuisine restaurant with take-away option.
Levantis (€€–€€€)
Odós Ágora, Páros Town tel: 22840 23613
Really good food inspired by Turkish and Middle Eastern cuisine in the Kastro.
Tsitsanas (€–€€)
between villages of Pródromos and Mármara
Though this restaurant is hard to find (ask for directions), the food is well worth the search.

Sérifos

I Platia (€€)
near the bus stop, Livádi tel: 22810 51261
Great *ouzeri* with a good selection of *mezedes*.

Sífnos

Apostolis to Koutouki (€€)
Apollonía tel: 22840 31186
The best of the tavernas. Also a great find for those seeking vegetarian dishes.
Captain Andreas (€–€€)
Kamáres tel: 22840 32356
Excellent fish and seafood taverna directly on the beach.
Liotrivi (€€)
Artemón tel: 22840 32051
Local specialities include caper salad and chickpea *beignets*. Only open in summer, but its sister restaurant, **Manganas** (€€), on the central square in Artemón, is open all year.

Sýros

Boubas (€)
left of the ferry landing, Ermoúpoli
Pleasant *ouzéri*.

Thalami Ouzerii (€€)
Odós Souri Agios Nikolaos Bay, Ermoúpoli
tel: 22810 85331
Excellent and extremely popular fish restaurant
in an old house on the waterfront.
Tou Arkontariki (€)
near Platía Minoúli, Ermoúpoli tel: 22810 81774
Small and very Greek place with tables spilling
over outside and tasty daily specials.

Thíra

1800 (€€€)
Odós Nikolaou Nomikou, Oia tel: 22860 71485
The best restaurant in town, run by three Greek
architects in a superb Venetian mansion, with
inventive Greek cuisine based on the best
produce.
Nikolas (€)
*Odós Erythou Stavrou, Thíra tel: 22860
24550*
Long-established taverna serving hearty Greek
dishes—as traditional as it gets.
Sélene (€)
Agiou Mina tel: 22860 22249
Exquisite modern Greek cuisine served in
spectacular surroundings.

Tínos

Drossia (€)
Ktikados tel: 22830 41215
Excellent taverna, popular with Tiniot families,
with really good local cuisine and a beautiful
terrace.
Ta Myronia (€€)
Pyrgos tel: 22830 31229
Well-prepared *mezedes* from the island, includ-
ing 'young pigeons'.
Ta Tsabia (€€)
*on the road from Tinos Town just before
arriving at Kionia tel: 22830 23142*
Popular with local families, particularly on week-
ends, for its honest Greek cuisine.

THE DODECANESE

Kálymnos

I Drosia (€–€€)
Melitsahas tel: 22430 48745
A wide choice of fish and seafood *mezedes*
in this excellent *ouzeri* overlooking the
harbour.
Stoukas (€)
Waterfront, Pothia tel: 22430 24546
Popular fish and seafood *ouzeri* with all the local
specialities. Book ahead.

Kárpathos

I Orea Kárpathos (€–€€)
*in the marina, Kárpathos Town
tel: 22450 22501*
Pikilia are the speciality here, larger portions
than *mezedes*, including all the best regional
specialities.
O Milos (€)
Olymbos tel: 22450 51333
Tiny restaurant in a restored windmill serving
delicious dishes and local sweets, with stunning
views over the sea.

Pelagia (€)
on the road from Menetes up to Amophi
tel: 22450 81135
Popular with local families who come for the
wonderful goat and lamb dishes served with salads and local produce.

Kós

Anatolia Hamam (€€€)
Plateia Diagora, Kos Town tel: 22420 28323
Superb Greek food and wine list, and excellent
service in an old private Turkish bathhouse.
Open May to October.
Arap (Platanio) (€–€€)
Platáni tel: 22420 28442
One of the few Turkish restaurants on the island:
excellent Turkish and Greek specialities. Open
summer only.
O Nikos O Psara (€€)
21 Odós Averof, Kos Town tel: 22420 23098
Good-value fish restaurant in the heart o
f town.
Petrino (€€)
Plateía Theológou 1, Kós Town
tel: 22420 27251
Lovely Greek specialities served on a quiet
terrace next to the Western Excavations.

Pátmos

Benetos (€€)
Sapsila tel: 22470 33089
Top-notch dining at this stylish farmhouse where
Greek *mezedes* go side by side with superb
sashimi of local fish with wasabi sauce.
Pantelis (€–€€)
one street back from the harbour in Skála
tel: 22470 31230
Long-established traditional restaurant, a
favourite with locals and foreign residents.
Friendly service. Open all the year round.

Ródos (Rhodes)

L'Auberge Bistro (€€)
*Praxitelous 21, Rhodes Old Town tel: 22410
34292*
Sophisticated courtyard setting and French-
Greek cuisine. Excellent food and wine list.
Fotis (€€–€€€)
8 Odós Menekléous, Old Town Rhodes
tel: 22410 27359
The best fish and seafood restaurant in town
with a long-standing reputation.
Nireas (€€)
Sophokleous 22 tel: 22410 21703
Seafood and shellfish specialist, straight from
the harbour.
To Kastrou tou Notou (€–€€)
Kiotari, on the road between Lardos and Gennadi
tel: 22440 47236
Excellent address if you want to get away from
the crowds. A beautiful stone house and a huge
terrace overlooking an enormous almost
deserted beach, with delicious Greek dishes.

Sými

Neraida (€–€€)
main square in Gialós, Sými Town
tel: 22460 71841

Atmospheric taverna with tasty grilled fish and an array of mouthwatering *mezedes*.

THE IONIAN ISLANDS

Itháki

Fatouros (€–€€)
main square in Stavrós tel: 26740 31385
Open all year for grilled meat and fish.
Gregory's (€€)
Paliocaravo, Itháki Town tel: 26740 32573
A little out of town, on Vathí bay. Good taverna food.
Symposium (€)
Fríkes
On the waterfront, this offers some imaginative dishes, with many vegetarian options.

Kefalloniá

Girvas Brothers (€–€€)
Odos Vassiléos Vandoroú 1, Argostóli tel: 26710 24259
Well-established, family-run taverna serving traditional dishes cooked by the owner himself to a loyal crowd of locals.

Kérkyra (Corfu)

Ninos (€)
Odós Chrisi, Corfu Town tel: 26610 46175
Simple, but very popular taverna, which has been running since the 1920s, serving a menu that changes daily.
Tripa (€€–€€€)
Kinopiastes, 7km (4 miles) southwest of Corfu Town tel: 26610 56333; www.tripas.gr
Celebrity visitors to the island are invariably taken here, for the wonderful banquet of seemingly endless Corfiot dishes served with a good folkloric show.
Venetian Well (€€)
Plateia Kremast, Corfu Town tel: 26610 44761
Charming restaurant in the back streets of the Old Town with is different menu each night. The inventive dishes may include lobster, wild boar and excellent stews.

Lefkáda

Regentos (€–€€)
Dimárchou Venióti 17, Lefkáda Town tel: 26450 22855
Fresh food simply prepared in a long-established family taverna. Excellent value.

Paxoí

Taka Taka (€€)
Gaios tel: 26620 32329
Up-market fish restaurant specializing in the freshest fish.
Vassilis (€€)
Longós tel: 26620 31587
Waterfront taverna serving exceptionally good food. Long wine list too.

Zákynthos

Arekia (€€)
Odós Kryeneniou (off Plateía Solómou) Zákynthos Town tel: 26950 26346

Greek food at good prices. Come early for a quiet dinner, or later to see the local musicians.
Kostas' Brother (€€)
Vasilikos Peninsula tel: 26950 35347
Atmospheric outdoor restaurant serving regional cuisine with produce from their own garden. Very popular and often live music.
Mantalena (€€)
Alikanás tel: 26950 83550
Some of the best food on the island.

NORTHERN AND EASTERN AEGEAN ISLANDS

Chíos

Akrigiali (€–€€)
Limnos tel: 22740 21777
Succulent grills served with salads and *mezedes*, served on an airy terrace near the sea.
Hotzas (€€)
3 Odós Kondyli, Chíos Town tel: 22710 42787
All year evening only
Beautiful traditional taverna where local families come to sample the delicious local cuisine.
Mesaionas I (€–€€)
main square in Mestá
Excellent food. Open all year round.

Lésvos

Averof (€€)
Odós Ermou and harbour, Mytilini tel: 22510 22180
Classic taverna, open since 1925, with good traditional fare to be chosen from the kitchen at all times of the day. Closed Sun in winter.
I Eftalou (€–€€)
Eftalou, 4km (2.5 miles) from Molivos tel: 22530 71049
Beautiful setting in an overgrown garden and excellent Greek food, near a small beach.
O Rigas (€–€€)
Petra tel: 22530 41405
This is the oldest taverna in the old town of Petra, on top of the rock. Very good authentic Greek food.

Límnos

Glaros (€€)
Mýrina harbour tel: 22540 24061
Typical harbour fish taverna. View of the *kástro*.
O Platanos (€–€€)
Odós P. Kyda Karatza, Myrina tel: 22540 22070
Popular taverna with a terrace on a delightful square with plane trees, serving mainly meat and vegetable stews.

Sámos

Christos (€–€€)
off Plateia Agiou Nikolao, Samos Town no phone
Simple and copious taverna food served on tables in the street.
Loukas (€)
Manolates tel: 22730 94541
Popular and cheap taverna with great views and a small selection of superb *mezedes* to be sampled with the local *moshato* (Muscat) wine.

Psaradés (€€)
*Agios Nikolaos, on the road from Samos to
Karlovassi tel: 22730 33489*
Superb fish and seafood restaurant on the edge
of the water. Perfect place to watch the sunset.
Open April to October.

Samothráki
I Asprovalta (€€)
*Kato Kariotes, 4km (2.5 miles) east of
Palaioplis tel: 25510 98250*
Small but very pleasant taverna on the sea, serv-
ing fish and seafood.
Klimitaria (€–€€)
waterfront in Kamariótissa tel: 255510 41535
Delightful restaurant serving good regional
dishes in the shade of vine leaves.

Thásos
O Andreas (€)
Kasaviti tel: 25930 71760
Family-run taverna under the trees on the square
with perfectly cooked regional food.

THE SARONIC ISLANDS

Aígina
Maridaki (€€)
Harbour, Aigina Town no phone
Good traditional Greek food and a large choice
of fresh fish.
To Proréon (€€)
Perdika tel: 22970 61577
Excellent fish restaurant in a garden filled with
flowers and cacti on the edge of the water.

Póros
Karavalos (€€)
*near the waterfront, Poros Town
tel: 22980 26158*
Speciality of snails, hence the name, but plenty
of other traditional fare, served on a quiet little
terrace.

Spétses
Exedra (€€)
Palaío Limáni, Spétses Town tel: 22980 73497
Excellent fish and seafood taverna overlooking
the Old Harbour.
Lazaros (€€)
*on the Dápia in Spétses Town
tel: 22980 72600*
Genuine taverna food, specialities of goat in
lemon sauce and chicken in tomato sauce, and
good barreled retsina.
Tasos (€€)
*near the beach at Agía Anargýri
tel 22980 73018*
Very popular and friendly taverna with good
typically Greek fare.

Ýdra
Léonidas (€–€€)
Kala Pigadia tel: 22980 53097
More a home than a restaurant with a friendly
welcome and delicious home-cooked food. Hard
to find so call beforehand, but worth the search.
Evening only.

To Steki (€€)
Odós Miaoúlis, Ýdra Town tel: 22980 53517
Friendly traditional taverna.

THE SPORADES AND ÉVVOIA

Skíathos
Amfiliki (€€)
Agia Triada, Skíathos Town tel: 24270 22839
Run by Christos, an old naval officer who tells
stories and cooks marvellously, while you can
take in the breathtaking views.
Ilias (€€–€€€)
*Skíathos Town (from Odós Papadiamánti, turn
right into Odós Evangelístrias and follow the
arrows to Ilias) tel: 24270 22664*
Traditional taverna dishes, excellent roast beef
with prunes and lamb with vegetables in filo.
The Windmill (€€)
Skíathos Town tel: 24270 24550
Superior cooking in a fabulous setting.

Skópelos
Anatoli Ouzeri (€)
*in the ruins of the Venetian kástro at the top of
Skópelos Old Town tel: 24240 22851*
Perfect *ouzéri*. Inexpensive *mezédes*.
O Pavlos (€€)
*Agnondas, 8km (5 miles) from Chora
tel: 24240 22409*
Excellent fish as well as other traditional dishes,
in a beautiful little cove.
Ta Kymata (€€)
*on the waterfront by the ferry landing in
Skópelos Town tel: 24240 22381*
The best of the waterfront tavernas.

Skýros
Filipeous (€)
Ferry dock, Linariá tel: 22220 93274
Delightful fish taverna overlooking the harbour.
Psariotis (€€)
Harbour, Linariá tel: 2220 93250
Renowned for its fish soup and lobster
spaghetti, but everything is good here.

Évvoia
Aegli (€€)
*Odós Paraliakis 18, Loutra Edipsoú tel: 22260
22215*
Charming taverna with good grills and salads,
served in the shade of trees.
Mesa-Exo (€) ·
Karistos tel: 22240 23997
Popular taverna where locals come for a plate of
grilled sardines, octopus or other *mezedes* with
a carafe of wine.
Paradosiako (€)
Main square, Límni tel: 22270 31479
Friendly taverna popular with local families for
its simple Greek food.

Index

Index

Index/Acknowledgements

Picture credits

The Automobile Association would like to thank the following photographers, libraries and associations for their assistance in the preparation of this book: **THE BRIDGEMAN ART LIBRARY** 28b Sculpture of Aphrodite (Hermitage, St. Petersburg); **THE BRITISH MUSEUM, LONDON** 26b, 108b, 126a, 126b, 219b, 240a; **BYZANTINE MUSEUM, ATHENS** 38a; **MARY EVANS PICTURE LIBRARY** 34a, 36a, 36b, 40b, 42b, 44a, 84/5, 86a, 116b, 182a, 182b, 183b, 210b, 211, 240b, 240/1; **R. GAULDIE** 102, 103; **GETTY IMAGES** 46b, 47a, 47b, 48t, 86b, 86/7, 87, 138a, 155b, 194a; **C. GORDON** 49b; **RONALD GRANT ARCHIVES** 135a, 135b; **TERRY HARRIS** 184, 185; **HISTORIC MUSEUM, CRETE** 42a, 70c; **THE HULTON GETTY PICTURE COLLECTION LTD** 44b, 44c, 49a, 194c; **NATIONAL ARCHAEOLOGICAL MUSEUM, ATHENS** 34b, 58, 59a, 218a; **NATURE PHOTOGRAPHERS LTD** 198 (J. Sutherland), 226b (P. R. Sterry), 226c (R. Tidman), 227a (P. R. Sterry); **PICTURES COLOUR LIBRARY LTD** 111, 117, 118, 120; **SPECTRUM COLOUR LIBRARY** 101, 192.
All other pictures are held in the Association's own library (**AA PHOTO LIBRARY**) with contributions from the following photographers: **S. L. DAY** 2b, 6, 8, 9b, 11, 12a, 13a, 14a, 16b, 17a, 19a, 20b, 21b, 25a, 25b, 40a, 43, 48b, 140a, 142/3, 144, 145, 147, 148b, 149, 150, 151, 152/3, 153, 154, 155a, 156, 157, 158, 159a, 159b, 160/1, 161, 164, 167, 168a, 168b, 168c, 169, 170, 171, 173, 174/5, 226a, 248b, 249a, 250/1, 255, 256/7, 259, 269a; **P. ENTICKNAP** 13b, 28a, 30a, 32a, 39a, 46a, 63, 68, 72/3, 72, 78a, 78b, 84b, 88, 91a, 92, 108a; **T. HARRIS** 3, 4a, 10a, 14b, 20a, 21a, 22a, 26a, 27b, 29a, 35b, 98/9, 104, 105a, 105b, 105c, 106/7, 107, 113, 114, 115a, 115b, 119, 121, 123, 124/5, 125, 128, 129, 130, 131, 133, 136, 137a, 138b, 139a, 139b, 140/1, 141, 209, 232/3, 236/7, 238/9, 253, 254, 261, 266, 268; **N. HICKS** 79t; **T. LARSEN-COLLINGE** 38b, 91b, 166, 172, 262, 265a; **R. MOORE** 10b, 19b, 183a, 234, 235, 242, 243, 244, 245a, 245b, 246a, 246b, 247; **K. PATERSON** 5, 12b, 15a, 15b, 17b, 18a, 18b, 23b, 24a, 27a, 33b, 35a, 62/3, 62, 64, 66, 69, 70a, 70b, 71a, 71b, 74, 75, 76/7, 77, 79b, 80, 81, 82, 89a, 89b, 90, 91c, 93, 94, 95, 96/7, 97, 140b, 188a, 197b; **A. SATTIN** 126c, 181a, 181b, 196, 197t, 199, 200/1, 204a, 204b, 205, 207, 208, 212, 213a, 213b, 214, 215, 216, 217, 219a, 249b, 265b; **C. SAWYER** 9a, 22b; **A. SOUTER** 37; **R. SURMAN** 29b, 39b, 50/1, 54, 60a, 127, 132a; **J. A. TIMS** 6/7, 16a, 45, 148a, 176/7, 176, 178, 186, 188b, 189, 190, 191, 193, 194b, 195a, 195b, 200/1, 224, 225, 229, 230a, 231, 263; **M. TRELAWNY** 260, 269b; **P. WILSON** 23a, 24b, 24c, 31a, 51, 53, 56, 57, 59b, 61a, 61b, 109, 132b, 222, 248a.

Acknowledgements

The authors would like to thank the following individuals and organizations for their help during the research of this book: Olympic Airways, Autohellas Hertz and National Tourist Office of Greece

Contributors

Verifier: Sylvie Franquet. Revisions design: Bookwork Creative Associates LImited